The Ten Commandments
& their Influence on American Law

A STUDY IN HISTORY

William J. Federer

The Ten Commandments
& their Influence on American Law

A STUDY IN HISTORY

William J. Federer

Amerisearch, Inc., P.O. Box 20163, St. Louis, MO 63123, 1-888-USA-WORD
314-487-4395 voice/fax, www.amerisearch.net, wjfederer@aol.com

CONTENTS

Contents

i.
INTRODUCTION

Matthew D. Staver is the founder of the Liberty Counsel in Orlando, Florida, a non-profit legal organization which defends First Amendment cases across America. In February of 2001, he asked me to serve as an expert witness in several United States District Court Cases regarding a prepared list of historical documents which influenced America's founding, approved to be used in public venues. This list included Colonial Documents, the Declaration of Independence, the Constitution, the Bill of Rights, etc., and the Ten Commandments.

The ACLU objected to the Ten Commandments being included in that list. Matthew Staver began preparations to take these cases to the Supreme Court, if necessary. The book you are about to read contains the expert witness testimony I prepared as a primary exhibit, along with legal commentary by Matthew D. Staver. Admittedly, this book is a collection of evidence rather than a typical book for reading.

This information was also provided to the attorneys for Grand Junction, Colorado, who were successful in defending a similar monument.

Others involved in the legal effort to preserve the historical truths of America's founding, including Jay Alan Sekulow - American Center for Law and Justice; Alan Sears - Alliance Defense Fund; Brad W. Dacus - Pacific Justice Institute; David C. Gibbs, Jr., & David C. Gibbs, III, - Christian Law Association; Larry Klayman - Judicial Watch; Gary Kreep - United States Justice Foundation; Gary S. Baylor - Center for Law and Religious Freedom; Stephen Crampton - Center for Law and Policy; James Bopp - James Madison Center for Free Speech; Christian Legal Society; Richard Thompson - Thomas More Law Center; Rutherford Institute; John Eidsmoe, Herb Titus, Steve Melchior and Chief Justice of the Alabama Supreme Court Roy Moore.

This information is presented not as a public policy recommendation, but rather as documentation that the historical record is replete with evidence that *the Ten Commandments have directly and indirectly influenced America's founders, leaders, system of government and legal code,* and, therefore, deserve to be included among the publicly acknowledged historical documents which have impacted the founding of America.

RECENT DECISIONS
JUDGE DISMISSES ACLU CHALLENGE to TEN COMMANDMENTS DISPLAY - January 24, 2003 www.lc.org

LEXINGTON, KY - Handing the ACLU a significant defeat, Federal District Court Judge Karl Forrester, in the Eastern District of Kentucky, held on Wednesday that a display of the Ten Commandments together with other historical documents in Mercer County, Kentucky, is constitutional. Mercer County is represented jointly by Liberty Counsel and the American Center for Law and Justice.

The ACLU sued Mercer County for its display in the county courthouse that contained the Ten Commandments. The display included the Ten Commandments, the Mayflower Compact, the Declaration of Independence, the Magna Carta, the Star Spangled Banner, the National Motto, the Preamble to the Kentucky Constitution, the Bill of Rights to the United States Constitution, and a picture of Lady Justice. Named the "Foundations of American Law and Government," the display is intended to depict several documents that have played a significant role in the founding of our system of law and government.

Judge Forrester had previously denied the ACLU's request for an injunction against the display. In a previous opinion denying the request for an Injunction, Judge Forrester stated, "for good or bad, right or wrong, the Ten Commandments did have an influence upon the development of United States law and it can be constitutional to display the Ten Commandments in the appropriate context."

Judge Forrester's decision Wednesday that ended the ACLU's challenge against Mercer County recognized that "The display clearly has a legitimate secular purpose of, including but not limited to, acknowledging the historical influence of the Commandments on the development of this country's laws and this record is devoid of any evidence indicating a religious purpose by the government." Based on this, Judge Forrester granted the County's Motion for Summary Judgment and issued a final judgment holding the display to be constitutional.

Mat Staver hailed today's decision as a great victory. Staver stated, "Today's decision begins to turn the tide against the ACLU, which has been on a search and destroy mission to remove all vestiges of our religious history from public view." Staver added, "Whether the ACLU likes it or not, history is crystal clear that each one of the Ten Commandments has played an important role in the founding of our system of law and government. Each one of the Ten Commandments was adopted as law by 12 of the 13 original American colonies."

Staver also added, "As long as a governmental entity displays the Ten Commandments together with other historical documents and does so for an educational or historical purpose, such displays will be constitutional." Staver concluded, "This case should be used as a model for other counties wishing to display historical documents, including the Ten Commandments. These displays are constitutional."i

TEN COMMANDMENTS MONUMENT ON TEXAS STATE CAPITOL GROUNDS IS CONSTITUTIONAL
November 13, 2003, Liberty Counsel

Austin, Texas – The Fifth Circuit Court of Appeals issued an opinion holding that a stand-alone Ten Commandments monument on the Texas State Capitol grounds in Austin, Texas, is constitutional. Liberty Counsel, a civil liberties education and legal defense organization with an extensive amount of experience in the constitutionality of the public display of the Ten Commandments, filed an Amicus Brief in support of the state of Texas. The Fifth Circuit covers the states of Texas, Louisiana and Mississippi.

The 42 year-old monument was originally donated to the State by the Fraternal Order of Eagles in 1961. The granite monolith is more than six feet high and three feet wide. It is one of 17 monuments and memorials on the grounds of the State Capitol. The donation of the Ten Commandments was part of a youth guidance project to give the youth of the nation a code of conduct by which to govern their actions. The monument sat in a small park-like subsection between the Supreme Court building and the Capitol building.

Thomas Van Orden filed the suit to have the monument removed because he claimed the sight of the Ten Commandments disturbed him. The Court began by noting that "The Ten Commandments have both a religious and secular message." Given that message, the Court held that the State of Texas had a secular purpose for displaying the monument.

The Court noted that, "Even those who would see the Decalogue as wise counsel born of man's experience rather than as divinely inspired religious teaching cannot deny its influence upon the civil and criminal laws of this country. That extraordinary influence has been repeatedly acknowledged by the Supreme Court and detailed by scholars. Equally so is its influence upon ethics and the ideal of a just society." The Court concluded its opinion by noting the Ten Commandments influence on American law and stating, "There is no constitutional right to be free of government endorsement of its own laws."

Mathew Staver, President and General Counsel of Liberty Counsel, stated, "This decision begins to turn the tide against the historical revisionism of groups like the ACLU who seek to remove all references to the Ten Commandments from our public life."

Staver added, "We are excited that the Court issued such a ringing endorsement of the Ten Commandments and their effect on our laws. This opinion energizes us to take our fight to preserve our history, including the Ten Commandments, to the highest levels."

Staver concluded "The Ten Commandments have both a secular and religious aspect. To ignore the influence of the Ten Commandments in the founding and shaping of American law and government would require significant historical revisionism."

Liberty Counsel is currently defending 10 separate Ten Commandment displays throughout the country. In the past 14 months, two federal courts of appeals and three federal district courts have found such displays to be constitutional.

COURT OKs TEN COMMANDMENTS DISPLAY
Federal judge says Texas Capitol exhibit constitutional
by Jon Dougherty, www.WorldNetDaily.com October 11, 2002

A federal judge in Austin, Texas, has ruled that a 42-year-old display of the Ten Commandments on the grounds of the state Capitol building is not an official endorsement of religion and can remain intact.

U.S. District Judge Harry Lee Hudspeth found that the six-feet-by-three-feet granite memorial - one of 17 monuments on state Capitol grounds - was appropriate as a tool "to promote youth morality and to stop the alarming increase in delinquency," and served a legitimate secular purpose.

The court also found that no reasonable observer would conclude that the state sought to advance or endorse religion. The Ten Commandments display did not contain the state seal or the Lone Star symbol, as other monuments do.

"The court was clear in noting that the display of the ... monument could not be interpreted by a reasonable observer as a state endorsement of religion," said Mathew Staver, president and general counsel of Liberty Counsel, a nonprofit legal group that defends religious-freedom cases.

Introduction

"Each of the Ten Commandments has played a significant role in the foundation of our system of law and government," he said, adding that the biblical edicts have "both a secular and religious aspect."

Liberty Counsel filed an amicus brief with the court in support of the state of Texas. Thomas Van Orden, a criminal defense lawyer who has temporarily lost his law license and is homeless, filed suit to have the display removed, claiming it was an official endorsement of religion. He could not be reached for comment.

"To ignore the influence of the Ten Commandments in the founding and shaping of American law and government would require significant historical revisionism," Staver told WorldNetDaily.com. He said they "take on an even greater secular aspect when placed in the context of other historical or legal documents, such as in the context of the state Capitol."

Texas Gov. Rick Perry also applauded the ruling. "Today's court ruling is a victory for those who believe, as I do, that the Ten Commandments are time-tested and appropriate guidelines for living a full and moral life," he said in a statement. "The Ten Commandments provide a historical foundation for our laws and principles as a free and strong nation, under God, and should be displayed at the Texas Capitol."

Staver said he was unsure whether Van Orden would appeal. The display was donated to the state by the Fraternal Order of Eagles in 1961 as part of a youth guidance project "to give the youth of the nation a code of conduct by which to govern their actions," said Staver.

The monument sits in a small park-like subsection between the state Supreme Court building and the Capitol. Display of the Ten Commandments has not fared well recently in other court venues.

On Wednesday, a federal court in Frankfort, Ky., rejected a plan to display a Ten Commandments monument near the state Capitol, saying it was a thinly disguised effort at government promotion of religion. However, the court said the state could display the edicts by presenting them in the context of other historical and non-religious material.

In 1997, then-Alabama state court Judge Roy Moore, over the objections of the American Civil Liberties Union, posted the Ten Commandments in his chambers. Moore has since been elevated to chief justice of the Alabama Supreme Court.ii
http://www.worldnetdaily.com/news/article.asp?ARTICLE_ID=29250

"Ten Commandment Return to Alabama Judicial Building" by Susan Jones CNSNews.com Morning Editor, February 06, 2004. "The Ten Commandments have returned to the Alabama Judicial Building.....'It gives me great pleasure...to see the constitutional public display of the Ten Commandments back in the Alabama Judicial Building,' said John Giles, president of the Christian Coalition of Alabama."

ii
FOREWORD

In his commentary, *The Ten Commandments in American Law and Government*, Matthew D. Staver writes:

> When a governmental practice has been "deeply embedded in the history and tradition of this country," such a practice will not violate the Establishment Clause because the practice has become part of the "fabric of our society." See Marsh v. Chambers, 463 U.S. 783, 786 (1983).

> The Ten Commandments played a significant role in the development of American law. The incorporation of the Ten Commandments in law and policy pre-dates the Constitution. This intermingling of the Ten Commandments into American law and government was long before the appearance of legislative prayers. The drafters of the First Amendment would never have dreamed they were abolishing the Decalogue.

> From time out of mind, courts, legislatures and our founding fathers have referred to the Ten commandments and their impact on our culture and legal system. The Supreme Court has often recognized the impact the Ten Commandments has played on our system of law and government.

> See:
> > Griswold v. Connecticut, 381 U.S. 479,529 n.2 (1965) (Stewart, J., dissenting) (most criminal prohibitions coincide with the prohibitions contained in the Ten Commandments);

> > McGowan v. Maryland, 366 U.S. 420, 459 (1961) (Frankfurter, J., concurring) ("Innumerable civil

regulations enforce conduct which harmonizes with religious canons. State prohibitions of murder, theft and adultery reinforce commands of the decalogue.");

Stone v. Graham, 449 U.S. 39, 45 (1980) (Rehnquist, J., dissenting) ("It is equally undeniable ... that the Ten Commandments have had a significant impact on the development of secular legal codes of the Western World.");

Lynch v. Donnelly, 465 U.S. 668, 677-78 (1984) (describing the depiction of Moses with the Ten Commandments on the wall of the Supreme Court chamber and stating that such acknowledgments of religion demonstrate that "our history is pervaded by expressions of religious beliefs....");

Edwards v. Aguillard, 482 U.S. 578, 593-94 (1987) (acknowledging that the Ten Commandments did not play an exclusively religious role in the history of Western civilization).

The Ten Commandments have been repeatedly used by government from the conception of America. Each of the Ten Commandments has played some significant role in the foundation of our system of law and government. Twelve of the thirteen original colonies adopted the entire Decalogue into their civil and criminal laws. Joseph Story, the eminent Supreme Court Justice who was the youngest Justice ever appointed and who served on the Supreme Court for thirty four years, from 1811 to 1845, remarked:

Now, there will probably be found few persons in this, or any other Christian country, who would deliberately contend, that it was unreasonable, or unjust to foster and encourage the Christian religion generally, as a matter of sound policy, as well as of revealed truth. In fact, every American colony, from its foundation down to the revolution, with the exception of Rhode Island, (if, indeed, that state be an exception,) did openly, by the whole course of its laws and institutions, support and sustain, in some form, the Christian religion; and almost invariably gave a peculiar sanction to some of its fundamental doctrines. And this has continued to be the case in some of the states down to the present period, without the slightest suspicion, that it was against the principles of public law, or republican liberty.

JOSEPH STORY, 3 COMMENTARIES ON THE CONSTITUTION OF THE UNITED STATES, § 1867 (1833). Rhode Island adopted the last six of the Commandments, but not the first four. See Alvin w. Johnson, Sunday Legislation, 23 KY. L.J. 131 n. 1 (1934-35) [1]

iii.
HISTORICAL REFERENCES

Showing the influence the Ten Commandments had on American law is akin to the task of showing their immense influence on Western Culture in general. The references listed in this book are just a small sampling of the thousands of supporting citations available in the historical record.

The Ten Commandments were referred to directly by America's founders and leaders as the: **Laws of God, Ordinances of God, Statutes of God, Divine Law, Revealed Law, Holy Law, Book of Laws, Eternal Laws, Laws given to Moses on the Mount, His Just and Holy Laws, the Decalogue, Foundation of Our Holy Religion, Immutable Laws of Good and Evil, Government of God, etc.** The Ten Commandments were referred to indirectly in statements made in the context of religion, virtue, principles and morals.

COMMENTARY

In his commentary *The Ten Commandments in American Law and Government,* Matthew D. Staver writes:

In 1950, the Florida Supreme Court declared:

A people unschooled about the sovereignty of God, the *Ten Commandments,* and the ethics of Jesus, could never have evolved the Bill of Rights, the Declaration of Independence, and the Constitution. There is not one solitary fundamental principle of our democratic policy that did not stem directly from the basic moral concepts as embodied in *the Decalogue......*

Florida v. City of Tampa, 48 So.2d 78, 79 (Fla. 1950); see also Commissioners of Johnston County v. Lacy, 93 S.E. 482,487 (N.C. 1917) ("Our laws are founded upon *the Decalogue......*).

To see the original Constitution and Declaration of Independence one must first view the *Ten Commandments* at the entrance to the National Archives. Moses is the only figure facing forward out of twenty-three other profiles of famous law givers and he occupies the central position in the United States House Chamber. Similarly, *Moses with the Ten Commandments* faces forward in the central position perched over the Chief Justice's seat in the United States Supreme Court. See Lynch v. Donnelly, 465 U.S. 668, 677 (1984).

The *Ten Commandments* in the New Displays was only one frame among many other secular historical and legal documents. The *Ten Commandments* by no means dominated the display. Viewed in its entirety, one may not conclude that the *Ten Commandments* is an establishment of religion. *The Decalogue* played a significant role in the foundation of American law. Any other conclusion would require erasing numerous pages of American history. [2]

INFLUENCE OF THE COMMANDMENTS
William J. Federer

JOHN ADAMS

"The *Ten Commandments* and the Sermon on the Mount contain my religion," wrote John Adams to Thomas Jefferson, Nov. 4, 1816. [3]

This admission by Adams is significant as he was a key founder. A graduate of Harvard, Adams was an original member of the Continental Congress and a signer of the Declaration of Independence. He recommended Thomas Jefferson pen the Declaration and George Washington be the Commander-in-Chief of the Continental Army. He helped write the Massachusetts Constitution. He was the second U.S. President, after having served eight years as Vice-President under Washington. He was the first President to live in the White House, and his administration began the Department of the Navy and the Library of Congress. He was the husband of Abigail Adams, whose letters are considered among the best accounts of the Revolutionary period. He was the father of sixth President John Quincy Adams and the cousin of Samuel Adams, known as the "Father of the Revolution."

John Adams' quote regarding the Ten Commandments was not isolated. Indeed, it was indicative of the belief and worldview of America's founder.

After reviewing an estimated 15,000 items, including newspaper articles, pamphlets, books, monographs, etc., written between 1760-1805 by the 55 men who wrote the Constitution, Professors Donald S. Lutz and Charles S. Hyneman, in their work "The Relative Influence of European Writers on Late Eighteenth-Century American Political Thought" published in the American Political Science Review (1984), revealed that the Bible, especially the book of Deuteronomy, contributed 34% of all quotations used by our Founding Fathers.

The other main sources cited include: Baron Charles Montesquieu 8.3 %, Sir William Blackstone 7.9%, John Locke 2.9%, David Hume 2.7%, Plutarch 1.5%, Beccaria 1.5%, Trenchard and Gordon 1.4%, Delolme 1.4%, Samuel von Pufendorf 1.3%, Cicero 1.2%, Hugo Grotius 0.9%, Shakespeare 0.8%, Vattel 0.5%, etc. These additional sources as well took 60% of their quotes directly from the Bible. Direct and indirect citations combined reveal that the majority of all quotations referenced by the Founding Fathers are derived from the Bible.[4]

John Adams wrote in his diary, February 22, 1756:

Suppose a nation in some distant Region should take the Bible for their only *law Book*, and every member should regulate his conduct by the precepts there exhibited! Every member would be obliged in conscience, to temperance, frugality, and industry; to justice, kindness, and charity towards his fellow men; and to piety, love, and reverence toward Almighty God...What a Eutopia, what a Paradise would this region be.[5]

In a letter to the officers of the First Brigade of the Third Division of the Militia of Massachusetts, October 11, 1798, President John Adams stated:

We have no government armed with power capable of contending with human passions unbridled by *morality and religion.* Avarice, ambition, revenge, or gallantry, would break the strongest cords of our Constitution as a whale goes through a net. Our Constitution was made only for a *moral and religious* people. It is wholly inadequate to the government of any other.[6]

On June 21, 1776, John Adams wrote:

> Statesmen, my dear Sir, may plan and speculate for liberty, but it is *Religion and Morality* alone, which can establish the Principles upon which Freedom can securely stand. The only foundation of a free Constitution is *pure Virtue*, and if this cannot be inspired into our People in a greater Measure, than they have it now, they may change their Rulers and the forms of Government, but they will not obtain a lasting liberty.[7]

On April 19, 1817, John Adams wrote to Thomas Jefferson:

> Without *religion*, this world would be something not fit to be mentioned in polite company....The most abandoned scoundrel that ever existed, never yet wholly extinguished his Conscience and while Conscience remains, there is some *religion.*[8]

On August 28, 1811, to Dr. Benjamin Rush, John Adams wrote:

> *Religion and virtue* are the only foundations, not only of republicanism and of all free government, but of social felicity under all governments and in all the combinations of human society.[9]

In a letter to Mr. Warren, John Adams stated:

> The Form of Government, which you admire, when its Principles are pure is admirable, indeed, it is productive of every Thing which is great and excellent among Men. But its Principles are as easily destroyed, as human Nature is corrupted.... A Government is only to be supported by *pure Religion or Austere Morals. Private and public Virtue* is the only Foundation of Republics.[10]

John Adams wrote to Thomas Jefferson:

> Have you ever found in history, one single example of a Nation thoroughly corrupted that was afterwards restored to *virtue*?... And without *virtue*, there can be no political liberty.[11]

On June 20, 1815, John Adams wrote to Thomas Jefferson:

The question before the human race is, whether
the God of nature shall govern the world by *His own laws*.[12]

During a threatened war with France, President John Adams imposed
upon the retired George Washington to once again assume command of the
Army, which he did. Adams also issued a National a Day of Humiliation,
Fasting, and Prayer, on Wednesday, March 6, 1799. In the proclamation,
Adams used the phrases "accountableness of men to Him" and "obligation to
Him" and "to yield a more suitable obedience to His righteous requisitions,"
which are undoubtedly implied references to keeping the Ten Commandments:

As no truth is more clearly taught in the *Volume
of Inspiration*, nor any more fully demonstrated by the
experience of all ages, than that a deep sense and a due
acknowledgment of the growing providence of a Supreme
Being and of the accountableness of men to Him as the
searcher of hearts and righteous distributor of rewards and
punishments are conducive equally to the happiness and
rectitude of individuals and to the well-being of
communities;

As it is also most reasonable in itself that men who
are made capable of social acts and relations, who owe their
improvements to the social state, and who derive their
enjoyments from it, should, as a society, make their
acknowledgments of dependence and *obligation to Him*
who hath endowed them with these capacities and elevated
them in the scale of existence by these distinctions;

As it is likewise a plain dictate of duty and a strong
sentiment of nature that in circumstances of great urgency
and seasons on imminent danger earnest and particular
supplications should be made to Him who is able to defend
or to destroy;

As, moreover, the most precious interests of the
people of the United States are still held in jeopardy by the
hostile designs and insidious acts of a foreign nation, as
well as by the dissemination among them of those
principles, subversive *to the foundations of all religious,
moral, and social obligations,* that have produced
incalculable mischief and misery in other countries;

And as, in fine, the observance of special seasons for public religious solemnities is happily calculated to avert the evils which we ought to deprecate, and to excite to the performance of the duties which we ought to discharge, by calling and fixing the attention of the people at large to the momentous truths already recited, by affording opportunity to teach and inculcate them by animating devotion and giving to it the character of a national act:

For these reasons I have thought proper to recommend, and I hereby recommend accordingly, that Thursday, the twenty-fifth day of April next, be observed throughout the United States of America as a day of solemn humiliation, fasting, and prayer;

That the citizens on that day abstain, as far as may be, from their secular occupation, and devote the time to the *sacred duties of religion*, in public and in private;

That they call to mind our numerous offenses against the Most High God, confess them before Him with the sincerest penitence, implore His pardoning mercy, through the Great Mediator and Redeemer, for our past transgressions, and that through the grace of His Holy Spirit, we may be disposed and enabled to yield a more suitable obedience to *His righteous requisitions* in time to come;

That He would interpose to arrest the progress of that impiety and licentiousness in principle and practice so offensive to Himself and so ruinous to mankind;

That He would make us deeply sensible that "righteousness exalteth a nation but sin is a reproach to any people"[Proverbs 14:34];

That He would turn us from our transgressions and turn His displeasure from us;

That He would withhold us from unreasonable discontent, from disunion, faction, sedition, and insurrection;

That He would preserve our country from the desolating sword;

That He would save our cities and towns from a repetition of those awful pestilential visitations under which they have lately suffered so severely, and that the health of our inhabitants generally may be precious in His sight;

That He would favor us with fruitful seasons and so bless the labors of the husbandman as that there may be food in abundance for man and beast;

That He would prosper our commerce, manufactures, and fisheries, and give success to the people in all their lawful industry and enterprise;

That He would smile on our colleges, academies, schools, and seminaries of learning, and make them nurseries of sound science, **morals, and religion;**

That He would bless all magistrates, from the highest to the lowest, give them the true spirit of their station, make them a terror to evil doers and a praise to them that do well;

That He would preside over the councils of the nation at this critical period, enlighten them to a just discernment of the public interest, and save them from mistake, division, and discord;

That He would make succeed our preparations for defense and bless our armaments by land and sea;

That He would put and end to the effusion of human blood and the accumulation of human misery among the contending nations of the earth by disposing them to justice, to equity, to benevolence, and to peace;

And that He would extend the blessings of knowledge, of true liberty, and *of pure and undefiled religion* throughout the world.

And I do also recommend that with these acts of humiliation, penitence, and prayer, fervent thanksgiving to the Author of All Good be united for the countless favors which He is still continuing to the people of the United States, and which render their condition as a nation eminently happy when compared with the lot of others. Given, etc.[13]

To emphasis that when John Adams mentions "accountableness," "obligation," or "obedience" to God, he is referring to the God of the Ten Commandment, he wrote to Judge F.A. Van der Kemp, February 16, 1809:

The Hebrews have done more to civilize men than any other nation....[God] ordered the Jews to preserve and propagate to all mankind *the doctrine of a Supreme, Intelligent, Wise, Almighty Sovereign of the Universe*....[which is] to be *the great essential principle of morality*, and consequently all civilization.[14]

NATHANIEL MORTON

Nathaniel Morton, in New England's Memorial, (Cambridge, SG and MJ for John Usher of Boston, 1669, p. 17), wrote:

> In the year 1602, divers godly Christians of our English nation...entered into covenant to walk with God, and one another, in the enjoyment of the ordinances of God, according to the primitive pattern in the word of God.

WILLIAM BRADFORD

William Bradford (March 1590-May 9, 1657) was a leader of the Plymouth Colony. Sailing in the Mayflower, he was chosen as governor of the colony in 1621, and was reelected 30 times until his death. In 1650, William Bradford wrote a history *Of Plymouth Plantation*, which is comparable to Shakespeare's works in literary and historical significance. In it he wrote:

> Though I am growne aged, yet I have had a longing desire, to see with my own eyes, something of the most ancient language, and holy tongue, in which *the Law, and oracles of God* were writ; and in which God, and angels, spoke to the holy patriarchs, of old time; and what names were given to things, from the creation. And though I cannot attaine to much herein, yet I am refreshed, to have seen some glimpse hereof; (as Moses saw the Land of Canaan afarr off) my aime and desire is, to see how the words, and phrases lye *in the holy texte*; and to dicerne somewhat of the same for my owne contente.[16]

JOHN COTTON

John Cotton, in God's Promise to His Plantation, (William Jones, London, 1630, pp. 13-14), wrote:

> Have special care that you ever have the Ordinances planted amongs you, or else never looke for security. As soone as God's Ordinances cease, your security ceaseth likewise; but if God plant his Ordinances among you, feare not, he will maintaine them. Isay4,5,6. Upon all their glory there shall be a defence; that is, upon all God's Ordinances: for so was the Arke called the glory of Israel, I Sam. 4:22.

Secondly, have a care to be planted into the Ordinances, that the word may be ingrafted into you, and you into it: If you take rooting in the Ordinances, grow up thereby, bring forth much fruite, continue and abide therein, then you are a vineyard of red wine, and the Lord will keepe you, Isay 27:2,3, that no sonnes of violence shall destroy you. Looke into all the stories whether divine or humane, and you shall never finde that God ever rooted out a people that had the Ordinances; never did God suffer such plants to be plucked up: on all their glory shall be defence.

THOMAS HOOKER

Thomas Hooker (July 7, 1586-July 7, 1647) founded Hartford, Connecticut in 1636. A Cambridge University graduate, he was persecuted in England for getting involved with the Puritans. Exiled from England for his religious beliefs, he fled to Holland, then to Massachusetts (1633), where he became the minister at the Cambridge (formerly New-Town) settlement. Disputes with the leadership drove him and his congregation to Connecticut (1635-36). In 1638, he stated to the Connecticut General Assembly that he believed people had a God-given right to choose their magistrates. He was a principal organizer of the New England colonies into the defensive confederation, known as the United Colonies of New England, 1643.

Thomas Hooker's sermon before the General Court of Connecticut put forth unprecedented democratic principles and inspired the Fundamental Constitutions of Connecticut, 1639, which promoted individual rights, "due process of law," "trial by a jury of peers," "no taxation without representation" and prohibitions against "cruel and unusual punishment." It became a model for all other colonial constitutions.[17] In 1638, Rev. Thomas Hooker stated:

The choice of public magistrates belongs unto the people, by God's allowance.... (T)he privilege of election, which belongs to the people, therefore must not be exercised according to their humours, but according to the blessed will and *law of God.*[18]

MASSACHUSETTS BODY OF LIBERTIES

65. No custome or prescription shall ever prevaile amongs us in any morall cause, our meaneing is maintaine anythinge that can prove to be morrallie sinfull by the word of God.

WILLIAM PENN

William Penn (October 14, 1644-July 30, 1718) was the founder of Pennsylvania. His father, British Navy Admiral William Penn, discovered Bermuda and helped strengthen King Charles II's throne. William Penn attended Oxford University, and later studied law. In 1667, at the age of 22, he was impressed by a sermon delivered by Thomas Loe, entitled, "The Sandy Foundation Shaken." He converted to the Society of Friends, or Quakers, who at that time were scorned and ridiculed.[19]

Beginning in 1668, William Penn suffered imprisonment three times for his faith. Once he was imprisoned in the Tower of London for eight months, during which time he wrote the classic book, *No Cross, No Crown* :

The false notion that they may be children of God while in a state of disobedience *to his holy commandments*, and disciples of Jesus though they revolt from his cross, and members of his true church, which is without spot or wrinkle, notwithstanding their lives are full of spots and wrinkles, is of all other deceptions upon themselves the most pernicious to their eternal condition for they are at peace in sin and under a security in their transgression.[20]

COLONIAL SCHOOLBOOK

New Guide to the English Tongue (1740), was published first in England by Thomas Dilworth, a distinguished educator and textbook writer. The book's popularity grew in the Colonies, until, by 1765, it was universally adopted in the New England schools. The book contained spelling, reading and grammar lessons, "adorned with proper Scriptures." Its first lesson, having words only three letters long or less, stated:

No Man may put off *the Law of God.*
The Way of God is no ill Way.
My Joy is in God all the Day.
A bad Man is a Foe to God.[15]

ROGER SHERMAN

Roger Sherman was distinguished as the only Founding Father to sign all four major founding documents: The Articles of Association, 1774; The Declaration of Independence, 1776; The Articles of Confederation, 1777; and The Constitution of the United States, 1787.

Representative Roger Sherman wrote a letter from New York to Samuel Hopkins, the Congregational minister of Newport, Rhode Island:

That a God of infinite Goodness can (through atonement) have mercy on whom He will, consistent with the honor of *His law and Government* and all of His perfections, is a much better ground of hope than the denial of self-love.[21]

SAMUEL ADAMS

On November 20, 1772, in the section of *The Rights of the Colonists* entitled, "The Rights of the Colonist as Men," Samuel Adams declared:

As neither reason requires nor religion permits the contrary, every man living in or out of a state of civil society has a right peaceably and quietly to worship God according to the dictates of his own conscience.

"Just and true liberty, equal and impartial liberty," in matters spiritual and temporal, is a thing that all men are clearly entitled to by *the eternal and immutable laws of God* and nature, as well as by the law of nations and all well-grounded municipal laws, which must have their *foundation in the former.*[22]

On November 20, 1772, in the section of *The Rights of the Colonists* entitled, "The Rights of the Colonist as Christians," Samuel Adams declared:

The right to freedom being the gift of God Almighty, the rights of the Colonists as Christians may best be understood by reading and carefully studying *the institutions of The Great Law Giver* and the Head of the Christian Church, which are to be found clearly written and promulgated in the New Testament[23]

GOUVERNOR MORRIS

Gouvernor Morris (January 31, 1752-November 6, 1816) was an attorney, politician, soldier and diplomat. He penned the final draft of the Constitution of the United States, being the head of the Committee on Style, and was the originator of the phrase "We the people of the United States." He was 35 years old when he served as one of the members of the Continental

Congress, and he spoke 173 times during the Constitutional debates (more than any other delegate).

He was the first U.S. Minister to France, a U.S. Senator, and helped to write the New York Constitution. A graduate of King's College (Columbia University), he was a merchant, lawyer, planter, financier and pioneer promoter of the Erie Canal.

In An Address on the Bank of North America, given in the Pennsylvania State Assembly, 1785, Gouverneur Morris stated:

> How can we hope for public peace and national prosperity, if the faith of governments so solemnly pledged can be so lightly infringed? Destroy this prop, which once gave us support, and where will you turn in the hour of distress? To whom will you look for succor? By what promise or vows can you hope to obtain confidence?
>
> This hour of distress will come. It comes to all, and the moment of affliction is known to Him alone, whose Divine Providence exalts or depresses states and kingdoms. Not by the blind dictates of arbitrary will. Not by a tyrannous and despotic mandate.
>
> But in proportion to their obedience or disobedience of *His just and holy laws*. It is He who commands us that we abstain from wrong. It is He who tells you, "do unto others as ye would that they would do unto you"[24]

ALEXIS DE TOCQUEVILLE

Alexis de Tocqueville (July 29, 1805-April 16, 1859) was a French statesman, historian and social philosopher. He arrived in New York, May 11, 1831, with Gustave de Beaumont, and began a nine month tour of the country for the purpose of observing the American prison system, the people and American institutions. His two-part work, which was published in 1835 and 1840, was entitled Democracy in America. It has been described as 'the most comprehensive and penetrating analysis of the relationship between character and society in America that has ever been written.'[25] In it, Alexis de Tocqueville related:

> Each sect adores the Deity in its own peculiar manner, but all sects preach *the same moral law in the name of God*....Moreover, all the sects of the United States

are comprised within the great unity of Christianity, and Christian morality is everywhere the same.[26]

DANIEL WEBSTER

Daniel Webster (January 18, 1782-October 24, 1852) had a political career which spanned almost four decades. Considered one of the greatest orators in American history, he served as Secretary of State for President William Henry Harrison, President John Tyler and President Millard Fillmore; was elected U.S. Senator, 1827; elected U.S. Representative, 1822; practiced law in Boston, 1816; elected U.S. Representative, 1812; admitted to the bar, 1805; and graduated from Dartmouth College, 1801. By a resolution of the Senate, Daniel Webster was esteemed as one of the five greatest senators in U.S. history.[27] Daniel Webster stated:

> If there is anything in my thoughts or style to commend, the credit is due to my parents for instilling in me an early love of the Scriptures. If we abide by *the principles taught in the Bible,* our country will go on prospering and to prosper; If we and our posterity shall be true to the Christian religion, if we and they shall live always in the fear of God and shall respect *His Commandments*...we may have the highest hopes of the future fortunes of our country;...
>
> But if we and our posterity neglect *religious instruction and authority;* violate *the rules of eternal justice,* trifle with *the injunctions of morality,* and recklessly destroy the political constitution which holds us together, no man can tell how sudden a catastrophe may overwhelm us and bury all our glory in profound obscurity.[28]

WILLIAM MCGUFFEY

William Holmes McGuffey (September 23, 1800-May 4, 1873) was an American educator. He was the president of Ohio University, professor at the University of Virginia and the department chairman at the Miami University of Ohio. He was responsible for forming the first teachers' association in that part of the nation.

Considered the "Schoolmaster of the Nation," McGuffey published the first edition of *his McGuffey's Reader* in 1836. This book was the mainstay in public education in America till 1920. As of 1963, 125 million copies had been sold, making it one of the most widely used and influential textbooks of all times. Millions of American children learned to read and write from it.

In the foreword of *McGuffey's Reader*, 1836, William H. McGuffey wrote:

> *The Ten Commandments* and the teachings of Jesus are not only basic but plenary.[29]

> The Christian religion is the religion of our country. From it are derived our prevalent notions of the character of God, *the great moral governor of the universe.* On *its doctrines* are founded the peculiarities of our free institutions.[30]

William H. McGuffey, in his Sixth Elective Reader, (American Gook Company, New York, 1879, p. 225), wrote:

> Whenever a few of them settled a town, they immediately gathered themselves into a church, and their elders were magistrates, and their code of laws was the Pentateuch.

MARK TWAIN

In the response to criticism of the authenticity of the Bible, Mark Twain remarked:

> If the *Ten Commandments* were not written by Moses, then they were written by another fellow of the same name.[31]

WILLIAM MCKINLEY

Twenty-fifth U.S. President William McKinley stated in his First Inaugural Address, Thursday, March 4, 1897:

> Our faith teaches that there is no safer reliance than upon the God of our fathers, who has so singularly favored the American people in every national trial, and who will not forsake us so long as we obey *His commandments* and walk humbly in His footsteps....[32]

ALFRED E. SMITH

Alfred Emanuel Smith (December 30, 1873-October 4, 1944) was the four-term Governor of New York, 1919-21, 1923-29; and the Democratic Presidential candidate in 1928. He served as Assemblyman in the New York State Legislature, 1903; Sheriff of New York City, 1915-17; and leader of the American Liberty League, 1939-44. Alfred Smith, a Catholic, came under attack during his campaign for the Presidency. He responded in May of 1927:

> I am unable to understand how anything I was taught to believe as a Catholic could possibly be in conflict with what is good citizenship. The essence of my faith is built upon *the Commandments of God.* The law of the land is built on *the Commandments of God.* There can be no conflict between them.[33]

HERBERT HOOVER

On September 17, 1935, in San Diego, California, Herbert Hoover expressed:

> Our Constitution is not alone the working plan of a great Federation of States under representative government. There is embedded in it also the vital principles of the American system of liberty. That system is based upon certain inalienable freedoms and protections which in no event the government may infringe and which we call the Bill of Rights.
> It does not require a lawyer to interpret those provisions. They are as clear as *the Ten Commandments.*[34]

CECIL B. DEMILLE

Cecil Blount DeMille (August 12, 1881-January 21, 1959), was an American motion-picture producer and director. He was know for the originality and accuracy of his epic productions, which utilized spectacular crowd scenes and special effects. His best-known films include: *Cleopatra* ; *Union Pacific* ; *The Crusades* ; *The Sign of the Cross* ; *Autobiography*; *The King of Kings* 1927; *Samson and Delilah* 1949; *The Ten Commandments* 1923, remade 1956; and *The Greatest Show on Earth,* for which he won the 1952 Academy Award for best film.

Born in Ashfield, Massachusetts, Cecil B. DeMille was educated at Pennsylvania Military Academy and at the American Academy of Dramatic

Arts. An actor, he wrote two plays, and from 1936 to 1945 produced numerous radio programs. His niece, Agnes de Mille (born 1909), was well-known for her choreography of the films and musicals: *Oklahoma!* (1943); *Paint Your Wagons* (1951); *Carousel* (1945); and *Rodeo* (1942). In 1956, at the New York opening of the film *The Ten Commandments*, Cecil B. DeMille stated:

> The *Ten Commandments* are not the laws. They are *THE LAW*. Man has made 32 million laws since *the Commandments were handed down to Moses on Mount Sinai* more than three thousand years ago, but he has never improved on *God's law*. The *Ten Commandments* are the principles by which man may live with God and man may live with man. They are the expressions of the mind of God for His creatures. They are the charter and guide of human liberty, for there can be no liberty without *the law*....
>
> What I hope for our production of *The Ten Commandments* is that those who see it shall come from the theater not only entertained and filled with the sight of a big spectacle, but filled with the spirit of truth. That it will bring to its audience a better understanding of the real meaning of this *pattern of life that God has set down for us to follow*.[35]

HARRY S TRUMAN

On February 15, 1950, at 10:05 a.m., President Harry S. Truman addressed the Attorney General's Conference on Law Enforcement Problems in the Department of Justice Auditorium, Washington. DC. In speaking to the organizations present, which included the Department Of Justice, the National Association of Attorneys, the U.S. Conference of Lawyers, and the National Institute of Municipal Law Officers, President Truman admonished:

> The *fundamental basis of this nation's laws was given to Moses on the Mount*. The fundamental basis of our Bill of Rights comes from the teachings we get from *Exodus* and St. Matthew, from Isaiah and St. Paul.
>
> I don't think we emphasize that enough these days. If we don't have a proper fundamental moral background, we will finally end up with a totalitarian government which does not believe in rights for anybody except the State![36]

CONRAD HILTON

Conrad Nicholson Hilton (December 25, 1887-January 3, 1979) was founder of the Hilton Hotel chain. After having served in World War I, he was involved in the banking business, and his father's mercantile concerns. In 1919, he purchased his first hotel in Cisco, Texas, which began his world-impacting career. On May 7, 1952, Conrad Hilton gave an address, entitled, A Battle for Peace:

OUR FATHER IN HEAVEN: WE PRAY that YOU save us from ourselves. The world that YOU have made for us, to live in peace, We have made into an armed camp. We live in fear of war to come. We are afraid of 'the terror that flies by night, and the arrow that flies by day, the pestilence that walks in darkness and the destruction that wastes at noon-day.' We have turned from YOU to go our selfish way. We have broken *YOUR Commandments* and denied YOUR truth. We have left YOUR altars to serve the false gods of money and pleasure and power. FORGIVE US AND HELP US[37]

DWIGHT D. EISENHOWER

In 1954, Thirty-fourth President Dwight David Eisenhower, said:

The purpose of a devout and united people was set forth in the pages of The Bible... (1) to live in freedom, (2) to work in a prosperous land...and (3) to obey *the commandments of God....* This Biblical story of the Promised land inspired the founders of America. It continues to inspire us.[38]

RONALD REAGAN

In 1973, as Governor of California, Ronald Reagan stated:

With freedom goes responsibility. Sir Winston Churchill once said you can have 10,000 regulations and still not have respect for the law. We might start with *the Ten Commandments.* If we lived by the Golden Rule, there would be no need for other laws.[39]

In 1974, as Governor of California, Ronald Reagan stated:

> If a bureaucrat had been writing *the Ten Commandments,* a simple rock slab would not have been near enough room. Those simple rules would have read: "Thou Shalt Not, unless you feel strongly to the contrary, or for the following stated exceptions, see paragraphs 1-10 subsection #A."[40]

On March 8, 1982, at the annual Washington Policy Meeting of the National Association of Manufacturers, fortieth U.S. President Ronald Reagan stated:

> The Lord's Prayer contains 57 words. Lincoln's Gettysburg Address has 266 words. *The Ten Commandments* are presented in just 297 words, and the Declaration of Independence has only 300 words. And...an Agriculture Department order setting the price of cabbage has 26,911 words.[41]

On January 31, 1983, at the annual convention of the National Religious Broadcasters, President Ronald Reagan stated:

> I read in the Washington Post about a young woman named Victoria. She's with child, and she said, "In this society we save whales, we save timber wolves and bald eagles and Coke bottles. Yet everyone wanted me to throw away my baby." Well, Victoria's story has a happy ending. Her baby will be born. Victoria has received assistance from a Christian couple, and from Sav-A-Life, a new Dallas group run by Jim McKee.... They're living the meaning of the two great *commandments:* "Thou shalt love the Lord thy God with all thy heart, and with all thy soul, and with all thy might" and "Thou shalt love they neighbor as thyself."[42]

On March 8, 1983, at the National Association of Evangelicals in Orlando, Florida, President Reagan stated:

> One recent survey by a Washington-based research council concluded that Americans were far more religious than the people of other nations. Ninety-five percent of those surveyed expressed a belief in God. A huge majority

believed *the Ten Commandments* had real meaning in their lives.[43]

On May 6, 1983, at the annual banquet of the National Rifle Association, Phoenix, Arizona, President Ronald Reagan stated:

Standing up for America also means standing up for the God who has blessed this land. If we could just keep remembering that Moses brought down from the mountain *the Ten Commandments*, not ten suggestions - and if those of us who live for the Lord could remember that He wants us to love our Lord and our neighbor, then there's no limit to the problems we could solve or the mountains we could move together as a mighty force for good.[44]

ROBERT BYRD

On June 27, 1962, Senator Robert Byrd delivered a message in Congress just two days after the Supreme Court declared prayer in schools unconstitutional:

Above the head of the Chief Justice of the Supreme Court are *the Ten Commandments,* with the great American eagle protecting them. Moses is included among the great lawgivers in Herman A MacNeil's marble sculpture group on the east front. The crier who opens each session closes with the words, "God save the United States and this Honorable Court."[45]

MARGARET THATCHER

Margaret Hilda Thatcher (b. October 13, 1925) became the first woman Prime Minister of the United Kingdom, 1979; after succeeding Robert Heath as the Conservative leader, 1975. She had worked as a research chemist before becoming a barrister and entering Parliament in 1959. She had served as minister of pensions and national insurance, 1961; opposition spokesman on education, 1969; and secretary of state for education and science, 1970. In her administration as Prime Minister, she instituted cuts in government spending, and regained control of the Falkland Islands, 1982.

On February 5, 1996, Margaret Thatcher was interviewed in New York City, while on her way to Utah for the U.K.-Utah Festival. Her statements were printed in *Human Events:*

> *The Decalogue* [Ten Commandments] are addressed to each and every person. This is the origin of our common humanity and of the sanctity of the individual. Each one has a duty to try to carry out *those commandments...*
>
> If you accept freedom, you've got to have principles about the responsibility. You can't do this without a biblical foundation. Your Founding Fathers came over with that. They came over with the *doctrines of the New Testament as well as the Old.* They looked after one another, not only as a matter of necessity, but as a matter of duty to their God. There is no other country in the world which started that way.[46]

WILLIAM GRAHAM

The United States Congress, Thursday, May 2, 1996, during the celebration of the National Day of Prayer, presented Dr. Billy Graham, and his wife Ruth, with the distinguished Congressional Gold Medal. This award, having been given to only 263 individuals in the history of the United States, is the highest honor which can be bestowed on an American citizen, the first recipient being President George Washington. Dr. Graham, who has the unique distinction of having personally counseled every President since Harry S. Truman, stated in his acceptance speech, entitled "The Hope for America":

> We must commit our lives to God, and to the moral and spiritual truths that have made this nation great. Think how different our nation would be if we sought to follow the simple and yet profound injunctions of *the Ten Commandments* and the Sermon on the Mount.[47]

FOB JAMES

Forrest Hood "Fob" James, Jr. (b. September 15, 1934) was the Governor of Alabama, 1978-82; reelected 1994. He graduated from Auburn University, 1955; served as lieutenant in the U.S. Army, 1957-58; founder and chairman of Diversified Products Corporation, 1962-78; is active in the Cystic Fibrosis Foundation, Boy Scouts of America, Alabama Saftey Council, Junior Achievement, Future Farmers of America, Young President's Organization; Alabama Road Builders Association, American Legion, Spade Honor Society; and Alpha Sigma Epsilon.

On Wednesday, February 5, 1997, Governor Fob James threatened to call out the National Guard to prevent those who were endeavoring to remove the Ten Commandments display from a Gadsden courtroom and prohibit the opening of court sessions with traditional invocations:

> The only way those *Ten Commandments* and prayer would be stripped from that courtroom is with the force of arms.[48]

U.S. CONGRESS

In the U.S. Congress, August 11, 1992, U.S. Representative Nick Joe Rahall II introduced legislation in the 102nd Congress to declare November 22 through November 28, 1992, as "America's Christian Heritage Week." (Reintroduce in the 103rd Congress as Christian Heritage Resolution, H.J. 113). As recorded in the Congressional Record, Vol 138, No. 1, Washington, Wednesday, August 12, 1992, the legislation reads:

> There is no better place than this great land of America for people to embrace and declare that our trust is in God, and that we look to *His commandments* and teachings for values that fortify and give direction to our families.[49]

The United States Congress, June 17, 1999, approved the amendment introduced by Rep. Robert Aderholt of Alabama to H.R. 1501, The Juvenile Justice Reform Act of 1999, by a roll call vote of 248-180. Included in the amendment is:

> SEC. 1202. RELIGIOUS LIBERTY RIGHTS DECLARED.
> (a) DISPLAY OF *TEN COMMANDMENTS* - The power to *display the Ten Commandments* on or within property owned or administered by the several States or political subdivisions thereof is hereby declared to be among the powers reserved to the States respectively.
> (b) EXPRESSION OF RELIGIOUS FAITH- The expression of religious faith by individual persons on or within property owned or administered by the several States or political subdivisions thereof is hereby:
> (1) declared to be among the rights secured against laws respecting an establishment of religion or prohibiting the free exercise of religion made or enforced by the United States Government or by any department or executive or

judicial officer thereof; and (2) declared to be among the liberties of which no State shall deprive any person without due process of law made in pursuance of powers reserved to the States respectively.

(c) EXERCISE OF JUDICIAL POWER- The courts constituted, ordained, and established by the Congress shall exercise the judicial power in a manner consistent with the foregoing declarations.[50]

U.S. SUPREME COURT

The U.S. Supreme Court (1973), in Anderson v. Salt Lake City Corp, 475 F. 2d 29, 33, 34 (10th Cir. 1973), cert. denied, 414 U.S. 879, stated:

But this creed does not include any element of coercion concerning these beliefs unless one considers it coercive to look upon *the Ten Commandments*. Although they are in plain view, no one is required to read or recite them. It does not seem reasonable to require removal of a passive monument, involving no compulsion, because its accepted precepts, as *a foundation for law*, reflect the religious nature of an ancient era.[51]

U.S. DISTRICT COURT

U.S. District Court (1983), Western District of Virginia, in Crockett v. Sorenson, 568 F.Supp. 1422, 1425-1430 (W.D. Va. 1983), stated:

Further, biblical influences pervade many specific areas of the law. The 'good Samaritan' laws use a phrase lifted directly out of one of Jesus' parables. The concept of the 'fertile octogenarian,' applicable to the law of wills and trusts, is in a large part derived from the book of Genesis where we are told that Sarah, the wife of the patriarch Abraham, gave birth to Isaac when she was 'past age.' In addition, *the Ten Commandments* have had immeasurable effect on Anglo-American legal development.[52]

iv.
THE TEN COMMANDMENTS

WEBSTER'S DICTIONARY

Noah Webster's original 1828 *Dictionary of the English Language* gives the definition:

COMMANDMENT, n.
1. A command; a mandate; an order or injunction given by authority; charge; precept.
Why do ye transgress the commandment of God. Matt. 15.
This is the first and great commandment. Matt. 22.
A new commandment I give to you, that you love one another. John 13.
2. By way of eminence, a precept of the decalogue, or moral law, written on tables of stone, at Mount Sinai; one of the ten commandments. Ex. 34.
3. Authority; coercive power.

In order to accurately assess the direct and indirect impact of the Ten Commandments, it is necessary to examine them one by one, studying the influence each of them individually had on America's founders, leaders and the system of government.

COMMANDMENTS

The Ten Commandments can be found in two places in the Scriptures, in the Book of Exodus, chapter 20, versus 2-17, and the Book of Deuteronomy, chapter 5, versus 6-21:

I.   I am the Lord thy God, which have brought thee out of the land of Egypt, out of the house of bondage. Thou shalt have no other gods before me.

II.   Thou shalt not make unto thee any graven image, or any likeness of any thing that is in heaven above, or that is in the earth beneath, or that is in the water under the earth. Thou shalt not bow down thyself to them, nor serve them: for I the Lord thy God am a jealous God, visiting the iniquity of the fathers upon the children unto the third and fourth generation of them that hate me; And shewing mercy unto thousands of them that love me, and keep my commandments.

III.   Thou shalt not take the name of the Lord thy God in vain; for the Lord will not hold him guiltless that taketh his name in vain.

IV.   Remember the sabbath day, to keep it holy. Six days shalt thou labour, and do all thy work: But the seventh day is the sabbath of the Lord thy God: in it thou shalt not do any work, thou, nor thy son, nor thy daughter, thy manservant, nor thy maidservant, nor thy cattle, nor thy stranger that is within thy gates: For in six days the Lord made heaven and earth, the sea, and all that in them is, and rested the seventh day: wherefore the Lord blessed the sabbath day, and hallowed it.

V.   Honour thy father and thy mother: that thy days may be long upon the land which the Lord thy God giveth thee.

VI.   Thou shalt not kill.

VII.   Thou shalt not commit adultery.

VIII.   Thou shalt not steal.

IX.   Thou shalt not bear false witness against thy neighbour.

X.   Thou shalt not covet thy neighbour's house, thou shalt not covet thy neighbour's wife, nor his manservant, nor his maidservant, nor his ox, nor his ass, nor any thing that is thy neighbour's.

I.
THE FIRST COMMANDMENT

"I am the Lord thy God, which have brought thee out of the land of Egypt, out of the house of bondage. Thou shalt have no other gods before me." – Ex. 20:2-3, Deut 5:6-7

WEBSTER'S DICTIONARY

Noah Webster's original 1828 *Dictionary of the English Language* gives the definition:

GOD, n.
1. The Supreme Being; Jehovah; the eternal and infinite spirit, the creator, and the sovereign of the universe.
 God is a spirit; and they that worship him, must worship him in spirit and in truth. John 4.
2. A false god; a heathen deity; an idol.
 Fear not the gods of the Amorites. Judges 6.
3. A prince; a ruler; a magistrate or judge; an angel. Thou shalt not revile the gods, nor curse the ruler of thy people. Ex. 22. Ps.97.
[Gods here is a bad translation.]
4. Any person or thing exalted too much in estimation, or deified and honored as the chief good.
 Whose god is their belly. Phil.3.

COMMENTARY

In his commentary "The Ten Commandments in American Law and Government," Matthew D. Staver writes:

The First Commandment states, "Thou shalt have no other gods before me."

In 1610, Virginia required its leaders to give "allegiance" to God, "from whom all power and authority is derived," and who is the "King of kings, the Commander of commanders, and Lord of hosts." The law stated the following:

> [S]ince we owe our highest and supreme duty, our greatest and all our allegiance to Him from whom all power and authority is derived, and flows as from the first and only fountain, and being especially soldiers impressed in this sacred cause, we must alone expect our success from Him who is only the blesser of all good attempts, the King of kings, the Commander of commanders, and Lord of hosts, I do strictly command and charge all Captains and Officers of what quality or nature soever, whether commanders in the field, or in town or towns, forts or fortresses, to have a care that the Almighty God be duly and daily served, and that they call upon their people to hear sermons, as that also they diligently frequent morning and evening prayer themselves by their own example and daily life and duties herein, encouraging others thereunto.

Articles, Laws, and Orders, Divine, Politic and Martial for the Colony of Virginia, reprinted in Donald S. Lutz, ed., COLONIAL ORIGINS OF THE AMERICAN CONSTITUTION: A DOCUMENTARY HISTORY at 315-16 (hereafter "COLONIAL ORIGINS").

In 1641, Massachusetts adopted a law that stated:

> If any man after legal conviction shall have or worship any other god but the Lord God, he shall be put to death. Deut. 13.6, 10, Deut. 17.2, 6, Ex. 22.20.

Massachusetts Body of Liberties (1641), reprinted in THE COLONIAL LAWS OF MASSACHUSETTS at 33 (W. H. Whitmore, 1890).

Even today, most every state constitution continues to reference God or a Supreme Being. See Capital Square, 243 F.3d at 296 n.6.

The preamble to Alabama's Constitution of 1901 states that the people are:

> invoking the favor and guidance of almighty God....

The 1820 Preamble to Maine's constitution describes God as:

> the Sovereign Ruler of the Universe.

West Virginia's Preamble to the 1872 constitution:

> reaffirms our faith in an constant reliance upon God.

These phrases are reflections of an idea and belief in the preeminence of God that flows directly from the First Commandment. This is not to advocate that the First Commandment be enacted and enforced today upon pain of death, but merely to demonstrate the Commandment was and is a major part of the development of law and government. Indeed, our national motto proclaims, "In God We Trust," not "In Gods We Trust." [53]

INFLUENCE OF THE FIRST COMMANDMENT
William J. Federer

The belief in a monotheistic God is so basic to America that it is almost unnecessary to discuss. We have to look no further than our National Coinage, National Currency, National Motto, National Anthem, Pledge of Allegiance, Inaugural Addresses, State Constitutions, the wall above the chair of the Speaker of the House, National Monuments, National Day of Thanksgiving Proclamations, etc., to see examples.

THE NATIONAL COINAGE

In a *Memorial Address* for President Lincoln, April 24, 1865, Speaker of the House Schuyler Colfax stated:

> Nor should I forget to mention here that the last act of Congress ever signed by him was one requiring that the motto, in which he sincerely believed, "In God We Trust," should hereafter be inscribed upon all our national coin.[54]

Salmon Portland Chase was the U.S. Secretary of the Treasury under President Lincoln. He served as the Governor of Ohio, a U.S. Senator and was appointed by President Abraham Lincoln as Chief Justice of the Supreme Court. He was a strong opponent of slavery, defending so many escaped slaves when he first started practicing law that he was given the nickname "Attorney-General of Fugitive Slaves."

On November 20, 1861, Secretary of the Treasury Salmon Portland Chase wrote to the Director of the Mint in Philadelphia:

> Dear Sir,
> No nation can be strong except in the strength of God or safe except in His defense. The trust of our people in God should be declared on our national coins.
> You will cause a device to be prepared without unnecessary delay with a motto expressing in the fewest and tersest words possible this national recognition.
> Yours truly,
> (Sgd). S.P. Chase"[55]

On December 9, 1863, Secretary of the Treasury Salmon Portland Chase, wrote to the Director of the Mint, James Pollock:

> I approve your mottos, only suggesting that on that with the Washington obverse, the motto should begin with the word "Our," so as to read:

"Our God and our Country." And on that with the shield, it should be changed so as to read: "In God We Trust.'"[56]

On March 3, 1865, the Congress of the United States of America approved the Treasury Secretary Salmon Portland Chase's instruction to the U.S. mint to prepare a "device" to inscribe U.S. coins with the motto:

In God We Trust.[57]

THE NATIONAL CURRENCY

In 1955, the Congress of the United States passed a bill, signed by President Eisenhower, providing that all U.S. currency should bear the words "In God We Trust."[58]

THE NATIONAL MOTTO

On October 30, 1949, in a radio address, President Harry S. Truman stated:

When the United States was established, its coins bore witness to the American faith in a benevolent deity. The motto then was 'In God We Trust.' That is still our motto and we, as a people, still place our firm trust in God.[59]

The United States Congress, July 20, 1956, in the 84th Congress, 2nd session, adopted House Joint Resolution 396, introduced by Rep. Charles E. Bennett (FL), providing that the national motto of the United States of America officially be "In God We Trust":

84th Congress, 2nd Session, H.J. 396;
IN THE SENATE OF THE UNITED STATES
April 18 (legislative day, April 9,) 1956
Read twice and referred to the Committee on the Judiciary

Joint Resolution
To establish a national motto of the United States.
Resolved by the Senate and House of Representatives of the United States of America in Congress Assembled, That the national motto of the United States is hereby declared to be "In God We Trust."

Passed the House of Representatives April 16, 1956.
Attest: Ralph R. Roberts, Clerk.[60]

On March 19, 1981, in a Proclamation of a National Day of Prayer,
President Ronald Reagan stated:

Our Nation's motto – "In God We Trust" - was
not chosen lightly. It reflects a basic recognition that there
is a divine authority in the universe to which this nation
owes homage.[61]

THE NATIONAL ANTHEM

The United States Congress, March 3, 1931, in the 71st Congress
adopted *The Star Spangled Banner* as our National Anthem, 36 U.S.C.
Sec.170, (H.R. 14; Public, No. 823; Session III, Chap. 436.):

1508 Seventy-First Congress. Sess. III. Chs. 436,
437. 1931.
Chap. 436. - An Act To make The Star-Spangled
Banner the national anthem of the United States of America.
Be it enacted by the Senate and House of
Representatives of the United States of America in Congress
assembled, That the composition consisting of the words
and music known as The Star-Spangled Banner is
designated the national anthem of the United States of
America.
Approved March 3, 1931.[62]

This anthem was written by Francis Scott Key, September 14, 1814,
at the Battle of Fort McHenry during the War of 1812. The fourth verse is as
follows:

O! thus be it ever when free men shall stand
Between their loved home and the war's
desolation;
Blest with vict'ry and peace, may the Heav'n-
rescued land
Praise the Pow'r that hath made and preserved us
a nation!
Then conquer we must, when our cause it is just;
And this be our motto, "In God is our trust!"

And the star spangled banner in triumph shall wave
O'er the land of the free and the home of the
brave![63]

THE PLEDGE OF ALLEGIANCE

The Unites States Congress, June 14, 1954, approved the Joint Resolution 243 (Public Law 83-396), which added the words "under God" to the *Pledge of Allegiance*. (The Pledge was initially adopted by the 79th Congress on December 28, 1945, as Public Law 287.):

Public Law 396; Chapter 297;
Joint Resolution
To amend the pledge of allegiance to the flag of the United States of America.

Resolved by the Senate and House of Representatives of the United States of America in Congress assembled, That section 7 of the joint resolution entitled "Joint resolution to codify and emphasize existing rules and customs pertaining to the display and use of the flag of the United States of America," approved June 22, 1942, as amended (36 U.S.C., sec. 172), is amended to read as follows:

Sec. 7. The following is designated as the pledge of allegiance to the flag: "I pledge allegiance to the flag of the United States of America and to the Republic for which it stands, one Nation under God, indivisible, with liberty and justice for all." Such pledge should be rendered by standing with the right hand over the heart. However, civilians will always show full respect to the flag when the pledge is given by merely standing at attention, men removing the headdress. Persons in uniform shall render the military salute.

Approved June 14, 1954.[64]

The *Pledge of Allegiance* was written in 1892 by a Baptist minister from Boston named Francis Bellamy, who was ordained in the Baptist Church of Little Falls, New York. He was a member of the staff of The Youth's Companion, which first published the Pledge on September 8, 1892, in Boston, Massachusetts. Public-school children first recited it during the National School Celebration on the 400th anniversary of Columbus' discovery of America, October 12, 1892, at the dedication of the 1892 Chicago World's

Fair. The words "under God" were taken from Abraham Lincoln's Gettysburg Address, "...that this nation, under God, shall have a new birth..."[65]

On June 14, 1954, President Eisenhower signed it into law:

> I pledge allegiance to the flag of the United States of America and to the Republic for which it stands, one Nation under God, indivisible, with liberty and justice for all."[66]

President Eisenhower gave his support to the Congressional Act, which added the phrase "under God" to the Pledge of Allegiance, saying:

> In this way we are reaffirming the transcendence of religious faith in America's heritage and future; in this way we shall constantly strengthen those spiritual weapons which forever will be our country's most powerful resource in peace and war.[67]

President Eisenhower then stood on the steps of the Capitol Building and recited *the Pledge of Allegiance* for the first time with the phrase, "one Nation under God."[68]

In 1979, a publication approved by and printed under authority of Congress entitled *The Capitol - A Pictorial History of the Capitol and of the Congress* (Washington, D.C.: U.S. Government Printing Office, 1979), p. 24, rendered the following comments regarding the pledge:

> This pledge attests what has been true about America from the beginning. Faith in the transcendent, sovereign God was in the public philosophy - the American consensus. America's story opened with the first words of the Bible, In the beginning God.... We are truthfully one nation under God "and our institutions presuppose a Divine Being," wrote Justice William O. Douglas in 1966.
>
> Only a nation founded on theistic pre-supposition would adopt a first amendment to ensure the free exercise of all religions or of none. The government would be neutral among the many denominations and no one church would become the state church. But America and its institutions of government could not be neutral about God.[69]

INAUGURAL ADDRESSES

Every President swore into office with their hand upon a Bible, ended their oath with the phrase "So help me, God," and acknowledged God in their address upon assuming office:

George Washington, 1st, "that **Almighty Being** who rules over the universe..."

John Adams, 2nd, "that **Being** who is supreme over all, the Patron of Order, the Fountain of Justice..."

Thomas Jefferson, 3rd, "that **Being** in whose hands we are, who led our forefathers, as Israel of old..."

James Madison, 4th, "that **Almighty Being** whose power regulates the destiny of nations..."

James Monroe, 5th, "with a firm reliance on the protection of **Almighty God...**"

John Quincy Adams, 6th, "knowing that 'Except **the Lord** keep the city, the watchman waketh in vain'..."

Andrew Jackson, 7th, "my fervent prayer to that **Almighty Being** before whom I now stand..."

Martin Van Buren, 8th, "that **Divine Being** whose strengthening support I humbly solicit..."

William Henry Harrison, 9th, "the **Beneficent Creator** has made no distinction amongst men..."

John Tyler, 10th, "the all-wise and **all-powerful Being** who made me..."

James Polk, 11th, "in their worship of **the Almighty** according to the dictates of their own conscience..."

Zachary Taylor, 12th, "to which the goodness of **Divine Providence** has conducted our common country..."

Millard Fillmore, 13th, "it has pleased **Almighty God** to remove from this life Zachary Taylor..."

Franklin Pierce, 14th, "humble, acknowledged dependence upon **God** and His overruling providence..."

James Buchanan, 15th, "In entering upon this great office I must humbly invoke the **God of our fathers...**"

Abraham Lincoln, 16th, "Both read the same Bible and pray to the same **God**, and each invokes His aid..."

Andrew Johnson, 17th, "grief on earth which can only be assuaged by communion with **the Father in heaven...**"

Ulysses S. Grant, 18th, "I do believe that **our Great Maker** is preparing the world, in His own good time..."

Rutherford B. Hayes, 19th, "guidance of that **Divine Hand** by which the destinies of nations and individuals are shaped..."

James Garfield, 20th, "**their fathers' God** that the Union was preserved, that slavery was overthrown..."

Chester Arthur, 21st, "I assume the trust imposed by the Constitution, relying for aid on **Divine Guidance...**"

Grover Cleveland, 22nd, "the power and goodness of **Almighty God** who presides over the destiny of nations..."

Benjamin Harrison, 23rd, "invoke and confidently extend the favor and help of **Almighty God** - that He will give me wisdom..."

Grover Cleveland, 24th, "I know there is a **Supreme Being** who rules the affairs of men and whose goodness and mercy have..."

William McKinley, 25th, "Our faith teaches that there is no safer reliance than upon **the God of our fathers...**"

Theodore Roosevelt, 26th, "with gratitude to **the Giver of Good** who has blessed us with the conditions which have enabled us..."

Howard Taft, 27th, "support of my fellow-citizens and the aid of **the Almighty God** in the discharge of my responsible duties..."

Woodrow Wilson, 28th, "I pray **God** I may be given the wisdom and the prudence to do my duty..."

Warren G. Harding, 29th, "that passage of Holy Writ wherein it is asked: "What doth **the Lord** require of thee..."

Calvin Coolidge, 30th, "[America] cherishes no purpose save to merit the favor of **Almighty God...**"

Herbert Hoover, 31st, "I beg your tolerance, your aid, and your cooperation. I ask the help of **Almighty God...**"

Franklin D. Roosevelt, 32nd, "In this dedication of a nation we humbly ask the blessing of **God...**"

Harry S. Truman, 33rd, "all men are created equal because they are created in the image of **God...**"

Dwight D. Eisenhower, 34th, "I ask that you bow your heads. **Almighty God**, as we stand here at this moment..."

John F. Kennedy, 35th, "the rights of man come not from the generosity of the state but from the hand of **God...**"

Lyndon B. Johnson, 36th, "the judgement of **God** is harshest on those who are most favored..."

Richard M. Nixon, 37th, "as all are born equal in dignity before **God**, all are born equal in dignity before man..."

Gerald Ford, 38th, "to uphold the Constitution, to do what is right as **God** gives me to see the right..."

Jimmy Carter, 39th, "what does **the Lord** require of thee, but to do justly, and to love mercy, and to walk humbly with thy **God...**"

Ronald Reagan, 40th, "one people under **God**, dedicated to the dream of freedom that He has placed in the human heart..."

George Bush, 41st, "**Heavenly Father**, we bow our heads and thank You for Your love..."

Bill Clinton, 42nd, "with **God**'s help, we must answer the call..."

George W. Bush, 43rd, "this story's **Author**, Who fills time and eternity with His purpose..."

STATE CONSTITUTIONS

Every one of the fifty State Constitutions acknowledge God:

Alabama 1901, Preamble. We the people of the State of Alabama...invoking the favor and guidance of **Almighty God**, do ordain and establish...[70]

Alaska 1956, Preamble. We, the people of Alaska, grateful to **God** and to those who founded our nation and pioneered this great land, in order to ...[71]

Arizona 1911, Preamble. We, the people of the State of Arizona, grateful to **Almighty God** for our liberties, do ordain this Constitution...[72]

Arkansas 1874, Preamble. We, the people of the State of Arkansas, grateful to **Almighty God** for the privilege of choosing our own form of government..[73]

California 1879, Preamble. We, the People of the State of California, grateful to **Almighty God** for our freedom, in order to secure and perpetuate its...[74]

Colorado 1876, Preamble. We, the people of Colorado, with profound reverence for the **Supreme Ruler** of Universe, in order to form a more...[75]

Connecticut 1818, Preamble. The People of Connecticut, acknowledging with gratitude the good Providence of **God** in permitting them to enjoy...[76]

Delaware 1897, Preamble. Through **Divine Goodness** all men have, by nature, the rights of worshipping and serving their Creator according to the dictates...[77]

Florida 1885, Preamble. We, the people of the State of Florida, grateful to **Almighty God** for our constitutional liberty...establish this Constitution...[78]

Georgia 1777, Preamble. We, the people of Georgia, relying upon protection and guidance of **Almighty God**, do ordain and establish this Constitution...[79]

Hawaii 1959, Preamble. We, the people of Hawaii, Grateful for **Divine Guidance**...establish this Constitution...[80]

Idaho 1889, Preamble. We, the people of the State of Idaho, grateful to **Almighty God** for our freedom, to secure its blessings and promote our...[81]

Illinois 1870, Preamble. We, the people of the State of Illinois, grateful to **Almighty God** for the civil, political and religious liberty which He hath so long permitted us to enjoy and looking to Him for a blessing on our endeavors[82]

Indiana 1851, Preamble. We, the People of the State of Indiana, grateful to **Almighty God** for the free exercise of the right to chose our form of govern...[83]

Iowa 1857, Preamble. We, the People of the State of Iowa, grateful to the **Supreme Being** for the blessings hitherto enjoyed, and feeling our dependence on Him for a continuation of these blessings...establish this Constitution...[84]

Kansas 1859, Preamble. We, the people of Kansas, grateful to **Almighty God** for our civil and religious privileges...establish this Constitution...[85]

Kentucky 1891, Preamble. We, the people of the Commonwealth of Kentucky, grateful to **Almighty God** for the civil, political and religious liberties...[86]

Louisiana 1921, Preamble. We, the people of the State of Louisiana, grateful to **Almighty God** for the civil, political and religious liberties we enjoy...[87]

Maine 1820, Preamble. We the People of Maine...acknowledging with grateful hearts the goodness of the **Sovereign Ruler of the Universe** in affording us an opportunity...and imploring His aid and direction...establish...[88]

Maryland 1776, Preamble. We, the people of the state of Maryland, grateful to **Almighty God** for our civil and religious liberty...[89]

Massachusetts 1780, Preamble...We the people of Massachusetts, acknowledging with grateful hearts, the goodness of **the great Legislator of the Universe**...in the course of His Providence, an opportunity...of entering into a solemn compact with each other..and devoutly imploring His direction.[90]

Michigan 1908, Preamble. We, the people of the State of Michigan, grateful to **Almighty God** for the blessings of freedom...establish this Constitution[91]

Minnesota, 1857, Preamble. We, the people of the State of Minnesota, grateful to **God** for our civil and religious liberty, and desiring to prepetuate its bless...[92]

Mississippi 1890, Preamble. We, the people of Mississippi in convention assembled, grateful to **Almighty God**, and invoking His blessing on our work[93]

Missouri 1945, Preamble. We, the people of Missouri, with profound reverence for **the Supreme Ruler of the Universe**, and grateful for His goodness...establish this Constitution.[94]

Montana 1889, Preamble. We, the people of Montana, grateful to **Almighty God** for the blessings of liberty...establish this Constitution.[95]

Nebraska 1875, Preamble. We, the people, grateful to **Almighty God** for our freedom...establish this Constitution.[96]

Nevada 1864, Preamble. We the people of the State of Nevada, grateful to **Almighty God** for our freedom...establish this Constitution.[97]

New Hampshire 1792, Part I. Art. I. Sec. V. Every individual has a natural and unalienable right to worship **God** according to the dictates of his own conscience.[98]

New Jersey 1844, Preamble. We, the people of the State of New Jersey, grateful to **Almighty God** for civil and religious liberty which He hath so long permitted us to enjoy, and looking to Him for a blessingon our endeavors[99]

New Mexico 1911, Preamble. We, the People of New Mexico, grateful to **Almighty God** for the blessings of liberty...[100]

New York 1846, Preamble. We, the people of the State of New York, grateful to **Almighty God** for our freedom, in order to secure its blessings...[101]

North Carolina 1868, Preamble. We the people of the State of North Carolina, grateful to **Almighty God, the Sovereign Ruler of Nations**, for...our civil, political, and religious liberties, and acknowledging our dependence upon Him for the continuanceof those...[102]

North Dakota 1889, Preamble. We, the people of North Dakota, grateful to **Almighty God** for the blessings of civil and religious liberty, do ordain...[103]

Ohio 1852, Preamble. We the people of the state of Ohio, grateful to **Almighty God** for our freedom, to secure its blessings and to promote our common...[104]

Oklahoma 1907, Preamble. Invoking the guidance of **Almighty God**, in order to secure and perpetuate the blessings of liberty...establish this...[105]

Oregon 1857, Bill of Rights, Article I. Section 2. All men shall be secure in the Natural right, to worship **Almighty God** according to the dictates of their consciences...[106]

Pennsylvania 1776, Preamble. We, the people of Pennsylvania, grateful to **Almighty God** for the blessings of civil and religious liberty, and humbly invoking His guidance...[107]

Rhode Island 1842, Preamble. We the People of the State of Rhode Island...grateful to **Almighty God** for the civil and religious liberty which He hath so long permitted us to enjoy, and looking to Him for a blessing...[108]

South Carolina, 1778, Preamble. We, the people of the State of South Carolina...grateful to **God** for our liberties, do ordain and establish this...[109]

South Dakota 1889, Preamble. We, the people of South Dakota, grateful to **Almighty God** for our civil and religious liberties...establish this...[110]

Tennessee 1796, Art. XI.III. That all men have a natural and indefeasible right to worship **Almighty God** according to the dictates of their conscience...[111]

Texas 1845, Preamble. We the People of the Republic of Texas, acknowledging, with gratitude, the grace and beneficence of **God**...[112]

Utah 1896, Preamble. Grateful to Almighty God for life and liberty, we...establish this Constitution...[113]

Vermont 1777, Preamble. Whereas all government ought to...enable the individuals who compose it to enjoy their natural rights, and other blessings which the **Author of existence** has bestowed on man...[114]

Virginia 1776, Bill of Rights, XVI...Religion, or the Duty which we owe **our Creator**...can be directed only by Reason...and that it is the mutual duty of all to practice Christian Forbearance, Love and Charity towards each other[115]

Washington 1889, Preamble. We the People of the State of Washington, grateful to **the Supreme Ruler of the Universe** for our liberties, do ordain...[116]

West Virginia 1872, Preamble. Since through Divine Providence we enjoy the blessings of civil, political and religious liberty, we, the people of West Virginia...reaffirm our faith in and constant reliance upon **God**...[117]

Wisconsin 1848, Preamble. We, the people of Wisconsin, grateful to **Almighty God** for our freedom, domestic tranquility...[118]

Wyoming 1890, Preamble. We, the people of the State of Wyoming, grateful to **God** for our civil, political, and religious liberties...establish this...[119]

GEORGE WASHINGTON

Did the first of the Ten Commandments have an influence on the founders? Did the founders believe in one God? Was that "one" God the "God of the Ten Commandments?" Below are examinations of some of prominent leaders.

George Washington was a Colonel in the Virginia Militia and fought alongside of British General Edward Braddock during the French and Indian War. He was justice of Fairfax County and a member of the Virginia House of Burgesses. He was a delegate to the First and Second Continental Congresses. He was Commander-in-Chief of the Continental Army. He was President of the Constitutional Convention where the U.S. Constitution was formulated, and he was the first President of the United States. Considered the most popular man in the Colonies, George Washington was described by Henry "Light Horse Harry" Lee in his now famous tribute, "First in war, first in peace, first in the hearts of his countrymen."

The son of Augustine Washington and his second wife, Mary Ball, George Washington was also a descendant of King John of England, and nine of the twenty-five Baron Sureties of the Magna Carta. His great-great grandfather, Rev. Lawrence Washington, was a clergyman in the Church of England. His great-grandfather, John Washington, moved to America in 1657, and helped found a parish in Virginia.

In his *Last Will and Testament*, John Washington left a gift to the church of a tablet with the Ten Commandments, on which he inscribed his testimony:

> Being heartily sorry from the bottome of my hart
> for my sins past, most humbly desiring forgiveness of the
> same from the Almighty God (my Saviour) and Redeemer,
> in whom and by the merits of Jesus Christ, I trust and believe
> assuredly to be saved, and to have full remission and
> forgiveness of all my sins.[120]

In addition to being a political leader, George Washington was also an active participant in the Episcopal Church. On January 6, 1759, George Washington was married to Martha Dandridge Custis by Rev. David Mossom, rector of Saint Peter's Episcopal Church, New Kent County, Virginia.

After having settled at Mount Vernon, George Washington became one of the twelve vestrymen in the Truro Parish, which included the Pohick

Church, the Falls Church, and the Alexandria Church. The old vestry book of Pohick Church contained the entry:

> At a Vestry held for Truro Parish, October 25, 1762, ordered, that George Washington, Esq. be chosen and appointed one of the Vestry-men of this Parish, in the room of William Peake, Gent. deceased.[121]

On February 15, 1763, the Fairfax County Court recorded:

> George Washington, Esq. took the oath according to Law, repeated and subscribed the Test and subscribed to the Doctrine and Discipline of the Church of England in order to qualify him to act as a Vestryman of Truro Parish.[122]

In his diary, George Washington recorded his attendance at numerous Church and Vestry meetings:

> 1768 - May 8th - Went to Church from Colonel Bassett's.
> May 22d - Went to Church at Nomini.
> May 29th - Church at St. Paul's.
> June 5th - to Church at Alexandria.
> June 12th - at Pohick.
> July 16th - Went by Muddy Hole and Dog Run to the vestry at Pohick Church – stayed there till after 3 o'clock and only four members coming, returned by Captain McCartys and dined there.
> August - Nomini in Westmoreland.
> September 9th - proceeded [through Alexandria] to the meeting of our Vestry at the new Church [Payne's] and lodged at Captain Edward Payne's.
> Nov. 15th - at Pohick.
> Nov. 28th - Went to Vestry at Pohick Church.
> 1769 - March 3rd - Went to the Vestry at Pohick Church and returned at 11 o'clock at night.
> Sept. 23rd - Captain Posey called here in the morning and we went to a Vestry.
> 1772 - June 5th - Met the Vestry at our new Church [Payne's] and came home in the afternoon.
> 1774 - Feb. 15th - I went to a Vestry at the new Church [Payne's] and returned in the afternoon.

Sept. 25th - Went to Quaker meeting in the forenoon, and
to St. Peter's in the afternoon; dined at my lodgings.
Oct. 2d - Went to Church, dined at the new tavern.
Oct. 9th - Went to the Presbyterian meeting in the afternoon;
dined at Bevan's.
Oct. 16th - Went to Christ Church in the morning; after
which rode to and dined at the Province Island; supped at
Byrn's."[123]

President James Madison stated:

Washington was constant in the observance of
worship, according to the received forms of the Episcopal
Church.[124]

Being in communion with the Anglican Church, serving for over
twenty years as a vestryman (trustee), and on at least three different occasions
serving as churchwarden, Washington would have regularly been at church
services and repeated the Apostle's Creed, which begins with a reference to
the first of the Ten Commandments:

I believe in God, the Father Almighty, Maker of heaven
and earth...[125]

Washington referred to God in the following terms:

"The Almighty" (Letter to the Hebrew Congregations of
Philadelphia, Newport, Charlestown and Richmond January
1790)[126]
**"Almighty Being who rules over the universe, who
presides in the councils of nations and whose
providential aids can supply every human defect"**
(Inaugural Address, New York City, New York, April 30,
1789)[127]
"Almighty Father" (From headquarters near the Hudson
River, June 1779)[128]
"Almighty God" (Orders to his troops, May 15, 1776)[129]
"Almighty and Merciful Sovereign of the Universe"
(from Philadelphia, letter to the Emperor of Germany May
15, 1796)[130]
"Almighty Ruler of the Universe" (Orders from Valley
Forge, May 5, 1778)[131]

"The Author of All Good" (Seventh Annual Message to Congress, Tuesday, December 8, 1795)[132]
"Divine Author of life and felicity" (To Episcopal Bishop William White, Rev. Ashabel Green, D.D., and twenty-three other clergymen of Philadelphia, March 3, 1797)[133]
"Divine Author of our blessed religion" (From his headquarters at Newburgh, New York, Circular Letter Addressed to the Governors of all the States on Disbanding the Army, June 14, 1783)[134]
"Great Author of all the care and good that have been extended in relieving us in difficulties" (From his headquarters at Valley Forge to Landon Carter May 30, 1778)[135]
"Great Author of every public and private good" (Inaugural Address, New York City, New York, April 30, 1789) [136]
"The kind Author of these blessings" (Proclamation of a National Day of Public Thanksgiving and Prayer, January 1, 1795)[137]
"Supreme Author of all good" (Orders to troops at Valley Forge, May 2, 1778)[138]
"The Great Arbiter of the Universe" (To the U.S. Senate Monday, May 18, 1789)[139]
"Great Governor of the Universe" (To General Benjamin Lincoln, his deputy in the War, who had accepted British General Cornwallis' sword at the surrender at Yorktown, June 29, 1788)[140]
"Lord and Giver of victory" (Orders to his troops, May 15, 1776)[141]
"The Lord and Giver of all victory" (From his headquarters at Cambridge, orders for a Day of Fasting, Prayer and Humiliation, March 6, 1776)[142]
"The Lord of hosts" (From his headquarters at Cambridge, orders for a Day of Fasting, Prayer and Humiliation, March 6, 1776)[143]
"The great Lord and Ruler of Nations" (From the city of New York, Proclamation of a National Day of Thanksgiving, October 3, 1789)[144]
"The Benign Parent of the Human Race" (Inaugural Address, New York City, April 30, 1789)[145]
"That great and glorious Being, who is the beneficent Author of all the good that was, that is, or that will be"

(From the city of New York, Proclamation of a National Day of Thanksgiving, October 3, 1789)[146]
"That Being in whose hands are all Human Events" (Handbill prepared by Washington at Cambridge given to Col. Benedict Arnold to be distributed to the inhabitants of Canada)[147]
"That Being who is powerful to save, and in whose hands is the fate of nations" (To the General Assembly of Massachusetts regarding the recent evacuation of General Howe and the British troops from Boston, March 17, 1776)[148]
"The same glorious Being" (to the Reformed German Congregation of New York, November 27, 1783)[149]
"Omnipotent Being" (From Mount Vernon to James McHenry, July 31, 1788)[150]
"The Supreme Being" (To P.A. Adet, the minister plenipotentiary of the French Republic, January 1, 1796)[151]
"The Supreme Being in whose hands victory is" (General Orders from his Head Quarters in New York, July 2, 1776)[152]
"The most Gracious Being, who has hitherto watched over the interests and averted the perils of the United States" (In addressing the mayor, recorder, aldermen and Common Council of the City of Philadelphia, April 20, 1789) [153]
"That beneficent Being" (To the mayor, corporation and citizens of Alexandria, Virginia, before leaving for his Inauguration in New York, April 16, 1789)[154]
"That Being on whose will the fate of nations depends to crown with success our mutual endeavors for the general happiness." (Fifth Annual Address to Congress, December 3, 1793)[155]
"The God to whom you commended me" (Letter to his mother, April 1755)[156]
"The Judge of the hearts of men" (To Colonel Benedict Arnold, September 14, 1775)[157]
"The God of Armies" (From Rock Hill, near Princeton, Farewell Orders to the Armies of the United States, November 2, 1783)[158]
"My God" (From Mount Vernon to Henry Lee in Congress, who had urged him to accept the presidency, September 22, 1788)[159]

"So help me, God" (Oath of office, Thursday, April 30, 1789, on the balcony of Federal Hall, in New York City, with his hand upon an open Bible)[160]
"The Deity" (To the Hebrew Congregations of the city of Savannah, Georgia)[161]
"That God who is alone able to protect them" (From Philadelphia to John Armstrong March 11, 1792)[162]
"Father of mercies, take me unto thyself" (Last words, as recorded by his secretary Tobias Lear, at about eleven o'clock in the evening, December 14, 1799)[163]
"In the Name of God, Amen...." (Last Will and Testament)[164]

George Washington's references were to the God of the who gave the Ten Commandments to the Jews. He wrote to the Hebrew Congregations of the city of Savannah, Georgia:

> May the same wonder-working Deity, who long since delivering the Hebrews from their Egyptian Oppressors planted them in the promised land - whose Providential Agency has lately been conspicuous in establishing these United States as an independent Nation - still continue to water them with the dews of Heaven and to make the inhabitants of every denomination participate in the temporal and spiritual blessings of that people whose God is Jehovah.[165]

On August 17, 1790, in an address to the Hebrew Congregation in Newport, Rhode Island, President Washington stated:

> May the children of the stock of Abraham who dwell in this land continue to merit and enjoy the good will of the other inhabitants - while every one shall sit in safety under his own vine and fig tree and there shall be none to make him afraid. May the Father of all mercies scatter light, and not darkness, upon our paths, and make us all in our several vocations useful here, and in His own due time and way everlastingly happy.[166]

WILLIAM PENN

On August 18, 1681, in a letter to the Indians in Pennsylvania, William Penn stated:

My Friends:
There is one great God and Power that hath made the world and all things therein, to whom you and I and all people owe their being and well-being, and to whom you and I must one day give an account, for all that we doe in the world; This great God hath written His law in our hearts by which we are taught and commanded to love and help and doe good to one another and not to doe harm and mischief one unto another.[167]

BENJAMIN FRANKLIN

In The Papers of Benjamin Franklin (Yale University Press, New Haven, 1959), Franklin listed topics and doctrines, which he considered of vital importance, to be shared and preached:

That there is one God, Father of the Universe.
That He [is] infinitely good, powerful and wise.
That He is omnipresent.
That He ought to be worshipped, by adoration, prayer and thanksgiving both in publick and private.
That He loves such of His creatures as love and do good to others: and will reward them either in this world or hereafter.
That men's minds do not die with their bodies, but are made more happy or miserable after this life according to their actions.
That virtuous men ought to league together to strengthen the interest of virtue, in the world: and so strengthen themselves in virtue.
That knowledge and learning is to be cultivated, and ignorance dissipated. That none but the virtuous are wise. That man's perfection is in virtue.[168]

On March 9, 1790, Benjamin Franklin wrote to Ezra Stiles, President of Yale University:

Here is my Creed. I believe in one God, the Creator of the Universe. That He governs it by His Providence. That He ought to be worshipped. That the most acceptable service we render to Him is in doing good to His other Children. That the soul of Man is immortal, and will be treated with Justice in another Life respecting its conduct in this. These I take to be the fundamental points in all sound Religion, and I regard them as you do in whatever Sect I meet with them.[169]

In 1754, in a pamphlet entitled Information to *Those Who Would Remove to America*, Benjamin Franklin wrote to Europeans interested in immigrating or sending their youth to this land:

Hence bad examples to youth are more rare in America, which must be a comfortable consideration to parents. To this may be truly added, that serious religion, under its various denominations, is not only tolerated, but respected and practised.

Atheism is unknown there; Infidelity rare and secret; so that persons may live to a great age in that country without having their piety shocked by meeting with either an Atheist or an Infidel.

And the Divine Being seems to have manifested his approbation of the mutual forbearance and kindness with which the different sects treat each other; by the remarkable prosperity with which he has been pleased to favor the whole country.[170]

ROGER SHERMAN

Roger Sherman was distinguished as the only Founding Father to sign all four major founding documents: The Articles of Association, 1774; The Declaration of Independence, 1776; The Articles of Confederation, 1777; and The Constitution of the United States, 1787.

In 1788, as a member of the White Haven Congregational Church, Roger Sherman, was asked to use his expertise in revising the wording of their creed. In his own handwriting, he wrote the following:

I believe that there is one only living and true God, existing in three persons, the Father, the Son, and the Holy Ghost, the same in substance equal in power and glory.[171]

THOMAS JEFFERSON

On Monday, March 4, 1805, in his Second Inaugural Address, President Thomas Jefferson stated:

> I shall need, too, the favor of that Being in whose hands we are, who led our forefathers, as Israel of old, from their native land and planted them in a country flowing with all the necessities and comforts of life, who has covered our infancy with His Providence and our riper years with His wisdom and power, and to whose goodness I ask you to join with me in supplications that He will so enlighten the minds of your servants, guide their councils and prosper their measures, that whatever they do shall result in your good, and shall secure to you the peace, friendship and approbation of all nations.[172]

Writing of Jesus in a letter to Dr. Benjamin Rush, April 21, 1803, President Thomas Jefferson referenced the belief in the One God of the Hebrew scriptures:

> His system of morals...if filled up in the style and spirit of the rich fragments He left us, would be the most perfect and sublime that has ever been taught by man....He corrected the deism of the Jews, confirming them in their belief of one only God, and giving them juster notions of His attributes and government....
>
> The precepts of philosophy, and of the Hebrew code, laid hold of actions only. He pushed his scrutinies into the hearts of man, erected his tribunal in the region of thoughts, and purified the waters at the fountainhead....
>
> Of all the systems of morality, ancient and modern, which have come under my observation, none appear to me so pure as that of Jesus.[173]

CHARLES COTESWORTH PINCKNEY

Charles Cotesworth Pinckney was a delegate to the Constitutional Convention and a signer of the United States Constitution. He was a Presidential and Vice-Presidential candidate, a successful lawyer, planter, statesman, soldier, a Brigadier General and an aide-de-camp to General Washington.

Charles Cotesworth Pinckney helped write the Constitution of the State of South Carolina, which contained the article:

SOUTH CAROLINA, 1778. Article XXXVIII. That all persons and religious societies who acknowledge that there is one God, and a future state of rewards and punishments, and that God is publicly to be worshipped, shall be freely tolerated.... That all denominations of Christian[s]...in this State, demeaning themselves peaceably and faithfully, shall enjoy equal religious and civil privileges.[174]

STATE DOCUMENTS

The Constitution of the State of Pennsylvania, adopted 1776, stated:

Frame of Government, Chapter 2, Section 10. And each member [of the legislature], before he takes his seat, shall make and subscribe the following declaration, viz: "I do believe in one God, the Creator and Governour of the Universe, the Rewarder of the good and Punisher of the wicked, and I do acknowledge the Scriptures of the Old and New Testament to be given by Divine Inspiration."[175]

In 1792, the Constitution of the State of Vermont stated:

Frame of Government, Chapter II, Section XII. And each member, before he takes his seat, shall make and subscribe the following declaration, viz: "You do believe in one God, the Creator and Governor of the Universe, the Rewarder of the good and Punisher of the wicked."[176]

ALEXIS DE TOCQUEVILLE

In August of 1831, while traveling through Chester County in New York, Alexis de Tocqueville had the opportunity to observe a court case. He wrote:

While I was in America, a witness, who happened to be called at the assizes of the county of Chester (state of New York), declared that he did not believe in the existence of God or in the immortality of the soul. The judge refused to admit his evidence, on the ground that the witness had destroyed beforehand all confidence of the court in what he was about to say. The newspapers related the fact without any further comment. The New York Spectator of August 23d, 1831, relates the fact in the following terms:

"The court of common pleas of Chester county (New York), a few days since rejected a witness who declared his disbelief in the existence of God. The presiding judge remarked, that he had not before been aware that there was a man living who did not believe in the existence of God; that this belief constituted the sanction of all testimony in a court of justice: and that he knew of no case in a Christian country, where a witness had been permitted to testify without such belief."[177]

GUSTAVE DE BEAUMONT

Gustave de Beaumont was a French historian, who traveled in America with Alexis de Tocqueville (May 1831-February 1832). He was commissioned by the French Government to study the American prisons, democracy, and religion. He published his work in Paris entitled, Marie ou l'Esclavage aux E'tas-Unis (1835). He wrote:

Religion in America is not only a moral institution but also a political institution. All of the American constitutions exhort the citizens to practice religious worship as a safeguard both to good morals and to public liberties. In the United States, the law is never atheistic.[178]

FRANCIS J. GRUND

Francis J. Grund, a publicist who was a contemporary of Alexis de Tocqueville, wrote in his work *The Americans in Their Moral, Social and Political Relations*, 1837:

Although the most perfect tolerance exists with regard to particular creeds, yet it is absolutely necessary that a man should belong to some persuasion of other, lest his fellow-citizens should consider him an outcast from society.

The Jews are tolerated in America with the same liberality as any denomination of Christians; but if a person were to call himself a Deist or an Atheist, it would excite universal execration.

Yet there are religious denominations in the United States whose creeds are very nearly verging on Deism; but taking their arguments from the Bible, and calling themselves followers of Christ, they and their doctrines are tolerated, together with their form of worship.[179]

II.
THE SECOND COMMANDMENT

"Thou shalt not make unto thee any graven image, or any likeness of any thing that is in heaven above, or that is in the earth beneath, or that is in the water under the earth. Thou shalt not bow down thyself to them, nor serve them: for I the Lord thy God am a jealous God, visiting the iniquity of the fathers upon the children unto the third and fourth generation of them that hate me; And shewing mercy unto thousands of them that love me, and keep my commandments." Ex. 20:4-6, Deut. 20:8-10

WEBSTER'S DICTIONARY

Noah Webster's original 1828 Dictionary of the English Language gives the definition:

WORSHIP, v.t.
1. To adore; to pay divine honors to; to reverence with supreme respect and veneration.
Thou shalt worship no other God. Exodus 34.
2. To respect; to honor; to treat with civil reverence.
Nor worshipd with a waxen epitaph.
3. To honor with extravagant love and extreme submission; as a lover.
With bended knees I daily worship her.

WORSHIP, n. [See Worth.]
1. Excellence of character; dignity; worth; worthiness.
—Elfin born of noble state, and muckle worship in his native land.
In this sense, the word is nearly or quite obsolete; but hence,
2. A title of honor, used in addresses to certain magistrates and other of respectable character.
My father desires your worships company.
3. A term of ironical respect.
4. Chiefly and eminently, the act of paying divine honors to the Supreme Being; or the reverence and homage paid

to him in religious exercises, consisting in adoration, confession, prayer, thanksgiving and the like.
The worship of God is an eminent part of religion.
Prayer is a chief part of religious worship.
5. The homage paid to idols or false gods by pagans; as the worship or Isis.
6. Honor; respect; civil deference.
Then shalt thou have worship in the presence of them that sit at meat with thee. Luke 14.
7. Idolatry of lovers; obsequious or submissive respect.

COMMENTARY

Matthew D. Staver writes:

The Second Commandment forbids the making of idols. In 1680, the New Hampshire colony enacted an idolatry law that stated:

Idolatry. It is enacted by ye Assembly and ye authority thereof, yet if any person having had the knowledge of the true God openly and manifestly have or worship any other god but the Lord God, he shall be put to death. Ex. 22.20, Deut. 13.6 and 10.

General Laws and Liberties of New Hampshire 1680, reprinted in COLONIAL ORIGINS at 6.

The 1780 Constitution of Massachusetts stated in Part I, Article II:

It is the right as well as the duty of all men in society, publicly, and at stated seasons, to worship the SUPREME BEING, the great creator and preserver of the universe.

How can a constitution declare that it is the duty of citizens to worship God without admitting the converse that the duty is breached when a one worships idols? [180]

INFLUENCE OF THE SECOND COMMANDMENT
William J. Federer

Our founders not only believed that God existed, but that He was to be worshipped. Citizens simply had the choice as to how they wanted to worship Him. It was not enough to acknowledge that One God existed, but our founders believe that citizens had a duty to worship this one God, as referenced in the sources below:

COLONIAL DOCUMENTS

The Second Charter of Virginia, May 23, 1609, granted by King James I, stated:

> And forasmuch, as it shall be necessary for all such our loving Subjects, as shall inhabit within the said Precincts of Virginia, aforesaid, to determine to live together, in the Fear and true Worship of Almighty God, Christian Peace, and civil Quietness, with each other, whereby every one may, with more Safety, Pleasure, and Profit, enjoy that, whereunto they shall attain with great Pain and Peril. [181]

The Body of Liberties, established by the Massachusetts General Court, December 1641, was the first code of laws established in New England. They were compiled by Nathaniel Ward (1578-1652), a leading English Puritan minister, who had been trained as a lawyer. He came to the Colony in 1634, and was for a time pastor at Ipswich. The Massachusetts Body of Liberties included:

> If any man after legall conviction shall have or worship any other god, but the Lord God, he shall be put to death. [182]

The Cambridge Platform of the Massachusetts Bay Colony, 1648 was recorded in the Plymouth Colony Records IX, 1663, listing the proposal of William Vassall and others. Item 8 recited:

> Idolatry, Blasphemy, Heresy, venting corrupt & pernicious opinions, that destroy the foundation, open contempt of the word preached, prophanation of the Lord's day, disturbing the peaceable administration & exercise of the worship & holy things of God, & the like, are to be restrayned, & punished by civil authority.[183]

The Code of the Connecticut General Court, 1650, in the Capital Laws Section, stated:

> 1. If any man after legal conviction shall have or worship any other God but the Lord God, he shall be put to death. Deut. 13:6, 17:2; Ex. 22:20.[184]

FOUNDERS

On June 6, 1753, Benjamin Franklin wrote from Philadelphia to Joseph Huey:

> The worship of God is a duty; the hearing and reading of sermons may be useful; but, if men rest in hearing and praying, as too many do, it is as if a tree should value itself on being watered and putting forth leaves, though it never produce any fruit.[185]

On November 20, 1772, in the section of *The Rights of the Colonists* entitled, "The Rights of the Colonist as Men," Samuel Adams declared:

> As neither reason requires nor religion permits the contrary, every man living in or out of a state of civil society has a right peaceably and quietly to worship God according to the dictates of his own conscience.[186]

In Thomas Jefferson's *Republican Notes on Religion and an Act Establishing Religious Freedom*, Passed in the Assembly of Virginia, in the Year 1786, reference is made to a law passed in 1705:

> By our own act of assembly of 1705, c. 30, if a person brought up in the Christian religion denies the being of a God, or the Trinity, or asserts there are more gods than one, or denies the Christian religion to be true, or the Scriptures to be of divine authority, he is punishable on the

first offense by incapacity to hold any office of employment, ecclesiastical, civil or military; on the second by disability to sue, to take any gift or legacy, to be guardian, executor, or administrator, and by three years' imprisonment without bail.[187]

On January 27, 1793, to the congregation of the New Church in Baltimore, President Washington wrote:

> We have abundant reason to rejoice that in this Land the light of truth and reason has triumphed over the power of bigotry and superstition, and that every person may here worship God according to the dictates of his own heart.[188]

ARTICLES IN STATE CONSTITUTIONS

The Constitution of the State of New Jersey, adopted 1776, stated:

> Article XVIII. That no person shall ever, within this Colony, be deprived of the inestimable privilege of worshipping Almighty God in a manner agreeable to the dictates of his own conscience.[189]

The Constitution of the State of Maryland, adopted 1776, stated:

> Article XIX; XXXIII. That, as it is the duty of every man to worship God in such a manner as he thinks most acceptable to him; all persons, professing the Christian religion, are equally entitled to protection in their religious liberty.[190]

The Constitution of the State of North Carolina, adopted 1776, stated:

> Article XIX. That all men have a natural and unalienable right to worship Almighty God according to the dictates of their own conscience.[191]
> Article XXXII. That no person who shall deny the being of God, or the truth of the Protestant religion, or the divine authority of the Old or New Testaments, or who shall hold religious principles incompatible with the freedom and safety of the State, shall be capable of holding

any office or place of trust or profit in the civil department within this State.[192]

The Constitution of the State of Vermont, adopted 1777, stated:

DECLARATION OF RIGHTS, III. That all men have a natural and Unalienable right to worship Almighty God according to the dictates of their own consciences and understanding, regulated by the word of GOD.[193]

The Constitution of the State of South Carolina, adopted 1778, stated:

Article XXXVIII. That all persons and religious societies, who acknowledge that there is one God, and a future state of rewards and punishments, and that God is publicly to be worshipped, shall be freely tolerated.[194]

The Constitution of Massachusetts, adopted 1780, stated:

Part I, Article II. It is the right, as well as the duty, of all men in society, publicly, and at stated seasons, to worship the Supreme Being, the Great Creator and Preserver of the Universe.[195]

The Constitution of the State of New Hampshire, adopted 1784 and 1792, stated:

Declaration of rights. The open denial of the being and existence of God or of the Supreme Being is prohibited by statute, and declared to be blasphemy.[196]

Part One, Article I, Section V. Every individual has a natural and unalienable right to worship God according to the dictates of his own conscience, and reason; and no subject shall be hurt, molested, or restrained in his person, liberty or estate for worshipping God.[197]

The Constitution of the State of Tennessee, adopted 1796, stated:

Article XI, Section III. That all men have a natural and indefeasible right to worship Almighty God according to the dictates of their own consciences.[198]

Article VIII, Section II. No person who denies the being of God, or a future state of rewards and punishments, shall hold any office in the civil department of this State.[199]

The Constitution of the State of Georgia, adopted 1798, stated:

Article IV, Section 10. No person within this State shall, upon any pretense, be deprived of the inestimable privilege of worshipping God.[200]

The Constitution of the State of Connecticut, adopted 1818, stated:

Article VII, Section 1. It being the duty of all men to worship the Supreme Being, the Great Creator and Preserver of the Universe, and their right to render that worship, in the mode most consistent with the dictates of their consciences.[201]

The Constitution of the State of Maine, adopted 1820, stated:

Article I, Section 3. All men have a natural and unalienable right to worship Almighty God according to the dictates of their own consciences.[202]

The Constitution of the State of Delaware, adopted 1831, stated:

It is the duty of all men frequently to assemble together for the public worship of the Author of the Universe; and piety and morality, on which the prosperity of communities depends, are thereby promoted.[203]

The Constitution of the State of Florida, adopted 1838, stated:

Bill of Rights. That all men have a natural and unalienable right to worship Almighty God according to the dictates of their own conscience; and that no preference shall ever be given by law to any religious establishment or mode of worship.[204]

The Constitution of the State of Texas, adopted 1845, stated:

> Article I, Section 4. All men have a natural and indefeasible right to worship God according to the dictates of their own consciences[205]

The Constitution of the State of Wisconsin, 1848, stated:

> Article I, Section 18. The right of every man to worship Almighty God according to the dictates of his own conscience shall never be infringed.[206]

The Constitution of the State of Indiana, adopted 1851, stated:

> Article I, Section 2. All men shall be secure in their natural right to worship Almighty God.[207]

The Constitution of the State of Ohio, adopted 1852, stated:

> Bill of Rights, Article I, Section 7. All men have a natural and indefeasible right to worship Almighty God according to the dictates of their own conscience.[208]

The Constitution of the State of Minnesota, adopted 1857, stated:

> Bill of Rights, Article I, Section 16. The right of every man to worship God according to the dictates of his own conscience shall never be infringed.[209]

The Constitution of the State of Oregon, adopted 1857, stated:

> Bill of Rights, Article I, Section 2. All men shall be secure in the Natural right, to worship Almighty God according to the dictates of their consciences.[210]

The Constitution of the State of Kansas, adopted 1859, stated:

> Bill of Rights, Section 7. The right to worship God according to the dictates of conscience shall never be infringed.[211]

The Constitution of the State of Pennsylvania, adopted 1874, stated:

Article I, Section 3. All men have a natural and indefeasible right to worship Almighty God according to the dictates of their own consciences.[212]

The Constitution of the State of Arkansas, adopted 1874, stated:

Article II, Section 24. All men have a natural and indefeasible right to worship Almighty God according to the dictates of their own consciences.[213]

Article XIX, Section 1. No person who denies the being of a God shall hold office in the civil departments of this State, nor be competent to testify as a witness in any court.[214]

The Constitution of the State of Nebraska, adopted 1875, stated:

Bill of Rights, Article I, Section 4. All persons have a natural and indefeasible right to worship Almighty God according to the dictates of their own consciences.[215]

The Constitution of the State of South Dakota, adopted 1889, stated:

Article VI, Section 3. The right to worship God according to the dictates of conscience shall never be infringed.[216]

The Constitution of the State of Michigan, adopted 1908, stated:

Article II, Section 3. Every person shall be at liberty to worship God according to the dictates of his own conscience.[217]

The Constitution of the State of New Mexico, adopted 1911, stated:

Article II, Section 2. Every man shall be free to worship God according to the dictates of his own conscience.[218]

The Constitution of the State of Louisiana, adopted 1921, stated:

> Article I, Section 4. Every person has the natural
> right to worship God according to the dictates of his own
> conscience.[219]

The Constitution of the State of Missouri, adopted 1945 stated:

> Bill of Rights, Article I, Section 5. That all men
> have a natural and indefeasible right to worship Almighty
> God according to the dictates of their own consciences.[220]

PRESIDENTS

On Tuesday, March 4, 1845, in his Inaugural Address, President
James Knox Polk stated:

> The Government of the United States....leaves
> individuals, over whom it casts its protecting influence,
> entirely free to improve their own condition by the
> legitimate exercise of all their mental and physical powers.
> It is a common protector of each and all the States; of every
> man who lives upon our soil, whether of native or foreign
> birth; of every religious sect, in their worship of the
> Almighty according to the dictates of their own
> conscience.[221]

On November 5, 1915, in an address celebrating the fiftieth
Anniversary of the Manhattan Club, at the Biltmore Hotel, New York,
President Woodrow Wilson stated:

> It does not become America that within her
> borders, where every man is free to follow the dictates of
> his conscience and worship God as he pleases, men should
> raise the cry of church against church. To do that is to strike
> at the very spirit and heart of America. We are a God-fearing
> people. We agree to differ about methods of worship, but
> we are united in believing in Divine Providence and in
> worshipping the God of Nations. We are the champions of
> religious right here and everywhere that it may be our
> privilege to give in our countenance and support.[222]

On January 6, 1941, President Franklin D. Roosevelt gave his Four Freedoms Speech to Congress:

> The second is freedom of every person to worship God in his own way.[223]

At noon on March 6, 1946, President Harry S. Truman addressed a Conference of the Federal Council of Churches given in Deshler-Wallick Hotel in Columbus, Ohio. In the speech, which was broadcast on national radio, he explained:

> We have just come though a decade in which the forces of evil in various parts of the world have been lined up in a bitter fight to banish from the face of the earth both these ideals - religion and democracy....
> In that long struggle between these two doctrines, the cause of decency and righteousness has been victorious. The right of every human being to live in dignity and freedom, the right to worship God in his own way, the right to fix his own relationship to his fellow men and to his Creator - these again have been saved for mankind.[224]

On Thursday, January 20, 1949, in his Inaugural Address, President Harry S. Truman stated:

> These differences between communism and democracy do not concern the United States alone. People everywhere are coming to realize that what is involved is material well-being, human dignity, and the right to believe in and worship God.[225]

III.
THE THIRD COMMANDMENT

*"Thou shalt not take the name of the Lord thy God
in vain; for the Lord will not hold him guiltless that taketh
his name in vain." – Ex. 20:7, Deut. 5:11*

WEBSTER'S DICTIONARY

Noah Webster's original 1828 Dictionary of the English Language
give the definition:

VAIN, a. [L. vanus; Eng. wan, wane, want.]
1. Empty; worthless; having no substance, value or
importance. 1Peter 1.
To your vain answer will you have recourse.
Every man walketh in a vain show. Ps. 39.
Why do the people imagine a vain thing? Ps. 2.
2. Fruitless; ineffectual. All attempts, all efforts were vain.
Vain is the force of man.
3. Proud of petty things, or of trifling attainments; elated
with a high opinion of one's own accomplishments, or with
things more showy than valuable; conceited.
The minstrels play'd on every side, vain of their art -
4. Empty; unreal; as a vain chimers.
5. Showy; ostentatious.
Load some vain church with old theatric state.
6. Light; inconstant; worthless. Prov. 12.
7. Empty; unsatisfying. The pleasures of life are vain.
8. False; deceitful; not genuine; spurious. James 1.
9. Not effectual; having no efficacy
Bring no more vain oblations. Is. 1.
In vain, to no purpose; without effect; ineffectual.
In vain they do worship me. Matt. 15.
To take the name of God in vain, to use the name of God
with levity or profaneness.

COMMENTARY

Matthew D. Staver writes:

The Third Commandment relates to not taking God's name in vain. The Third Commandment was adopted by Virginia in 1610:

> That no man blaspheme God's
> holy name upon the pain of death

and by Connecticut in 1639

> If any person shall blaspheme the name of God the Father, Son, or Holy Ghost ... he shall be put to death.

See COLONIAL ORIGINS at 316; THE CODE OF 1650 at 28-29.

In a 1921 case from the Supreme Court of Maine stated:

> To curse God means to scoff at God; to use profanely insolent and reproachful language against him. This is one form of blasphemy under the authority of standard lexicographers. To contumeliously reproach God, His Creation, government, final judgment of the world, Jesus Christ, the Holy Ghost, or the Holy Scriptures as contained in the canonical books of the Old and New Testament, under the same authorities, is to charge Him or Them with fault, to rebuke, to censure, to upbraid, doing the same with scornful insolence, with disdain, with contemptuousness in act or speech. This is another form of blasphemy. But as particularly applicable, perhaps, to the present case,

it is blasphemy to expose any of these enumerated Beings or Scriptures to contempt and ridicule. To have done any one of these things is blasphemy under the statute as well as at common law. It was not necessary for the state to prove that the respondent did them all.

State v. Mockus, 113 A. 39, 42 (Me. 1921).

Other colonies passed similar laws:

Massachusetts in 1641, Massachusetts Body Of Liberties (1641), reprinted in William MacDonald ed., SELECT CHARTERS AND OTHER DOCUMENTS ILLUSTRATIVE OF AMERICAN HISTORY, 1606-1775 (1993) at 87 (hereafter SELECT CHARTERS);

Connecticut in 1642, Capital Laws of Connecticut (1642), reprinted in COLONIAL ORIGINS at 230;

New Hampshire in 1680, General Laws and Liberties of New Hampshire (1680), reprinted in COLONIAL ORIGINS at 6;

Pennsylvania in 1682, An Act for Freedom of Conscience (1682), reprinted in COLONIAL ORIGINS at 289; Pennsylvania in 1700, Collinson Read ed., AN ABRIDGMENT OF THE LAWS OF PENNSYLVANIA (1801) at 32; Pennsylvania in 1741, An Act to Prevent the Grievous Sins of Cursing and Swearing within this Province and Territories, reprinted in 1 LAWS OF THE COMMONWEALTH OF PENNSYLVANIA (1810) at 7;

South Carolina in 1695, Joseph
Brevard ed., Blasphemy-Profaneness
(1695), reprinted in I ALPHABETICAL
DIGEST OF THE PUBLIC STATUTE
OF SOUTH CAROLINA (1814) at 87-
88;

and North Carolina in 1741,
Vice and Immorality (1741), reprinted in
John Haywood ed., A MANUAL OF
THE LAWS OF NORTH CAROLINA,
ARRANGED UNDER DISTINCT
HEADS, IN ALPHABETICAL ORDER
(1814) at 264.

Additionally, the Florida Supreme Court in 1944
stated:

This court has never defined the
legal meaning of the word "profanity" so
far as this writer has been able to
discover, but a number of other courts of
last resort have done so, and practically
all of them, following pretty closely the
dictionary meaning, define it as the use
of words importing "an imprecation of
Divine vengeance," of "implying Divine
condemnation," or words denoting
"irreverence of God and holy things,"—
blasphemous. These decisions doubtless
hark back to the third Commandment of
the decalogue: "Thou shalt not take the
name of the Lord thy God in vain."

Cason v. Baskin, 20 So.2d 243, 247 (Fla. 1944)
(en banc).

Commander-in-Chief George Washington issued
numerous military orders during the American Revolution
that first prohibited swearing and then ordered an attendance
on Divine worship, thus relating the prohibition against

profanity to a religious duty. Typical of these orders, on July 4, 1775, Washington declared:

> The General most earnestly requires and expects a due observance of those articles of war established for the government of the army which forbid profane cursing, swearing, and drunkenness; and in like manner requires and expects of all officers and soldiers not engaged on actual duty, a punctual attendance on Divine Service to implore the blessings of Heaven upon the means used for our safety and defense.

> John C. Fitzpatrick, ed., General Orders, Head-Quarters, Cambridge, July 4, 1775, THE WRITINGS OF GEORGE WASHINGTON (Washington: U. S. Government Printing Office, 1931) at 309.

Washington began issuing such orders to his troops as early as 1756 during the French and Indian War, and continued the practice throughout the American Revolution, issuing similar orders in 1776, 1777, 1778 and other years. See Jared Sparks, ed., 2 The Writings of George Washington (Boston: Ferdinand Andrews, 1836) at 167 (from his "Orderly Book," an undated order issued between June 25 and August 4, 1756.). See also General Orders, Head-Quarters, New York, August 3, 1776, Fitzpatrick, ed., 4 Writings of George Washington (1932) at 367.

The Third Commandment also affected the history of American jurisprudence. Judge Zephaniah Swift, author of the first legal text published in America, explained why civil authorities enforced the third commandment's prohibition against blasphemy and profane swearing:

> Crimes of this description are not punishable by the civil arm merely because they are against religion. Bold and presumptuous must he be who would attempt to wrest the thunder of heaven

from the hand of God and direct the bolts of vengeance where to fall. The Supreme Deity is capable of maintaining the dignity of His moral government and avenging the violations of His holy laws. His omniscient mind estimates every act by the standard of perfect truth and His impartial justice inflicts punishments that are accurately proportioned to the crimes. But short-sighted mortals cannot search the heart and punish according to the intent. They can only judge by overt acts and punish them as they respect the peace and happiness of civil society. This is the rule to estimate all crimes against civil law and is the standard of all human punishments. It is on this ground only that civil tribunals are authorized to punish offences against religion.

Zephaniah Swift, 2 A System of the Laws of the State of Connecticut (1976) at 320.

The laws against blasphemy and profanity based on the Third Commandment continued beyond the Founding Era. During the eighteenth and nineteenth century, several states passed laws based on the Third Commandment:

Connecticut in 1784, An Act for the Punishment of Divers Capital and Other Felonies, 1 THE PUBLIC STATUTE LAWS of THE STATE of CONNECTICUT (1808) at 295-96;

New Hampshire in 1791, An Act for the Punishment of Profane Cursing and Swearing (passed February 6, 1791),THE LAWS OF THE STATE OF NEW HAMPSHIRE, THE CONSTITUTION OF THE STATE OF NEW HAMPSHIRE, AND THE

CONSTITUTION OF THE UNITED STATES, WITH ITS PROPOSED AMENDMENTS (1797) at 280-281, 286-287 (a separate act passed February 10,1791); see also An Act for the Punishment of Certain Crimes not Capital (passed February 16, 1791), CONSTITUTION AND LAWS OF THE STATE OF NEWHAMPSHIRE TOGETHER WITH THE CONSTITUTION OF THE UNITED STATES (1805) at 277;

Vermont in 1791, An Act for the Punishment of Drunkenness, Gaming, and Profane Swearing (passed February 28,1787), STATUTES OF THE STATE OF VERMONT (1791) at 51; An Act for the Punishment of Divers Capital and other Felonies (passed March 8, 1787), STATUTES OF THE STATE OF VERMONT at 75;

Virginia in 1792, Joseph Tate ed., A DIGEST OF THE LAWS OF VIRGINIA, WHICH ARE OF A PERMANENT CHARACTER AND GENERAL OPERATION (1823) at 453-454; see also An Act for the Effectual Suppression of Vice, and Punishing the Disturbers of Religious Worship and Sabbath Breakers, 1 THE REVISED CODE OF THE LAWS OF VIRGINIA: BEING A COLLECTION OF ALL SUCH ACTS OF THE GENERAL ASSEMBLY, OF A PUBLIC AND PERMANENT NATURE AS ARE NOW IN FORCE (1819) at 554-556;

Pennsylvania in 1794, Act of April 22, 1794, AN ABRIDGMENT OF

THE LAWS OF PENNSYLVANIA 380 (1801);

MAINE IN 1821, Jeremiah Perley, 7 THE MAINE JUSTICE: CONTAINING THE LAWS RELATIVE TO THE POWERS AND DUTIES OF JUSTICES OF THE PEACE (1823) at 236; see also An Act Against Blasphemy and Profane Cursing and Swearing (passed February 24, 1821), LAWS OF THE STATE OF MAINE (1822) at 66-67;

Tennessee in 1834, Breaking the Sabbath, reprinted in James Coffield Mitchell, THE TENNESSEE JUSTICE'S MANUAL AND CIVIL OFFICER'S GUIDE (1834) at 428;

Massachusetts in 1835, Title 7, §76, Of Towns and Town Officers (passed November 4, 1835), THE REVISED STATUTES OF THE COMMONWEALTH OF MASSACHUSETTS (1836) at 185;

and New York in 1836, Of Profane Cursing and Swearing, Rev. Stat. 673, Art 6, reprinted in George C. Edwards, TREATISE OF THE POWERS AND DUTIES OF THE JUSTICES OF THE PEACE AND THE TOWN OFFICERS IN THE STATE OF NEW YORK (1836) at 379-380.

In 1824, the Supreme Court of Pennsylvania (in a decision subsequently invoked authoritatively and endorsed by the U. S. Supreme Court, See Church of the Holy Trinity v. U. S., 143 U. S. 457, 470-471 (1892)), reaffirmed that the civil laws against blasphemy were derived from divine law:

The true principles of natural religion are part of the common law; the essential principles of revealed religion are part of the common law; so that a person vilifying, subverting or ridiculing them may be prosecuted at common law.

Updegraph v. Commonwealth, 11 Serg. & Rawle 393, 401 (Penn. 1824), 1824 WL 2393 (Pa.).

The court then noted that its State's laws against blasphemy had been drawn up by James Wilson, a signer of the Constitution and original Justice on the U. S. Supreme Court:

The late Judge Wilson, of the Supreme Court of the United States, Professor of Law in the College in Philadelphia, was appointed in 1791, unanimously by the House of Representatives of this State to "revise and digest the laws of this commonwealth...... He had just risen from his seat in the Convention which formed the Constitution of the United States, and of this State; and it is well known that for our present form of government we are greatly indebted to his exertions and influence. With his fresh recollection of both constitutions, in his course of Lectures (3d vol. of his works, 112), he states that profaneness and blasphemy are offences punishable by fine and imprisonment, and that Christianity is part of the common law. It is vain to object that the law is obsolete; this is not so; it has seldom been called into operation because this, like some other offences, has been rare. It has been retained in our recollection of laws now in force, made by the direction of the legislature, and it has not been a dead letter.

Id. at 403.

In a 1921 case, the Supreme Court of Maine stated:

To curse God means to scoff at God; to use profanely insolent and reproachful language against him. This is one form of blasphemy under the authority of standard lexicographers. To contumeliously reproach God, His Creation, government, final judgment of the world, Jesus Christ, the Holy Ghost, or the Holy Scriptures as contained in the canonical books of the Old and New Testament, under the same authorities, is to charge Him or Them with fault, to rebuke, to censure, to upbraid, doing the same with scornful insolence, with disdain, with contemptuousness in act or speech. This is another form of blasphemy. But as particularly applicable, perhaps, to the present case, it is blasphemy to expose any of these enumerated Beings or Scriptures to contempt and ridicule. To have done any one of these things is blasphemy under the statute as well as at common law. It was not necessary for the state to prove that the respondent did them all.

State v. Mockus, 113 A. 39, 42 (Me. 1921).

Additionally, the Florida Supreme Court in 1944 stated:

This court has never defined the legal meaning of the word "profanity", so far as this writer has been able to discover, but a number of other courts of

last resort have done so, and practically
all of them, following pretty closely the
dictionary meaning, define it as the use
of words importing "an imprecation of
Divine vengeance," of "implying Divine
condemnation," or words denoting
"irreverence of God and holy things,"—
blasphemous. These decisions doubtless
hark back to the third Commandment of
the decalogue: "Thou shalt not take the
name of the Lord thy God in vain."

Cason v. Baskin, 20 So.2d 243, 247 (Fla. 1944)
(en banc).

Noah Webster, an American legislator and judge,
affirmed that both of these categories of law were derived
from the third commandment:

When in obedience to the third
commandment of the Decalogue you
would avoid profane swearing, you are
to remember that this alone is not a full
compliance with the prohibition which
[also] comprehends all irreverent words
or actions and whatever tends to cast
contempt on the Supreme Being or on His
word and ordinances [i.e., blasphemy].

Noah Webster, 8 LETTERS TO A YOUNG
GENTLEMAN (1823); see also Noah Webster, A
COLLECTION of PAPERS (1843) at 296. [226]

THE INFLUENCE OF THE THIRD COMMANDMENT
William J. Federer

The influence of the Third Commandment, not taking the name of
God in vain, can be seen in laws, military orders, court decisions, etc., as
referenced below:

COLONIAL DOCUMENTS

The Body of Liberties of Massachusetts, December 1641, was the first code of laws established in New England. It was established by the Massachusetts General Court and compiled by Nathaniel Ward (1578-1652). The Massachusetts Body of Liberties stated:

> 3. If any man shall Blaspheme the Name of God, the Father, Sonne or Holie Ghost, with direct, expresse, presumptous or high handed blasphemie, or shall curse God in the like manner he shall be put to death.[227]

Cambridge Platform of the Massachusetts Bay Colony, 1648, recorded in the Plymouth Colony Records IX, 1663, listed the proposal of William Vassall and others:

> 8. Idolatry, Blasphemy, Heresy, venting corrupt & pernicious opinions, that destroy the foundation, open contempt of the word preached, prophanation of the Lord's day, disturbing the peaceable administration & exercise of the worship & holy things of God, & the like, are to be restrayned, & punished by civil authority.[228]

Code of the Connecticut General Court, 1650, in the Capital Laws Section of the Code, stated:

> 3. If any person shall blaspheme the Name of God the Father, Son or Holy Ghost with direct, express, presumptuous, or high-handed blasphemy, or shall curse in the like manner, he shall be put to death. Lev. 24:15, 16.[229]

The Colonial Legislature of New York Colony, 1665, enacted:

> Church wardens to report twice a year all misdemeanors, such as swearing, profaneness, Sabbath-breaking, drunkenness, fornication, adultery, and all such abominable sins.[230]

STATE CONSTITUTION

The Constitution of the State of New York, adopted 1777 and 1821, stated:

Blasphemy is a crime at common law and is not abrogated by the constitution.[231]

MILITARY

On August 3, 1776, General Washington issued the orders:

Parole Uxbridge. Countersign Virginia.
The General is sorry to be informed that the foolish, and wicked practice, of profane cursing and swearing (a Vice heretofore little known in an American Army) is growing into fashion; he hopes the officers will, by example, as well as influence, endeavour to check it, and that both they, and the men will reflect, that we can have little hopes of the blessing of Heaven on our Arms, if we insult it by our impiety, and folly; added to this, it is a vice so mean and low, without any temptation, that every man of sense, and character, detests and despises it.[232]

COURTS

Sir William Blackstone stated:

Blasphemy against the Almighty is denying his being or providence, or uttering contumelious reproaches on our Savior Christ. It is punished, at common law by fine and imprisonment, for Christianity is part of the laws of the land.[233]

Massachusetts Supreme Court (1838), heard the case of Commonwealth v. Abner Kneeland, 37 Mass. (20 Pick) 206, 216-217 1838, which involved a Universalist who claimed the right of "freedom of the press" as a defense for publishing libelous and defamatory remarks about Christianity and God. The Court delivered its decision, stating that "freedom of press" was not a license to print without restraint, otherwise:

According to the argument...every act, however injurious or criminal, which can be committed by the use of language may be committed...if such language is printed. Not only therefore would the article in question become a general license for scandal, calumny and falsehood against individuals, institutions and governments, in the form of publication...but all incitation to treason, assassination, and all other crimes however atrocious, if conveyed in printed language, would be dispunishable.[234]

The statute, on which the question arises, is as follows:

That if any person shall willfully blaspheme the holy name of God, by denying, cursing, or contumeliously reproaching God, his creation, government, or final judging of the world, &.... In general, blasphemy [libel against God] may be described, as consisting in speaking evil of the Deity...to alienate the minds of others from the love and reverence of God. It is purposely using words concerning God...to impair and destroy the reverence, respect, and confidence due him....

It is a wilful and malicious attempt to lessen men's reverence of God by denying his existence, of his attributes as an intelligent creator, governor and judge of men, and to prevent their having confidence in him....

But another ground for arresting the judgement, and one apparently most relied on and urged by the defendant, is, that this statute itself is repugnant to the constitution...and therefore wholly void....

[This law] was passed very soon after the adoption of the constitution, and no doubt, many members of the convention which framed the constitution, were members of the legislature which passed this law....

In New Hampshire, the constitution of which State has a similar declaration of [religious] rights, the open denial of the being and existence of God or of the Supreme Being is prohibited by statute, and declared to be blasphemy.

In Vermont, with a similar declaration of rights, a statute was passed in 1797, by which it was enacted, that if any person shall publicly deny the being and existence of God or the Supreme Being, or shall contumeliously reproach his providence and government, he shall be deemed a disturber of the peace and tranquility of the State, and an offender against the good morals and manners of society, and shall be punishable by fine....

The State of Maine also, having adopted the same constitutional provision with that of Massachusetts, in her declaration of rights, in respect to religious freedom, immediately after the adoption of the constitution reenacted, the Massachusetts statue against blasphemy....

In New York the universal toleration of all religious professions and sentiments, is secured in the most ample manner. It is declared in the constitution...that the free exercise and enjoyment of religious worship, without discrimination or preference, shall for ever be allowed in this State to all mankind....

Notwithstanding this constitutional declaration carrying the doctrine of unlimited toleration as far as the peace and safety of any community will allow, the courts have decided that blasphemy was a crime at common law and was not abrogated by the constitution [People v. Ruggles].[235]

In the 1844 case of Vidal v. Girard's Executor, Justice Joseph Story delivered the U.S. Supreme Court's unanimous opinion:

Christianity...is not to be maliciously and openly reviled and blasphemed against, to the annoyance of believers or the injury of the public.[236]

New York Supreme Court (1811), in the case of the People v. Ruggles, 8 Johns 545-547, Chief Justice Chancellor Kent rendered:

The defendant was indicted...in December, 1810, for that he did, on the 2nd day of September, 1810...wickedly, maliciously, and blasphemously, utter, and with a loud voice publish, in the presence and hearing of divers good and Christian people, of and concerning the Christian religion, and of and concerning Jesus Christ, the false, scandalous, malicious, wicked and blasphemous words following: "Jesus Christ was a bastard, and his mother must be a whore," in contempt of the Christian religion...the defendant was tried and found guilty, and was sentenced by the court to be imprisoned for three months, and to pay a fine of $500.[237]

The argument which the prosecuting attorney had presented to the court, explained:

> While the constitution of the State has saved the rights of conscience, and allowed a free and fair discussion of all points of controversy among religious sects, it has left the principal engrafted on the body of our common law, that Christianity is part of the laws of the State, untouched and unimpaired.[238]

Chief Justice Kent delivered the courts decision in this case:

> Such words uttered with such a disposition were an offense at common law. In Taylor's case the defendant was convicted upon information of speaking similar words, and the Court...said that Christianity was parcel of the law, and to cast contumelious reproaches upon it, tended to weaken the foundation of moral obligation, and the efficacy of oaths.
> And in the case of Rex v. Woolston, on a like conviction, the Court said...that whatever strikes at the root of Christianity tends manifestly to the dissolution of civil government....the authorities show that blasphemy against God and...profane ridicule of Christ or the Holy Scriptures (which are equally treated as blasphemy), are offenses punishable at common law, whether uttered by words or writings...because it tends to corrupt the morals of the people, and to destroy good order.
> Such offenses have always been considered independent of any religious establishment or the rights of the Church. They are treated as affecting the essential interests of civil society....
> We stand equally in need, now as formerly, of all the moral discipline, and of those principles of virtue, which help to bind society together.
> The people of this State, in common with the people of this country, profess the general doctrines of Christianity, as the rule of their faith and practice; and to scandalize the author of these doctrines is not only, in a

religious point of view, extremely impious, but, even in respect to the obligations due to society, is a gross violation of decency and good order.

Nothing could be more injurious to the tender morals of the young, than to declare such profanity lawful....

The free, equal, and undisturbed enjoyment of religious opinion, whatever it may be, and free and decent discussions on any religious subject, is granted and secured; but to revile....the religion professed by almost the whole community, is an abuse of that right....

We are a Christian people, and the morality of the country is deeply engrafted upon Christianity, and not upon the doctrines or worship of those impostors [other religions]....

[We are] people whose manners are refined and whose morals have been elevated and inspired with a more enlarged benevolence, by means of the Christian religion. Though the constitution has discarded religious establishments, it does not forbid judicial cognizance of those offenses against religion and morality which have no reference to any such establishment....[offenses which] strike at the root of moral obligation, and weaken the security of the social ties....

This [constitutional] declaration (noble and magnanimous as it is, when duly understood) never meant to withdraw religion in general, and with it the best sanctions of moral and social obligation from all consideration and notice of the law....

To construe it as breaking down the common law barriers against licentious, wanton, and impious attacks upon Christianity itself, would be an enormous perversion of its meaning....

Christianity, in its enlarged sense, as a religion revealed and taught in the Bible, is not unknown to our law....

The Court are accordingly of opinion that the judgement....must be affirmed.[239]

IV.
THE FOURTH COMMANDMENT

"Remember the sabbath day, to keep it holy. Six days shalt thou labour, and do all thy work: But the seventh day is the sabbath of the Lord thy God: in it thou shalt not do any work, thou, nor thy son, nor thy daughter, thy manservant, nor thy maidservant, nor thy cattle, nor thy stranger that is within thy gates: For in six days the Lord made heaven and earth, the sea, and all that in them is, and rested the seventh day: wherefore the Lord blessed the sabbath day, and hallowed it." – Ex. 20:8-11, Deut. 5:12-15

WEBSTER'S DICTIONARY

Noah Webster's original 1828 Dictionary of the English Language, gave the following definitions:

SABBATH, n.
1. The day which God appointed to be observed by the Jews as a day of rest from all secular labor or employments, and to be kept holy and consecrated to his service and worship. This was originally the seventh day of the week, the day on which God rested from the work of creation; and this day is still observed by the Jews and some Christians, as the sabbath. But the Christian church very early begun and still continue to observe the first day of the week, in commemoration of the resurrection of Christ on that day, by which the work of redemption was completed. Hence it is often called the Lords day. The heathen nations in the north of Europe dedicated this day to the sun, and hence their Christian descendants continue to call the day Sunday. But in the United States, Christians have to a great extent discarded the heathen name, and adopted the Jewish name sabbath.
2. Intermission of pain or sorrow; time of rest.
Peaceful sleep out the sabbath of the tomb.
3. The sabbatical year among the Israelites. Lev. 25.

SABBATH-BREAKER, n. One who profanes the sabbath by violating the laws of God or man which enjoin the religious observance of that day.

SABBATH-BREAKING, n. A profanation of the sabbath by violating the injunction of the fourth commandment, or the municipal laws of a state which require the observance of that day as holy time. All unnecessary secular labor, visiting, traveling, sports, amusements and the like are considered as sabbath-breaking.

HO'LY, a.
1. Properly, whole, entire or perfect, in a moral sense. Hence, pure in heart, temper or dispositions; free from sin and sinful affections. Applied to the Supreme Being, holy signifies perfectly pure, immaculate and complete in moral character; and man is more or less holy, as his heart is more or less sanctified, or purified from evil dispositions. We call a man holy, when his heart is conformed in some degree to the image of God, and his life is regulated by the divine precepts. Hence, holy is used as nearly synonymous with good, pious, godly.
 Be ye holy; for I am holy. 1 pet.1.
2. Hallowed; consecrated or set apart to a sacred use, or to the service or worship of God; a sense frequent in Scripture; as the holy sabbath; holy oil; holy vessels; a holy nation; the holy temple; a holy priesthood.
3. Proceeding from pious principles, or directed to pious purposes; as holy zeal.
4. Perfectly just and good; as the holy law of God.
5. Sacred; as a holy witness.

COMMENTARY

Matthew D. Staver writes:

The Fourth Commandment states, "Remember the sabbath day to keep it holy." The Fourth Commandment was adopted by Virginia in 1610, New Haven in 1653, New Hampshire in 1680, Pennsylvania in 1682 and 1705, South

Carolina in 1712, North Carolina in 1741 and Connecticut in 1751.

See:

Articles, Laws, and Order, Divine, Politic and Martial for the Colony of Virginia (1610-1611), COLONIAL ORIGINS at 316-317;

Charles J. Hoadly, RECORDS OF THE COLONY OR JURISDICTION OF NEW HAVEN, FROM MAY, 1653, To THE UNION, TOGETHER WITH THE NEW HAVEN CODE OF 1656 (Lockwood and Company, 1858) at 605;

General Laws and Liberties of New Hampshire (1680), COLONIAL ORIGINS at 10-11;

An Act for Freedom of Conscience (Pennsylvania 1682), COLONIAL ORIGINS at 288;

An Act to Restrain People from Labor on the First Day of the Week (passed October 4, 1705), 1 LAWS OF THE COMMONWEALTH OF PENNSYLVANIA (1810) at 25-26; see also ABRIDGEMENT OF THE LAWS OF PENNSYLVANIA (1801) at 362;

Title 160: Sunday, 2 ALPHABETICAL DIGESTOF THE PUBLIC STATUTE LAW of SOUTH CAROLINA (1814) at 272-275 (1814);

Vice and Immorality (1741), A MANUAL OF THE LAWS OF NORTH CAROLINA (1814) at 264;

An Act for the Due Observation
of the Sabbath, or Lord's Day, 1 THE
PUBLIC STATUTE LAWS OF THE
STATE OF CONNECTICUT at 577-578
(Hartford: Hudson and Goodwin, 1808);
see also Swift, 2 A System of the Laws
at 325-326.

In 1775, and throughout the American Revolution,
Commander-in-Chief George Washington issued military
orders directing that the Sabbath be observed. His order of
May 2, 1778, at Valley Forge was typical:

The Commander in Chief
directs that divine service be performed
every Sunday at 11 o'clock in those
brigades to which there are chaplains;
those which have none to attend the
places of worship nearest to them. It is
expected that officers of all ranks will by
their attendance set an example to their
men.

Fitzpatrick, ed., General Orders, Head-Quarters,
Valley Forge, Saturday, May 2, 1778, 9 WRITINGS OF
GEORGE WASHINGTON (1934) at 342.

In the Federal Era and well beyond, states
continued to enact and reenact Sabbath laws. In fact, the
States went to impressive lengths to uphold the Sabbath.

For example:

in 1787, Vermont enacted a ten-
part law to preserve the Sabbath;

in 1791, Massachusetts enacted
an eleven-part law;

in 1792, Virginia enacted an
extensive eight-part law -a law Written

by Thomas Jefferson and sponsored by James Madison;

in 1798, New Jersey enacted a twenty-one-part law;

in 1799, New Hampshire enacted a fourteen-part law;

in 1821, Maine enacted a thirteen-part law.

See An Act for the Due Observation of the Sabbath (passed March 9, 1787), STATUTES OF THE STATE OF VERMONT (1791) at 155-157;

Of the Observance of the Lord's Day and the Prevention and Punishment of Immorality, THE REVISED STATUTES OF THE COMMONWEALTH OF MASSACHUSETTS (passed November 4, 1835) at 385-386 (1836);

An Act for the Effectual Suppression of Vice, and Punishing the Disturbers of Religious Worship, and Sabbath Breakers (passed December 26, 1792), THE REVISED CODE Of THE LAWS OF VIRGINIA (1819) at 554-556; see also A DIGEST OF THE LAWS OF VIRGINIA (1823) at 453-445; Robert A. Rutland, ed., Bills for a Revised State Code of Laws, 8 THE PAPERS OF JAMES MADISON (Chicago: University of Chicago Press, 1973) at 391-396; Julian P. Boyd, ed., The Revisal of the Laws, 1776-1786, 2 THE PAPERS OF THOMAS

JEFFERSON (Princeton: Princeton University Press, 1950) at 322;

An Act for Suppressing Vice and Immorality (passed March 16, 1798), LAWS OF THE STATE OF NEW JERSEY (1800) at 329-333;

An Act for the Better Observation of the Lord's Day, and for Repealing All the Laws Heretofore Made for that Purpose (passed December 24, 1799), CONSTITUTION AND LAWS OF THE STATE OF NEW HAMPSHIRE (1805) at 290-293;

An Act Providing for the Due Observation of the Lord's Day, LAWS Of THE STATE OF MAINE (1822) at 67-71.

The Sabbath day has been recognized in the U.S. Constitution under Article 1, Section 7, Paragraph 2 which states, in part:

If any Bill shall not be returned by the President within ten days (Sundays excepted) after it shall have been presented to him, the Same shall be a Law....

The Missouri Supreme Court observed the following:

It is provided that if the Governor does not return a bill within 10 days (Sundays excepted), it shall become a law without his signature. Although it may be said that this provision leaves it optional with the Governor whether he will consider bills or not on Sunday, yet, regard being had to the circumstances under which it was inserted, can any impartial mind deny that it contains a recognition of the Lord's Day as a day exempted by law from all worldly pursuits? The framers of the Constitution, then, recognized Sunday as a day to be observed, acting themselves under a law which exacted a compulsive observance of it. If a compulsive observance of the Lord" s Day as a day of rest had been deemed inconsistent with the principles contained in the Constitution, can anything be clearer than, as the matter was so plainly and palpably before the Convention, a specific condemnation of the Sunday law would have been engrafted upon it? So far from it, Sunday was recognized as a day of rest.

See also Missouri v. Chicago B. & Q. R. Co., 143 S.W. 785, 803 (Mo. 1912).

The Supreme Court ruled that Sunday closing laws are Constitutional. See McGowan v. Maryland, 366 U.S. 420 (1961). These laws originate from the Fourth Commandment as the Pennsylvania Supreme Court stated:

Remember the Sabbath day to keep it holy; six days shalt thou labor and do all thy work; but the seventh day is the Sabbath of the Lord thy God. In it thou shalt not do any work." This divine pronouncement became part of the Common Law inherited by the thirteen American colonies and by the sovereign States of the American union.

Bertera's Hopewell Foodland, Inc. v. Masters, 236 A.2d 197, 200-01 (Pa. 1967); see also Theisen v. McDavid, 16 So. 321, 323 (Fla. 1894); Gillooley v. Vaughn, 110 So. 653, 655 (Fla 1926); Rogers v. Georgia, 4 S.E.2d 918, 919 (Ga. App. 1939); Paramount-Richards Theatres v. City of

Hattiesburg, 49 So.2d 574, 577 (Miss. 1950)("Sunday laws have a divine origin").

The Fourth Commandment remains part of American law. Many states have recognized the Sabbath as influencing in their civil process laws.

For example, a 1830 New York law declared that:

Civil process cannot, by statute, be executed on Sunday, and a service of such process on Sunday is utterly void and subjects the officer to damages.

General Rules Applicable to a Summons, Warrant of Attachment, Rev. Stat. 675, reprinted in Edwards, JUSTICES OF THE PEACE IN THE STATE OF NEW YORK at 38.

Similar laws may be found in:

Pennsylvania in 1862, see Charter of Liberties and Frame of Government of the Province of Pennsylvania in America (1682), reprinted in COLONIAL ORIGINS at 281; Pennsylvania in 1705, An Act to Restrain People from Labor on the First Day of the Week (passed October 14, 1705), 1 LAWS OF THE COMMONWEALTH OF PENNSYLVANIA (1810) at 25;

Vermont in 1787, An Act for the Due Observation of the Sabbath (passed March 9, 1787), STATUTES OF THE STATE OF VERMONT (1791) at 157;

Connecticut in 1796, Of Crimes Against Religion, reprinted in Swift, 2 A SYSTEM OF THE LAWS (1796) at 326;

and New Jersey in 1798, William Paterson ed., An Act for Suppressing Vice and Immorality (passed March 16,1798), LAWS OF THE STATE OF NEW JERSEY, REVISED AND PUBLISHED UNDER THE AUTHORITY OF THE LEGISLATURE (1800) at 329-330.

The Fourth Commandment was also enacted into law. Examples of the early implementation of the fourth commandment into law are seen in the:

Virginia laws of 1610, Articles, Laws, and Orders, Divine, Politic and Martial for the Colony of Virginia, reprinted in COLONIAL ORIGINS at 316-17;

the New Haven laws of 1653, Charles J. Hoadly, RECORDS OF THE COLONY OR JURISDICTION OF NEW HAVEN, FROM MAY, 1653, TO THE UNION, TOGETHER WITH THE NEW HAVEN CODE OF 1656, AT 605 (1858); THE NEW HAMPSHIRE LAWS OF 1680, General Laws and Liberties of New Hampshire, reprinted in COLONIAL ORIGINS at 10-11;

the Pennsylvania laws of 1682, An Act for Freedom of Conscience, reprinted in COLONIAL ORIGINS at 288; and the Pennsylvania laws of 1705, An Act to Restrain People from Labor on the First Day of the Week (passed October 4, 1705), 1 LAWS OF THE COMMONWEALTH OF PENNSYLVANIA (1810) at 25-26 (1810), see also ABRIDGEMENT OF THE LAWS OF PENNSYLVANIA (1801) at 362;

the South Carolina laws of 1712, Title 160: Sunday, 2 ALPHABETICAL DIGEST OF THE PUBLIC STATUTE LAW OF SOUTH CAROLINA (1814) at 272-275;

the North Carolina laws of 1741, Vice and Immorality, A MANUAL OF THE LAWS OF NORTH CAROLINA (1814) at 264;

the Connecticut laws of 1751, An Act for the Due Observation of the Sabbath, or Lords Day, 1 THE PUBLIC STATUTE LAWS OF THE STATE OF CONNECTICUT (1808) at 577-578, see also Swift, 2 A SYSTEM OF THE LAWS (1796) at 325-26.

During the Federal Era and well beyond, states continued to enact and reenact Sabbath laws. In fact, the States went to impressive lengths to uphold the Sabbath. For example:

in 1787, Vermont enacted a ten-part law to preserve the Sabbath. See An Act for the Due Observation of the Sabbath (passed March 9, 1787), STATUTES OF THE STATE OF VERMONT (1791) at 155-15.

In 1791, Massachusetts enacted an eleven-part law. See Of the Observance of the Lord's Day and the Prevention and Punishment of Immorality (passed November 4, 1835), THE REVISED STATUTES OF THE COMMONWEALTH OF MASSACHUSETTS (1836) at 385-386.

In 1792, Virginia enacted an extensive eight-part law. See An Act for the Effectual Suppression of Vice, and Punishing the Disturbers of Religious Worship, and Sabbath Breakers (passed December 26,1792), 1 THE REVISED CODE OF THE LAWS OF VIRGINIA (1819) at 554556; see also A DIGEST OF THE LAWS OF VIRGINIA (1823) 453-454.

In 1798, New Jersey enacted a twenty-one-part law. See An Act for Suppressing Vice and Immorality (passed March 16, 1798), LAWS OF THE STATE OF NEW JERSEY (1800) at 329-333.

In 1799, New Hampshire enacted a fourteen-part law. See An Act for the Better Observation of the Lord's Day, and for Repealing All the Laws Heretofore Made for that Purpose (passed December 24,1799), reprinted in CONSTITUTION AND LAWS OF THE STATE OF NEW HAMPSHIRE (1805) at 290-293.

In 1821, Maine enacted a thirteen-part law. See An Act Providing for the Due Observation of the Lords Day (passed December 24, 1799), reprinted in LAWS OF THE STATE Of MAINE (1822) at 67-71 (1822).

The Fourth Commandment clearly shaped and influenced American law. The Fourth Commandment is still found today in many laws throughout the country. [240]

THE INFLUENCE OF THE FOURTH COMMANDMENT
William J. Federer

The influence of the Fourth Commandment to keep the Sabbath holy can be seen in early Colonial Documents, statements of the Founders, Leaders in Education, Constitutions, Presidents, Military, Courts, etc., as referenced below:

COLONIAL DOCUMENTS

Colony of Virginia, 1623, enacted legislation requiring civil magistrates:

To see that the Sabbath was not profaned by working or any employments, or journeying from place to place.[241]

Commonwealth of Virginia, 1662, enacted:

Enacted that the Lord's Day be kept holy, and no journeys be made on that day, unless upon necessity. And all persons inhabiting in this country, having no lawful excuse, shall, every Sunday, resort to the parish church or chapel, and there abide orderly during the common prayer, preaching, and divine service.[242]

The Colonial Legislature of New York Colony, 1665, enacted:

Whereas, The public worship of God is much discredited for want of painful [serious] and able ministers to instruct the people in the true religion, it is ordered that a church shall be built in each parish, capable of holding two hundred persons; that ministers of every church shall preach every Sunday, and pray for the king, queen, the Duke of York, and the royal family; and to marry persons after legal publication of license...
Sunday is not to be profaned by traveling, by laborers, or vicious persons... Church wardens to report twice a year all misdemeanors, such as swearing, profaneness, Sabbath-breaking, drunkenness, fornication, adultery, and all such abominable sins.[243]

In Colony of New Jersey, 1697, Governor Basse stated:

It being very necessary for the good and prosperity of this province that our principal care be, in obedience to the laws of God, to endeavor as much as in us lyeth the extirpation of all sorts of looseness and profanity, and to unite in the fear and love of God and one another,...
Take due care that all laws made and provided for the suppression of vice and encouraging of religion and virtue, particularly the observance of the Lord's day, be duly put into execution.[244]

The Frame of Government of Pennsylvania, April 25, 1682, composed by William Penn, stated:

Article XXII. That as often as any day of the month, mentioned in any article of this charter, shall fall upon the first day of the week, commonly called the Lord's Day, the business appointed for that day shall be deferred till the next day, unless in the case of emergency.[245]

FOUNDERS

James Warren (September 28, 1726-November 28, 1808), was the president of the Massachusetts Provincial Congress, following Joseph Warren's death. He was a Major-General in the Provincial Militia; a member of the Navy board for the Eastern Department, a member of the Governor's Council, 1792-94; and a presidential elector from Massachusetts, 1804. He was married to Mercy Otis Warren, 1724-1814, a remarkable author of the Revolutionary period, whose correspondence with numerous founding fathers has granted invaluable insight into our nation's history. In 1805, she wrote the History of the Rise, Progress and Termination of the American Revolution, in 3 volumes.

It was James Warren who first proposed the Committees of Correspondence to Samuel Adams, which were of inestimable influence in inspiring the spirit of freedom among the Colonies. On June 16, 1775, President James Warren and the Massachusetts Provincial Congress resolved:

IN Provincial Congress, Watertown, June 16TH, 1775.
As it has pleased Almighty GOD in his Providence to suffer the Calamities of an unnatural War to take Place among us, in Consequence of our sinful Declensions from

Him, and our great abuse of those inestimable Blessings bestowed upon us. And as we have Reason to fear, that unless we become a penitent and reformed People, we shall feel still severer Tokens of his Displeasure.

And as the most effectual Way to escape those desolating Judgements, which so evidently hang over us, and if it may be obtain the Restoration of our former Tranquility, will be - That we repent and return every one from his Iniquities, unto him that correcteth us, which if we do in Sincerity and Truth, we have no Reason to doubt but he will remove his Judgements - cause our Enemies to be at Peace with us - and prosper the Work of our Hands.

And as among the prevailing Sins of this Day, which threaten the Destruction of this Land, we have Reason to lament the frequent Prophanation of the Lord's-Day, or Christian Sabbath; many spending their Time in Idleness and Sloth, others in Diversion, and others in Journeying of Business, which is not necessary on said Day:

And as we earnestly desire that a Stop might be put to this great and prevailing Evil: It is therefore RESOLVED, That it be recommended by this Congress, to the People of all Ranks and Denominations throughout this Colony, that they not only pay a religious Regard to that Day, and to the public Worship of God thereon; but that they also use their Influence to discountenance and suppress any Prophanations thereof in others.

And it is further RESOLVED, That it be recommended to the Ministers of the Gospel to read this Resolve to their several Congregations, accompanied with such Exhortations as they shall think proper.

And whereas there is great Danger that the Prophanation of the Lord's-Day will prevail in the Camp:

We earnestly recommend to all the Officers, not only to set good Examples; but that they strictly require of their Soldiers to keep up a religious Regard to that Day, and attend upon the public Worship of God thereon, so far as may be consistent with other Duties.

A true Copy from the Minutes,
Attest. SAMUEL FREEMAN, Secry.
By Order of the Congress,
JAMES WARREN, President.[246]

In a letter dated June 25, 1775, Abigail wrote to her husband, John Adams regarding the battle at Charlestown, Massachusetts:

> They [British] delight on molesting us on the Sabbath. Two Sabbaths we have been in such Alarms that we have had no meetings.[247]

In 1751, George Washington accompanied his older brother, Lawrence Washington, who, on the advice of physicians, spent the winter in the West Indies in a desperate attempt to regain his health. The illness nevertheless grew worse, and before he died, Lawrence left his estate at Mount Vernon to George. In his journal of the trip, George entered:

> Sunday, November 11th - Dressed in order for Church but got to town too late. Dined at Major Clarke's with ye SeG. Went to Evening Service and return'd to our lodgings.[248]

On Sunday, November 8, 1789, while in Connecticut, President Washington entered in his diary:

> It being contrary to law and disagreeable to the People of this State to travel on the Sabbath Day - and my horses, after passing through such intolerable roads, wanting to rest, I stayed at Perkins' tavern (which, by the by, is not a good one) all day - and a meeting-house being within a few rods of the door, I attended morning and evening service, and heard very lame discourses from a Mr. Pond [Reverend Enoch Pond].[249]

In his Autobiography, Benjamin Franklin stated:

> I had been religiously educated as a Presbyterian; and tho' some of the dogmas of that persuasion, such as the eternal degrees of God, election, reprobation, etc., appeared to me unintelligible, others doubtful, and I early absented myself from the public assemblies of the sect, Sunday being my studying day, I never was without some religious principles.
>
> I never doubted, for instance, the existence of the Deity; that He made the world, and govern'd it by His Providence; that the most acceptable service of God was

the doing good to man; that our souls are immortal; and that all crime will be punished, and virtue rewarded, either here or hereafter.[250]

Benjamin Rush (January 4, 1745-April 19, 1813) was a member of the Continental Congress, signed the Declaration of Independence, was Surgeon General of the Continental Army and Treasurer of the U.S. Mint. He helped found Dickinson College and joined the staff of the Pennsylvania Hospital. In 1774, Rush helped found the Pennsylvania Society for Promoting the Abolition of Slavery, the Philadelphia Bible Society; was a principal promoter of the American Sunday School Union. Dr. Benjamin Rush wrote his estimation of Roger Sherman, another signer of the Declaration in 1777:

He was not less distinguished for his piety than his patriotism. He once objected to a motion for Congress sitting on a Sunday upon an occasion which he thought did not require it, and gave as a reason for his objection a regard for the commands of his Maker.[251]

EDUCATION

Columbia University (1754), founded in New York City. Originally named Kings College in honor of King George II, it was renamed Columbia College, 1784, and Columbia University, 1896. It has grown to become one of the most influential universities in America.

Admission requirements for Columbia College, which John Jay, the first Chief Justice of the U.S. Supreme Court, passed at the age of fourteen, included translating from Greek the first ten chapters of the Gospel of John and attending worship on Sundays:

No candidate shall be admitted into the College...unless he shall be able to render into English...the Gospels from the Greek....It is also expected that all students attend public worship on Sunday.[252]

Timothy Dwight (May 14, 1752-January 11, 1817) was an American educator and author. He was the president of Yale, 1795-1817. He was the grandson of Jonathan Edwards, the New England minister and president of Princeton University. Timothy Dwight's grandson, also named Timothy Dwight, was president of Yale from 1886 to 1898. On July 4th, 1798, in New Haven, President Timothy Dwight delivered an address entitled, The Duty of Americans, at the Present Crisis, Illustrated in a Discourse, in which stated:

To destroy us therefore, in this dreadful sense, our enemies must first destroy our Sabbath and seduce us from the house of God.[253]

William Holmes McGuffey, in McGuffey's Fifth Eclectic Reader (Cincinnati and New York: Van Antwerp, Bragg & Co., revised edition, 1879), included lesson XIII, "Respect for the Sabbath Rewarded":

In the city of Bath, not many years since, lived a barber who made a practice of following his ordinary occupation on the Lord's day. As he was on the way to his morning's employment, he happened to look into some place of worship just as the minister was giving out his text - "Remember the Sabbath day, to keep it holy." He listened long enough to be convinced that he was constantly breaking the laws of God and man by shaving and dressing his customers on the Lord's day. He became uneasy, and went with a heavy heart to his Sabbath task....

He discontinued his Sabbath work, went constantly and early to the public services of religion, and soon enjoyed that satisfaction of mind which is one of the rewards of doing our duty, and that peace which the world can neither give nor take away....

Providence had now thrown him in his way in a most extraordinary manner, and he had great pleasure in transferring a great many thousand pounds to a worthy man, the rightful heir of the property. Thus was man's extremity God's opportunity.[254]

Henry Opukahai'a (d.1818) was the first Hawaiian convert to Christianity. Orphaned at age 10, he was raised by his uncle to be a pagan priest (kahuna) of the Hawaiian religion. He grew disillusioned with the rituals and chants, and left on an American ship bound for New England with his Hawaiian friend, Thomas Hopu. There he was befriended by students and professors of Yale College and soon became a Christian. He studied Greek and Hebrew and translated sections of the Bible into the Hawaiian language. In his memoirs, which sold 500,000 copies after his death, Henry Opukahai'a wrote:

My poor countrymen, without knowledge of the true God, and ignorant of the future world, have no Bible to read, no Sabbath.[255]

John Wanamaker (July 11, 1838-December 12, 1922) was a U.S. Postmaster General, 1889-93; a financier; and founder of one of the first American department stores. He had served as secretary of the Philadelphia YMCA, 1857-61. In 1861, he formed a clothing business with Nathan Brown; in 1869 he founded John Wanamaker and Company.

John Wanamaker helped found the Bethany Presbyterian Church and served as a senior elder. He led a John Wesley Class Meeting, with attendance growing to over 5,000 people, and was an active Sunday school superintendent for nearly 70 years.[256]

Dallas High Schools (September 1946), published a Bible Study Course - New Testament, Bulletin No. 170. It was authorized by the Board of Education, April 23, 1946, and printed in The Dallas Public Schools Printshop, Dallas, Texas:

Foreword....the Dallas public schools allowed one-half credit toward high-school graduation for the successful completion of a general survey course in the Bible, given in the churches and Sunday schools of the city. In 1939, it was decided to provide separate courses in the Old and the New Testaments, each course carrying one-half unit of credit toward high-school graduation.
E.B. Comstock,
Assistant Superintendent
in Charge of High Schools.[257]

CONSTITUTIONS

The Constitution of the State of Vermont, adopted 1777, stated:

DECLARATION OF RIGHTS, III...Every sect or denomination of people ought to observe the Sabbath, or the Lord's day, and keep up, and support, some sort of religious worship, which to them shall seem most agreeable to the revealed will of GOD.[258]

On October 31, 1785, James Madison introduced legislation in the Virginia Legislature entitled, "Bill for Punishing Disturbers of Religious Worship and Sabbath Breakers," which was passed in 1789:

> If any person on Sunday shall himself be found laboring at his own or any other trade or calling, or shall employ the apprentices, servants or slaves in labor, or other business, except it be in the ordinary household offices of daily necessity, or other work of necessity or charity, he shall forfeit the sum of ten shillings for every such offense, deeming every apprentice, servant, or slave so employed, and every day he shall be so employed as constituting a distinct offense.[259]

United States Congress, 1789, during the period when Congress first met in the new capitol of Washington, D.C., the House and Senate Chaplains, which traditionally have always been Christian, regularly led service every Sunday in the House Chamber."[260]

The Constitution of the State of Alabama, adopted 1901, stated:

> Article V, Section 125. Approval, Veto of Bills....If any bill shall not be returned by the governor within six days, Sunday excepted, after if shall have been presented, the same shall become a law in like manner as if he had signed it.[261]

PRESIDENTS

In his diary, which he kept meticulously, John Quincy Adams made note of his Sunday church attendance:

> Scarcely a Sunday passes [that I fail to] hear something of which a pointed application to my own situation and circumstances occurs to my thoughts. It is often consolation, support, encouragement - sometimes warning and admonition, sometimes keen and trying remembrance of deep distress. The lines [of Isaac Watts' hymn sung] are of the cheering kind.[262]

On July 11, 1841, his seventy-fourth birthday, John Quincy Adams wrote in his diary:

> My birthday happens this day upon the Sabbath. Every return of the day comes with a weight of solemnity more and more awful. How peculiarly impressive ought it then be when the annual warning of the shortening thread sounds in tones deepened by the church bell of the Lord's Day! The question comes with yearly aggravation upon my conscience, "What have I done with the seventy-four years that I have been indulged with the blessings of life."[263]

In honor of the Sabbath, President William H. Harrison stated to visitors:

> We shall be happy to see you at any time except on the Sabbath.[264]

Refusing to be inaugurated on the Sabbath, Zachary Taylor was sworn into office the following day, Monday, March 5, 1849.[265]

President Millard Fillmore, who was a member of the Episcopalian Church,[266] stated:

> The Sabbath day I always kept as a day of rest. Besides being a religious duty, it was essential to health. On commencing my Presidential career, I found that the Sabbath had frequently been employed by visitors for private interviews with the President. I determined to put an end to this custom, and ordered my doorkeeper to meet all Sunday visitors with an indiscriminate refusal.[267]

On September 3, 1864, President Abraham Lincoln issued a Proclamation of a National Day of Thanksgiving on a Sunday:

> The signal success that Divine Providence has recently vouchsafed to the operations of the United States fleet and army in the harbor of Mobile, and the reduction of Fort Powell, Fort Gaines, and Fort Morgan, and the glorious achievements of the army under Major-General Sherman in the State of Georgia, resulting in the capture of the city of Atlanta, call for devout acknowledgment to the Supreme Being, in whose hands are the destinies of nations.

It is therefore requested that on next Sunday, in all places of public worship in the United States, thanksgiving be offered to Him for His mercy in preserving our national existence against the insurgent rebels who so long have been waging a cruel war against the Government of the United States for its overthrow; and also that prayer be made for the divine protection to our brave soldiers and their leaders in the field, who have so often and so gallantly periled their lives in battling with the enemy, and for blessing and comfort from the Father of Mercies to the sick, wounded, and prisoners, and to the orphans and widows of those who have fallen in the service of their country; and that He will continue to uphold the Government of the United States against all the efforts of public enemies and secret foes.[268]

On June 6, 1876, President Ulysses S. Grant wrote from Washington to the Editor of the Sunday School Times in Philadelphia:

Your favor of yesterday asking a message from me to the children and the youth of the United States, to accompany your Centennial number, is this morning received.

My advice to Sunday schools, no matter what their denomination, is: Hold fast to the Bible as the sheet anchor of your liberties; write its precepts in your hearts, and practice them in your lives.

To the influence of this Book are we indebted for all the progress made in true civilization, and to this must we look as our guide in the future. "Righteousness exalteth a nation; but sin is a reproach to any people."

Yours respectfully,
U.S. Grant.[269]

In 1884, while fighting throat cancer, Ulysses S. Grant began writing his Memoirs at the behest of Mark Twain, who agreed to publish them. Encouraged by the affection and honor of the people of the country during his illness, Ulysses S. Grant, who was a Methodist, wrote:

I believe in the Holy Scriptures, and whoso lives by them will be benefited thereby. Men may differ as to the interpretation, which is human, but the Scriptures are man's best guide....

I did not go riding yesterday, although invited and permitted by my physicians, because it was the Lord's day, and because I felt that if a relapse should set in, the people who are praying for me would feel that I was not helping their faith by riding out on Sunday....

Yes, I know, and I feel very grateful to the Christian people of the land for their prayers in my behalf. There is no sect or religion, as shown in the Old or New Testament, to which this does not apply.[270]

On November 2, 1966, after touring many Asian and Pacific nations, President Lyndon B. Johnson arrived in Dulles Airport where he recalled, to those waiting, a prayer offered ten days earlier while they attended Sunday service in the Cathedral Church of St. James, Townsville, northern Australia:

O God, Who has bound us together in the bundle of life, give us grace to understand how our lives depend upon the courage, the industry, the honesty, and the integrity of our fellow men; that we may be mindful of their needs and grateful for their faithfulness, and faithful in our responsibilities to them.[271]

On Sunday, March 31, 1968, after attending church at St. Dominic's in Washington D.C., President Lyndon B. Johnson noted his feeling concerning his daughter Lynda's husband, Chuck Robb, and his daughter Luci's husband, Pat Nugent:

They were so very young, and they had such promising and happy lives ahead of them, if they were lucky. Pat already had his orders for Vietnam. In a matter of days, by his own insistence, he would be with Chuck Robb in action in Vietnam. The good Lord had blessed us with two brave sons-in-law, and no man could have been prouder of them than I. Now, for a year or more, their wives would wait and pray, as other wives across America would, for their husbands to return to them and their babies.[272]

On March 6, 1984, at the annual convention of the National Association of Evangelicals, President Ronald Reagan stated:

There was minister who put his sermon text on the pulpit a half an hour before service. And one Sunday a smart aleck hid the last page. And the minister preached powerfully, but when he got to the words, "So Adams said to Eve," he was horrified to discover that the final sheet was gone. And riffling through the other pages, he stalled time by repeating, "So Adam said to Eve" - and then in a low voice he said, "There seems to be a missing leaf.".

Talking to a church audience like this reminds me of a little church in a little town in Illinois - Dixon, Illinois - that I used to attend as a boy. One sweltering Sunday morning in July, the minister told us he was going to preach the shortest sermon he had ever given. And then he said a single sentence: 'If you think it's hot today, just wait.'[273]

MILITARY

On August 3, 1776, General Washington issued the orders:

Parole Uxbridge. Countersign Virginia.

That the Troops may have an opportunity of attending public worship, as well as take some rest after the great fatigue they have come through; The General in future excuses them from fatigue duty on Sundays (except at the Ship Yards, or special occasions until further orders.[274]

On May 2, 1778, General George Washington issued these orders to his troops at Valley Forge:

The Commander-in-Chief directs that Divine service be performed every Sunday at 11 o'clock, in each Brigade which has a Chaplain. Those Brigades which have none will attend the places of worship nearest to them.

It is expected that officers of all ranks will, by their attendance, set an example for their men. While we are zealously performing the duties of good citizens and soldiers, we certainly ought not to be inattentive to the higher duties of religion. To the distinguished character of Patriot, it should be our highest Glory to laud the more distinguished Character of Christian.[275]

On March 22, 1783, from Newburg, New York, as recorded in the Orderly Book, General Washington directed:

> In justice to the zeal and ability of the Chaplains, as well as to his own feelings, the Commander-in-Chief thinks it a duty to declare that the regularity and decorum with which Divine Service is performed every Sunday, will reflect great credit on the army in general, tend to improve the morals, and the same time increase the happiness of the soldiery, and must afford the most pure, rational entertainments for every serious and well-disposed mind.[276]

The House Judiciary Committee Report of 1854 referenced the orders United States Congress to the U.S. Navy:

> The commanders of all ships and vessels in the navy having chaplains on board shall take care that divine service be performed in an orderly and reverent manner twice a day, and a sermon preached on Sunday, except bad weather or other extraordinary accident prevent it, and that they cause all, or as many of the ship's company as can be spared from duty, to attend every performance of the worship of Almighty God.
>
> Chap. 204. - An Act for the better government of the navy of the United States. Be it enacted by the Senate and House of Representatives of the United States of America in Congress assembled, That, from and after the first day of September next, the following articles be adopted and put in force for the government of the navy of the United States...
>
> Article 2. The commanders of vessels and naval stations to which chaplains are attached shall cause divine service to be performed on Sunday, whenever the weather and other circumstances will allow it to be done; and it is earnestly recommended to all officers, seamen, and others in the naval service diligently to attend at every performance of the worship of Almighty God. Any irreverent or unbecoming behavior during divine service shall be punished as a general or summary court-martial shall direct.[277]

On a Sunday in 1853, on his way to Japan to protect American seamen, Commodore Matthew Calbraith Perry set his Bible on the capstan, read Psalm 100, then sang:

> Before Jehovah's awful throne
> Ye nations bow with sacred joy.[278]

On November 15, 1862, from his Executive Mansion in Washington, President Lincoln issued a General Order Respecting the Observance of the Sabbath Day in the Army and Navy:

> The President, Commander in Chief of the Army and Navy, desires and enjoins the orderly observance of the Sabbath by the officers and men in the military and naval service. The importance for man and beast of the prescribed weekly rest, the sacred rights of Christian soldiers and sailors, a becoming deference to the best sentiment of a Christian people, and a due regard for the Divine Will demand that Sunday labor in the Army and Navy be reduced to the measure of strict necessity.
> The discipline and character of the national forces should not suffer nor the cause they defend be imperiled by the profanation of the day or name of the Most High. "At this time of public distress," adopting the words of Washington in 1776, "men may find enough to do in the service of God and their country without abandoning themselves to vice and immorality."
> The first general order issued by the Father of his Country after the Declaration of Independence indicates the spirit in which our institutions were founded and should ever be defended: "The General hopes and trusts that every officer and man will endeavor to live and act as becomes a Christian soldier defending the dearest rights and liberties of his country."
> Abraham Lincoln.[279]

William Starke Rosecrans (September 6, 1819-March 11, 1898) was a Union General during the Civil War. He was noted for having increased the number of chaplains in his company, insisting that his troops not fight on the Sabbath, and conversed often with his staff in religious discussions, once till 4 a.m. for ten nights in a row. Having been a significant part of many major battles, General Rosecrans motto was: "God never fails those who truly trust."[280]

Oliver Otis Howard (November 8, 1830-1909) was a Union General during the Civil War. He served as Superintendent of West Point Academy, and was appointed by President Lincoln to lead the Freedmen's Bureau, assisting former slaves after the war, 1866-72. In 1867, he founded Howard University for freed slaves, serving as its president, 1869-73, and later founded Lincoln Memorial University, Cumberland Gap, Tennessee. General Oliver Otis Howard, whose understanding of the Gospel created controversy when he integrated a church, also served as the Chairman of the American Tract Society. He was known by his soldiers as the "Old Prayer Book," as he never drank, smoke or swore. In 1869, as Superintendent of West Point, he personally presented each incoming cadet with a Bible, initiating the practice.

In 1863, Major-General Oliver Otis Howard addressed the officers and troops of the 127th Pennsylvania Volunteers:

> I am glad to see so many of you out to hear preaching this Sabbath morning, and I would to God, that all the men of my command were true followers of Christ Jesus, the Lord. Soldiers, allow me to express, with your chaplain, the sincere desire of my heart, that we may meet at the right hand of the Great Judge in that day, which he has described to us.[281]

General Stonewall Jackson had faithfully taught an African-American Sunday school class in Lexington. He wrote to his pastor, the Reverend Dr. White:

> My dear Pastor,
> In my tent last night, after a fatiguing day's service, I remembered that I had failed to send you my contribution for our colored Sunday School. Enclosed you will find my check for that object, which please acknowledge at your earliest convenience and oblige yours faithfully,
> T. Jackson.[282]

On Friday, June 7, 1889, from his Executive Mansion, President Benjamin Harrison wrote:

In November, 1862, President Lincoln quoted the words of Washington to sustain his own views, and announced in a general order that -

"The President, Commander in Chief of the Army and Navy, desires and enjoins the orderly observance of the Sabbath by the officers and men in the military and naval service. The importance for man and beast of the prescribed weekly rest, the sacred rights of Christian soldiers and sailors, a becoming deference to the best sentiment of a Christian people, and a due regard for the divine will demand that Sunday labor in the Army and Navy be reduced to the measure of strict necessity."

The truth so concisely stated can not be too faithfully regarded, and the pressure to ignore it is far less now than in the midst of war. To recall the kindly and considerate spirit of the orders issued by these great men in the most trying times of our history, and to promote contentment and efficiency, the President directs that Sunday-morning inspection will be merely of the dress and general appearance, without arms; and the more complete inspection under arms, with all men present, as required in paragraph 950, Army Regulations, 1889, will take place on Saturday.

Benj. Harrison.

By the President: Ronald Proctor, Secretary of War.[283]

On Sunday, January 20, 1918, in an Executive Order to the Army and Navy enjoining Sabbath observance, President Woodrow Wilson stated:

The President, commander in chief of the Army and Navy, following the reverent example of his predecessors, desires and enjoins the orderly observance of the Sabbath by the officers and men in the military and naval service of the United States. The importance for man and beast of the prescribed weekly rest, the sacred rights of Christian soldiers and sailors, a becoming deference to the best sentiment of a Christian people, and a due regard for the Divine Will demand that Sunday labor in the Army and Navy be reduced to the measure of strict necessity.

Such an observance of Sunday is dictated by the best traditions of our people and by the convictions of all who look to Divine Providence for guidance and protection, and, in repeating in this order the language of President Lincoln, the President in confident that he is speaking alike to the hearts and to the consciences of those under his authority.[284]

On August 10, 1941, President Franklin D. Roosevelt attended the Mid-Atlantic Conference, as recorded by British Prime Minister Winston Churchill:

> On Sunday morning, August 10, Mr. Roosevelt came aboard H.M.S. Prince of Wales and, with his Staff officers and several hundred representatives of all ranks of the United States Navy and Marines, attended Divine Service on the quarterdeck.
> This service was felt by us all to be a deeply moving expression of the unity of faith of our two peoples, and none who took part in it will forget the spectacle presented that sunlit morning on the crowded quarterdeck – the symbolism of the Union Jack and the Stars and Stripes draped side by side on the pulpit; the American and British chaplains sharing in the reading of the prayers; the highest navel, military, and air officers of Britain and the United States grouped in one body behind the President and me; the close-packed ranks of British and American sailors, completely intermingled, sharing the same books and joining fervently together in the prayers and hymns familiar to both.
> I chose the hymns myself - 'For Those in Peril on the Sea' and 'Onward Christian Soldiers.' We ended with 'Oh God, Our Help in Ages Past,' which Macaulay reminds us the Ironsides had chanted as they bore John Hampden's body to the grave.
> It was a great hour to live. Nearly half of those who sang were soon to die.[285]

On Sunday, September 2, 1945, aboard the battleship USS Missouri in Tokyo Bay, General Douglas MacArthur met with leaders of Allied forces to sign the treaty of the surrender of Japan. After signing, he offered a prayer:

> Let us pray that peace be now restored to the world and that God will preserve it always.[286]

United States Corp of Cadets (1947), contained in their regulations:

> Attendance at chapel is part of a cadet's training; no cadet will be exempted. Each cadet will receive religious training in one of the three particular faiths: Protestant, Catholic or Jewish.[287]

The U.S. Naval Academy required:

> All Midshipmen, except those on authorized outside church parties, shall attend Sunday services in the chapel.[288]

COURTS

David Josiah Brewer (June 20, 1837-March 28, 1910) was a Justice of the United State Supreme Court, 1889-1910. He had been appointed by President Chester A. Arthur as a circuit court judge, 1884; and served as Justice of the Kansas Supreme Court, 1870-84. His uncle was Supreme Court Justice Stephen J. Field, with whom he serve 9 years on the bench. Justice David Josiah Brewer gave the court's opinion in the 1892 case of Church of the Holy Trinity v. United States, (143 U.S. 457-458, 465-471, 36 L ed 226):

> If we pass beyond these matters to a view of American life as expressed by its laws, its business, its customs and its society, we find everywhere a clear recognition of the same truth. Among other matters note the following:
> The form of oath universally prevailing, concluding with an appeal to the Almighty;
> the custom of opening sessions of all deliberative bodies and most conventions with prayer;
> the prefatory words of all wills, "In the name of God, amen";
> the laws respecting the observance of the Sabbath, with the general cessation of all secular business, and the closing of courts, legislatures, and other similar public assemblies on that day;
> the churches and church organizations which abound in every city, town and hamlet;

the multitude of charitable organizations existing everywhere under Christian auspices;
the gigantic missionary associations, with general support, and aiming to establish Christian missions in every quarter of the globe.[289]

South Carolina Supreme Court (1846), in the case of City of Charleston v. S.A. Benjamin, cites an individual who willfully broke an Ordinance which stated:

No person or persons whatsoever shall publicly expose to sale, or sell...any goods, wares or merchandise whatsoever upon the Lord's day.[290]

The prosecuting attorney astutely explained the premise, stating:

Christianity is a part of the common law of the land, with liberty of conscience to all. It has always been so recognized....If Christianity is a part of the common law, its disturbance is punishable at common law. The U.S. Constitution allows it as a part of the common law. The President is allowed ten days [to sign a bill], with the exception of Sunday. The Legislature does not sit, public offices are closed, and the Government recognizes the day in all things....
The observance of Sunday is one of the usages of the common law, recognized by our U.S. and State Governments....
The Sabbath is still to be supported; Christianity is part and parcel of the common law....Christianity has reference to the principles of right and wrong....it is the foundation of those morals and manners upon which our society is formed; it is their basis. Remove this and they would fall....[Morality] has grown upon the basis of Christianity.[291]

The Supreme Court of South Carolina delivered its decision, declaring:

The Lord's day, the day of the Resurrection, is to us, who are called Christians, the day of rest after finishing a new creation. It is the day of the first visible triumph over death, hell and the grave! It was the birth day of the believer in Christ, to whom and through whom it opened up the way which, by repentance and faith, leads unto everlasting life and eternal happiness! On that day we rest, and to us it is the Sabbath of the Lord - its decent observance, in a Christian community, is that which ought to be expected.[292]

United States Congress (January 19, 1853), as part of a Congressional investigation, records the report of Mr. Badger of the Senate Judiciary Committee:

> How comes it that Sunday, the Christian Sabbath, is recognized and respected by all the departments of Government? In the law, Sunday is a "dies non;" it cannot be used for the service of legal process, the returns of writs, or other judicial purposes. The executive departments, the public establishments, are all closed on Sundays; on that day neither House of Congress sits....
>
> Here is a recognition by law, and by universal usage, not only of a Sabbath, but of the Christian Sabbath, in exclusion of the Jewish or Mohammedan Sabbath. Why, then, do the petitioners exclaim against this invasion of their religious rights? Why do they not assert that a national Sabbath, no less than a national Church, is an establishment of religion?...The recognition of the Christian Sabbath is complete and perfect. The officers who receive salaries, or per-diem compensation, are discharged from duty on this day, because it is the Christian Sabbath, and yet suffer no loss or diminution of pay on that account.[293]

William Strong (May 6, 1808-August 19, 1895) was an Associate Justice of U.S. Supreme Court, 1870-80. He had previously served as a U.S. Representative, 1847-51, and as a justice on the Supreme Court of Pennsylvania, 1857-68. He was also president of the American Sunday School Union, 1883-95.

V.
THE FIFTH COMMANDMENT

"Honour thy father and thy mother: that thy days may be long upon the land which the Lord thy God giveth thee." - Ex. 20:12, Deut. 5:16

WEBSTER'S DICTIONARY

Noah Webster's original 1828 Dictionary of the English Language gave this definition:

HON'OR, v.t on'or. [L. honoro.]
1. To revere; to respect; to treat with deference and submission, and perform relative duties to.
 Honor thy father and thy mother. Ex.20.
2. To reverence; to manifest the highest veneration for, in words and actions; to entertain the most exalted thoughts of; to worship; to adore.
 That all men should honor the Son, even as they honor the Father. John 5.
3. To dignify; to raise to distinction or notice; to elevate in rank or station; to exalt. Men are sometimes honored with titles and offices, which they do not merit.
 Thus shall it be done to the man whom the king delighteth to honor.
 Esth.6.
4. To glorify; to render illustrious.
 I will be honored upon Pharaoh, and upon all his host. Ex.14.
5. To treat with due civility and respect in the ordinary intercourse of life. The troops honored the governor with a salute.
6. In commerce, to accept and pay when due; as, to honor a bill of exchange.

COMMENTARY

Matthew D. Staver writes:

The Fifth Commandment exhorts children to honor their parents. A 1642 Connecticut law cited to the Fifth Commandment for the proposition that children should honor their parents:

> If any child or children above sixteen years old, and of sufficient understanding shall curse or smite their normal father or mother, he or they shall be put to death; unless it can be sufficiently testified that the parents have been very unchristianly negligent in the education of such children, or so provoke them by extreme and cruel correction that they have been forced thereunto to preserve themselves from death (or) maiming. Ex. 21:17, Lev. 20, Ex. 20:15.

THE CODE OF 1650 at 29; see also COLONIAL ORIGINS at 230; See also THE CODE OF 1650 at 29; COLONIAL ORIGINS at 230.

The Louisiana Court of Appeals referred specifically to the Ten Commandments when making the following observation:

> "Honor thy father and thy mother," is as much a command of the municipal law as it is a part of the Decalogue, regarded as holy by every Christian people. "A child," says the code, "whatever be his age, owes honor and respect to his father and mother."

Ruiz v. Clancy, 157 So. 737, 738 (La. Ct. App. 1934); see also Pierce v. Yerkovich, 363 N.Y.S.2d 403, 414 (N.Y. Fam. Ct. 1974); Mileski v. Locker, 178 N.Y.S.2d

911, 916 (N.Y. Sup. Ct. 1958); Beaty v. McGoldrick, 121
N.Y.S.2d 431, 432 (N.Y. Sup. Ct. 1953). [294]

THE INFLUENCE OF THE FIFTH COMMANDMENT
William J. Federer

The influences of the Fifth Commandment to honor parents are
referenced below:

MASSACHUSETTS BODY OF LIBERTIES

81. When parents dye interstate, the Elder sonne
shall have a double portion of his whole estate reall and
personall, unlesse the General Court upon just cause
alleadged shall judge otherwise.

FOUNDERS

As a youth, George Washington copied in his own handwriting 110
Rules of Civility and Decent Behavior in Company and Conversation, which
included:

108) When you speak of God, or His Attributes,
let it be Seriously & Reverence, Honor & Obey your Natural
Parents altho they be poor.[295]

On February 21, 1825, in a letter to Thomas Jefferson Smith, the
son of a friend, Thomas Jefferson gave the admonition:

Adore God. Reverence and cherish your parents.
Love your neighbor as yourself. Be just. Be true. Murmur
not at the ways of Providence. So shall the life into which
you have entered be the Portal to one of eternal and ineffable
bliss.[296]

In 1754, in a pamphlet entitled Information to Those Who Would
Remove to America, Benjamin Franklin wrote to Europeans interested in
immigrating or sending their youth to this land:

Hence bad examples to youth are more rare in
America, which must be a comfortable consideration to
parents.[297]

EDUCATION

The Rules and Precepts observed at Harvard, September 26, 1642, stated:

> 6. None shall...frequent the company and society of such men as lead an unfit, and dissolute life. Nor shall any without his Tutors leave, or without the call of Parents or Guardians, goe abroad to other Townes.[298]

Colony of Connecticut, 1690, in the legislature, passed the law:

> This [legislature] observing that...there are many persons unable to read the English tongue and thereby incapable to read the holy Word of God or the good laws of this colony...it is ordered that all parents and masters shall cause their respective children and servants, as they are capable, to be taught to read distinctly the English tongue.[299]

In A Manual of Useful Studies, published in New Haven, 1839, Noah Webster stated:

> In the family are formed the elements of civil governments; the family discipline is the model of all social order;...The respect for the law and the magistrate begins in the respect for parents....
> Families are the nurseries of good and bad citizens. The parent who neglects to restrain and govern his child, or who, by his example, corrupts him, is the enemy of the community to which he belongs; the parent who instructs his child in good principles, and subjects him to correct discipline, is the guardian angel of his child, and the best benefactor of society.[300]

Noah Webster stated:

> To give children a good education in manners, arts and science, is important; to give them a religious education is indispensable; and an immense responsibility rests on parents and guardians who neglect these duties.[301]

PRESIDENTS

In September of 1811, John Quincy Adams wrote a letter to his son from St. Petersburg, Russia, while serving for the second time in the U.S. Ministry to that country:

> So great is my veneration for the Bible, and so strong my belief, that when duly read and meditated on, it is of all books in the world, that which contributes most to make men good, wise, and happy - that the earlier my children begin to read it, the more steadily they pursue the practice of reading it throughout their lives, the more lively and confident will be my hopes that they will prove useful citizens of their country, respectable members of society, and a real blessing to their parents.[302]

On May 1, 1926, before the National Council of the Boy Scouts of America, Washington, D.C., President Calvin Coolidge stated:

> Such thought as I have been able to give to the subject and such observations as have come within my experience have convinced me that there is no substitute for the influences of the home and of religion. These take hold of the innermost nature of the individual and play a very dominant part in the formation of personality and character. This most necessary and most valuable service has to be performed by the parents.[303]

On May 20, 1981, in a Proclamation of Father's Day, President Ronald Reagan stated:

> "Train up a child in the way he should go: and when he is old, he will not depart from it," Solomon tells us. Clearly, the future is in the care of our parents. Such is the responsibility, promise, and hope of fatherhood. Such is the gift that our fathers give us.[304]

On March 8, 1983, at the National Association of Evangelicals in Orlando, Florida, President Reagan stated:

> I've watched TV panel shows discuss this issue, seen columnists' pontification on our error, but no one seems to mention morality as playing a part in the subject of sex. Is the Judeo-Christian tradition wrong? Are we to believe that something so sacred can be looked upon as a pure physical thing with no potential for emotional and psychological harm?
>
> And isn't it the parents' right to give counsel and advice to keep their children from making mistakes that may affect their entire lives? Many of us in government would like to know what parents think about this intrusion into their families by government. We're going to fight in the courts.
>
> The right of parents and the rights of family take precedence over those of Washington-based bureaucrats and social engineers.[305]

LEADERS

Jedediah Strong Smith (June 24, 1798-May 27, 1831) was an American trader and explorer. His expeditions were exceeded in importance only by those of Lewis and Clark. He helped lead expeditions up the Missouri River, with characters such as keelboatmen Mike Fink, Talbot, and Carpenter. He led expeditions across the Rocky Mountains, 1822-26; from California to the Oregon coast; across the Mojave desert and the Sierra Nevadas; and along the Santa Fe Trail, 1826-29. Jedediah Strong Smith, along with two other partners, operated the successful fur-trading company of Smith, Jackson and Sublette, in Salt Lake City He discovered the South Pass through the Rockies and established the first land route to California.

Jedediah's honor for his parents can be seen in his letter to his parents in Ohio, December 24, 1829, written from Wind River on the east side of the Rocky Mountains:

> It is a long time since I left home & many times I have been ready, to bring my business to a close & endeavor to come home; but have been hindered hitherto....
>
> However I will endeavor, by the assistance of Divine Providence, to come home as soon as possible...but whether I shall ever be allowed the privilege, God only

knows, I feel the need of the watch & care of a Christian Church.

You may well suppose that our Society is of the roughest kind. Men of good morals seldom enter into business of this kind - I hope you will remember me before the Throne of Grace....

May God in His infinite mercy allow me soon to join My Parents is the Prayer of your undutiful Son, Jedediah S. Smith.[306]

On Tuesday, February 5, the U.S. Representative from Oklahoma, J.C. Watts, delivered the Republican response to President Clinton's State of the Union Address:

I didn't get my values from Washington. I got my values from my parents, from Buddy and Helen Watts, in Eufaula, Oklahoma. I got my values growing up in a poor black neighborhood on the east side of the railroad tracks, where money was scarce but dreams were plentiful and love was all around.

I got my values from a strong family, a strong church and a strong neighborhood. I wasn't raised to be a Republican or Democrat.

My parents just taught by example. They taught me and my brothers and sisters that, if you lived under their roof, you were going to work. They taught us, if you made a mistake, as we all do, you've got to own up to it, you call it what it is, and you try to turn it around. They taught us, if you spend more money than you make, you're on a sure road to disaster.[307]

On February 5, 1996, Margaret Thatcher stated:

Responsibility to your parents, to your children, to your God. This really binds us together in a way that nothing else does. If you accept freedom, you've got to have principles about the responsibility. You can't do this without a biblical foundation. Your Founding Fathers came over with that. They came over with the doctrines of the New Testament as well as the Old.[308]

COURTS

New York Supreme Court (December 30, 1993), in the Appellate Division, stated in the case of Alfonso v. Fernandez, that the public schools in New York City are:

> [Parents should not be] compelled by state authority to send their children into an environment where they will be permitted, even encouraged, to obtain a contraceptive device, which the parents disfavor as a matter of private belief.
>
> The amici miss the point. The primary purpose of the Board of Education is not to serve as a health provider. Its reason for being is education.
>
> No judicial or legislative authority directs or permits teachers and other public school educators to dispense condoms to minor, unemancipated students without the knowledge or consent of their parents. Nor do we believe that they have any inherent authority to do so....
>
> [Parents] enjoy a well-recognized liberty interest in rearing and educating their children to accord with their own views, [citing U.S. Supreme Court cases from the 1920's, Pierce v. Society of Sisters and Meyer v. Nebraska]
>
> The Constitution gives parents the right to regulate their children's sexual behavior as best they can, [a contraceptive decision] is clearly within the purview of the petitioners' constitutionally protected right to rear their children.[309]

VI.
THE SIXTH COMMANDMENT

"Thou shalt not kill." - Ex. 20:13, Deut. 5:17

WEBSTER'S DICTIONARY

Noah Webster's original 1828 Dictionary of the English Language gives the definition:

MUR'DER, n. [L. mors.]
1. The act of unlawfully killing a human being with premeditated malice, by a person of sound mind. To constitute murder in law, the person killing another must be of sound mind or in possession of his reason, and the act must be done with malice prepense, aforethought or premeditated; but malice may be implied, as well as express.
2. An outcry, when life is in danger.

MUR'DER, v.t.
1. To kill a human being with premeditated malice. [See the Noun.]
2. To destroy; to put an end to.
Canst thou murder thy breath in middle of a word?

MUR'DERED, pp. Slain with malice prepense.

MUR'DERER, n. A person who in possession of his reason, unlawfully kills a human being with premeditated malice.
1. A small piece of ordnance.

COMMENTARY

Matthew D. Staver writes:

Th Sixth Commandment simply states, "Thou shalt not kill." Citations to the incorporation of this Commandment from colonial times to the present are legion. Courts have been very candid in tracing the prohibition against murder back to the Sixth Commandment. For instance, a Kentucky appeals court stated:

> The rights of society as well as those of appellant are involved and are also to be protected, and to that end all forms of governments following the promulgation of Moses at Mt. Sinai has required of each and every one of its citizens that "Thou shalt not murder." If that law is violated, the one guilty of it has no right to demand more than a fair trial, and if, as a result thereof, the severest punishment for the crime is visited upon him, he has no one to blame but himself.

Young v. Commonwealth, 52 S.W. 963, 966 (Ky. Ct. App. 1932).

As recently as 1998, a Wisconsin appeals court quoted a 1974 Indiana Supreme Court opinion which stated:

> Virtually all criminal laws are in one way or another the progeny of Judeo-Christian ethics. We have no intention to overrule the Ten Commandments.

Wisconsin, v. Schultz, 582 N.W.2d 112, 117 (Wis. App. 1998) (quoting Sumpter v. Indiana, 306 N.E.2d 95, 101 (Ind. 1974)). [310]

THE INFLUENCE OF THE SIXTH COMMANDMENT
William J. Federer

The influence of the Sixth Commandment on America was and is felt in courts across the land, and is so obvious as to not require additional citations, but a few are offered below:

MASSACHUSETTS BODY OF LIBERTIES

94,4. If any person commit any wilfull murder, which is manslaughter, committed upon premeditated malice, hatred, or Crueltie, not in a mans necessarie and just defence, nor by mere casualtie against his will, he shall be put to death.

FOUNDERS

George Washington's father, Augustine Washington, who was an active vestryman in Truro Parish, Virginia, recorded the baptism of George in his own handwriting in the old family Bible, April of 1732:

George William, son to Augustine Washington and Mary, his wife, was born the eleventh day of February, 1731-32, about ten in the morning, and was baptized the 3rd April following, Mr. Bromley Whiting, and Captain Christopher Brooks godfathers, and Mrs. Mildred Gregory godmother.[311]

Augustine Washington, George's father, was a man of large stature. He died on April 12, 1743, at the age of forty-nine, when George was only eleven years old. His last words were:

I thank God that in all my life I never struck a man in anger; for had I done so I am sure (so great is my strength) that I would have killed my antagonist. Then his blood, at this awesome moment, would lie heavily on my soul. As it is, I die at peace with all mankind.[312]

EDUCATION

Noah Webster's 1828 edition of the American Dictionary of the English Language contained numerous Scripture verses from the Old and New Testaments to clarify the context in which a word was to be used. The word Law had the definition:

Law of Nature ....is a rule or conduct arising out of the natural relations of human beings established by the Creator, and existing prior to any positive precept. Thus it is a law of nature, that one man should not injure another, and murder and fraud would be crimes, independent of any prohibition from a supreme power.... A rule of direction; a directory; as reason and natural conscience. "These, having not the law, are a law to themselves." Rom.ii.[313]

On July 4th, 1798, in New Haven, Yale President Timothy Dwight delivered an address entitled, The Duty of Americans, at the Present Crisis, Illustrated in a Discourse, in which stated:

The great and good ends proposed by the Illuminati as the ultimate objects of their union are the overthrow of religion, government, and human society, civil and domestic. These they pronounce to be so good that murder, butchery, and war, however extended and dreadful, are declared by them to be completely justifiable if necessary for these great purposes.[314]

William Linn, May 1, 1789, was elected Chaplain of U.S. House of Representatives and given a salary of $500 from the Federal Treasury. He was a respected minister in New York City, and the father of the poet John Blair Linn (1777-1804). Reverend William Linn stated:

Let my neighbor once persuade himself that there is no God, and he will soon pick my pocket, and break not only my leg but my neck. If there be no God, there is no law, no future account; government then is the ordinance of man only, and we cannot be subject for conscience sake.[315]

STATE LAWS

The Constitution of the State of Alabama, adopted 1901, stated:

Article VIII, Section 182. Disqualification of voters. The following persons shall be disqualified both from registering, and from voting, namely: All idiots and insane persons; those who shall be reason of conviction of crime be disqualified from voting at the time of the ratification of this Constitution; those who shall be convicted of treason, murder...[316]

Article IV, Section 86. Dueling. The legislature shall pass such penal laws as it may deem expedient to suppress the evil practice of dueling.[317]

The Constitution of the State of Texas, adopted August 27, 1845), stated:

Article VII, Section 1. Members of the Legislature, and all officers, before they enter upon the duties of their offices, shall take the following oath or affirmation: "....and I do further solemnly swear (or affirm,) that since the adoption of this Constitution by the Congress of the United States, I being a citizen of this State, have not fought a duel with deadly weapons within this State, nor out of it; nor have I sent or accepted a challenge to fight a duel with deadly weapons; nor have I acted as second in carrying a challenge, or aided, advised, or assisted any person thus offending - So Help Me God."[318]

Since Alexander Hamilton had been successful in helping to outlaw dueling in New York, he and Aaron Burr took their places on the New Jersey side of the Hudson River. On July 11, 1804, Hamilton was fatally shot. He suffered for thirty-one hours before death. The Reverend Benjamin Moore, Episcopalian Bishop of New York, stayed with him, ministering the last rites.[319]

California Supreme Court, May 16, 1994, delivered a landmark 6-1 decision giving California one of the toughest fetal murder laws in the nation. In the majority opinion, Chief Justice Malcolm Lucas stated:

The third-party killing of a fetus with malice aforethought is murder...as long as the state can show that the fetus has progressed beyond the embryonic stage of seven to eight weeks.[320]

PRESIDENTS

On December 3, 1906, in his Sixth Annual Message to Congress, President Theodore Roosevelt stated:

A great many white men are lynched, but the crime is peculiarly frequent in respect to black men. The greatest existing cause of lynching is the perpetration, especially by black men, of the hideous crime of rape – the most abominable in all the category of crimes, even worse than murder.

Mobs frequently avenge the commission of this crime by themselves torturing to death the man committing it; thus avenging in bestial fashion a bestial deed, and reducing themselves to a level with the criminal....

Moreover, in my judgement, the crime of rape should always be punished with death, as is the case with murder; assault with intent to commit rape should be made a capital crime.[321]

On February 2, 1984, a National Prayer Breakfast, President Ronald Reagan stated:

This power of prayer can be illustrated by the story that goes back to the fourth century - the monk living in a little remote village, spending most of his time in prayer or tending the garden from which he obtained his sustenance....

One day he thought he heard the voice of God telling him to go to Rome. And believing that he had heard, he set out. Weeks and weeks later, he arrived there, having traveled most of the way on foot. It was at a time of a festival in Rome. They were celebrating over the Goths. He followed a crowd into the Colosseum, and then, there in the midst of this great crowd, he saw the gladiators come forth, stand before the Emperor, and say, 'We who are about to die salute you.'

And he realized they were going to fight to the death for the entertainment of the crowds. He cried out, "In the Name of Christ, stop!" And his voice was lost in the tumult there in the great Colosseum.

And as the games began, he made his way down through the crowd and climbed over the wall and dropped to the floor of the arena. Suddenly the crowds saw this scrawny little figure making his way out to the gladiators and saying, over and over again, "In the Name of Christ, stop!"

And they thought it was part of the entertainment, and at first they were amused. But then, when they realized it wasn't, they grew belligerent and angry. And as he was pleading with the gladiators, "In the Name of Christ, stop!" one of them plunged his sword into his body. And as he fell to the sand of the arena in death, his last words were, "In the Name of Christ, stop!"

And suddenly, a strange thing happened. The gladiators stood looking at this tiny form lying in the sand. A silence fell over the Colosseum. And then, someplace up in the upper tiers, an individual made his way to an exit and left, and the others began to follow. And in the dead silence, everyone left the Colosseum. That was the last battle to the death between gladiators in the Roman Colosseum. Never again did anyone kill or did men kill each other for the entertainment of the crowd.

One tiny voice that could hardly be heard above the tumult. "In the Name of Christ, stop!" It is something we could be saying to each other throughout the world today.[322]

VII.
THE SEVENTH COMMANDMENT

*"Thou shalt not commit adultery." - Ex. 20:14,
Deut. 5:18*

WEBSTER'S DICTIONARY

Noah Webster's original 1828 Dictionary of the English Language gives the following definitions:

ADUL'TERY, n. [L. adulterium. See Adulterate.]
1. Violation of the marriage bed; a crime, or a civil injury, which introduces, or may introduce, into a family, a spurious offspring.
By the laws of Connecticut, the sexual intercourse of any man, with a married woman, is the crime of adultery in both: such intercourse of a married man, with an unmarried woman, is fornication in both, and adultery of the man, within the meaning of the law respecting divorce; but not a felonious adultery in either, or the crime of adultery at common law, or by statute. This latter offense is, in England, proceeded with only in the ecclesiastical courts. In common usage, adultery means the unfaithfulness of any married person to the marriage bed. In England, Parliament grant absolute divorces for infidelity to the marriage bed in either party; and the spiritual courts divorce a mensa et thoro.
2. In a scriptural sense, all manner of lewdness or unchastity, as in the seventh commandment.
3. In scripture, idolatry, or apostasy from the true God. Jer. 3.
4. In old laws, the fine and penalty imposed for the offense of adultery.
5. In ecclesiastical affairs, the intrusion of a person into a bishopric, during the life of the bishop.
6. Among ancient naturalists, the grafting of trees was called adultery, being considered as an unnatural union.

ADUL'TERER, n. [L. adulter.]

1. A man guilty of adultery; a man who has sexual commerce with any married woman, except his wife. [See Adultery.]
2. In scripture, an idolator. Ezek. 23.
3. An apostate from the true faith, or one who violates his covenant engagements; a very wicked person. Jer. 9 and 23.
4. One devoted to earthly things. James, 4.

ADUL'TERESS, n. A married woman guilty of incontinence.

ADUL'TERINE, a. Proceeding from adulterous commerce; spurious.

ADUL'TERINE, n. In the civil law, a child issuing from an adulterous connection.

ADUL'TEROUS, a.
1. Guilty of adultery; pertaining to adultery.
2. In scripture, idolatrous, very wicked. Mat. 12 and 16. Mark, 8.

COMMENTARY

Matthew D. Staver writes:

The seventh Commandment states, "Thou shalt not commit adultery." A 1641 Massachusetts law declared:

If any person committeth adultery with a married or espoused wife, the adulterer and the adulteress shall surely be put to death. Ex. 30.14.

COLONIAL ORIGINS at 84.

Similar laws were enacted by Connecticut in 1642, Rhode Island in 1647, New Hampshire in 1680 and Pennsylvania in 1705.

The Texas Criminal Appeals court has stated:

The accused would insist upon the defense that the female consented. The state would reply that she could not consent. Why? Because the law prohibits, with a penalty, the completed act. "Thou shalt not commit adultery" is our law as well as the law of the Bible.

Hardin v. State, 46 S.W. 803, 808 (Tex. Crim. App. 1898).

The Washington Supreme Court stated,

Adultery, whether promiscuous or not, violates one of the Ten Commandments and the statutes of this State.

Schreifels v. Schreifels, 287 P.2d 1001, 1005 (Wash. 1955). [323]

THE INFLUENCE OF THE SEVENTH COMMANDMENT
William J. Federer

The influence of the Seventh Commandment is shown in Colonial Documents, State Documents, Court Decisions, Historians, Presidents, etc., as referenced below:

COLONIAL DOCUMENTS

Code of the Connecticut General Court, 1650, in the Capital Laws Section of the Code, stated:

6. If any man or woman shall lie with any beast or brute creature, by carnal copulation,
they shall surely be put to death, and the beast shall be slain and buried. Lev. 20:15, 16.
7. If any man lies with mankind as he lies with a woman, both of them have committed

abomination, they both shall surely be put to death. Lev. 20:13.[324]

The Colonial Legislature of New York Colony, 1665, enacted:

It is ordered that a church shall be built in each parish, capable of holding two hundred persons; that ministers of every church shall preach every Sunday, and pray for the king, queen, the Duke of York, and the royal family; and to marry persons after legal publication of license...

Church wardens to report twice a year all misdemeanors, such as swearing, profaneness, Sabbath-breaking, drunkenness, fornication, adultery, and all such abominable sins.[325]

STATE DOCUMENTS

The Constitution of the State of New York, adopted 1777, stated:

Article XXXVIII. The free exercise and enjoyment of religious profession and worship, without discrimination or preference, shall forever hereafter be allowed, within this State, to all mankind: Provided, that the liberty of conscience, hereby granted, shall not be so construed as to excuse acts of licentiousness.[326]

The Constitution of the State of Arizona, adopted December 12, 1911, stated:

Second. Polygamy. Polygamous or plural marriages, or polygamous co-habitation, are forever prohibited within the State.[327]

The Constitution of the State of Texas, adopted August 27, 1845), stated:

Article VII, Section 18. No divorce shall be granted by the Legislature.[328]

The Constitution of the State of Alabama, adopted 1901, stated:

Article VIII, Section 182. Disqualification of voters. The following persons shall be disqualified both from registering, and from voting, namely: All idiots and insane persons; those who shall be reason of conviction of crime be disqualified from voting at the time of the ratification of this Constitution; those who shall be convicted of treason, murder, arson, embezzlement, malfeasance in office, larceny, receiving stolen property, obtaining property or money under false pretenses, perjury, subordination of perjury, robbery, assault with intent to rob, burglary, forgery, bribery, assault and battery on the wife, bigamy, living in adultery, sodomy, incest...[329]

COURTS

Pennsylvania Supreme Court (1824), in the case of Updegraph v. The Commonwealth, 11 Serg. & R. 393-394, 398-399, 402-407 (1824), recorded the court's declaration that:

The act against cursing and swearing, and breach of the Lord's day; the act forbidding incestuous marriages, perjury by taking a false oath upon the book, fornication and adultery...for all these are founded on Christianity - for all these are restraints upon civil liberty.[330]

United States Supreme Court (1885), in the case of Murphy v. Ramsey & Others, 144 U.S. 15, 45 (1885), gave its opinion:

Every person who has a husband or wife living...and marries another...is guilty of polygamy, and shall be punished....
Certainly no legislation can be supposed more wholesome and necessary in the founding of a free, self-governing commonwealth...than that which seeks to establish it on the basis of the idea of the family, as consisting in and springing from the union for life of one man and one woman in the holy estate of matrimony;
[Marriage is] the sure foundation of all that is stable and noble in our civilization; the best guarantee of that reverent morality which is the source of all beneficent progress in social and political improvement.[331]

United States Supreme Court (1889), stated in the case of Davis v. Beason, 133 U.S. 333, 341-343, 348 (1890), that the U.S. considers bigamy and polygamy as crimes. The State of Idaho also declared bigamy and polygamy illegal, and declared that anyone who commits it, teaches it or even encourages it, is forbidden from voting or holding office in that Territory.

A man named Samuel Davis was caught in the crime, fined and jailed. He argued that he was being imprisoned for his religious belief and that he should have the freedom to commit bigamy and polygamy under the First Amendment. The decision of the Court was delivered by Justice Stephen Field, who had been appointed by President Abraham Lincoln in 1863. It stated:

> Bigamy and polygamy are crimes by the laws of all civilized and Christian countries. They are crimes by the laws of the United States, and they are crimes by the laws of Idaho. They tend to destroy the purity of the marriage relation, to disturb the peace of families, to degrade woman and debase man...,
>
> To extend exemption from punishment for such crimes would be to shock the moral judgement of the community. To call their advocacy a tenet of religion is to offend the commons sense of mankind.
>
> There have been sects which denied as a part of their religious tenets that there should be any marriage tie, and advocated promiscuous intercourse of the sexes as prompted by the passions of its members....
>
> Should a sect of either of these kinds ever find its way into this country, swift punishment would follow the carrying into effect of its doctrines, and no heed would be given to the pretence that...their supporters could be protected in their exercise by the Constitution of the United States.
>
> Probably never before in the history of this country has it been seriously contended that the whole punitive power of the government for acts, recognized by the general consent of the Christian world...must be suspended in order that the tenets of a religious sect...may be carried out without hindrance.
>
> The constitutions of several States, in providing for religious freedom, have declared expressly that such freedom shall not be construed to excuse acts of licentiousness.....

The constitution of New York of 1777 provided:
The free exercise and enjoyment of religious profession
and worship, without discrimination or preference, shall
forever hereafter be allowed, within this State, to all
mankind: Provided, That the liberty of conscience, hereby
granted, shall not be so construed as to excuse acts of
licentiousness....The constitutions of California, Colorado,
Connecticut, Florida, Georgia, Illinois, Maryland,
Minnesota, Mississippi, Missouri, Nevada and South
Carolina contain a similar declaration.[332]

United States Supreme Court (1878), rendered its opinion on the
case of Reynolds v. United States, 98 U.S. 145, 165 (1878). The same men
that passed the act creating religious freedom in Virginia, also passed very
strict laws against polygamy and sexual immorality, as documented in the
Supreme Court's decision of 1878:

It is a significant fact that on the 8th of December,
1788, after the passage of the act establishing religious
freedom, and after the convention of Virginia had
recommended as an amendment to the Constitution of the
United States the declaration in a bill of rights that 'all men
have an equal, natural, and unalienable right to the free
exercise of religion, according to the dictates of
conscience,'[that] the legislature of that State substantially
enacted the...death penalty...[for polygamy].[333]

United States Supreme Court (1890), in the case of The Church of
Jesus Christ of Latter Day Saints v. United States, 136 U.S. 1 (1890), forbade
the practice of polygamy in the United States, stating:

It is contrary to the spirit of Christianity and the
civilization which Christianity has produced in the Western
world.[334]

United States Supreme Court (1986), in the case of Bowers v.
Hardwick, 478 U.S. 186, 92 L Ed 2d 140, 106 S. Ct. 2841, p. 149, Chief
Justice Warren E. Burger delivered the Court's decision censuring the act of
sodomy:

Condemnation of those practices is firmly rooted
in Judeo-Christian moral and ethical standards.[335]

Sodomy was a criminal offense at common law and was forbidden by the laws of the original 13 States when they ratified the Bill of Rights. In 1868, when the Fourteenth Amendment was ratified, all but five of the 37 States in the Union had criminal sodomy laws. In fact, until 1961, all 50 states outlawed sodomy... provid[ing] criminal penalties for sodomy performed in private and between consenting adults.[336]

HISTORIANS

Alexis de Tocqueville, in his work Democracy in America (1835, 1840) stated:

I do not question that the great austerity of manners that is observable in the United States arises, in the first instance, from religious faith....Women are the protectors of morals. There is certainly no country in the world where the tie of marriage is more respected than in America or where conjugal happiness is more highly or worthily appreciated.[337]

Horace Greeley (February 3, 1811-November 29, 1872) was an American journalist, newspaper editor and politician. He made famous the phrase, "Go West, Young Man!" Horace Greeley founded and edited the New York Tribune daily paper and The New Yorker magazine.

Called by the poet, John Greenleaf Whittier, "our later Franklin," Greeley's strong anti-slavery editorials helped to stir the North to oppose slavery. He was one of the founders of the Republican Party and used his influence to secure the nomination of Abraham Lincoln for the Presidency. In his Autobiography, Horace Greeley wrote:

I must consider Jesus of Nazareth a better authority as to what is Christian and what pleases God than you are. His testimony on the subject is expressed and unequivocal (Matt. xix. 9) that a marriage can be ruthfully dissolved because of adultery alone.[338]

PRESIDENTS

On May 26, 1777, in a circular to the brigadier-generals, General Washington wrote:

Let vice and immorality of every kind be discouraged as much as possible in your brigade; and, as a chaplain is allowed to each regiment, see that the men regularly attend divine worship. Gaming of every kind is expressly forbidden, as being the foundation of evil, and the cause on many a brave and gallant officer's ruin. Games of exercise for amusement may not only be permitted but encouraged.[339]

On March 10, 1778, as recorded in The Writings of George Washington (March 1-May 31, 1778, 11:83-84, published by the U.S. Government Printing Office, 1934), George Washington issued the order:

At a General Court Marshall whereof Colo. Tupper was President (10th March 1778) Lieutt. Enslin of Colo. Malcom's Regiment tried for attempting to commit **sodomy**, with John Monhort a soldier; Secondly, For Perjury in swearing to false Accounts, found guilty of the charges exhibited against him, being breaches of 5th. Article 18th. Section of the Articles of War and do sentence him to be dismiss'd the service with Infamy. His Excellency the Commander-in-Chief approves the sentence and with Abhorrence and Detestation of such Infamous Crimes orders Liett. Enslin to be drummed out of Camp tomorrow morning by all the Drummers and Fifers in the Army never to return; The Drummers and Fifers to attend on the Grand parade at Guard mounting for that Purpose.[340]

On December 4, 1871, in his Third Annual Message to Congress, President Ulysses S. Grant stated:

In Utah there still remains a remnant of barbarism, repugnant to civilization, to decency, and to the laws of the United States. Territorial officers, however, have been found who are willing to perform their duty in a spirit of equity and with a due sense of the necessity of sustaining the majesty of the law.

Neither polygamy nor any other violation of existing statutes will be permitted within the territory of the United States. It is not with the religion of the self-styled Saints that we are now dealing, but with their practices.

They will be protected in the worship of God

according to the dictates of their consciences, but they will not be permitted to violate the laws under the cloak of religion. It may be advisable for Congress to consider what, in the execution of the laws against polygamy, is to be the status of plural wives and their offspring.

The propriety of Congress passing an enabling act authorizing the Territorial legislature of Utah to legitimize all children born prior to a time fixed in the act might be justified by its humanity to these innocent children.[341]

On December 7, 1875, in his Seventh Annual Message to Congress, President Ulysses S. Grant stated:

In nearly every annual message that I have had the honor of transmitting to Congress I have called attention to the anomalous, not to say scandalous, condition of affairs existing in the Territory of Utah, and have asked for definite legislation to correct it.

That polygamy should exist in a free, enlightened, and Christian country, without the power to punish so flagrant a crime against decency and morality, seems preposterous.

True, there is no law to sustain this unnatural vice; but what is needed is a law to punish it as a crime, and at the same time to fix that status of the innocent children, the offspring of this system, and of the possibility innocent plural wives. But as an institution polygamy should be banished from the land....

I deem of vital importance [to]....drive out licensed immorality, such as polygamy and the importation of women for illegitimate purposes.[342]

On Tuesday, December 6, 1881, in his First Annual Message to Congress, President Chester A. Arthur stated:

For many years the Executive, in his annual message to Congress, has urged the necessity of stringent legislation for the suppression of polygamy in the Territories, and especially in the Territory of Utah. The existing statute for the punishment of this odious crime, so revolting to the moral and religious sense of Christendom, has been persistently and contemptuously violated ever since its enactment.[343]

On Tuesday, December 8, 1885, in his First Annual Message to Congress, President Grover Cleveland stated:

The strength, the perpetuity, and the destiny of the nation rest upon our homes, established by the law of God, guarded by parental care, regulated by parental authority, and sanctified by parental love....

The mothers of our land, who rule the nation as they mold the characters and guide the actions of their sons, live according to God's holy ordinances, and each, secure and happy in the exclusive love of the father of her children, sheds the warm light of true womanhood, unperverted and unpolluted, upon all within her pure and wholesome family circle....

The fathers of our families are the best citizens of the Republic. Wife and children are the sources of patriotism, and conjugal and parental affection beget devotion to the country.

The man who, undefiled...is surrounded in his single home with his wife and children has a stake in the country which inspires him with respect for its laws and courage for its defense.[344]

On January 30, 1905, in a message to Congress, President Theodore Roosevelt stated:

The institution of marriage is, of course, at the very foundation of our social organization, and all influences that affect that institution are of vital concern to the people of the whole country. There is a widespread conviction that the divorce laws are dangerously lax and indifferently administered in some of the States, resulting in the diminishing regard for the sanctity of the marriage relation. The hope is entertained that co-operation amongst the several States can be secured to the end that there may be enacted upon the subject of marriage and divorce uniform laws, containing all possible safeguards for the security of the family.[345]

On December 3, 1906, in his Sixth Annual Message to Congress, President Theodore Roosevelt stated:

> I am well aware of how difficult it is to pass a constitutional amendment. Nevertheless in my judgement the whole question of marriage and divorce should be relegated to the authority of the National Congress....
>
> There is nothing so vitally essential to the welfare of the nation, nothing around which the nation should so bend itself to throw every safeguard, as the home life of the average citizen....
>
> When home ties are loosened; when men and women cease to regard a worthy family life, with all its duties fully performed, and all its responsibilities lived up to, as the life best worth living; then evil days for the commonwealth are at hand....
>
> Surely it should need no demonstration to show that wilful sterility is, from the standpoint of the nation, from the standpoint of the human race, the one sin for which the penalty is national death, race death; a sin for which there is no atonement; a sin which is the more dreadful exactly in proportion as the men and women guilty thereof are in other respects, in character, and bodily and mental powers, those whom for the sake of the state it would be well to see the fathers and mothers of many healthy children, well brought up in homes made happy by their presence. No man, no woman, can shirk the primary duties of life, whether for love of ease and pleasure, or for any other cause, and retain his or her self-respect.[346]

The magazine, Episcopal Churchnews asked President Dwight D. Eisenhower to write a summery of his ideas on religion. He responded with a lesson in America's founding principles and with comments on his reaction to the invasion of Normandy in June of 1944:

> It was part of the privilege into which I was born that my home was a religious home. My father and mother believed that 'the fear of God is the beginning of wisdom.'...
>
> The history of our country is inseparable from the history of such God-fearing families. In this fact we accept the explanation of the miracle of America....
>
> The founding fathers had to refer to the Creator in

order to make their revolutionary experiment make sense; it was because 'all men are endowed by their Creator with certain inalienable rights' that men could dare to be free.[347]

On December 5, 1950, in an address at the Mid-Century White House Conference on Children and Youth, President Harry S. Truman stated:

> The basis of mental and moral strength for our children lies in spiritual things. It lies first of all in the home.
> And next, it lies in the religious and moral influences which are brought to bear on the children. If children have a good home - a home in which they are loved and understood - and if they have good teachers in the first few grades of school, I believe they are well started on the way toward being useful and honorable citizens....
> I no not think I am being old fashioned when I say that children ought to have religious training when they are young, and that they will be happier for it and better for it the rest of their lives.[348]

On March 8, 1983, at the National Association of Evangelicals in Orlando, Florida, President Reagan stated:

> One recent survey by a Washington-based research council concluded that Americans were far more religious than the people of other nations. Ninety-five percent of those surveyed expressed a belief in God. A huge majority believed the Ten Commandments had real meaning in their lives. Another study has found that an overwhelming majority of Americans disapprove of adultery, teenage sex, pornography, abortion, and hard drugs. And this same study showed A deep reverence for the importance of family ties and religious belief.[349]

The March 6, 1980, issue of The Los Angeles Times quoted Ronald Reagan as he spoke on the question of Gay Rights:

> A fellow asked me if I believe that they should have the same civil rights, and I said I think they do, and should have, but that my criticism of the gay rights movement - it is asking for a recognition and acceptance

of an alternative life style which I do not believe society can condone, nor can I.

You could find that in the Bible. It says that in the eyes of the Lord, this is an abomination.[350]

In a July 12, 1984, response to a questionnaire by The Scoreboard, Ronald Reagan gave his views on values:

In part the erosion of these values has given way to a celebration of forms of sexual expression most people reject. We will resist the efforts of some to obtain government endorsement of homosexuality.

Like so many Americans I have been disturbed at attempts to water down traditional values and even abrogate the original terms of American democracy with respect to religious freedom

I firmly believe that freedom prospers when religion is vibrant and the rule of law under God is acknowledged.[351]

On May 7, 1983, in a Radio address to the Nation, President Ronald Reagan stated:

We also first learn at home, and, again, often from our mothers, about the God who will guide us through life....

The progress we're making with the economy, just like the national renewal we're seeing spring up all around us, is the product of our reliance again on good old-fashioned common sense, renewed belief in ourselves, and faith in God.

Now and then I find guidance and direction in the worn brown Bible I used to take the oath of office. It's been the Reagan family Bible, and, like many of yours, has its flyleaf filled with important events; its margins are scrawled with insights and passages underlined for emphasis. My mother, Nelle, made all those marks in that book.

She used it to instruct her two young sons, and I look to it still. A passage in Proverbs describes the ideal woman, saying: "Strength and dignity are her clothing, and she smiles at the future. She opens her mouth in wisdom, and the teaching of kindness is on her tongue. Give her the product of her hands, and let her work praise her in the gates."[352]

VIII.
THE EIGHTH COMMANDMENT

"Thou shalt not steal." - Ex. 20:15, Deut. 5:19

WEBSTER'S DICTIONARY

Noah Webster's original 1828 Dictionary of the English Language gave this definition:

STEAL, v.i.
1. To withdraw or pass privily; to slip along or away unperceived.
Fixed of mind to fly all company, one night she stole away.
From whom you now must steal and take no leave.
A soft and solemn breathing sound rose like a steam of rich distilld perfumes, and stole upon the air.
2. To practice theft; to take feloniously. He steals for a livelihood.
Thou shalt not steal. Exodus 20.

STEAL, v.t. pret. stole; pp. stolen, stole. [G. L, to take, to lift.]
1. To take and carry away feloniously, as the personal goods of another. To constitute stealing or theft, the taking must be felonious, that is, with an intent to take what belongs to another, and without his consent.
Let him that stole, steal no more. Ephesians 4.
2. To Withdraw or convey without notice or clandestinely.
They could insinuate and steal themselves under the same by submission.
3. To gain or win by address or gradual and imperceptible means.
Variety of objects has a tendency to steal away the mind from its steady pursuit of any subject.
So Absalom stole the hearts of the men of Israel. 2 Sam.15.

COMMENTARY

Matthew D. Staver writes:

The Eighth Commandment states, "Thou shalt not steal." This Command is too numerous to trace in this brief. James Kent, who together with Justice Joseph Story was considered as one of the two "Fathers of American Jurisprudence," wrote:

> To overturn justice by plundering others tended to destroy civil society, to violate the law of nature, and the institutions of Heaven.

James Kent, 1 COMMENTARIES ON AMERICAN LAW (1826) at 7.

Not only have the laws against theft been derived from the Eighth Commandment, see Hollywood Motion Picture Equipment Co. v. Furer, 105 P.2d 299, 301 (Cal. 1940), but also laws protecting the integrity of elections, see Doll v. Bender, 47 S.E. 293, 300 (W.Va. 1904) (Dent, J. concurring), as well as the U.S. Constitution's Takings Clause. See Pennsylvania Co. v. United States, 214 F. 445, 455 (W.D. Pa. 1914). See Utah v. Donaldson, 99 P. 447, 449 (Utah 1909); De Rinzie v. Colorado, 138 P. 1009, 1010 (Colo. 1913); Addison v. Florida, 116 So 629 (Fla 1928); Missouri v. Gould, 46 S.W.2d 886,889-890 (Mo. 1932); Succession of Onorato, 51 So.2d 804, 810 (La. 1951); Anderson v. Maddox, 65 So.2d 299, 301-302 (Fla. 1953).[353]

THE INFLUENCE OF THE EIGHTH COMMANDMENT
William J. Federer

The influence of the Eighth Commandment is shown in the following references:

MASSACHUSETTS BODY OF LIBERTIES

23. No man shall be adjudged to pay for detaining any debt from any Creditor above eight pounds in the

hundred for one yeare, And not above that rate proportionable for all somes what so ever, neither shall this be a coulour or countenance to allow any usurie amongst us contrarie to the law of God.

ROGER SHERMAN

Roger Sherman, in A Caveat Against Injustice or, An Inquiry into the Evils of a Fluctuating Medium of Exchange, 1752). wrote:

Section 13. For in the year 1743, it appears by the Face of the Bills then emitted that Twenty-seven Shillings Old-Tenor was equal to one Ounce of Silver. And by an Act of their General Assembly pass'd in March last, the stated Fifty-four Shilling Old-Tenor Bills equal to one Ounce of Silver, which sunk their Value one half. And by another Act in June last, (viz. 1751) they stated Sixty-four Shillings in their Old-Tenor Bills equal to one Ounce of Silver. And by another Act in August last they gave Order and Direction to the Courts in that Colony to make Allowance to the Creditors in making up Judgement from Time to Time as the Bills shall depreciate for the Future, which shews that they expect their Bills of Credit to depreciate for the Future.

Section 20. But if what is us'd as a Medium of Exchange is fluctuating in its Value it is no better than unjust Weights and Measures, both which are condemn'd by the Law of GOD and Man, and therefore the longest and most universal Custom could never make the Use of such a Medium either lawful or reasonable.

U.S. CONSTITUTION

Article 1, Section 8, Paragraph 5. The Congress shall have power...to coin money, regulate the value thereof, and of foreign coin, and fix the standard of weights and measures...Article 1, Section 10, Paragraph 1. No State shall...coin money, emit bills of credit, make any thing but gold and silver coin a tender in payment of debts.

THOMAS JEFFERSON

Thomas Jefferson, as quoted in The Writings of Thomas Jefferson, edited by Albert E. Bergh, vol. 13, 1907, p. 430), stated:

Specie [gold and silver coin] is the most perfect medium, because it will preserve its own level; because, having intrinsic and universal value, it can never die in our hands; and it is the surest resource of reliance in time of war...The trifling economy of paper as a cheaper medium, or its convenience for transmission, weighs nothing in opposition to the advantages of the precious metals...[Paper money} is liable to be abused, has been, is, and forever will be abused, in every country in which it is permitted.

GEORGE WASHINGTON

George Washington, as quoted by Charles Warren, The Making of the Constitution, (Little, Brown and Company, Boston, 1937, p. 551) stated:

If we mean to be honest, debts and taxes must be paid with the substance and not the shadow.

DANIEL WEBSTER

Daniel Webster, in the Congressional Record, March 4, 1846:

Of all the contrivances for cheating the laboring classes of mankind, none has been more effectual than that which deludes them with paper money. This is the most effectual of inventions to fertilize the rich man's field by the sweat of the poor man's brow. Ordinary tyranny, oppression, excessive taxation, there bear lightly on the happiness of the mass of the community, compared with the fraudulent currencies and the robberies committed by depreciated paper. Our own history has recorded for our instruction enough, and more than enough, of the demoralizing tendency, the injustice, and the intolerable oppression on the virtuous and well disposed, or a degraded paper currency, authorized by law, or any way counteranced by government.

JAMES MADISON

James Madison, in Federalist Paper #44, wrote:

The extension of the prohibition to bills of credit

must give pleasure to every citizen in proportion to his love of justice and his knowledge of the true springs of public prosperity.

THOMAS JEFFERSON

Thomas Jefferson, in writing to John Taylor, November 26, 1798, (as quoted by Paul L. Ford, editor, The Writings of Thomas Jefferson, vol. 7., 1896, p. 310):

> I wish it were possible to obtain a single amendment to our constitution. I would be willing to depend on that alone for the reduction of the administration of our government to the genuine principles of it's constitution; I mean an additional article, taking from the federal government the power of borrowing.

JAMES RUSSELL LOWELL

James Russell Lowell (February 22, 1819-August 12, 1891) was an American poet, editor and diplomat. He was the son of Charles Lowell, minister of the West Church in Boston. A graduate of Harvard Law School, James Russell Lowell wrote poetry and prose which received wide acclaim. His well-known works include: *Fable For Critics*, 1848; and *Biglow Papers*, 1848-67. He edited the *Atlantic Monthly*, 1857-61; and the *North American Review*, 1862-72.

He received honorary degrees from both Oxford and Cambridge, and became a professor at Harvard. Lowell was appointed by President Rutherford B. Hayes as U.S. Minister to Spain, 1877-80, and England, 1880-85, where he was immensely popular.

On November 20, 1885, in his International Copyright, James Russell Lowell stated:

> In vain we call old notions fudge,
> And bend our conscience to our dealing;
> The Ten Commandments will not budge,
> And stealing will continue stealing.[354]

MARK TWAIN

In The Adventures of Tom Sawyer, 1876, chapter 13, Mark Twain wrote:

There was no getting around the stubborn fact that taking sweetmeats was only "hooking," while taking bacon and hams and such valuables was plain simple stealing - and there was a command against that in the Bible. So they inwardly resolved that so long as they remained in the business, their piracies should not again be sullied with the crime of stealing.[355]

IX.
THE NINTH COMMANDMENT

"Thou shalt not bear false witness against thy neighbour." - Ex. 20:16, Deut. 5:20

WEBSTER'S DICTIONARY

Noah Webster's original 1828 Dictionary of the English Language give the following definitions:

LIE, n.
1. A criminal falsehood; a falsehood uttered for the purpose of deception; an intentional violation of truth. Fiction, or a false statement or representation, not intended to deceive, mislead or injure, as in fables, parables and the like, is not a lie.

It is willful deceit that makes a lie. A man may act a lie, as by pointing his finger in a wrong direction, when a traveler inquires of him his road.
2. A fiction; in a ludicrous sense.
3. False doctrine. 1John 2.
4. An idolatrous picture of God, or a false god. Romans 1.
5. That which deceives and disappoints confidence. Micah1
To give the lie, to charge with falsehood. A man's actions may give the lie to his words.

LIE, v.i.
1. To utter falsehood with an intention to deceive, or with an immoral design.
Thou hast not lied to men, but to God. Acts 5.
2. To exhibit a false representation; to say or do that which deceives another, when he has a right to know the truth, or when morality requires a just representation.
LIE, v.i. pret. lay; pp. lain, [lien, obs.] [The Gr. word usually signifies to speak, which is to utter or throw out sounds.

COMMENTARY

Matthew D. Staver writes:

The Ninth Commandment prohibits perjury or bearing "false witness". This Commandment became the foundation our judicial system. Connecticut enacted a perjury law in 1642. See THE CODE OF 1650 at 28-29; see also COLONIAL ORIGINS at 230.

Similar laws declaring their basis in the Decalogue were enacted by Massachusetts in 1641, by Rhode Island in 1647, and by New Hampshire in 1680. See COLONIAL ORIGINS at 7, 84, 88, 190-91.

The Oregon Supreme Court stated:

No official is above the law. "Thou shalt not bear false Witness" is a command of the Decalogue, and that forbidden act is denounced by the statute as a felony.

Watts v. Gerking, 228 P. 135, 141 (Or. 1924); see Hosford v. Mississippi, 525 So.2d 789, 799 (Miss. 1998).[356]

THE INFLUENCE OF THE NINTH COMMANDMENT
William J. Federer

The influence of the Ninth Commandment is shown in the references:

MASSACHUSETTS BODY OF LIBERTIES

47. No man shall be put to death without the testimony of two or three witnesses or that which is equivalent thereunto.

(See Deut 17:6: "At the mouth of two witnesses, or three witnesses, shall he that is worthy of death be put to death; but at the mouth of one witness he shall not be put to death." Deut 19:15: "One witness shall not rise up against a man for any iniquity, or for any sin, in any sin that he sinneth: at the mouth of two witnesses, or at the mouth of three witnesses, shall the matter be established.")

GEORGE WASHINGTON

George Washington, in his Farewell Address, 1796:

Let it simply be asked where is the security for prosperity, for reputation, for life, if the sense of religious obligation desert the oaths, which are the instruments of investigation in the Courts of Justice?

DAVID JOSIAH BREWER

Supreme Court Justice David Josiah Brewer, in the case of Church of the Holy Trinity vs the United States, wrote:

The form of oath universally prevailing, concluding with an appeal to the Almighty;

PENNSYLVANIA SUPREME COURT

Pennsylvania Supreme Court (1817), in the case of The Commonwealth v. Wolf, 3 Serg. & R. 48, 50 (1817), stated:

Laws cannot be administered in any civilized government unless the people are taught to revere the sanctity of an oath, and look to a future state of rewards and punishments for the deeds of this life. It is of the utmost moment, therefore, that they should be reminded of their religious duties at stated periods."

STATE OF ALABAMA

The Constitution of the State of Alabama, 1901, stated:

"Article VIII, Section 186...The board shall have power to examine, under oath...and to take testimony...in the following form...: 'I solemnly swear (or affirm) that...I will speak the truth, the whole truth, and nothing but the truth, so help me God.'"

BENJAMIN FRANKLIN

Benjamin. Franklin, 1728, in his "Articles of Belief and Acts of Religion.," referenced treachery and deceit:

Thou abhorrest in Thy creatures treachery and *deceit*, malice, revenge, Intemperance and every other hurtful Vice; but Thou art a Lover of justice and sincerity, of friendship, benevolence and every virtue. Thou art my Friend, my Father, and my Benefactor. Praised be Thy Name, O God, forever. Amen.[357]

In his Autobiography, published in complete form in 1868, Franklin mentioned a small book he carried, listing 13 virtues, of which one was:

7) Sincerity: Use no hurtful *deceit*; think innocently.[358]

THOMAS JEFFERSON

On August 19, 1785, Thomas Jefferson wrote to Peter Carr:

He who permits himself to tell a *lie* once, finds it much easier to do it a second and third time, till at length it becomes habitual; he tells *lies* without attending to it, and truths without the world's believing him. This *falsehood of the tongue* leads to that of the heart, and in time depraves all its good dispositions.[359]

GEORGE WASHINGTON CARVER

In a letter to L. Robinson, January 9, 1922, George Washington Carver listed virtues for his students, of which one was:

Who is too brave to lie.

GOUVERNOR MORRIS

Gouverneur Morris, in an address on the Bank of North America, given in the Pennsylvania State Assembly, 1785, stated:

How can we hope for public peace and national prosperity, *if the faith of governments so solemnly pledged can be so lightly infringed*? Destroy this prop, which once gave us support, and where will you turn in the hour of distress?...This hour of distress will come. It comes to all, and the moment of affliction is known to Him alone, whose

Divine Providence exalts or depresses states and kingdoms. Not by the blind dictates of arbitrary will. Not by a tyrannous and despotic mandate.

But in proportion to their obedience or disobedience of His just and holy laws. It is He who commands us that we abstain from wrong. It is He who tells you, 'do unto others as ye would that they would do unto you'[360]

BENJAMIN HILL

In a tribute to Robert E. Lee, Senator Benjamin Harvey Hill (1823-1882), described him as:

He was a foe without hate, a friend without *treachery.*[361]

WOODROW WILSON

In 1911, Woodrow Wilson stated:

The man whose faith is rooted in the Bible knows that reform cannot be stayed, that the finger of God that moves upon the face of the nations is against every man that plots the nation's downfall or the people's *deceit*;

that these men are simply groping and staggering in their ignorance to a fearful day of judgement; and that whether one generation witnesses it or not, the glad day of revelation and of freedom will come in which men will sing by the host of the coming of the Lord in His glory, and all of those will be forgotten - those little scheming, contemptible creatures that forgot the image of God and tried to frame men according to the image of the evil one.[362]

WILLIAM BLACKSTONE

Sir William Blackstone, whose Commentaries on the Laws of England were widely read in America, wrote:

The belief of a future state of rewards and punishments, the entertaining just ideas of the main attributes of the Supreme Being, and a firm persuasion that

He superintends and will finally compensate every action in human life (all which are revealed in the doctrines of our Savior, Christ), these are the grand foundations of all judicial oaths, which call God to witness the truth of those facts which perhaps may be only known to Him and the party attesting; all moral evidences, therefore, all confidence in human veracity, must be weakened by apostasy, and overthrown by total infidelity.

Wherefore, all affronts to Christianity, or endeavors to depreciate its efficacy, in those who have once professed it, are highly deserving of censure.[363]

STATE DOCUMENTS

Massachusetts Supreme Court (1838), case of Commonwealth v. Abner Kneeland, 37 Mass. (20 Pick) 206, 216-217 1838, involved the publishing libelous remarks about Christianity and God. The Court stated that "freedom of press" was not a license to print without restraint, otherwise:

According to the argument...every act, however injurious or criminal, which can be committed by the use of language may be committed...if such language is printed. Not only therefore would the article in question become a general license for scandal, calumny and falsehood against individuals, institutions and governments, in the form of publication...but all incitation to treason, assassination, and all other crimes however atrocious, if conveyed in printed language, would be dispunishable.[364]

The Constitution of South Carolina, 1778, stated:

Article XXXVIII. V. That it is lawful and the duty of every man being thereuntocalled by those that govern, to bear witness to truth. That every inhabitant of this State, when called to make an appeal to God as a witness to truth, shall be permitted to do it in that way which is most agreeable to the dictates of his own conscience.[365]

In August of 1831, after observing a trial in Chester County, New York, Alexis de Tocqueville wrote:

While I was in America, a witness, who happened to be called at the assizes of the county of Chester (state of

New York), declared that he did not believe in the existence of God or in the immortality of the soul. The judge refused to admit his evidence, on the ground that the witness had destroyed beforehand all confidence of the court in what he was about to say. The newspapers related the fact without any further comment. The New York Spectator of August 23d, 1831, relates the fact in the following terms:

"The court of common pleas of Chester county (New York), a few days since rejected a witness who declared his disbelief in the existence of God. The presiding judge remarked, that he had not before been aware that there was a man living who did not believe in the existence of God; that this belief constituted the sanction of all testimony in a court of justice: and that he knew of no case in a Christian country, where a witness had been permitted to testify without such belief."[366]

The Constitution of the State of Arkansas, 1874, stated:

Article XIX: No person who denies the being of a God shall hold office in the civil departments of this State, nor be competent to testify as a witness in any court.[367]

South Carolina Supreme Court (1846), in City of Charleston v. S.A. Benjamin, cites an individual who willfully broke an Ordinance which stated:

In the Courts over which we preside, we daily acknowledge Christianity as the most solemn part of our administration. A Christian witness, having no religious scruple about placing his hand upon the book, is sworn upon the holy Evangelists - the books of the New Testament, which testify of our Savior's birth, life, death, and resurrection; this is so common a matter, that it is little thought of as an evidence of the part which Christianity has in the common law.[368]

POLITICAL LEADERS

In his Farewell Address, 1796, President George Washington said:

Of all the dispositions and habits which lead to political prosperity, Religion and Morality are indispensable supports. In vain would that man claim the tribute of

Patriotism, who should labor to subvert these great Pillars of human happiness, these firmest props of the duties of Men and Citizens. The mere Politician, equally with the pious man, ought to respect and to cherish them. A volume could not trace all their connections with private and public felicity.[369]

On July 23, 1813, President James Madison issued a Proclamation of a National Day of Public Humiliation and Prayer:

To Him whom no hypocrisy can deceive and no forced sacrifices propitiate.[370]

On March 4, 1837, in his Farewell Address, President Jackson stated:

The men who profit by the abuses and desire to perpetuate them will continue to besiege the halls of legislation in the General Government...and will seek by every artifice to mislead and deceive the public servants....[371]

On March 28, 1860, President James Buchanan sent a formal Protest to the House of Representatives:

I defy all investigations. Nothing but the basest perjury can sully my good name. I do not fear even this, because I cherish an humble confidence that the gracious Being who has hitherto defended and protected me against the shafts of falsehood and malice will not desert me now when I have become 'old and gray headed.' I can declare before God and my country that no human being (with an exception scarcely worthy of notice) has at any period of my life dared to approach me with a corrupt or dishonorable proposition.[372]

On March 30, 1863, President Abraham Lincoln issued a Proclamation of a National Day of Humiliation, Fasting and Prayer:

We have grown in numbers, wealth and power as no other nation has ever grown. But we have forgotten God. We have forgotten the gracious Hand which preserved us in peace, and multiplied and enriched and strengthened us; and we have vainly imagined, in the deceitfulness of our hearts, that all these blessings were produced by some superior wisdom and virtue of our own.[373]

Schuyler Colfax (1823-1885) was Vice-President under Ulysses S. Grant, 1869-73; a U.S. Representative seven terms, 1855-69, and Speaker of the House, 1863-69. Schuyler Colfax said:

Man derives his greatest happiness not by that which he does for himself, but by what he accomplishes for others. This is a sad world at best - a world of sorrow, of suffering, of injustice, and falsification; men stab those whom they hate with the stiletto of slander, but it is for the followers of our Lord to improve it, and to make it more as Christ would have it. The most precious crown of fame that a human being can ask is to kneel at the bar of God and hear the beautiful words, 'Well done, good and faithful servant.'[374]

On January 20, 1953, in his Inaugural Address, President Dwight D. Eisenhower stated:

My fellow citizens....We are summoned by this honored and historic ceremony to witness more than the act of one citizen swearing his oath of service, in the presence of God. We are called as a people to give testimony in the sight of the world our faith that the future shall belong to the free.[375]

On February 22, 1990, President George Bush, at the request of Congress, Joint Resolution 164, issued a Presidential Proclamation declaring 1990 the International Year of Bible Reading:

President Woodrow Wilson likewise recognized the importance of the Bible to its readers. "The Bible is the word of life," he once said. Describing its contents, he added:
"You will find it full of real men and women not only but also of the things you have wondered about and been troubled about all your life, as men have been always; and the more you will read it the more it will become plain to you what things are worth while and what are not, what things make men happy - loyalty, right dealing speaking the truth..."[376]

WRITERS

Josiah Gilbert Holland (1819-1881) was editor of Scribner's Monthly (later Century Magazine) and the Springfield Republican. A celebrated speaker on social topics, Josiah Gilbert Holland wrote under the pen name "Timothy Titcomb." His narratives include Kathrina and Bitter-Sweet. In Wanted, 1872, Josiah Holland penned:

God give us men! A time like this demands
Strong minds, great hearts, true faith, and ready hands;
Men whom the lust of office does not kill;
Men whom the spoils of office cannot buy;
Men who possess opinions and a will;
Men who have honor; men who will not lie.[377]

William McGuffey was considered the "Schoolmaster of the nation" as his Readers sold 125 million copies between 1836 and 1963. In McGuffey's Third Eclectic Reader, Lesson 31 is entitled "On Speaking Truth":

Every action and every thought of your life will then be fresh in your mind. You know it is written in the Bible, "God will bring every work into judgement, with every secret thing, whether it be good or whether it be evil." How must the child then feel who has been guilty of falsehood and deception, who sees it brought to light.[378]

On July 4th, 1798, in New Haven, Yale President Timothy Dwight delivered an address entitled, The Duty of Americans, at the Present Crisis, Illustrated in a Discourse, in which stated:

In societies of Illuminati, doctrines were taught which strike at the root of all human happiness and virtue; and every such doctrine was either expressly or implicitly involved in their system. The being of God was denied and ridiculed....The possession of property was pronounced robbery. Chastity and natural affection were declared to be nothing more than groundless prejudices. Adultery, assassination, poisoning, and other crimes of the like infernal nature, were taught as lawful and even as virtuous actions. To crown such a system of falsehood and horror, all means were declared to be lawful, provided the end was good.[379]

X.
THE TENTH COMMANDMENT

"Thou shalt not covet thy neighbour's house, thou
shalt not covet thy neighbour's wife, nor his manservant,
nor his maidservant, nor his ox, nor his ass, nor any thing
that is thy neighbour's." - Ex. 20:17, Deut. 5:21

WEBSTER'S DICTIONARY

Noah Webster's original 1828 Dictionary of the English Language gives the following definitions

COVET, v.t.
1. To desire or wish for, with eagerness; to desire earnestly to obtain or possess; in a good sense.
Covet earnestly the best gifts. 1 Corinthians 12.
2. To desire inordinately; to desire that which it is unlawful to obtain or possess; in a bad sense.
Thou shalt not covet thy neighbors house, wife or servant. Exodus 20.

COVET, v.i. To have an earnest desire. 1 Timothy 6.

COVETABLE, a. That may be coveted.

COVETED, pp. Earnestly desired; greatly wished or longed for.

COVETING, n. Inordinate desire.

COVETISE, n. Avarice. [Not in use.]

COVETOUS, a.
1. Very desirous; eager to obtain; in a good sense; as covetous of wisdom, virtue or learning.
2. Inordinately desirous; excessively eager to obtain and possess; directed to money or goods, avaricious.
A bishop must not be covetous. 1 Timothy 3.

COVETOUSLY, adv. With a strong or inordinate desire to obtain and possess; eagerly; avariciously.

COVETOUSNESS, n.
1. A strong or inordinate desire of obtaining and possessing some supposed good; usually in a bad sense, and applied to an inordinate desire of wealth or avarice.
Out of the heart proceedeth covetousness. Mark 7.
Mortify your members—and covetousness which is idolatry. Colossians 3.
2. Strong desire; eagerness.

COMMENTARY

Matthew D. Staver writes:

The Tenth Commandment prohibits coveting. John Adams, the first Vice President and second President, talked about property rights, and stated:

> If "Thou shalt not covet" and "Thou shalt not steal" were not commandments of Heaven, they must be made inviolable precepts in every society before it can be civilized or made free.

John Adams, 4 THE WORKS OF JOHN ADAMS, SECOND PRESIDENT OF THE UNITED STATES 9 (Francis Adams, ed. 1851).

This Commandment has been cited as the basis of civil laws against defamation, See Weinstock, Lubin & Co. v. Marks, 42 P. 142, 145 (Cal, 1895), laws preventing election fraud, See Doll v. Bender, 47 S.E. 293, 300-01 (W. Va. 1904) (Dent, J. concurring), laws targeting white collar crime. See Chisman v. Moylan, 105 So. 2d 186, 189 (Fla. App. Ct. 1958), and laws targeting modern forms of cattle rustling. See Swift & Co. v. Peterson, 233 P.2d 216, 231 (Or. 1951). [380]

THE INFLUENCE OF THE TENTH COMMANDMENT
William J. Federer

The influence of the Tenth Commandment is shown in the following references:

JOHN ADAMS

On October 11, 1798, President John Adams stated in a letter to the officers of the First Brigade of the Third Division of the Militia of Massachusetts:

We have no government armed with power capable of contending with human passions unbridled by morality and religion. *Avarice (covetousness)*, ambition, revenge, or gallantry, would break the strongest cords of our Constitution as a whale goes through a net. Our Constitution was made only for a moral and religious people. It is wholly inadequate to the government of any other.[381]

NOAH WEBSTER

In 1823, in an article entitled, Letters to a Young Gentleman Commencing His Education, published in New Haven, Noah Webster wrote:

In selecting men for office, let principle be your guide....It is alleged by men of loose principles, or defective views of the subject, that religion and morality are not necessary or important qualifications for political stations.
But the Scriptures teach a different doctrine. They direct that rulers should be men who rule in the fear of God, able men, such as fear God, men of truth, hating *covetousness.*
But if we had no divine instruction on the subject, our own interest would demand of us a strict observance of the principle of these injunctions. And it is to the neglect of this rule of conduct in our citizens, that we must ascribe the multiplied frauds, breeches of trust, peculations and embezzlements of public property which astonish even ourselves; which tarnish the character of our country; which disgrace a republican government; and which will tend to

reconcile men to monarchs in other countries and even our own.[382]

GROVER CLEVELAND

Grover Cleveland's father died when he was sixteen years of age. Grover helped to support his family by teaching at the New York Institute for the Blind. It was during this time that he heard a sermon by Henry Ward Beecher, of which he described:

> He captivated my youthful understanding and pictured, to my aroused imagination, the entrance of two young men upon the world's jostling activities - one laden like a beast of burden with *avaricious (covetous)* plans and sordid expectations, and the other with a light step and cheerful determination, seeking the way of duty and usefulness and striving for the reward of those who love and serve God, and labor for humanity....
> What this sermon has been for me in all these years I alone know.[383]

V.
PHILOSOPHY OF LAW
William J. Federer

The direct and indirect influence of the Ten Commandments on American law goes back in time to the development of English Common Law, and before that to the origins of Western Civilization. The Ten Commandments were the embodiment of the philosophy of government that a *nation with more internal laws can exist with less external laws*. That if a population had a commonly accepted internal code of conduct, then that population could exist with less of an external legal codes. The more internal restraints a citizenry had, the less external restraints were needed, and thus they could be "free."

SIR FRANCIS BACON

Sir Francis Bacon (January 22, 1561-April 9, 1626), was the Baron Verulam, Viscount St. Albans and Lord Keeper of the Great Seal under King James I. As Lord Chancellor of England (1618-21), he was significantly responsible for the formulation and acceptance of the scientific method, which stressed gathering data from experimentation and induction rather than through the practice of philosophical deduction promulgated by Aristotle. Sir Francis Bacon was responsible for helping to found the Royal Society of London. He wrote:

There never was found, in any age of the world, either philosophy, or sect, or religion, or law, or discipline, which did so highly exalt the good of the community, and increase private and particular good as the holy Christian faith. Hence, it clearly appears that it was one and the same God that gave the Christian law to men, who gave the laws of nature to the creatures.[384]

HUGO GROTIUS

President James Madison described Hugo Grotius as "the father of the modern code of nations."[385] Hugo Grotius (April 10, 1583-August 28, 1645), was a Dutch jurist, theologian and statesman, who was considered the founder of the science of International Law. In 1607, being 24 years old, he was appointed Advocate General for the provinces of Holland and Zealand. In 1613, at the age of 30, he became the Chief Magistrate of Rotterdam. In

1619, Prince Maurice of Nassau sentenced him to life imprisonment for his support of the Arminian faith. Three years later, with his wife's help, he escaped to France hidden in a linen chest. Hugo Grotius (or Huig de Groot in the Dutch language), published *De Jure Belli et Pacis* (On the Law of War and Peace), in 1625, which was a study of the laws of mankind in reference to individuals, nations and states. From 1635 till his death he served as the Swedish ambassador to France.

In his work, On the Law of War and Peace, Hugo Grotius stated:

> Among all good men one principle at any rate is established beyond controversy, that if the authorities issue any order that is contrary to the law of nature or to *the commandments of God*, the order should not be carried out. For when the Apostles said that obedience should be rendered to God rather than men, they appealed to an infallible rule of action, which is written in the hearts of all men.[386]

John Cotton (December 1585-December 23, 1652), was a powerful Puritan minister and scholar in Boston, Massachusetts. Born in England, he fled to the colonies in 1632 to avoid religious persecution. There he rose to become perhaps the most influential leader in shaping the destiny of Puritan New England, serving at the First Church of Boston, 1633-52. Known for his didactic writings, the principles stated in his sermons were frequently put into immediate practice by civil authorities.

In 1636, Rev. John Cotton gave the outline for a code of laws, which included the phrase:

> The Law of Nature, delivered by God.[387]

JOHN LOCKE

John Locke (August 29, 1632-October 28, 1704) was an English philosopher, diplomat and educator, whose writings had a profound influence on America's Founding Fathers. He received his master's degree from the Christ Church College of Oxford University, 1658, and lectured there on Greek, philosophy and rhetoric. He served as a diplomat to Madrid, 1665, moved to France, 1675, then Holland, 1683, and returned to England, 1688. His works include: A Letter Concerning Toleration, 1689; Two Treatises of Government, 1690; An Essay Concerning Human Understanding, 1693; Some Thoughts Concerning Education, 1693; and The Reasonableness of Christianity, 1695. Of nearly 15,000 items of the Founding Fathers which were reviewed; including books, newspaper articles, pamphlets, monographs, etc., John Locke was the third most frequently quoted author.[388] In his Two Treatises of Government, 1690, he cited 80 references to the Bible in the first treatise and 22 references to the Bible in the second.

John Locke elaborated on fundamental concepts, such as: parental authority, separation of powers, private property, the right to resist unlawful authority, unalienable rights, and government by consent, whereby governments "derive their just powers from the consent of the governed." Concerning the idea of a "social compact," a constitution between the people and the government, John Locke trace its origins to:

> That Paction which God made with Noah after the Deluge.[389]

John Locke classified the basic natural rights of man as the right to "life, liberty and property." This not only influenced Thomas Jefferson, who penned the Declaration of Independence, but also elements in the Fifth and Fourteenth Amendments.

In The Second Treatise on Civil Government, 1690, John Locke stated:

> Human Laws are measures in respect of Men whose Actions they must direct, albeit such measures they are as have also their higher Rules to be measured by, which Rules are two, *the Law of God,* and the Law of Nature; so that Laws Human must be made according to the general Laws of Nature, and without contradiction to any positive Law of Scripture, otherwise they are ill made.[390]

SIR WILLIAM BLACKSTONE

Sir William Blackstone (July 10, 1723-February 14, 1780), was an English jurist who deeply influenced the growth of Common Law, jurisprudence and the basis of law in America. In 1758, he was honored by being elected Oxford's first Vinerian lecturer, and in 1770, he became one of the Judges of the Common Pleas. From 1765 to 1770, Sir William Blackstone published his highly influential work entitled, Commentaries on the Laws of England. These were so universally accepted in America that by 1775 they had sold more copies in America than in England. This work set the foundation for America's great legal minds including Chief Justice John Marshall.[391]

Sir William Blackstone expressed the presuppositional base for law in his Commentaries on the Laws of England, 1765-70:

Law of Nature. This will of his Maker is called the law of nature. For as God, when He created matter, and endued it with a principle of mobility, established certain rules for the perpetual direction of that motion; so, when He created man, and endued him with free will to conduct himself in all parts of life, He laid down certain immutable laws of human nature, whereby that free will is in some degree regulated and restrained, and gave him also the faculty of reason to discover the purport of those laws.

Considering the Creator only a Being of infinite power, He was able unquestionably to have prescribed whatever laws He pleased to His creature, man, however unjust or severe. But as He is also a Being of infinite wisdom, He has laid down only such laws as were founded in those relations of justice, that existed in the nature of things antecedent to any positive precept.

These are the eternal, immutable laws of good and evil, to which the Creator Himself in all his Dispensations conforms; and which He has enabled human reason to discover, so far as they are necessary for the conduct of human actions. Such among others, are these principles: that we should live honestly, should hurt nobody, and should render to everyone his due; to which three general precepts Justinian has reduced the whole doctrine of law....

This law of nature, being coeval with mankind and dictated by God Himself, is of course superior in obligation to any other. It is binding over all the globe in all countries, and at all times: no human laws are of any validity, if contrary to this.[392]

Revealed Law. This has given manifold occasion for the interposition of divine providence; which in compassion to the frailty, the imperfection, and the blindness of human reason, hath been pleased, at sundry times and in divers manners, to discover and enforce *its laws* by an immediate and direct revelation.

The doctrines thus delivered we call *the revealed or divine law*, and they are to be found only in the Holy Scriptures. These precepts, when revealed, are found upon comparison to be really a part of the original law of nature as they tend in all their consequences to man's felicity.

But we are not from thence to conclude that the knowledge of these truths was attainable by reason, in its present corrupted state; since we find that, until they were revealed, they were hid from the wisdom of the ages.

As then the moral precepts of *this law* are indeed of the same original with those of the law of nature, so their intrinsic obligation is of equal strength and perpetuity. Yet *undoubtedly the revealed law* is of infinitely more authenticity than that moral system, which is framed by ethical writers, and denominated the natural law.

Because one is the law of nature, expressly declared so to be by God Himself; the other is only what, by the assistance of human reason, we imagine to be that law. If we could be as certain of the latter as we are of the former, both would have an equal authority; but, till then, they can never be put in any competition together.

Upon these two foundations, the law of nature and *the law of revelation*, depend all human laws; that is to say, no human laws should be suffered to contradict these.[393]

FUNDAMENTAL ORDERS OF CONNECTICUT

Fundamental Orders (Constitution) of Connecticut, January 14, 1639, was the first constitution written in America, establishing a pattern which all others followed, including the United States Constitution.[394] It was penned by Roger Ludlow, 1638, after hearing a sermon by Thomas Hooker, the Puritan minister who founded Hartford, Connecticut. So important was this work that Connecticut became known as "The Constitution State."[395]

The committee responsible to frame the orders was charged to make the laws:

As near the *law of God* as they can be.[396]

MONTESQUIEU

Baron Charles Louis Joseph de Secondat Montesquieu (January 18, 1689-February 10, 1755) was a French political philosopher who greatly influenced nineteenth century thought America.

In the beginning of his work *The Spirit of the Laws*, 1748, Baron Montesquieu wrote:

> God is related to the universe, as Creator and Preserver; the laws by which He created all things are those by which He preserves them....
>
> But the intelligent world is far from being so well governed as the physical. For though the former has also its laws, which of their own nature are invariable, it does not conform to them so exactly as the physical world.
>
> This is because, on the one hand, particular intelligent beings are of a finite nature, and consequently liable to error; and on the other, their nature requires them to be free agents. Hence they do not steadily conform to their primitive laws; and even those of their own instituting they frequently infringe....
>
> Man, as a physical being, is like other bodies governed by invariable laws. As an intelligent being, he incessantly transgresses the laws established by God, and changes those of his own instituting. He is left to his private direction, though a limited being, and subject, like all finite intelligences, to ignorance and error: even his imperfect knowledge he loses; and as a sensible creature, he is hurried away by a thousand impetuous passions.
>
> Such a being might every instant forget his Creator; God has therefore reminded him of his duty by the laws of religion. Such a being is liable every moment to forget himself; philosophy has provided against this by the laws of morality. Formed to live in society, he might forget his fellow-creatures; legislators have therefore, by political and civil laws, confined him to his duty.[397]

BENJAMIN FRANKLIN

In 1790, Benjamin Franklin wrote to Thomas Paine regarding his copy of the manuscript *of The Age of Reason:*

> I have read your manuscript with some attention. By the argument it contains against a particular Providence, though you allow a general Providence, you strike at the foundation of all religion. For without the belief of a

Providence that takes cognizance of, guards, and guides, and may favor particular persons, there is no motive to worship a Deity, to fear his displeasure, or to pray for his protection.

I will not enter into any discussion of your principles, though you seem to desire it. At present I shall only give you my opinion that...the consequence of printing this piece will be a great deal of odium drawn upon yourself, mischief to you, and no benefit to others. He that spits into the wind, spits in his own face. But were you to succeed, do you imagine any good would be done by it?...

Think how great a portion of mankind consists of weak and ignorant men and women and of inexperienced, inconsiderate youth of both sexes who have need of the motives of religion to restrain them from vice, to support their virtue....

I would advise you, therefore, not to attempt unchaining the tiger, but to burn this piece before it is seen by any other person....

If men are so wicked with religion, what would they be without it? I intend this letter itself as a proof of my friendship.[398]

EDMUND BURKE

In 1791, Edmund Burke stated in "A Letter to a Member of the National Assembly":

What is liberty without wisdom and without virtue? It is the greatest of all possible evils; for it is folly, vice, and madness, without restraint.

Men are qualified for civil liberty in exact proportion to their disposition to put moral chains upon their own appetites; in proportion as they are disposed to listen to the counsels of the wise and good in preference to the flattery of knaves.

Society cannot exist, unless a controlling power upon will and appetite be placed somewhere; and the less of it there is within, the more there must be without.

It is ordained in the eternal constitution of things, that men of intemperate minds cannot be free. Their passions forge their fetters.[399]

GEORGE WASHINGTON

On September 19, 1796, in his Farewell Address, President George Washington said:

The name of AMERICAN, which belongs to you, in your national capacity, must always exalt the just pride of Patriotism, more than any appellation derived from local discriminations. With slight shades of difference, you have the same Religion, Manners, Habits, and political Principles....

Of all the dispositions and habits which lead to political prosperity, Religion and Morality are indispensable supports. In vain would that man claim the tribute of Patriotism, who should labor to subvert these great Pillars of human happiness, these firmest props of the duties of Men and Citizens.

The mere Politician, equally with the pious man, ought to respect and to cherish them. A volume could not trace all their connections with private and public felicity. Let it simply be asked where is the security for prosperity, for reputation, for life, if the sense of religious obligation desert the oaths, which are the instruments of investigation in the Courts of Justice?

And let us with caution indulge the supposition, that morality can be maintained without religion. Whatever may be conceded to the influence of refined education on minds of peculiar structure, reason and experience both forbid us to expect that national morality can prevail in exclusion of religious principle.

Tis substantially true, that virtue or morality is a necessary spring of popular government. The rule indeed extends with more or less force to every species of Free Government. Who that is a sincere friend to it, can look with indifference upon attempts to shake the foundation of the fabric?...

Observe good faith and justice towards all Nations. Cultivate peace and harmony with all. Religion and Morality enjoin this conduct; and can it be that good policy does not equally enjoin it?...

Can it be, that Providence has not connected the permanent felicity of a Nation with its virtue?[400]

ABIGAIL ADAMS

Near November 5, 1775, Abigail wrote to her friend, Mercy Warren:

A patriot without religion in my estimation is as great a paradox as an honest Man without the fear of God. Is it possible that he whom no moral obligations bind, can have any real Good Will towards Men?

Can he be a patriot who, by an openly vicious conduct, is undermining the very bonds of Society, corrupting the Morals of Youth, and by his bad example injuring the very Country he professes to patronize more than he can possibly compensate by intrepidity, Generosity and honour? The Scriptures tell us "righteousness exalteth a Nation."[401]

ABRAHAM BALDWIN

Abraham Baldwin (November 22, 1754-March 4, 1807) was a signer of the Constitution of the United States, member of Congress and U.S. Senator.

He graduated from Yale University and, in 1781, was offered the professorship of divinity there. He served as chaplain in the Continental Army during the Revolutionary War and later studied law. In 1783 he was admitted to the bar, elected to the state assembly, and later chosen as a representative from Georgia to the Constitutional Convention.

In 1785, he founded and became the first President of the University of Georgia, which was the first state-chartered university in the United States. Through his far-sighted efforts, he secured for the university 40,000 acres of land. His expertise in law and ministry was manifest in his writing of the Charter of the College of Georgia :

As it is the distinguishing happiness of free governments that civil order should be the result of choice and not of necessity, and the common wishes of the people become the laws of the land, their public prosperity and even existence very much depend upon suitably forming the minds and morals of their citizens.

When the minds of the people in general are viciously disposed and unprincipled, and their conduct disorderly, a free government will be attended with greater confusions and evils more horrid than the wild, uncultivated state of nature.

It can only be happy when the public principles and opinions are properly directed, and their manners regulated. This is an influence beyond the reach of laws and punishments, and can be claimed only by religion and education.

It should therefore be among the first objects of those who wish well to the national prosperity to encourage and support the principles of religion and morality, and early to place the youth under the forming hand of society, that by instruction they may be molded to the love of virtue and good order.[402]

JEDEDIAH MORSE

Jedediah Morse (August 23, 1761-June 9, 1826) was a pioneer American educator and geographer. Called the "Father of American Geography," his son was Samuel F.B. Morse, the inventor of the telegraph and the Morse Code. Jedediah Morse taught in the New Haven schools for several years, compiled his notes and published them in a successful work entitled, Geography Made Easy, 1784. He set a standard for American Geography, authoring numerous books, including: The American Geography, 1789; Elements of Geography, 1795; The American Gazetteer, 1797; A New Gazetteer of the Eastern Continent, 1802; A Compendious History of New England, 1804; and Annals of the American Revolution. He also founded the New England Tract Society, 1814; The American Bible Society, 1816; and was a member of the American Board of Commissioners for Foreign Missions, 1811-19.

In an "Election Sermon" given at Charleston, Massachusetts, April 25, 1799, Jedediah Morse stated:

To the kindly influence of Christianity we owe that degree of civil freedom, and political and social happiness which mankind now enjoys. In proportion as the genuine effects of Christianity are diminished in any nation, either through unbelief, or the corruption of its doctrines, or the neglect of its institutions; in the same proportion will the people of that nation recede from the blessings of genuine freedom, and approximate the miseries of complete despotism.

I hold this to be a truth confirmed by experience. If so, it follows, that all efforts to destroy the foundations of our holy religion, ultimately tend to the subversion also of our political freedom and happiness.

Whenever the pillars of Christianity shall be overthrown, our present republican forms of government, and all the blessings which flow from them, must fall with them.[403]

JAMES MADISON

In Federalist Paper #39, James Madison stated:

That honourable determination which animates every votary of freedom, to rest all our political experiments on the capacity of mankind for self-government.[404]

A similar statement that has sometimes been attributed to James Madison, but nevertheless reflects the views of founders, is:

We have staked the whole future of American civilization, not upon the power of government, far from it. We have staked the future of all of our political institutions upon the capacity of mankind for self-government; upon the capacity of each and all of us to govern ourselves, to control ourselves, to sustain ourselves according to *the Ten Commandments of God*.[405]

NOAH WEBSTER

In 1832, in his History of the United States, Noah Webster wrote:

The moral principles and precepts contained in the Scriptures ought to form the basis of all of our civil constitutions and laws....

All the miseries and evils which men suffer from vice, crime, ambition, injustice, oppression, slavery and war, proceed from their despising or neglecting the precepts contained in the Bible.[406]

In his 1834 work entitled, Value of the Bible and Excellence of the Christian Religion, Noah Webster wrote:

The Bible must be considered as the great source of all the truths by which men are to be guided in government, as well as in all social transactions....The Bible [is] the instrument of all reformation in morals and religion.[407]

Moral evils constitute or produce most of the miseries of mankind and these may be prevented or avoided. Be it remembered then that disobedience to God's law, or sin is the procuring cause of almost all the sufferings of mankind.

God has so formed the moral system of this world, that a conformity to His will by men produces peace, prosperity and happiness; and disobedience to His will or laws inevitably produces misery. If men are wretched, it is because they reject the government of God, and seek temporary good in that which certainly produces evil.[408]

In A Manual of Useful Studies, published in New Haven, 1839, Noah Webster stated:

Without religious and moral principles deeply impressed on the mind, and controlling the whole conduct, science and literature will not make men what the laws of God require them to be; and without both kinds of knowledge, citizens can not enjoy the blessings which they seek, and which a strict conformity to rules of duty will enable them to obtain.[409]

Noah Webster stated"

God's Word, contained in the Bible, has furnished all necessary rules to direct our conduct.[410]

SAMUEL ADAMS

On November 20, 1772, in the section of The Rights of the Colonists entitled, "The Rights of the Colonist as Men," Samuel Adams declared:

"Just and true liberty, equal and impartial liberty," in matters spiritual and temporal, is a thing that all men are clearly entitled to by *the eternal and immutable laws of God* and nature, as well as by the law of nations and all well-grounded municipal laws, which must have their foundation in the former.[411]

JOHN QUINCY ADAMS

In September of 1811, John Quincy Adams wrote a letter to his son from St. Petersburg, Russia, while serving for the second time in the U.S. Ministry to that country:

It is essential, my son, in order that you may go through life with comfort to yourself, and usefulness to your fellow-creatures, that you should form and adopt certain rules or principles, for the government of your own conduct and temper....It is in the Bible, you must learn them.[412]

John Quincy Adams stated:

From the day of the Declaration...they (the American people) were bound by the laws of God, which they all, and by the laws of The Gospel, which they nearly all, acknowledge as the rules of their conduct.[413]

JAMES MCHENRY

James McHenry (November 16, 1753-May 3, 1816) was a physician, soldier and politician. He was one of the signers of the Constitution of the United States, a member of the Continental Congress, a state legislator, and the U.S. Secretary of War, who supervised the establishment of the U.S. Military Academy at West Point. He studied medicine under the renowned Dr. Benjamin Rush, himself a signer of the Declaration of Independence. James McHenry served with distinction under General Washington on the medical staff during the Revolutionary War. Fort McHenry, where, in 1812, the battle with Britain occasioned the writing of our national anthem, was named after him.

In 1813, he became the president of the first Bible society in Baltimore, Maryland. He conveys the urgency of distributing Bibles to the public in an article to solicit funds for the society:

Neither, in considering this subject, let it be overlooked, that public utility pleads most forcibly for the general distribution of the Holy Scriptures.

The doctrine they preach, the obligations they impose, the punishment they threaten, the rewards they promise, the stamp and image of divinity they bear, which produces a conviction of their truths, can alone secure to society, order and peace, and to our courts of justice and constitutions of government, purity, stability and usefulness.

In vain, without the Bible, we increase penal laws and draw intrenchments around our institutions. Bibles are strong intrenchments. Where they abound, men cannot pursue wicked courses, and at the same time enjoy quiet conscience.

Consider also, the rich do not possess aught more precious than their Bible, and that the poor cannot be presented by the rich with anything of greater value. Withhold it not from the poor. It is a book of councils and directions, fitted to every situation in which man can be placed.

It is an oracle which reveals to mortals the secrets of heavens and the hidden will of the Almighty....

It is an estate, whose title is guaranteed by Christ, whose delicious fruits ripen every season, survive the worm, and keep through eternity. It is for the purpose of distributing this divine book more effectually and extensively among the multitudes, whose circumstances render such a donation necessary, that your cooperation is most earnestly requested.[414]

ALEXIS DE TOCQUEVILLE

Charles Alexis Henri Maurice Clèrel de Tocqueville (July 29, 1805-April 16, 1859) arrived in New York, May 11, 1831, with Gustave de Beaumont, and began a nine month tour of the country for the purpose of observing the American prison system, the people and American institutions. His two-part work, entitled Democracy in America, Was published in 1835 and 1840. It has been described as "the most comprehensive and penetrating analysis of the relationship between character and society in America that has ever been written."[415] In it, Alexis de Tocqueville related:

In France I had almost always seen the spirit of religion and the spirit of freedom marching in opposite directions. But in America I found they were intimately united and that they reigned in common over the same country.[416]

Religion in America...must be regarded as the foremost of the political institutions of that country; for if it does not impart a taste for freedom, it facilitates the use of it. Indeed, it is in this same point of view that the inhabitants of the United States themselves look upon religious belief.... They hold it to be indispensable to the maintenance of republican institutions. This opinion is not peculiar to a class of citizens or a party, but it belongs to the whole nation and to every rank of society.[417]

Each sect adores the Deity in its own peculiar manner, but all sects *preach the same moral law in the name of God*....Moreover, all the sects of the United States are comprised within the great unity of Christianity, and Christian morality is everywhere the same.[418]

In the United States the sovereign authority is religious....There is no country in the whole world where the Christian religion retains a greater influence over the souls of men than in America, and there can be no greater proof of its utility and of its conformity to human nature than that its influence is powerfully felt over the most enlightened and free nation of the earth.[419]

America is still the place where the Christian religion has kept the greatest real power over men's souls; and nothing better demonstrates how useful and natural it is to man, since the country where it now has the widest sway is both the most enlightened and the freest.[420]

The Americans show by their practice that they feel the high necessity of imparting morality to democratic communities by means of religion. What they think of themselves in this respect is a truth of which every democratic nation ought to be thoroughly persuaded.[421]

In the United States the influence of religion is not confined to the manners, but it extends to the intelligence of the people....Christianity, therefore reigns without obstacle, by universal consent; the consequence is, as I have before observed, that every principle of the moral world is fixed and determinate.[422]

The Americans combine the notions of Christianity and of liberty so intimately in their minds, that it is impossible to make them conceive the one without the other.[423]

I think that the state of religion in America is one of the things that most powerfully helps us to maintain our republican institutions. The religious spirit exercises a direct power over political passions, and also an indirect power by sustaining morals.[424]

LYMAN BEECHER

Lyman Beecher (October 12, 1775-January 10, 1863) was a renowned Presbyterian clergyman in New England. He preached in Boston and Cincinnati, where he later became President of Lane Theological Seminary. He was the father of both Henry Ward Beecher, one of the most eloquent preachers of his time, and Harriet Beecher Stowe, author of the book Uncle Tom's Cabin, which greatly precipitated the abolition of slavery.

In 1831, Lyman Beecher wrote in the newspaper, The Spirit of the Pilgrims:

The Government of God is the only government which will hold society, against depravity within and temptation without; and this it must do by the force of its own law written upon the heart.

This is that unity of the Spirit and that bond of peace which can alone perpetuate national purity and tranquility - that law of universal and impartial love by which alone nations can be kept back from ruin.

There is no safety for republics but in self-government, under the influence of a holy heart, swayed by the government of God.[425]

DANIEL WEBSTER

In a speech, July 4, 1851, Daniel Webster stated:

> Let the religious element in man's nature be neglected, let him be influenced by no higher motives than low self-interest, and subjected to no stronger restraint than the limits of civil authority, and he becomes the creature of selfish passion or blind fanaticism.
>
> On the other hand, the cultivation of the religious sentiment represses licentiousness...inspires respect for law and order, and gives strength to the whole social fabric, at the same time that it conducts the human soul upward to the Author of its being.[426]

Daniel Webster stated:

> I have read the Bible through many times, and now make it a practice to read it through once every year. - It is a book of all others for lawyers, as well as divines; and I pity the man who cannot find in it a rich supply of thought and of rules for conduct. It fits man for life - it prepares him for death.[427]

> The Bible is our only safe guide. So long as we take it as our instructor for conduct and character, we will go on prospering in the future as in the past. But the moment we relegate it from our lives a catastrophe will come to us such as we have never known.[428]

FRANCIS WAYLAND

Francis Wayland (March 11, 1796-September 30, 1865) was the president of Brown University, 1827-55, and the first president of the American Institute of Instruction, 1830. He was instrumental in devising the school system for Providence, Rhode Island. A graduate of Union College and Harvard University, Francis Wayland wrote: Elements of Moral Science, 1835; Elements of Political Economy, 1837; Thoughts on the Present Collegiate System in the United States, 1842; and A Memoir of the Life of the Rev. Adoniram Judson, D.D., 1842. Francis Wayland stated:

The truths of the Bible have the power of awakening an intense moral feeling in every human being; they make bad men good, and send a pulse of healthful feeling through all the domestic, civil, and social relations;

they teach men to love right, and hate wrong, and seek each other's welfare as children of a common parent;

they control the baleful passions of the heart, and thus make men proficient in self government;

and finally they teach man to aspire after conformity to a Being of infinite holiness, and fill him with hopes more purifying, exalted, and suited to his nature than any other book the world has ever known -

these are facts as incontrovertible as the laws of philosophy, or the demonstrations of mathematics.[429]

WILLIAM CULLEN BRYANT

William Cullen Bryant (November 3, 1794-June 12, 1878) was an American poet and editor. He known as the "Father of American Poets," and wrote such titles as: *Thanatopsis*; *To a Waterfowl*; *The Death of the Flowers*; and *To the Fringed Gentian*. He was the editor in chief of the New York Evening Post for 50 years, lending its support in the formation of the Republican Party and the fight against slavery. William Cullen Bryant wrote:

The very men who, in the pride of their investigations into the secrets of the internal world, turn a look of scorn upon the Christian system of belief, are not aware how much of the peace and order of society, how much the happiness of households, and the purest of those who are the dearest to them, are owing to the influence of that religion extending beyond their sphere.[430]

THEODORE PARKER

Theodore Parker (August 24, 1810-May 10, 1860) was an American abolitionist, clergyman, and graduate of Harvard. Strongly opposed slavery, Parker stated:

The Bible goes equally to the cottage of the peasant, and the palace of the king. It is woven into literature, and colors the talk of the street. The bark of the merchant cannot sail without it; and no ship of war goes to the conflict but it is there. It enters men's closets; directs their conduct, and mingles in all the grief and cheerfulness of life.[431]

ROBERT WINTHROP

Robert Charles Winthrop (May 12, 1809-November 16, 1894), was a U.S. Representative, author and orator. He served as the Speaker of the House of Representatives, 1847-49. He was a descendant of Governor John Winthrop. On May 28, 1849, Robert Charles Winthrop spoke at the Annual Meeting of the Massachusetts Bible Society in Boston, stating:

> The voice of experience and the voice of our own reason speak but one language....Both united in teaching us, that men may as well build their houses upon the sand and expect to see them stand, when the rains fall, and the winds blow, and the floods come, as to found free institutions upon any other basis than that of morality and virtue, of which the Word of God is the only authoritative rule, and the only adequate sanction.
>
> All societies of men must be governed in some way or other. The less they have of stringent State Government, the more they must have of individual self-government. The less they rely on public law or physical force, the more they must rely on private moral restraint.
>
> Men, in a word, must necessarily be controlled either by a power within them, or a power without them; either by the word of God, or by the strong arm of man; either by the Bible or by the bayonet. It may do for other countries, and other governments to talk about the State supporting religion. Here, under our own free institutions, it is Religion which must support the State.[432]

WESLEY MERRITT

Wesley Merritt (June 16, 1836-1910) was a Major General in the Union Army during the Civil War. He was the superintendent of the U.S. Military Academy at West Point, 1882-87, and Commander of the first Philippine expedition to occupy Manila in August of 1898. He stated:

> The principles of life as taught in the Bible, the inspired Word, and exemplified in the matchless Life of Him 'who spake as never man spake,' are the rules of moral action which have resulted in civilizing the world.

The testimony of great men, like Gladstone and his fellow statesmen; like Havelock and his fellow soldiers, who have made the teachings of the Scriptures their rule of conduct in life, are wonderful helps to men of lesser note and smaller intellectual and moral powers.

One example, even of the smallest of these, more than offsets the efforts of an hundred unbelievers in active opposition. They are the worthy followers of the religion of the Bible, and in their daily lives interpret the inimitable example and Divine precepts of the Son of God, our Saviour.[433]

On Tuesday, December 5, 1905, in his Fifth Annual Message to Congress, President Theodore Roosevelt stated:

The Golden Rule should be, and as the world grows in morality it will be, the guiding rule of conduct among nations as among individuals.[434]

WOODROW WILSON

On October 24, 1914, in an address entitled "The Power of Christian Young Men," delivered at the 70th Anniversary of the Young Men's Christian Association in Pittsburgh, Pennsylvania, President Woodrow Wilson stated:

The only way your powers can become great is by exerting them outside the circle of your own narrow, special, selfish interests. And that is the reason of Christianity. Christ came into the world to save others, not to save himself; and no man is a true Christian who does not think constantly of how he can lift his brother, how he can assist his friend, how he can enlighten mankind, how he can make virtue the rule of conduct in the circle in which he lives.[435]

JOHN FOSTER DULLES

John Foster Dulles (February 25, 1888-May 24, 1959) was the U.S. Secretary of State, 1953-59, during the Eisenhower administration, where he helped negotiate the Peace Treaty with Japan after World War II, 1950-51. A graduate of Princeton University and George Washington University, he served as an international attorney with the law firm of Sullivan and Cromwell in New York, 1911-49. He was instrumental in the creation of the United

Nations, to which he was the U.S. ambassador, 1945-49, and was an interim U.S. Senator, 1949.

On April 11, 1955, Secretary of State John Foster Dulles delivered a speech before the Fifth Annual All-Jesuit Alumni Dinner, in which he stated:

> Peace is a goal which men above always sought. It is a goal which we particularly think of at this Easter Season when we commemorate the resurrection of the Prince of Peace....
>
> One cannot but shrink from buying peace at the price of extending over human beings the rule of those who believe that men are in fact nothing more than animated bits of matter and that, to insure harmony and conformity, they should be deprived of the capacity for moral and intellectual judgment.
>
> Man, we read in the Holy Scriptures, was made a little lower than the angels. Should man now be made little, if any, higher than domesticated animals which serve the purpose of their human masters?
>
> So men face the great dilemma of when and whether to use force to resist aggression which imposes conditions which violate the moral law and the concept that man has his origins and his destiny in God....
>
> The government of the United States has, I like to believe, a rather unique tradition in this respect. Our nation was founded as an experiment in human liberty.
>
> Our institutions reflect the belief of our founders that all men were endowed by their Creator with inalienable rights and had duties prescribed by moral law. They believed that human institutions ought primarily to help men develop their God-given possibilities and that our nation, by its conduct and example, could help men everywhere to find the way to a better and more abundant life. Our nation realized that vision. There developed here an area of spiritual and economic vigor the like of which the world had never seen.[436]

JOHN COURNEY MURRAY

John Courtney Murray, S.J., (1904-1967) was a renown theologian and philosopher. Engraved on an outside portico wall at St. Louis University Highschool, St. Louis, Missouri, is his statement:

It is not an American belief that free government is inevitable, only that it is possible, and that its possibility can be realized only when the people are inwardly governed by the universal moral law.

J. EDGAR HOOVER

J. (John) Edgar Hoover (January 1, 1895-May 2, 1972) was the director of the Federal Bureau of Investigation, 1924-1972. He graduated from George Washington University, 1916; earned a Masters Degree in Law, 1917; served as assistant to Attorney General A. Mitchell Palmer. He became famous for his dramatic campaigns to stop organized crime. In writing the introduction to Edward L.R. Elson's book, *America's Spiritual Recovery*, 1954, J. Edgar Hoover expressed:

We can see all too clearly the devastating effects of the resultant Secularism on our Christian way of life. The period when it was smart to "debunk" our traditions undermined inspiring customs and high standards of conduct.

A rising emphasis on materialism caused a decline of "God-centered" deeds and thoughts. The American home became a place of transient, furtive living and ceased to be a school of moral and spiritual education....

When spiritual guidance is at a low ebb, moral principles are accordingly is a state of deterioration. Secularism advances in periods when men forget God....

But there are hopeful signs for a better day. There was hope in the words of General Eisenhower when he bowed his head on Inaugural Day and asked in part, "Give us, we pray, the power to discern right from wrong and allow all our words and actions to be governed thereby and by the laws of this land."

This humble prayer touched Americans from coast to coast. Here was hope manifested in a manner which inspired the hearts of countless millions. A President with such a deep religious sense and with such a sincere spiritual motivation, seeking to be guided by the right, sets an example for all the people.[437]

vi.
FUTURE REWARDS AND PUNISHMENTS
William J. Federer

An integral yet easily overlooked aspect of how the Ten Commandments indirectly influenced our democratic form of government is a underlying concept that these laws should be obeyed because, as our founders referred to it, there would be "a future state of rewards and punishments." This was key to the experiment of "self-government," as to believe in such a future state resulted in one acting with internal restraint, requiring less external restraint from the government.

U.S. CONGRESS

United States Congress, March 27, 1854, received the report of Mr. Meacham of the House Committee on the Judiciary:

> It must be considered as the foundation on which the whole structure rests. Laws will not have permanence or power without the sanction of religious sentiment, - without a firm belief that there is a Power above us that will **reward our virtues and punish our vices**. In this age there can be no substitute for Christianity: that, in its general principles, is the great conservative element on which we must rely for the purity and permanence of free institutions. That was the religion of the founders of the republic, and they expected it to remain the religion of their descendants. There is a great and very prevalent error on this subject in the opinion that those who organized this Government did not legislate on religion.[438]

STATE OF PENNSYLVANIA

The Pennsylvania Supreme Court, in the case of *The Commonwealth v. Wolf*, 3 Serg. & R. 48, 50 (1817), stated:

> Laws cannot be administered in any civilized government unless the people are taught to revere the sanctity of an oath, and look to **a future state of rewards and punishments** for the deeds of this life.[439]

STATE OF MARYLAND

The Constitution of the State of Maryland, adopted 1851, declared that no other test or qualification for admission to any office of trust or profit shall be required than the official oath and:

A declaration of belief in the Christian religion; and if the party shall profess to be a Jew the declaration shall be of his belief in **a future state of rewards and punishments.**[440]

The Constitution of the State of Maryland, adopted 1864, required all State officers to make:

A declaration of belief in the Christian religion, or of the existence of God, and in **a future state of rewards and punishments.**[441]

STATE OF SOUTH CAROLINA

The Constitution of the State of South Carolina, adopted 1778, stated:

Article XII. ...The qualifications of electors shall be that every...person, who acknowledges the being of a God, and believes **in the future state of rewards and punishments**...[is eligible to vote].[442]

Article XXXVIII. That all persons and religious societies, who acknowledge that there is one God, **and a future state of rewards and punishments,** and that God is publicly to be worshipped, shall be freely tolerated.[443]

The Constitution of the State of South Carolina, adopted 1790, stated:

Article XXXVIII. That all persons and religious societies, who acknowledge that there is one God, **and a future state of rewards and punishments,** and that God is publicly to be worshipped, shall be freely tolerated.[444]

STATE OF TENNESSEE

The Constitution of the State of Tennessee, adopted 1796, stated:

Article VIII, Section II. No person who denies the being of God, or **a future state of rewards and punishments,** shall hold any office in the civil department of this State.

Article XI, Section IV. That no religious test shall ever be required as a qualification to any office or public trust under this State.[445]

The Constitution of the State of Tennessee, adopted 1870, stated:

Article IX, Section 2. No person who denies the being of God, or **a future state of rewards and punishments**, shall hold any office in the civil department of this State.[446]

STATE OF MISSISSIPPI

The Constitution of the State of Mississippi, adopted 1817, stated:

No person who denies the being of God **or a future state of rewards and punishments** shall hold any office in the civil department of the State[447]

GUSTAVE DE BEAUMONT

The French historian Gustave de Beaumont traveled in America with Alexis de Tocqueville, May 1831-February 1832. He was commissioned by the French Government to study the American prisons, democracy, and religion. He published his report in Paris under the title, *Marie ou l'Esclavage aux E'tas-Unis* (1835). He wrote:

Sometimes the American constitutions offer religious bodies some indirect assistance: thus, Maryland law declares that, to be admitted to public office, it is necessary to be a Christian. The Pennsylvania constitution requires that one believe in the existence of God and in **a future life of punishment or rewards.**[448]

BENJAMIN FRANKLIN

Benjamin Franklin listed topics and doctrines, which he considered of vital importance, to be shared and preached:

That there is one God, Father of the Universe.

That He [is] infinitely good, powerful and wise.

That He is omnipresent.

That He ought to be worshipped, by adoration, prayer and thanksgiving both in publick and private.

That He loves such of His creatures as love and do good to others: and will **reward them either in this world or hereafter.**

That men's minds do not die with their bodies, but are made more happy or miserable after this life according to their actions.[449]

SIR WILLIAM BLACKSTONE

Sir William Blackstone (July 10, 1723-February 14, 1780), was an English jurist who deeply influenced the growth of Common Law, jurisprudence and the basis of law in America. In 1758, he was honored by being elected Oxford's first Vinerian lecturer, and in 1770, he became one of the Judges of the Common Pleas. From 1765 to 1770, Sir William Blackstone published his highly influential work entitled, *Commentaries on the Laws of England*. These were so universally accepted in America that by 1775 they had sold more copies in America than in England. This work set the foundation for America's great legal minds including Chief Justice John Marshall. When scholars examined nearly 15,000 items written by the Founding Fathers from 1760 to 1805 (including books, newspapers articles, monographs, pamphlets, etc.), it was found that Sir William Blackstone was quoted more than any other author except one.

Sir William Blackstone stated:

The belief of a future state of rewards and punishments, the entertaining just ideas of the main attributes of the Supreme Being, and a firm persuasion that He superintends and will finally compensate every action in human life (all which are revealed in the doctrines of our Savior, Christ), these are the grand foundations of all judicial oaths, which call God to witness the truth of those facts which perhaps may be only known to Him and the party attesting; all moral evidences, therefore, all confidence in human veracity, must be weakened by apostasy, and overthrown by total infidelity. Wherefore, all affronts to Christianity, or endeavors to depreciate its efficacy, in those who have once professed it, are highly deserving of censure.[450]

JAMES MCHENRY

In 1813, James McHenry became the president of the first Bible society in Baltimore, Maryland. He conveys the urgency of distributing Bibles to the public in an article to solicit funds for the society:

> Neither, in considering this subject, let it be overlooked, that public utility pleads most forcibly for the general distribution of the Holy Scriptures. The doctrine they preach, the obligations they impose, **the punishment they threaten, the rewards they promise,** the stamp and image of divinity they bear, which produces a conviction of their truths, can alone secure to society, order and peace, and to our courts of justice and constitutions of government, purity, stability and usefulness. In vain, without the Bible, we increase penal laws and draw intrenchments around our institutions. Bibles are strong intrenchments. Where they abound, men cannot pursue wicked courses, and at the same time enjoy quiet conscience.[451]

SAMUEL ADAMS

On April 30, 1776, Samuel Adams wrote to John Scollay of Boston:

> Revelation assures us that "Righteousness exalteth a nation." Communities are dealt with in this world by the wise and just Ruler of the Universe. **He rewards or punishes them according to their general character.**
> The diminution of public virtue is usually attended with that of public happiness, and the public liberty will not long survive the total extinction of morals. 'The Roman Empire,' says the historian, 'must have sunk, though the Goths had not invaded it. Why? Because the Roman virtue was sunk.'
> Could I be assured that America would remain virtuous, I would venture to defy the utmost efforts of enemies to subjugate her.
> You will allow me to remind you, that the morals of that city which has borne so great a share in the American

contest, depend much upon the vigilance of the respectable body of magistrates, of which you are a member.[452]

JOHN ADAMS

On Wednesday, March 6, 1799, President John Adams issued a Proclamation of a National a Day of Humiliation, Fasting, and Prayer:

> As no truth is more clearly taught in the Volume of Inspiration, nor any more fully demonstrated by the experience of all ages, than that a deep sense and a due acknowledgment of the growing providence of a Supreme Being and of the accountableness of men to Him as the searcher of hearts and **righteous distributor of rewards and punishments** are conducive equally to the happiness and rectitude of individuals and to the well-being of communities...[453]

John Adams wrote to Judge F.A. Van der Kemp, January 13, 1815:

> My religion is founded on the love of God and my neighbor; in the hope of pardon for my offenses; upon contrition; upon the duty as well as the necessity of supporting with patience the inevitable evils of life; in the duty of doing no wrong, but all the good I can, to the creation, of which I am but an infinitesimal part. **I believe, too, in a future state of rewards and punishments.**...[454]

John Adams wrote to Judge F.A. Van de Kemp, December 27, 1816;

> As I understand the Christian religion, it was, and is, a revelation.... Let it once be revealed or demonstrated that there is no **future state,** and my advice to every man, woman, and child, would be, as our existence would be in our own power, to take opium. For, I am certain there is nothing in this world worth living for but hope, and every hope will fail us, if the last hope, that of **a future state**, is extinguished.[455]

John Adams wrote:

That you and I shall meet in a better world I have no doubt than we now exist on the same globe; if my reason did not convince me of this, Cicero's Dream of Scipio, and his Essay on Friendship and Old Age would have been sufficient for that purpose. But Jesus taught us that a **future state** is a social state, when He promised to prepare places in His Father's house of many mansions, for His disciples.[456]

THOMAS JEFFERSON

Thomas Jefferson wrote:

1. The doctrines of Jesus are simple and tend to the happiness of man.

2. There is only one God, and He is all perfect.

3. **There is a future state of rewards and punishment.**

4. To love God with all the heart and thy neighbor as thyself is the sum of all. These are the great points on which to reform the religion of the Jews.[457]

BENJAMIN RUSH

Benjamin Rush (January 4, 1745-April 19, 1813) was a physician, educator and philanthropist. He was a member of the Continental Congress, 1776-77, and signed the Declaration of Independence. In 1774, he helped found and was president of the Pennsylvania Society for Promoting the Abolition of Slavery. He helped found and was vice-president of the Philadelphia Bible Society; was a principal promoter of the American Sunday School Union; and a member of the Abolition Society. He also served as the Surgeon General of the Continental Army, 1777-78; helped to write the Pennsylvania Constitution, 1789-90; and was Treasurer of the U.S. Mint, 1797-1813. In 1783, Dr. Benjamin Rush helped found Dickinson College and joined the staff of the Pennsylvania Hospital. In 1786, he established the first free medical clinic.

In 1786, Dr. Benjamin Rush wrote *Thoughts Upon the Mode of Education Proper in a Republic*, in which he stated:

I beg leave to remark that the only foundation for a useful education in a republic is to be laid on the foundation of religion. Without this there can be no virtue, and without virtue there can be no liberty, and liberty is the object and life of all republican governments.

Such is my veneration for every religion that reveals the attributes of the Deity, **or a future state of rewards and punishments,** that I had rather see the opinions of Confucius or Mohamed inculcated upon our youth than to see them grow up wholly devoid of a system of religious principles. But the religion I mean to recommend in this place is that of the New Testament.

It is not my purpose to hint at the arguements which establish the truth of the Christian revelation. My only business is to declare that all its doctrines and precepts are calculated to promote the happiness of society and the safety and well-being of civil government.

A Christian cannot fail of being a republican... for every precept of the Gospel inculcates those degrees of humility, self-denial, and brotherly kindness which are directly opposed to the pride of monarchy....

A Christian cannot fail of being useful to the republic, for his religion teaches him that no man "liveth to himself." And lastly a Christian cannot fail of being wholly inoffensive, for his religion teaches him in all things to do to others what he would wish, in like circumstances, they should do to him.[458]

JAMES KENT

James Kent (July 31, 1763-December 12, 1847) was the Chief Justice of the Supreme Court of New York, 1804. He was the Head of the New York Court of Chancery, 1814-23; professor of law at Columbia College, 1793; member of the New York Legislature; admitted to the bar, 1785; graduated from Yale, 1781, and after his death he was elected to the American Hall of Fame, 1900. Considered the premier jurist in the development of the legal practice in the United States, James Kent is known for having compiled the work, Commentaries on American Law, 1826-30.

In an address before the American Bible Society, Chief Justice Kent expressed:

The Bible is equally adapted to the wants and infirmities of every human being.... It brings life and immortality to light, which until the publication of the Gospel, were hidden from the scrutiny of the ages. The gracious Revelation of **a future state** is calculated to solve the mysteries of Providence in the dispensations of this life, to reconcile us to the inequalities of our present condition, and to inspire unconquerable fortitude and the most animating consolations when all other consolations fail....[459]

CHARLES COTESWORTH PINCKNEY

Charles Cotesworth Pinckney (February 25, 1746-August 16, 1825) was a signer of the United States Constitution. He was a delegate to the Constitutional Convention and helped to write the Constitution of the State of South Carolina. A Presidential and Vice-Presidential candidate, he was a successful lawyer, planter, statesman, soldier, aide-de-camp to General Washington and Brigadier General.

Pinckney turned down many offers from President Washington for positions within government, including several cabinet appointments and a place on the U.S. Supreme Court, though he finally accepted the position of U.S. Minister to France. He helped found the Charleston Bible Society and served as its first president. He studied for his military career at the Royal Military Academy of France, after having studied law at the Westminster School at Oxford, under Sir William Blackstone.

Charles Cotesworth Pinckney was very involved in forming the Constitution of the State of South Carolina, which contained the article:

SOUTH CAROLINA, 1778. Article XXXVIII. That all persons and religious societies who acknowledge that there is one God, and **a future state of rewards and punishments**, and that God is publicly to be worshipped, shall be freely tolerated....That all denominations of Christian[s]... in this State, demeaning themselves peaceably and faithfully, shall enjoy equal religious and civil privileges.[460]

NOAH WEBSTER

In Noah Webster's 1828 edition of the American Dictionary of the English Language, the word *Religion* has the definition:

Religion .... In its most comprehensive sense, includes a belief in the being and perfection of God, in the revelation of his will to man, and in man's obligation to obey his commands, **in a state of rewards and**

punishment, and in man's accountableness to God; and also true godliness or piety of life, with the practice of all moral duties....The practice of moral duties without belief in a divine lawgiver, and without reference to his will or commands, is not religion.[461]

vii.
CONCLUSION

As was initially stated, the purpose of this study is not to propose public policy, but to simply demonstrate that the historical record is replete with evidence that the Ten Commandments have directly and indirectly influenced America's founders, leaders, system of government and legal code.

In his commentary, *The Ten Commandments in American Law and Government,* Matthew D. Staver writes:

> One would have to rewrite American history to conclude that the Ten Commandments played an insignificant role in the foundation of our system of law and government.

William Findley observed that the Ten Commandments were:

> incorporated in the judicial law.

William Findley, OBSERVATIONS ON "THE TWO SONS OF OIL" 36 (1812).

John Quincy Adams, the sixth president, stated:

> The law given on Sinai was a
> civil and municipal as well as a moral
> and religious code.

John Quincy Adams, LETTERS OF JOHN QUINCY ADAMS, TO HIS SON, ON THE BIBLE AND ITS TEACHINGS 61 (Auburn: James M Alden 1850). [462]

TEN COMMANDMENTS AND THEIR INFLUENCE
William J. Federer

The information presented herein is evidence beyond a reasonable doubt that the historical record demonstrates the Ten Commandments have directly and indirectly influenced America's founders, leaders, system of government and legal code.

The Ten Commandments, therefore, deserve to be included among the list of publicly acknowledged historical documents which have impacted the founding of America.

An honest and objective examination of this information gives an enlightened insight into the minds of the leaders who founded the freest and most prosperous nation the world has ever seen.

viii.
ENDNOTES

1On August 22, 2002, Federal District Court Judge Karl Forrester in the Eastern District of Kentucky held that a display of the Ten Commandments together with other historical documents in Rowan and Mercer Counties in Kentucky are constitutional. Rowan and Mercer Counties were sued by the ACLU of Kentucky. The ACLU requested the judge to issue an injunction requiring the Ten Commandments to be taken down while the cases were pending in court.

Judge Forrester denied the request for an Injunction and instead stated that the displays were constitutional. Rowan County is represented by Mathew D. Staver, President and General Counsel of Liberty Counsel, and Erik W. Stanley, Litigation Counsel for Liberty Counsel. Mercer County is represented jointly by Liberty Counsel and the American Center for Law and Justice.

Rowan, Mercer, Garrard & Grayson counties in Kentucky were sued simultaneously by the ACLU for displays containing the Ten Commandments in county courthouses. Displays include the Ten Commandments, the Mayflower Compact, the Declaration of Independence, the Magna Charta, the Star Spangled Banner, the National Motto, the Preamble to the Kentucky Constitution, the Bill of Rights to the United States Constitution, and a picture of Lady Justice.

Named the "Foundations of American Law and Government," the display is intended to show several documents that have played a significant role in the founding of our system of law and government. The County's display was previously ordered removed in May. Decision on Garrard County's display is pending before Judge Forrester. Four lawsuits followed a lawsuit filed by the ACLU in 2000 against McCreary, Pulaski and Harlan counties in Kentucky.

In those cases, Judge Jennifer Coffman ordered that the displays, which are identical to the Rowan and Mercer County displays, be taken down. McCreary, Pulaski and Harlan Counties are also represented by Liberty Counsel and have appealed the case to the Sixth Circuit. Argument on the McCreary case is expected before the Sixth Circuit Court of Appeals in December. Judge Forrester's decision today will be followed by a written opinion. Judge Forrester commented in Court that there are two issues in deciding the constitutionality of Ten Commandments displays.

The first issue is whether the display was erected for an entirely religious purpose. Forrester stated that the displays in Rowan and Mercer counties were educational in nature and that there was no evidence that they were erected for an entirely religious purpose.

The second issue is whether a reasonable observer would view the display as an endorsement of religion. The ACLU had argued that the Ten Commandments are an entirely religious document that played no role in the foundation of our system of law and government. Judge Forrester rejected that argument and said that the Ten Commandments are historical and did have a role to play in our system of law and government, therefore, they may be constitutionally displayed.

Judge Forrester also commented that he specifically disagreed with the decisions ordering the Ten Commandments to be taken down in Grayson and McCreary Counties. Mat Staver hailed today's decision as a great victory. Staver stated, "Today's decision begins to turn the tide against the ACLU who has been on a search and destroy mission to remove all vestiges of our religious history from public view."

"The ACLU's attempts to remove the Ten Commandments from public display are nothing more than historical revisionism at its worst." Staver added, "Whether the ACLU likes it or not, history is crystal clear that each one of the Ten Commandments has played an important role in the founding of our system of law and government. Each one of the Ten Commandments was adopted as law by 12 of the 13 original American colonies." Staver also added, "As long as a governmental entity displays the Ten Commandments together with other historical documents and does so for an educational or historical purpose, such displays will be constitutional."

Staver concluded, "We are pleased that Judge Forrester found these displays constitutional and are confident that the Sixth Circuit will do likewise when it takes this issue up in December in the McCreary county case."

II FEDERAL COURT RULES THAT TEN COMMANDMENTS ARE CONSTITUTIONAL 10/9/2002 WWW.LC.ORG

Austin, Texas - Federal Judge Harry Lee Hudspeth has ruled that a Ten Commandments monument on the Texas State Capitol grounds in Austin, Texas, is constitutional. Liberty Counsel, a civil liberties education and legal defense organization with an extensive amount of experience in the constitutionality of the public display of the Ten Commandments, filed an Amicus Brief in support of the state of Texas.

The 42 year-old monument was originally donated to the State by the Fraternal Order of Eagles in 1961. The granite monolith is more than six feet high and three feet wide. It is one of 17 monuments and memorials on the grounds of the State Capitol. The donation of the Ten Commandments was part of a youth guidance project to give the youth of the nation a code of conduct by which to govern their actions. The monument sat in a small park-like subsection between the Supreme Court building and the Capitol building.

Thomas Van Orden, a criminal defense lawyer who temporarily lost his license to practice law and is homeless, filed the suit to have the monument removed because he claimed the sight of the Ten Commandments disturbed him. The Court found that the State's desire "to promote youth morality and to help stop the alarming increase in delinquency" served a legitimate secular purpose. The Court then ruled that no reasonable observer would conclude that the State sought to advance or endorse religion. Unlike some of the other monuments, the Ten Commandments did not bear the State seal or the Lone Star symbol.

Mathew Staver, President and General Counsel of Liberty Counsel, stated, "The court was clear in noting that the display of the Ten Commandments monument could not be interpreted by a reasonable observer as a state endorsement of religion. Each of the Ten Commandments has played a significant role in the foundation of our system of law and government.

Staver added, "The Ten Commandments have both a secular and religious aspect. The Ten Commandments take on an even greater secular aspect when placed in the context of other historical or legal documents, such as in the context of the State Capitol." Staver concluded, "To ignore the influence of the Ten Commandments in the founding and shaping of American law and government would require significant historical revisionism."

[1] Matthew D. Staver, "The Ten Commandments in American Law and Government" (Orlando, FL: The Liberty Counsel, P.O. Box 540774, Orlando, FL 32854, 407-875-2100, 407-875-0770 Fax, http://www.lc.org, liberty@lc.org, 2002), pp. 1-2.
[2] Matthew D. Staver, "The Ten Commandments in American Law and Government" (Orlando, FL: The Liberty Counsel, P.O. Box 540774, Orlando, FL 32854, 407-875-2100, 407-875-0770 Fax, http://www.lc.org, liberty@lc.org, 2002), p. 1.
[3] Adams, John. November 4, 1816, in a letter to Thomas Jefferson. Paul Wilstach, ed., The Correspondence of John Adams and Thomas Jefferson, 1812-1826 (Indianapolis: The Bobbs-Merrill Publishers, 1925), p. 112. Norman Cousins, In God We Trust - The Religious Beliefs and Ideas of the American Founding Fathers (NY: Harper & Brothers, 1958), p. 280.
[4] Donald S. Lutz and Charles S. Hyneman, "The Relative Influence of European Writers on Late Eighteenth-Century American Political Thought," American Political Science Review 189 (1984): 189-197. (Courtesy of Dr. Wayne House of Dallas Theological Seminary.) John Eidsmoe, Christianity and the Constitution - The Faith of Our Founding Fathers (Grand Rapids, MI: Baker Book House, A Mott Media Book, 1987; 6th printing, 1993), pp. 51-53. Origins of American Constitutionalism, (1987). Stephen K. McDowell and Mark A. Beliles, America's Providential History (Charlottesville, VA: Providence Press, 1988), p. 156.
[5] Adams, John. February 22, 1756, in a diary entry. L.H. Butterfield, ed., Diary and Autobiography of John Adams (Cambridge, MA: Belknap Press of Harvard Press, 1961), Vol. III, p. 9. L.H. Butterfield, The Earliest Diary of John Adams (Cambridge, MA: The Belknap Press of Harvard University Press, 1966), Vol. 1, p. 9. Life and Works of John Adams, Vol. XI, pp. 6-7. Stephen Abbott Northrop, D.D., A Cloud of Witnesses (Portland, OR: American Heritage Ministries, 1987; Mantle Ministries, 228 Still Ridge, Bulverde, Texas, 78163), p. 2. D.P. Diffine, Ph.D., One Nation Under God - How Close a Separation? (Searcy, Arkansas: Harding University, Belden Center for Private Enterprise Education, 6th

Endnotes

edition, 1992), p. 6.
6 Adams, John. October 11, 1798, in a letter to the officers of the First Brigade of the Third Division of the Militia of Massachusetts. Charles Francis Adams (son of John Quincy Adams and grandson of John Adams), ed., The Works of John Adams - Second President of the United States: with a Life of the Author, Notes, and Illustration (Boston: Little, Brown, & Co., 1854), Vol. IX, pp. 228-229. Charles E. Rice, The Supreme Court and Public Prayer (New York: Fordham University Press, 1964), p. 47. Senator A. Willis Robertson, "Report on Prayers in Public Schools and Other Matters, Senate Committee on the Judiciary (87th Congress, 2nd Session), 1962, 32. Richard John Neuhaus, The Naked Public Square (Grand Rapids, MI: William B. Eerdman Publishing Company, 1984), p. 95. War on Religious Freedom (Virginia Beach, Virginia: Freedom Council, 1984), p. 1. A. James Reichley, Religion in American Public Life (Washington, D.C.: The Brookings Institute, 1985), p. 105. Pat Robertson, America's Dates With Destiny (Nashville, TN: 1986), pp. 93-95. Charles Colson, Kingdoms in Conflict (Grand Rapids, MI: Zondervan Publishing House, 1987), pp. 47, 120. Tim LaHaye, Faith of Our Founding Fathers (Brentwood, TN: Wolgemuth & Hyatt, Publishers, Inc., 1987), p. 194. John Eidsmoe, Christianity and the Constitution - The Faith of Our Founding Fathers (Grand Rapids, MI: Baker Book House, A Mott Media Book, 1987; 6th printing, 1993), pp. 273, 292, 381. Gary DeMar, "Is the Constitution Christian?" (Atlanta, GA: The Biblical Worldview, An American Vision Publication - American Vision, Inc., December 1989), p. 2. Peter Marshall and David Manuel, The Glory of America (Bloomington, MN: Garborg's Heart 'N Home, 1991), 8.11. Kerby Anderson, "Christian Roots of the Declaration" (Dallas, TX: Freedom Club Report, July 1993), p. 6. Rush H. Limbaugh III, See, I Told You So (New York, NY: reprinted by permission of Pocket Books, a division of Simon & Schuster Inc., 1993), pp. 73-76. Stephen McDowell and Mark Beliles, "The Providential Perspective" (Charlottesville, VA: The Providence Foundation, P.O. Box 6759, Charlottesville, Va. 22906, January 1994), Vol. 9, No. 1, p. 4.
7 Adams, John. June 21, 1776. Charles Francis Adams (son of John Quincy Adams and grandson of John Adams), ed., The Works of John Adams - Second President of the United States (Boston: Little, Brown, & Co., 1854), Vol. IX, p. 401. "Our Christian Heritage," Letter from Plymouth Rock (Marlborough, NH: The Plymouth Rock Foundation), p. 3. Russ Walton, One Nation Under God (NH: Plymouth Rock Foundation, 1993), p. 115.
8 Adams, John. April 19, 1817, in a letter to Thomas Jefferson. Norman Cousins, In God We Trust - The Religious Beliefs and Ideas of the American Founding Fathers (NY: Harper & Brothers, 1958), p. 282. Edmund Fuller and David E. Green, God in the White House - The Faiths of American Presidents (NY: Crown Publishers, Inc., 1968), p. 26. Richard K. Arnold, ed., Adams to Jefferson/Jefferson to Adams - A Dialogue from their Correspondence (San Francisco: Jerico Press, 1975), p. 25.
9 Adams, John. August 28, 1811, to Dr. Benjamin Rush. Charles Francis Adams (son of John Quincy Adams and grandson of John Adams), ed., The Works of John Adams - Second President of the United States (Boston: Little, Brown, & Co., 1854), Vol. IX, p. 636. Norman Cousins, In God We Trust - The Religious Beliefs and Ideas of the American Founding Fathers (NY: Harper & Brothers, 1958), p. 101.
10 Adams, John. In a letter to Mr. Warren. Warren-Adams Letters (Boston, MA: Massachusetts Historical Society, 1917), Vol. I, p. 222. Verna M. Hall, The Christian History of the American Revolution - Consider and Ponder (San Francisco: Foundation for American Christian Education, 1976), p. 615. Philip Greven, The Protestant Temperament - Patterns of Childrearing, Religious Experience, and Self in Early America (NY: Alfred A. Knopf, 1977), p. 346. Gary DeMar, America's Christian History: The Untold Story (Atlanta, GA: American Vision Publishers, Inc., 1993), p. 96. Stephen McDowell and Mark Beliles, "The Providential Perspective" (Charlottesville, VA: The Providence Foundation, P.O. Box 6759, Charlottesville, Va. 22906, January 1994), Vol. 9, No. 1, p. 5.
11 Adams, John. In a letter to Thomas Jefferson. Richard K. Arnold, ed., Adams to Jefferson/ Jefferson to Adams - A Dialogue from their Correspondence (San Francisco: Jerico Press,

1975), pp. 330-31.

[12] Adams, John. June 20, 1815, in a letter to Thomas Jefferson. Paul Wilstach, ed., The Correspondence of John Adams and Thomas Jefferson, 1812-1826 (Indianapolis: The Bobbs-Merrill Publishers, 1925), p. 112.

[13] Adams, John. March 6, 1799, in a Proclamation of a National Day of Humiliation, Fasting, and Prayer. James D. Richardson (U.S. Representative from Tennessee), ed., A Compilation of the Messages and Papers of the Presidents 1789-1897, 10 vols. (Washington, D.C.: U.S. Government Printing Office, published by Authority of Congress, 1897, 1899; Washington, D.C.: Bureau of National Literature and Art, 1789-1902, 11 vols., 1907, 1910), Vol. 1, pp. 284-286. Benjamin Franklin Morris, The Christian Life and Character of the Civil Institutions of the United States (Philadelphia: George W. Childs, 1864), pp. 547-548. Gary DeMar, The Biblical Worldview (Atlanta, GA: An American Vision Publication - American Vision, Inc., 1992), Vol. 8, No. 12, p. 9. Gary DeMar, America's Christian History: The Untold Story (Atlanta, GA: American Vision Publishers, Inc., 1993), p. 78. Stephen McDowell and Mark Beliles, "The Providential Perspective" (Charlottesville, VA: The Providence Foundation, P.O. Box 6759, Charlottesville, Va. 22906, January 1994), Vol. 9, No. 1, pp. 4, 6.

[14] Adams, John. February 16, 1809, in a letter to Judge F.A. Van der Kemp. Norman Cousins, ed., 'In God We Trust': The Religious Beliefs and Ideas of the American Founding Fathers (New York: Harper & Brothers, 1958), pp. 102-103. Russell Kirk, Roots of American Order (LaSalle, IL.: Open Court, 1974), p. 17. Charles Colson, Kingdoms in Conflict (Grand Rapids, MI: Zondervan Publishing House, 1987), p. 228. Gary DeMar, America's Christian History: The Untold Story (Atlanta, GA: American Vision Publishers, Inc., 1993), p. 96.

[15] New Guide to the English Tongue. 1740, Thomas Dilworth, London. H.R. Warfel, Noah Webster-Schoolmaster to America (New York: Octagon Press, 1966), pp. 11-13. Tim LaHaye, Faith of Our Founding Fathers (Brentwood, TN: Wolgemuth & Hyatt, Publishers, Inc., 1987), pp. 75-76. D.P. Diffine, Ph.D., One Nation Under God - How Close a Separation? (Searcy, Arkansas: Harding University, Belden Center for Private Enterprise Education, 6th edition, 1992), p. 5.

[16] Bradford, William. 1650, in his work entitled, The History of Plymouth Plantation 1608-1650 (Boston, Massachusetts: Massachusetts Historical Society, 1856; Boston, Massachusetts: Wright and Potter Printing Company, 1898, 1901, from the Original Manuscript, Library of Congress Rare Book Collection, Washington, D.C.; rendered in Modern English, Harold Paget, 1909; NY: Russell and Russell, 1968; NY: Random House, Inc., Modern Library College edition, 1981; San Antonio, TX: American Heritage Classics, Mantle Ministries, 228 Still Ridge, Bulverde, Texas, 1988).

[17] Hooker, Thomas. Rush H. Limbaugh III, See, I Told You So (New York, NY: reprinted by permission of Pocket Books, a division of Simon & Schuster Inc., 1993), pp. 72-73.

[18] Hooker, Thomas. 1638. Collections of the Connecticut Historical Society, 1:20. Benjamin Fletcher Wright, Jr., American Interpretations of Natural Law (New York: Russell & Russell, 1962), p. 23. John Eidsmoe, Christianity and the Constitution - The Faith of Our Founding Fathers (Grand Rapids, MI: Baker Book House, A Mott Media Book, 1987, 6th printing 1993), p. 35.

[19] Penn, William. The World Book Encyclopedia, 18 vols. (Chicago, IL: Field Enterprises, Inc., 1957; W.F. Quarrie and Company, 8 vols., 1917; World Book, Inc., 22 vols., 1989), Vol. 13, pp. 6181-6183, 6192-6195.

[20] Penn, William. From his writing No Cross, No Crown, written while imprisoned in the Tower of London for 8 months. Thomas Pyrn Cope, ed., Passages from the Life and Writings of William Penn (Philadelphia: Friends Bookstore, 1882).

[21] Sherman, Roger. circa 1789-91, in a letter to the Congregational minister of Newport, Rhode Island, Samuel Hopkins. Timothy Dwight, Statistical Account of the City of New Haven (New Haven, Connecticut: Connecticut Academy of Arts and Sciences, 1811). Roger Sherman Boardman, Roger Sherman - Signer and Statesman (NY: DaCapo Press, 1971), pp.

Endnotes

318-319. John Eidsmoe, Christianity and The Constitution - The Faith of Our Founding Fathers (Baker Book House, 1987), p. 322.

[22] Adams, Samuel. November 20, 1772, in a report for the Committees of Correspondence, entitled, The Rights of the Colonists; in the section: "The Rights of the Colonist as Men." Old South Leaflets. David C. Whitney, Signers of the Declaration of Independence - Founders of Freedom (1964), p. 49. The Annals of America, 20 vols. (Chicago, IL: Encyclopedia Britannica, 1968), Vol. 2, p. 217. Lucille Johnston, Celebrations of a Nation (Arlington, VA: The Year of Thanksgiving Foundation, 1987), p. 79.

[23] Adams, Samuel. November 20, 1772, in his pamphlet entitled, The Rights of the Colonists, in section: "The Rights of the Colonist as Christians." The Rights of the Colonists (Boston: Old South Leaflets), Vol. VII, 1772. Adams, Writings. Selim H. Peabody, ed., American Patriotism - Speeches, Letters, and Other Papers Which Illustrate the Foundation, the Development, the Preservation of the United States of America (NY: American Book Exchange, 1880), p. 34. Charles E. Kistler, This Nation Under God (Boston: Richard T. Badger, 1924), p. 73. The Annals of America, 20 vols. (Chicago, IL: Encyclopedia Britannica, 1968), Vol. 2, pp. 218-219. Verna M. Hall, The Christian History of the Constitution of the United States of America - Christian Self-Government (San Francisco: Foundation for American Christian Education, 1976), p. xiii. Marshall Foster and Mary-Elaine Swanson, The American Covenant - The Untold Story (Roseburg, OR: Foundation for Christian Self-Government, 1981; Thousand Oaks, CA: The Mayflower Institute, 1983, 1992), p. 112. Pat Robertson, America's Dates with Destiny (Nashville: Thomas Nelson Publishers, 1986), p. 91. John Eidsmoe, Christianity and the Constitution - The Faith of Our Founding Fathers (Grand Rapids, MI: Baker Book House, A Mott Media Book, 1987; 6th printing, 1993), p. 254. "Our Christian Heritage," Letter from Plymouth Rock (Marlborough, NH: The Plymouth Rock Foundation), pp. 2, 4. Peter Marshall and David Manuel, The Glory of America (Bloomington, MN: Garborg's Heart 'N Home, 1991), 1.19. D.P. Diffine, Ph.D., One Nation Under God - How Close a Separation? (Searcy, Arkansas: Harding University, Belden Center for Private Enterprise Education, 6th edition, 1992), p. 5.

[24] Morris, Gouverneur. 1785, in An Address on the Bank of North America given in the Pennsylvania State Assembly. Jared Sparks, ed., The Life of Gouverneur Morris, with Selections from His Correspondence and Miscellaneous Papers, 3 vols. (Boston: Gray and Bowen, 1832), Vol. III, p. 465. Stephen McDowell and Mark Beliles, "The Providential Perspective" (Charlottesville, VA: The Providence Foundation, P.O. Box 6759, Charlottesville, Va. 22906, January 1994), Vol. 9, No. 1, p. 5. John Eidsmoe, Christianity and The Constitution - The Faith of Our Founding Fathers (Baker Book House, 1987), pp. 183-84.

[25] Tocqueville, Alexis de. Robert N. Bellah, et. al., Habits of the Heart, p. viii. Gary DeMar, The Biblical Worldview (Atlanta, GA: An American Vision Publication - American Vision Inc., 1993), Vol. 9, No. 2, p. 14.

[26] Tocqueville, Alexis de. Alexis de Tocqueville, The Republic of the United States of America and Its Political Institutions, Reviewed and Examined, 2 vols. (New York: Alfred A. Knopf, 1945), Vol. I, p. 303. Alexis de Tocqueville, Democracy in America (New York: Vintage Books, 1945), Vol. I, pp. 314-315. Gary DeMar, The Biblical Worldview (Atlanta, GA: An American Vision Publication - American Vision, Inc., 1993), Vol. 9, No. 2, p. 14. "Our Christian Heritage," Letter from Plymouth Rock (Marlborough, NH: The Plymouth Rock Foundation), p. 5. Tim LaHaye, Faith of Our Founding Fathers (Brentwood, TN: Wolgemuth & Hyatt, Publishers, Inc., 1987), p. 97.

[27] Webster, Daniel. Esteemed as one of the five greatest senators in U.S. history, by a resolution of the United States Senate. The Capitol: A Pictorial History of the Capitol and of the Congress, 8th ed., House Doc. 96-374, 96th Congress, pp. 112-113. Gary L. Bauer, Family Research Council Newsletter (Washington, D.C.: Family Research Council, 1996), p. 2.

[28] Webster, Daniel. Benjamin Franklin Morris, The Christian Life and Character of the Civil

Institutions of the United States of America (Philadelphia: George W. Childs, 1864), p. 270. Henry H. Halley, Halley's Bible Handbook (Grand Rapids, MI: Zondervan Publishing House, 1927, 1965), p. 18. Alfred Armand Montapert, Distilled Wisdom (Englewood Cliffs, NJ: Prentice Hall, Inc., 1965), p. 37. D.P. Diffine, Ph.D., One Nation Under God - How Close a Separation? (Searcy, Arkansas: Harding University, Belden Center for Private Enterprise Education, 6th edition, 1992), p. 13. Stephen McDowell and Mark Beliles, "The Providential Perspective" (Charlottesville, VA: The Providence Foundation, P.O. Box 6759, Charlottesville, Va. 22906, January 1994), Vol. 9, No. 1, p. 7.

[29] McGuffey, William Holmes. Eclectic Reader. D. James Kennedy, What's Happened to American Education. Robert Flood, The Rebirth of America (Philadelphia: Arthur S. DeMoss Foundation, 1986), p. 122.

[30] McGuffey, William Holmes. 1836. in the Forward to his McGuffey's Reader. "Our Christian Heritage," Letter from Plymouth Rock (Marlborough, NH: The Plymouth Rock Foundation), p. 5. Stephen McDowell and Mark Beliles, "The Providential Perspective" (Charlottesville, VA: The Providence Foundation, P.O. Box 6759, Charlottesville, Va. 22906, January 1994), Vol. 9, No. 1, p. 8.

[31] Twain, Mark. Henry and Dana Thomas, 1942. Charles E. Jones, The Books You Read (Harrisburg, PA: Executive Books, 1985), p. 133.

[32] McKinley, William. March 4, 1897, in his First Inaugural Address. A Compilation of the Messages and Papers of the Presidents 20 vols. (New York: Bureau of National Literature, Inc., prepared under the direction of the Joint Committee on Printing, of the House and Senate, pursuant to an Act of the Fifty-Second Congress of the United States, 1893, 1923), Vol. XIII, pp. 6236-6244. Inaugural Addresses of the Presidents of the United States - From George Washington 1789 to Richard Milhous Nixon 1969 (Washington, D.C.: United States Government Printing Office; 91st Congress, 1st Session, House Document 91-142, 1969), pp. 169-177. Davis Newton Lott, The Inaugural Addresses of the American Presidents (NY: Holt, Rinehart and Winston, 1961), p. 171. Charles E. Rice, The Supreme Court and Public Prayer (New York: Fordham University Press, 1964), pp. 187-188. Arthur Schlesinger Jr., ed., The Chief Executive (NY: Chelsea House Publishers, 1965), p. 189. Benjamin Weiss, God in American History: A Documentation of America's Religious Heritage (Grand Rapids, MI: Zondervan, 1966) p. 115. Willard Cantelon, Money Master of the World (Plainfield, NJ: Logos International, 1976), p. 120. Proclaim Liberty (Dallas, TX: Word of Faith), p. 2. Stephen Abbott Northrop, D.D., A Cloud of Witnesses (Portland, OR: American Heritage Ministries, 1987; Mantle Ministries, 228 Still Ridge, Bulverde, Texas), p. 313. J. Michael Sharman, J.D., Faith of the Fathers (Culpepper, Virginia: Victory Publishing, 1995), p. 79.

[33] Smith, Alfred E. May 1927. Alfred E. Smith, Atlantic Monthly, May 1927. The Annals of America, 20 vols. (Chicago, IL: Encyclopedia Britannica, 1968), Vol. 14, p. 536. The National Experience, (second edition), p. 655.

[34] Hoover, Herbert Clark. September 17, 1935, in a speech in San Diego, California. Charles Hurd, ed., A Treasury of Great American Speeches (NY: Hawthorne Books, 1959), pp. 229-231.

[35] DeMille, Cecil Blount. 1956, at the New York opening of the film The Ten Commandments.

[36] Truman, Harry S. February 15, 1950, at 10:05 a.m., in an address given to the Attorney General's Conference on Law Enforcement Problems in the Department of Justice Auditorium, Washington. DC.; organizations present included the Department of Justice, the National Association of Attorneys, the United States Conference of Lawyers, and the National Institute of Municipal Law Officers. Public Papers of the Presidents: Harry S. Truman, 1950 - Containing Public Messages, Speeches, and Statements of the President, January 1 to December 31, 1950 (Washington, DC: United States Government Printing Office, 1965), Item 37, p. 157. Steve C. Dawson, God's Providence in America's History (Rancho Cordova, CA: Steve Dawson, 1988), p. 13:1. Gary DeMar, America's Christian History: The Untold Story (Atlanta, GA: American Vision Publishers, Inc., 1993), p. 60.

Endnotes

[37] Hilton, Conrad Nicholson. May 7, 1952, in an address entitled "The Battle for Peace." Mrs. James Dobson (Shirley), chairman, The National Day of Prayer Information Packet (Colorado Springs, CO: National Day of Prayer Task Force, May 6, 1993).

[38] Eisenhower, Dwight David. 1954. "Our Christian Heritage," Letter from Plymouth Rock (Marlborough, NH: The Plymouth Rock Foundation), p. 7.

[39] Reagan, Ronald Wilson. 1973, as Governor of California. Frederick J. Ryan, Jr., ed., Ronald Reagan - The Wisdom and Humor of the Great Communicator (San Francisco: Collins Publishers, A Division of Harper Collins Publishers, 1995), p. 115.

[40] Reagan, Ronald Wilson. 1974, as Governor of California. Frederick J. Ryan, Jr., ed., Ronald Reagan - The Wisdom and Humor of the Great Communicator (San Francisco: Collins Publishers, A Division of Harper Collins Publishers, 1995), p. 91.

[41] Reagan, Ronald Wilson. March 8, 1982, at the annual Washington Policy Meeting of the National Association of Manufacturers. Frederick J. Ryan, Jr., ed., Ronald Reagan - The Wisdom and Humor of the Great Communicator (San Francisco: Collins Publishers, A Division of Harper Collins Publishers, 1995), p. 87.

[42] Reagan, Ronald Wilson. January 31, 1983, at the annual convention of the National Religious Broadcasters. David R. Shepherd, ed., Ronald Reagan: In God I Trust (Wheaton, Illinois: Tyndale House Publishers, Inc., 1984), pp. 33-34, 83-84, 105-106.

[43] Reagan, Ronald Wilson. March 8, 1983, in a speech to the National Association of Evangelicals. William Safire, ed., Lend Me Your Ears - Great Speeches in History (NY: W.W. Norton & Company 1992), p. 464. David R. Shepherd, ed., Ronald Reagan: In God I Trust (Wheaton, Illinois: Tyndale House Publishers, Inc., 1984), pp. 35-38, 133-134. Frederick J. Ryan, Jr., ed., Ronald Reagan - The Wisdom and Humor of The Great Communicator (San Francisco: Collins Publishers, A Division of Harper Collins Publishers, 1995), p. 42.

[44] Reagan, Ronald Wilson. May 6, 1983, at the annual banquet of the National Rifle Association, Phoenix, Arizona. Frederick J. Ryan, Jr., ed., Ronald Reagan - The Wisdom and Humor of The Great Communicator (San Francisco: Collins Publishers, A Division of Harper Collins Publishers, 1995), p. 16.

[45] Byrd, Robert. July 27, 1962, in a message delivered in Congress by United States Senator from West Virginia two days after the Supreme Court declared prayer in schools unconstitutional. Robert Flood, The Rebirth of America (Philadelphia: Arthur S. DeMoss Foundation, 1986), pp. 66-69.

[46] Thatcher, Margaret Hilda. February 5, 1996, in New York City, prior to her trip to Utah where she addressed the U.K. - Utah Festival, in an interview with Joseph A. Cannon, entitled "The Conservative Vision of Margaret Thatcher," published in Human Events - The National Conservative Weekly, (Potomac, Maryland: Human Events Publishing, Inc., 7811 Montrose Road, Potomac, MD, 20854, 1-800-787-7557; Eagle Publishing, Inc.), March 29, 1996, Vol. 52, No. 12, pp. 12-14.

[47] Graham, William Franklin "Billy". May 2, 1996, Thursday, in his speech entitled "The Hope for America," delivered upon his acceptance of the Congressional Gold Medal, presented during the celebration of the National Day of Prayer, Washington, D.C. (Compliments of Billy Graham Association, A. Larry Ross, Director of Media/Public Relations, 4835 LBJ Freeway, Suite 800, Dallas, Texas, 75244, USA, 214-387-0700, Fax 214-387-0755.)

[48] James, Forrest Hood "Fob", Jr. February 5, 1997, Wednesday. "Alabama governor ready to defend prayer in Court" - Nationline (USA Today, Thursday, February 6, 1997), p. 3A.

[49] United States Congress. August 11, 1992, Congressman Nick Joe Rahall II of West Virginia introduced legislation in the 102nd Congress to declare November 22 through November 28, 1992, as "America's Christian Heritage Week"; reintroduce in the 103rd Congress as Christian Heritage Resolution, H.J. 113, with 55 cosponsors. Congressional Record, Vol 138, No. 1, Washington, Wednesday, August 12, 1992. Russ Walton, Executive Director, Plymouth Rock Foundation, Gen Off Fisk Mill, Marlborough, New Hampshire

03455. Courtesy of Bruce Barilla, Christian Heritage Week Ministry (P.O. Box 58, Athens, W.V. 24712; 304-384-7707, 304-384-9044 fax).

[50] United States Congress, June 17, 1999, approved by a roll call vote of 248-180 the amendment introduced by Rep. Robert Aderholt of Alabama to H.R. 1501, The Juvenile Justice Reform Act of 1999. The full bill was approved by a roll call vote of 287-139.

[51] United States Supreme Court. 1973, Anderson v. Salt Lake City Corp, 475 F.2d 29, 33, 34 (10th Cir. 1973), cert. denied, 414 U.S. 879.

[52] United States District Court. 1983, Western District of Virginia, in the case of Crockett v. Sorenson, 568 F.Supp. 1422, 1425-1430 (W.D. Va. 1983). Elizabeth Ridenour, Public Schools - Bible Curriculum (Greensboro, N.C.: National Council On Bible Curriculum, 1996), pp. 29-31, 42-43. Robert K. Skolrood, The National Legal Foundation, letter to National Council on the Bible Curriculum in Public Schools, Sept. 13, 1994, pp. 3-5.

[53] Matthew D. Staver, "The Ten Commandments in American Law and Government" (Orlando, FL: The Liberty Counsel, P.O. Box 540774, Orlando, FL 32854, 407-875-2100, 407-875-0770 Fax, http://www.lc.org, liberty@lc.org, 2002), pp. 2-3.

[54] Lincoln, Abraham. April 24, 1865, a Memorial Address delivered by Schuyler Colfax, Speaker of the House of Representatives. Colfax, Lincoln, p. 180. Peter Marshall and David Manuel, The Glory of America (Bloomington, MN: Garborg's Heart 'N Home, Inc., 1991), 4.24. D.P. Diffine, Ph.D., One Nation Under God - How Close a Separation? (Searcy, Arkansas: Harding University, Belden Center for Private Enterprise Education, 6th edition, 1992), p. 15. In 1955, the Congress of the United States passed a bill, signed by President Eisenhower, providing that all United States currency should bear the words "In God We Trust." The World Book Encyclopedia, 18 vols. (Chicago, IL: Field Enterprises, Inc., 1957; W.F. Quarrie and Company, 8 vols., 1917; World Book, Inc., 22 vols., 1989), Vol. 11, p. 5182.

[55] Chase, Salmon Portland. November 20, 1861, in correspondence to the Director of the Mint, Philadelphia.

[56] Chase, Salmon Portland. December 9, 1863, in correspondence to the James Pollock, Director of the Mint, Philadelphia.

[57] Chase, Salmon Portland. "Our Christian Heritage," Letter from Plymouth Rock (Marlborough, NH: The Plymouth Rock Foundation), p. 6. Keith J. Hardman, Christianity & The Civil War-The Christian History Timeline (Carol Stream, IL: Christian History, 1992), Vol. XI, No. 1, p. 33. In 1955, the Congress of the United States passed a bill, signed by President Eisenhower, providing that all United States currency should bear the words "In God We Trust." The World Book Encyclopedia, 18 vols. (Chicago, IL: Field Enterprises, Inc., 1957; W.F. Quarrie and Company, 8 vols., 1917; World Book, Inc., 22 vols., 1989), Vol. 11, p. 5182.

[58] United States Congress. 1955, in an Act of Congress signed by President Eisenhower approved that U.S. currency should bear the words "In God We Trust." The World Book Encyclopedia, 18 vols. (Chicago, IL: Field Enterprises, Inc., 1957; W.F. Quarrie and Company, 8 vols., 1917; World Book, Inc., 22 vols., 1989), Vol. 11, p. 5182.

[59] Truman, Harry S. October 30, 1949, in a radio address. T.S. Settel, and the staff of Quote, editors, The Quotable Harry Truman introduction by Merle Miller (NY: Droke House Publishers, Inc., Berkley Publishing Corporation, 1967), pp. 25, 147.

[60] United States Congress. July 20, 1956, bill for national motto, in the 84th Congress, 2nd session, adopted House Joint Resolution 396, introduced by Rep. Charles E. Bennett's (FL); April 18 (legislative day, April 9,) 1956; read twice and referred to the Committee on the Judiciary. Passed the House of Representatives April 16, 1956. Attest: Ralph R. Roberts, Clerk. Courtesy of Bruce Barilla, Christian Heritage Week Ministry (P.O. Box 58, Athens, W.V. 24712; 304-384-7707, 304-384-9044 fax).

[61] Reagan, Ronald Wilson. March 19, 1981, in a Proclamation of a National Day of Prayer. David R. Shepherd, ed., Ronald Reagan: In God I Trust (Wheaton, Illinois: Tyndale House Publishers, Inc., 1984), pp. 57-59. Frederick J. Ryan, Jr., ed., Ronald Reagan - The Wisdom

Endnotes

and Humor of the Great Communicator (San Francisco: Collins Publishers, A Division of Harper Collins Publishers, 1995), p. 123.

[62] United States Congress. March 3, 1931, adopted The Star Spangled Banner as our National Anthem, 36 U.S.C. Sec.170, (H.R. 14; Public, No. 823; Session III; 1508 Seventy-First Congress. Sess. III. Chs. 436, 437. 1931. Chap. 436. - An Act To make The Star-Spangled Banner the national anthem of the United States of America. Courtesy of Bruce Barilla, Christian Heritage Week Ministry (P.O. Box 58, Athens, W.V. 24712; 304-384-7707, 304-384-9044 fax).

[63] United States Congress. March 3, 1931, the United States National Anthem, Francis Scott Key's The Star Spangled Banner. (36 U.S.C. Sec.170). Hearings before Subcommittee No. 4 of the Committee Judiciary, 85th Congress, 2nd. Session. May 21, 22 & 28, 1958, p. 6. Tim LaHaye, Faith of Our Founding Fathers (Brentwood, TN: Wolgemuth & Hyatt, Publishers, Inc., 1987), p. 95. United States Congress. "Our Christian Heritage," Letter from Plymouth Rock (Marlborough, NH: The Plymouth Rock Foundation), p. 6. D.P. Diffine, Ph.D., One Nation Under God - How Close a Separation? (Searcy, Arkansas: Harding University, Belden Center for Private Enterprise Education, 6th edition, 1992), p. 17.

[64] Congress of the Unites States. June 14, 1954, approved the Joint Resolution 243, signed by President Eisenhower. (Public Law 83-396; Chapter 297; Sec. 7), June 22, 1942, 36 U.S.C. sec. 172); December 28, 1945, as Public Law 287.) Courtesy of Bruce Barilla, Christian Heritage Week Ministry (P.O. Box 58, Athens, W.V. 24712; 304-384-7707, 304-384-9044 fax). D.P. Diffine, Ph.D., One Nation Under God - How Close a Separation? (Searcy, Arkansas: Harding University, Belden Center for Private Enterprise Education, 6th edition, 1992), p. 17.

[65] Congress of the Unites States. June 14, 1954, approved the Joint Resolution 243, signed by President Eisenhower. (Public Law 83-396; Chapter 297; Sec. 7), June 22, 1942, 36 U.S.C. sec. 172); December 28, 1945, as Public Law 287.) Courtesy of Bruce Barilla, Christian Heritage Week Ministry (P.O. Box 58, Athens, W.V. 24712; 304-384-7707, 304-384-9044 fax). D.P. Diffine, Ph.D., One Nation Under God - How Close a Separation? (Searcy, Arkansas: Harding University, Belden Center for Private Enterprise Education, 6th edition, 1992), p. 17. United States Congress. September 8, 1892, Pledge of Allegiance. The World Book Encyclopedia, 18 vols. (Chicago, IL: Field Enterprises, Inc., 1957; W.F. Quarrie and Company, 8 vols., 1917; World Book, Inc., 22 vols., 1989), Vol. 13, p. 6419.

[66] United States Congress. June 14, 1954, President Eisenhower signed House Joint Resolution 243 into law as Public Law 83-396, which added the phrase, "under God," to the Pledge of Allegiance (Public Law 287). "Our Christian Heritage," Letter from Plymouth Rock (Marlborough, NH: The Plymouth Rock Foundation), p. 7. Gary DeMar, America's Christian History: The Untold Story (Atlanta, GA: American Vision Publishers, Inc., 1993), p. 104. D.P. Diffine, Ph.D., One Nation Under God - How Close a Separation? (Searcy, Arkansas: Harding University, Belden Center for Private Enterprise Education, 6th edition, 1992), p. 17.

[67] United States Congress. June 14, 1954, in a speech confirming the Act of Congress which added the phrase Under God to the Pledge of Allegiance. U.S. Marine Corps, How to Respect and Display Our Flag (Washington: U.S. Government Printing Office, 1977), p. 31.

[68] Congress of the United State. June 14, 1954, President Eisenhower on the steps of the Capitol Building. The Capitol (Washington D.C.: United States Government Printing Office, 7th edition, 1979), pp. 24-25. Gary DeMar, America's Christian History: The Untold Story (Atlanta, GA: American Vision Publishers, Inc., 1993), p. 53.

[69] Congress of the Unites States. June 14, 1954, approved the Joint Resolution 243 (Public Law 83-396), which added the words "under God" to the Pledge of Allegiance, (initially adopted by the 79th Congress on December 28, 1945, as Public Law 287.). The Capitol - A Pictorial History of the Capitol and of the Congress (Washington, D.C.: United States Government Printing Office, 1979), p. 24. Gary DeMar, "Censoring America's Christian History" (Atlanta: The Biblical Worldview, An American Vision Publication - American

Vision, Inc., July 1990), p. 10.
[70] Alabama, State of. 1901, Constitution, Preamble. Constitutions of the United States - National and States (Dobbs Ferry, New York: Oceana Publications, Inc., published for Legislative Drafting Research Fund of Columbia University, Release 96-4, Issued November 1996), Vol. 1, Alabama, Booklet 1(March 1996), p. 1. Charles E. Rice, The Supreme Court and Public Prayer (New York: Fordham University Press, 1964), p. 167; "Hearings, Prayers in Public Schools and Other Matters," Committee on the Judiciary, U.S. Senate (87th Cong., 2nd Sess.), 1962, pp. 268 et seq. Executive Proclamations declaring "Christian Heritage Week," signed September 28, 1994, and August 13, 1993 by Governor Jim Folsom; and December 23, 1992, by Governor Guy Hunt in the city of Montgomery. Courtesy of Bruce Barilla, Christian Heritage Week Ministry (P.O. Box 58, Athens, W.V. 24712; 304-384-7707, 304-384-9044 fax).
[71] Alaska, State of. 1956, Constitution, Preamble. Constitutions of the United States - National and State (Dobbs Ferry, New York: Oceana Publications, Inc., published for Legislative Drafting Research Fund of Columbia University, Release 95-5, Issued December 1995), Vol. 1, Alaska(June 1992), p. 1. Charles E. Rice, The Supreme Court and Public Prayer (New York: Fordham University Press, 1964), p. 167; "Hearings, Prayers in Public Schools and Other Matters," Committee on the Judiciary, U.S. Senate (87th Cong., 2nd Sess.), 1962, pp. 268 et seq.
[72] Arizona, State of. 1912, Constitution, Preamble. Constitutions of the United States - National and State (Dobbs Ferry, New York: Oceana Publications, Inc., published for Legislative Drafting Research Fund of Columbia University, Issued September 1993), Vol. 1, Arizona(September 1993), p. 1. Charles E. Rice, The Supreme Court and Public Prayer (New York: Fordham University Press, 1964), p. 167; "Hearings, Prayers in Public Schools and Other Matters," Committee on the Judiciary, U.S. Senate (87th Cong., 2nd Sess.), 1962, pp. 268 et seq.
[73] Arkansas, State of. 1874, Constitution, Preamble. Frances Newton Thorpe, ed., Federal and State Constitutions, Colonial Charters, and Other Organic Laws of the States, Territories, and Colonies now or heretofore forming the United States, 7 vols. (Washington: Government Printing Office, 1905; 1909; St. Clair Shores, MI: Scholarly Press, 1968). Constitutions of the United States - National and State (Dobbs Ferry, New York: Oceana Publications, Inc., published for Legislative Drafting Research Fund of Columbia University, Release 94-4, Issued October 1994), Vol. 1, Arkansas(October 1994), p. 1. Charles E. Rice, The Supreme Court and Public Prayer (New York: Fordham University Press, 1964), p. 167; "Hearings, Prayers in Public Schools and Other Matters," Committee on the Judiciary, U.S. Senate (87th Cong., 2nd Sess.), 1962, pp. 268 et seq. Miller, The First Liberty - Religion and the American Republic, p. 109. Gary DeMar, "God and the Constitution" (Atlanta, GA: Biblical Worldview, An American Vision Publication - American Vision, Inc., December 1993), p. 11. Cited August 21, 1996, in an Executive Proclamation declaring November 24 - November 30, 1994, as "Christian Heritage Week," signed by Governor Mike Huckabee and Secretary of State Sharon Priest. Courtesy of Bruce Barilla, Christian Heritage Week Ministry (P.O. Box 58, Athens, W.V. 24712; 304-384-7707, 304-384-9044 fax).
[74] California, State of. 1849, Constitution, Preamble. Constitutions of the United States - National and State (Dobbs Ferry, New York: Oceana Publications, Inc., published for Legislative Drafting Research Fund of Columbia University, Release 96-4, Issued November 1996), Vol. 1, California(November 1996), p. 1. Charles E. Rice, The Supreme Court and Public Prayer (New York: Fordham University Press, 1964), p. 168; "Hearings, Prayers in Public Schools and Other Matters," Committee on the Judiciary, U.S. Senate (87th Cong., 2nd Sess.), 1962, pp. 268 et seq.
[75] Colorado, State of. 1876, Constitution, Preamble. Constitutions of the United States - National and State (Dobbs Ferry, New York: Oceana Publications, Inc., published for Legislative Drafting Research Fund of Columbia University, Issued October 1992), Vol. 1, Colorado(October 1992), p. 1. Charles E. Rice, The Supreme Court and Public Prayer (New

Endnotes

York: Fordham University Press, 1964), p. 168; "Hearings, Prayers in Public Schools and Other Matters," Committee on the Judiciary, U.S. Senate (87th Cong., 2nd Sess.), 1962, pp. 268 et seq.
[76] Connecticut, State of. 1818, Constitution, Preamble. Frances Newton Thorpe, ed., Federal and State Constitutions, Colonial Charters, and Other Organic Laws of the States, Territories, and Colonies now or heretofore forming the United States, 7 vols. (Washington: Government Printing Office, 1905; 1909; St. Clair Shores, MI: Scholarly Press, 1968). Charles E. Rice, The Supreme Court and Public Prayer (New York: Fordham University Press, 1964), p. 168; "Hearings, Prayers in Public Schools and Other Matters," Committee on the Judiciary, U.S. Senate (87th Cong., 2nd Sess.), 1962, pp. 268 et seq. Gary DeMar, "God and the Constitution," (Atlanta, GA: The Biblical Worldview, An American Vision Publication, American Vision, Inc., December 1993). William Miller, The First Liberty - Religion and the American Republic (NY: 1986), p. 109.
[77] Delaware, State of. 1897, Constitution, Preamble. Frances Newton Thorpe, ed., Federal and State Constitutions, Colonial Charters, and Other Organic Laws of the States, Territories, and Colonies now or heretofore forming the United States, 7 vols. (Washington: Government Printing Office, 1905; 1909; St. Clair Shores, MI: Scholarly Press, 1968). Charles E. Rice, The Supreme Court and Public Prayer (New York: Fordham University Press, 1964), p. 168; "Hearings, Prayers in Public Schools and Other Matters," Committee on the Judiciary, U.S. Senate (87th Cong., 2nd Sess.), 1962, pp. 268 et seq. Edwin S. Gaustad, Neither King nor Prelate - Religion and the New Nation, 1776-1826 (Grand Rapids, MI: William B. Eerdmans Publishing Company, 1993), pp. 161-162. Gary DeMar, God and Government, A Biblical and Historical Study (Atlanta, Georgia: American Vision Press), Vol. 1, pp. 164-165. Church of the Holy Trinity v. U.S., 143 U.S. 457, 469-470. Recorded in The State of Delaware Executive Proclamation of November 14 - 20, 1993, as "Christian Heritage Week," signed by Governor Thomas R. Caper, and Lieutenant Governor Ruth Ann Minner. Courtesy of Bruce Barilla, Christian Heritage Week Ministry (P.O. Box 58, Athens, W.V. 24712; 304-384-7707, 304-384-9044 fax).
[78] Florida, State of. 1885, Constitution, Preamble. Frances Newton Thorpe, ed., Federal and State Constitutions, Colonial Charters, and Other Organic Laws of the States, Territories, and Colonies now or heretofore forming the United States, 7 vols. (Washington: Government Printing Office, 1905; 1909; St. Clair Shores, MI: Scholarly Press, 1968), Vol. II, p. 733. Charles E. Rice, The Supreme Court and Public Prayer (New York: Fordham University Press, 1964), p. 168; "Hearings, Prayers in Public Schools and Other Matters," Committee on the Judiciary, U.S. Senate (87th Cong., 2nd Sess.), 1962, pp. 268 et seq. Anson Phelps Stokes and Leo Pfeffer, Church and State in the United States (NY: Harper and Row, Publishers, 1950, revised one-volume edition, 1964), p. 156.
[79] Georgia, State of. 1777, Constitution, Preamble. Charles E. Rice, The Supreme Court and Public Prayer (New York: Fordham University Press, 1964), p. 169; "Hearings, Prayers in Public Schools and Other Matters," Committee on the Judiciary, U.S. Senate (87th Cong., 2nd Sess.), 1962, pp. 268 et seq. Benjamin Weiss, God in American History: A Documentation of America's Religious Heritage (Grand Rapids, MI: Zondervan, 1966), p. 155. Gary DeMar, America's Christian History: The Untold Story (Atlanta, GA: American Vision Publishers, Inc., 1993), p. 65.
[80] Hawaii, State of. 1959, Constitution, Preamble. Charles E. Rice, The Supreme Court and Public Prayer (New York: Fordham University Press, 1964), p. 169; "Hearings, Prayers in Public Schools and Other Matters," Committee on the Judiciary, U.S. Senate (87th Cong., 2nd Sess.), 1962, pp. 268 et seq. Recorded in an Executive Proclamation declaring February 12 - 22, 1994, as "Christian Heritage Week," signed by Governor John Waihee, in the Capitol City of Honolulu, December 30, 1993. Courtesy of Bruce Barilla, Christian Heritage Week Ministry (P.O. Box 58, Athens, W.V. 24712; 304-384-7707, 304-384-9044 fax).
[81] Idaho, State of. 1889, Constitution, Preamble. Charles E. Rice, The Supreme Court and Public Prayer (New York: Fordham University Press, 1964), p. 169; "Hearings, Prayers in

Public Schools and Other Matters," Committee on the Judiciary, U.S. Senate (87th Cong., 2nd Sess.), 1962, pp. 268 et seq. Recorded in the Executive Proclamation declaring October 16 - 22, 1994, as "Christian Heritage Week," signed in the Capitol City of Boise by Governor Cecil D. Andrus and Secretary of State Pete T. Cenarrusa. Courtesy of Bruce Barilla, Christian Heritage Week Ministry (P.O. Box 58, Athens, W.V. 24712; 304-384-7707, 304-384-9044 fax).

[82] Illinois, State of. 1870, Constitution, Preamble. Charles E. Rice, The Supreme Court and Public Prayer (New York: Fordham University Press, 1964), p. 169; "Hearings, Prayers in Public Schools and Other Matters," Committee on the Judiciary, U.S. Senate (87th Cong., 2nd Sess.), 1962, pp. 268 et seq. Church of the Holy Trinity v. United States 143 U.S. 457, (1892). Gary DeMar, God and Government-A Biblical and Historical Study (Atlanta: GA: American Vision Press, 1984), p. 143.

[83] Indiana, State of. 1851, Constitution, Preamble. Charles E. Rice, The Supreme Court and Public Prayer (New York: Fordham University Press, 1964), p. 169; "Hearings, Prayers in Public Schools and Other Matters," Committee on the Judiciary, U.S. Senate (87th Cong., 2nd Sess.), 1962, pp. 268 et seq.

[84] Iowa, State of. 1857, Constitution, Preamble. Charles E. Rice, The Supreme Court and Public Prayer (New York: Fordham University Press, 1964), p. 169; "Hearings, Prayers in Public Schools and Other Matters," Committee on the Judiciary, U.S. Senate (87th Cong., 2nd Sess.), 1962, pp. 268 et seq.

[85] Kansas, State of. 1859, Constitution, Preamble. Charles E. Rice, The Supreme Court and Public Prayer (New York: Fordham University Press, 1964), pp. 169-170; "Hearings, Prayers in Public Schools and Other Matters," Committee on the Judiciary, U.S. Senate (87th Cong., 2nd Sess.), 1962, pp. 268 et seq.

[86] Kentucky, State of. 1891, Constitution, Preamble. Charles E. Rice, The Supreme Court and Public Prayer (New York: Fordham University Press, 1964), p. 170; "Hearings, Prayers in Public Schools and Other Matters," Committee on the Judiciary, U.S. Senate (87th Cong., 2nd Sess.), 1962, pp. 268 et seq. Executive Proclamation by Governor Brereton C. Jones and Secretary of State Robert Babbage, declaring November 21 - November 27, 1993, as "Christian Heritage Week," signed November 1, 1993, in the Capitol City of Frankfort. Courtesy of Bruce Barilla, Christian Heritage Week Ministry (P.O. Box 58, Athens, W.V. 24712; 304-384-7707, 304-384-9044 fax).

[87] Louisiana, State of. 1921, Constitution, Preamble. Charles E. Rice, The Supreme Court and Public Prayer (New York: Fordham University Press, 1964), p. 170; "Hearings, Prayers in Public Schools and Other Matters," Committee on the Judiciary, U.S. Senate (87th Cong., 2nd Sess.), 1962, pp. 268 et seq.

[88] Maine, State of. 1819, Constitution, Preamble. Charles E. Rice, The Supreme Court and Public Prayer (New York: Fordham University Press, 1964), p. 170; "Hearings, Prayers in Public Schools and Other Matters," Committee on the Judiciary, U.S. Senate (87th Cong., 2nd Sess.), 1962, pp. 268 et seq.

[89] Maryland, State of. 1776, Constitution, Preamble. Benjamin Weiss, God in American History: A Documentation of America's Religious Heritage (Grand Rapids, MI: Zondervan, 1966), p. 155. Gary DeMar, America's Christian History: The Untold Story (Atlanta, GA: American Vision Publishers, Inc., 1993), p. 65.

[90] Massachusetts, State of. 1780, Constitution, Preamble. Henry Steele Commager, ed., Documents of American History, 2 vols. (NY: F.S. Crofts and Company, 1934; Appleton-Century-Crofts, Inc., 1948, 6th edition, 1958; Englewood Cliffs, NJ: Prentice Hall, Inc., 9th edition, 1973), Vol. I, pp. 107-108. The Annals of America, 20 vols. (Chicago, IL: Encyclopedia Britannica, 1968), Vol. I, pp. 322-333. Jacob C. Meyer, Church and State in Massachusetts from 1740-1833 (Cleveland: Western Reserve Press, 1930) pp. 234-235. Anson Phelps Stokes and Leo Pfeffer, Church and State in the United States (NY: Harper and Row, Publishers, 1950, revised one-volume edition, 1964), p. 77. The Constitutions of All the United States According to the Latest Amendments (Lexington, KY: Thomas T.

Endnotes

Skillman, 1817), p. 89. The Constitutions of the Several Independent States of America (Philadelphia: Bailey, published by order of the U.S. Continental Congress, 1781, in the Evans Collection, #17390), p. 138. Gary DeMar, "Censoring America's Christian History" (Atlanta, GA: The Biblical Worldview, An American Vision Publication - American Vision, Inc., July 1990), p. 7. Benjamin Weiss, God in American History: A Documentation of America's Religious Heritage (Grand Rapids, MI: Zondervan, 1966), p. 155. Gary DeMar, America's Christian History: The Untold Story (Atlanta, GA: American Vision Publishers, Inc., 1993), p. 65. Frances Newton Thorpe, ed., Federal and State Constitutions, Colonial Charters, and Other Organic Laws of the States, Territories, and Colonies now or heretofore forming the United States, 7 vols. (Washington: Government Printing Office, 1905; 1909; St. Clair Shores, MI: Scholarly Press, 1968), Vol. V, p. 38.

[91] Michigan, State of. 1908, Constitution, Preamble. Charles E. Rice, The Supreme Court and Public Prayer (New York: Fordham University Press, 1964), p. 171; "Hearings, Prayers in Public Schools and Other Matters," Committee on the Judiciary, U.S. Senate (87th Cong., 2nd Sess.), 1962, pp. 268 et seq.

[92] Minnesota, State of. 1857, Constitution, Preamble. Charles E. Rice, The Supreme Court and Public Prayer (New York: Fordham University Press, 1964), p. 171; "Hearings, Prayers in Public Schools and Other Matters," Committee on the Judiciary, U.S. Senate (87th Cong., 2nd Sess.), 1962, pp. 268 et seq.

[93] Mississippi, State of. 1890, Constitution, Preamble. Charles E. Rice, The Supreme Court and Public Prayer (New York: Fordham University Press, 1964), pp. 171-172; "Hearings, Prayers in Public Schools and Other Matters," Committee on the Judiciary, U.S. Senate (87th Cong., 2nd Sess.), 1962, pp. 268 et seq.

[94] Missouri, Constitution of the State of. 1945, Preamble. Charles E. Rice, The Supreme Court and Public Prayer (New York: Fordham University Press, 1964), p. 172; "Hearings, Prayers in Public Schools and Other Matters," Committee on the Judiciary, U.S. Senate (87th Cong., 2nd Sess.), 1962, pp. 268 et seq.

[95] Montana, State of. 1889, Constitution, Preamble. Charles E. Rice, The Supreme Court and Public Prayer (New York: Fordham University Press, 1964), p. 172; "Hearings, Prayers in Public Schools and Other Matters," Committee on the Judiciary, U.S. Senate (87th Cong., 2nd Sess.), 1962, pp. 268 et seq.

[96] Nebraska, State of. June 12, 1875, Constitution, Preamble. Charles E. Rice, The Supreme Court and Public Prayer (New York: Fordham University Press, 1964), p. 172; "Hearings, Prayers in Public Schools and Other Matters," Committee on the Judiciary, U.S. Senate (87th Cong., 2nd Sess.), 1962, pp. 268 et seq.

[97] Nevada, State of. 1864, Constitution, Preamble. Charles E. Rice, The Supreme Court and Public Prayer (New York: Fordham University Press, 1964), p. 172; "Hearings, Prayers in Public Schools and Other Matters," Committee on the Judiciary, U.S. Senate (87th Cong., 2nd Sess.), 1962, pp. 268 et seq.

[98] New Hampshire, State of. 1784, 1792, Part One, Article I, Section V. The Constitutions of All the United States According to the Latest Amendments (Lexington, KY: Thomas T. Skillman, 1817), pp. 27, 29. The Constitutions of the Several Independent States of America, Published by Order of Congress (Boston: Norman & Bowen, 1785) p. 3-4. Frances Newton Thorpe, ed., Federal and State Constitutions, Colonial Charters, and Other Organic Laws of the States, Territories, and Colonies now or heretofore forming the United States, 7 vols. (Washington: Government Printing Office, 1905; 1909; St. Clair Shores, MI: Scholarly Press, 1968). Charles E. Rice, The Supreme Court and Public Prayer (New York: Fordham University Press, 1964), p. 172; "Hearings, Prayers in Public Schools and Other Matters," Committee on the Judiciary, U.S. Senate (87th Cong., 2nd Sess.), 1962, pp. 268 et seq. New Hampshire Manuel (1937), pp. 9-10.5. Edwin S. Gaustad, Neither King nor Prelate - Religion and the New Nation, 1776-1826 (Grand Rapids, MI: William B. Eerdmans Publishing Company, 1993), p. 166.

[99] New Jersey, State of. 1844, 1947, Constitution, Preamble. Charles E. Rice, The Supreme

Court and Public Prayer (New York: Fordham University Press, 1964), pp. 172-173; "Hearings, Prayers in Public Schools and Other Matters," Committee on the Judiciary, U.S. Senate (87th Cong., 2nd Sess.), 1962, pp. 268 et seq. Tim LaHaye, Faith of Our Founding Fathers (Brentwood, TN: Wolgemuth & Hyatt, Publishers, Inc., 1987), p. 92.

100 New Mexico, State of. 1911, Constitution, Preamble. Charles E. Rice, The Supreme Court and Public Prayer (New York: Fordham University Press, 1964), p. 173; "Hearings, Prayers in Public Schools and Other Matters," Committee on the Judiciary, U.S. Senate (87th Cong., 2nd Sess.), 1962, pp. 268 et seq.

101 New York, State of. 1846, Constitution, Preamble. Frances Newton Thorpe, ed., Federal and State Constitutions, Colonial Charters, and Other Organic Laws of the States, Territories, and Colonies now or heretofore forming the United States, 7 vols. (Washington: Government Printing Office, 1905; 1909; St. Clair Shores, MI: Scholarly Press, 1968). Charles E. Rice, The Supreme Court and Public Prayer (New York: Fordham University Press, 1964), p. 173; "Hearings, Prayers in Public Schools and Other Matters," Committee on the Judiciary, U.S. Senate (87th Cong., 2nd Sess.), 1962, pp. 268 et seq. Benjamin Weiss, God in American History: A Documentation of America's Religious Heritage (Grand Rapids, MI: Zondervan, 1966), p. 155. Tim LaHaye, Faith of Our Founding Fathers (Brentwood, TN: Wolgemuth & Hyatt, Publishers, Inc., 1987), p. 93. Gary DeMar, America's Christian History: The Untold Story (Atlanta, GA: American Vision Publishers, Inc., 1993), p. 66. Gary DeMar, "Censoring America's Christian History" (Atlanta, GA: The Biblical Worldview, An American Vision Publication - American Vision, Inc., July 1990).

102 North Carolina, State of. 1868, Constitution, Preamble. Charles E. Rice, The Supreme Court and Public Prayer (New York: Fordham University Press, 1964), p. 173; "Hearings, Prayers in Public Schools and Other Matters," Committee on the Judiciary, U.S. Senate (87th Cong., 2nd Sess.), 1962, pp. 268 et seq.Tim LaHaye, Faith of Our Founding Fathers (Brentwood, TN: Wolgemuth & Hyatt, Publishers, Inc., 1987), p. 92.

103 North Dakota, State of. 1889, Constitution, Preamble. Charles E. Rice, The Supreme Court and Public Prayer (New York: Fordham University Press, 1964), p. 173; "Hearings, Prayers in Public Schools and Other Matters," Committee on the Judiciary, U.S. Senate (87th Cong., 2nd Sess.), 1962, pp. 268 et seq.

104 Ohio, State of. 1852, Constitution, Preamble. The Constitutions of the United States of America with the Latest Amendments (Trenton: Moore & Lake, 1813), p. 334. Frances Newton Thorpe, ed., Federal and State Constitutions, Colonial Charters, and Other Organic Laws of the States, Territories, and Colonies now or heretofore forming the United States, 7 vols. (Washington: Government Printing Office, 1905; 1909; St. Clair Shores, MI: Scholarly Press, 1968). Charles E. Rice, The Supreme Court and Public Prayer (New York: Fordham University Press, 1964), pp. 173-174; "Hearings, Prayers in Public Schools and Other Matters," Committee on the Judiciary, U.S. Senate (87th Cong., 2nd Sess.), 1962, pp. 268 et seq.

105 Oklahoma, State of. 1907, Constitution, Preamble. Charles E. Rice, The Supreme Court and Public Prayer (New York: Fordham University Press, 1964), p. 174; "Hearings, Prayers in Public Schools and Other Matters," Committee on the Judiciary, U.S. Senate (87th Cong., 2nd Sess.), 1962, pp. 268 et seq.

106 Oregon, State of. 1857, Constitution, Bill of Rights, Article I, Section 2. Charles E. Rice, The Supreme Court and Public Prayer (New York: Fordham University Press, 1964), p. 174; "Hearings, Prayers in Public Schools and Other Matters," Committee on the Judiciary, U.S. Senate (87th Cong., 2nd Sess.), 1962, pp. 268 et seq.

107 Pennsylvania, State of. 1776, Constitution, Preamble. Charles E. Rice, The Supreme Court and Public Prayer (New York: Fordham University Press, 1964), p. 174; "Hearings, Prayers in Public Schools and Other Matters," Committee on the Judiciary, U.S. Senate (87th Cong., 2nd Sess.), 1962, pp. 268 et seq. Benjamin Weiss, God in American History: A Documentation of America's Religious Heritage (Grand Rapids, MI: Zondervan, 1966), p. 155. Gary DeMar, America's Christian History: The Untold Story (Atlanta, GA: American

Endnotes

Vision Publishers, Inc., 1993), p. 65.
[108] Rhode Island and Providence Plantations, State of. 1842, Constitution, Preamble. Charles E. Rice, The Supreme Court and Public Prayer (New York: Fordham University Press, 1964), p. 174; "Hearings, Prayers in Public Schools and Other Matters," Committee on the Judiciary, U.S. Senate (87th Cong., 2nd Sess.), 1962, pp. 268 et seq. Benjamin Weiss, God in American History: A Documentation of America's Religious Heritage (Grand Rapids, MI: Zondervan, 1966), p. 155. Tim LaHaye, Faith of Our Founding Fathers (Brentwood, TN: Wolgemuth & Hyatt, Publishers, Inc., 1987), p. 92. Gary DeMar, America's Christian History: The Untold Story (Atlanta, GA: American Vision Publishers, Inc., 1993), pp. 64-64.
[109] South Carolina, State of. 1778, Constitution, Preamble. Frances Newton Thorpe, ed., Federal and State Constitutions, Colonial Charters, and Other Organic Laws of the States, Territories, and Colonies now or heretofore forming the United States, 7 vols. (Washington: Government Printing Office, 1905; 1909; St. Clair Shores, MI: Scholarly Press, 1968). Charles E. Rice, The Supreme Court and Public Prayer (New York: Fordham University Press, 1964), pp. 174-175; "Hearings, Prayers in Public Schools and Other Matters," Committee on the Judiciary, U.S. Senate (87th Cong., 2nd Sess.), 1962, pp. 268 et seq. Benjamin Weiss, God in American History: A Documentation of America's Religious Heritage (Grand Rapids, MI: Zondervan, 1966), p. 155. Gary DeMar, "Censoring America's Christian History" (Atlanta, GA: The Biblical Worldview, An American Vision Publication - American Vision, Inc., July 1990), p. 7. Gary DeMar, America's Christian History: The Untold Story (Atlanta, GA: American Vision Publishers, Inc., 1993), p. 66.
[110] South Dakota, State of. 1889, Constitution, Preamble. Charles E. Rice, The Supreme Court and Public Prayer (New York: Fordham University Press, 1964), p. 175; "Hearings, Prayers in Public Schools and Other Matters," Committee on the Judiciary, U.S. Senate (87th Cong., 2nd Sess.), 1962, pp. 268 et seq.
[111] Tennessee, State of. 1796, Constitution, Article XI, Section 3. Frances Newton Thorpe, ed., Federal and State Constitutions, Colonial Charters, and Other Organic Laws of the States, Territories, and Colonies now or heretofore forming the United States, 7 vols. (Washington: Government Printing Office, 1905; 1909; St. Clair Shores, MI: Scholarly Press, 1968). Edwin S. Gaustad, Neither King nor Prelate - Religion and the New Nation, 1776-1826 (Grand Rapids, MI: William B. Eerdmans Publishing Company, 1993), pp. 172-73. Governor Ned McWherter and Secretary of State Riley C. Darnell, Proclamation declaring Christian Heritage Week, August 29 - September 4, 1993, signed June 21, 1993, in the Capitol City of Nashville. Courtesy of Bruce Barilla, Christian Heritage Week Ministry (P.O. Box 58, Athens, W.V. 24712; 304-384-7707, 304-384-9044 fax).
[112] Texas, State of. August 27, 1845, Constitution, Preamble. Journals of the Convention, Assembled at the City of Austin on the Fourth of July, 1845, for the purpose of framing a Constitution for the State of Texas (Austin, TX: Miner & Cruger, Printers to the Convention, 1845; A Facsimile Reproduction of the 1845 Edition with a Preface by Mary Bell Hart, Shoal Creek Publishers, 1974), p. 338.
[113] Utah, State of. 1896, Constitution, Preamble. Charles E. Rice, The Supreme Court and Public Prayer (New York: Fordham University Press, 1964), p. 175; "Hearings, Prayers in Public Schools and Other Matters," Committee on the Judiciary, U.S. Senate (87th Cong., 2nd Sess.), 1962, pp. 268 et seq.
[114] Vermont, State of. July 8, 1777, Constitution. Perley Poore, ed., The Federal and State Constitutions, Colonial Charters, and Other Organic Laws of the United States (Washington, 1877), Vol. II, p. 1857. Frances Newton Thorpe, ed., Federal and State Constitutions, Colonial Charters, and Other Organic Laws of the States, Territories, and Colonies now or heretofore forming the United States, 7 vols. (Washington: Government Printing Office, 1905; 1909; St. Clair Shores, MI: Scholarly Press, 1968). The Annals of America, 20 vols. (Chicago, IL: Encyclopedia Britannica, 1968), Vol. 2, p. 483.
[115] Virginia, State of. July 12, 1776; 1830; 1851; 1868; 1902; 1928, Constitution, Bill of Rights, Article I, Section 16. Frances Newton Thorpe, ed., Federal and State Constitutions,

Colonial Charters, and Other Organic Laws of the States, Territories, and Colonies now or heretofore forming the United States, 7 vols. (Washington: Government Printing Office, 1905; 1909; St. Clair Shores, MI: Scholarly Press, 1968), Vol. VII, p. 3814. Benjamin Franklin Morris, The Christian Life and Character of the Civil Institutions of the United States (Philadelphia, PA: L. Johnson & Co., 1863; George W. Childs, 1864), p. 232. Henry Steele Commager, ed., Documents of American History, 2 vols. (NY: F.S. Crofts and Company, 1934; Appleton-Century-Crofts, Inc., 1948, 6th edition, 1958; Englewood Cliffs, NJ: Prentice Hall, Inc., 9th edition, 1973), pp. 103-104. Charles Fadiman, ed., The American Treasury (NY: Harper & Brothers, Publishers, 1955), p. 121. Charles E. Rice, The Supreme Court and Public Prayer (New York: Fordham University Press, 1964), pp. 175-176; "Hearings, Prayers in Public Schools and Other Matters," Committee on the Judiciary, U.S. Senate (87th Cong., 2nd Sess.), 1962, pp. 268 et seq. The Annals of America, 20 vols. (Chicago, IL: Encyclopedia Britannica, 1968), Vol. 2, p. 433. Pat Robertson, America's Dates with Destiny (Nashville: Thomas Nelson Publishers, 1986), pp. 80-81. "Our Christian Heritage," Letter form Plymouth Rock (Marlborough, NH: The Plymouth Rock Foundation), p. 3. Stephen McDowell and Mark Beliles, "The Providential Perspective" (Charlottesville, VA: The Providence Foundation, P.O. Box 6759, Charlottesville, Va. 22906, January 1994), Vol. 9, No. 1, p. 2. Edwin S. Gaustad, Neither King nor Prelate - Religion and the New Nation, 1776-1826 (Grand Rapids, MI: William B. Eerdmans Publishing Company, 1993), p. 174.

[116] Washington, State of. 1889, Constitution, Preamble. Charles E. Rice, The Supreme Court and Public Prayer (New York: Fordham University Press, 1964), p. 176; "Hearings, Prayers in Public Schools and Other Matters," Committee on the Judiciary, U.S. Senate (87th Cong., 2nd Sess.), 1962, pp. 268 ct scq.

[117] West Virginia, State of. 1872, Constitution, Preamble. Charles E. Rice, The Supreme Court and Public Prayer (New York: Fordham University Press, 1964), p. 176; "Hearings, Prayers in Public Schools and Other Matters," Committee on the Judiciary, U.S. Senate (87th Cong., 2nd Sess.), 1962, pp. 268 et seq.

[118] Wisconsin, State of. 1848, Constitution, Preamble. Charles E. Rice, The Supreme Court and Public Prayer (New York: Fordham University Press, 1964), p. 176; "Hearings, Prayers in Public Schools and Other Matters," Committee on the Judiciary, U.S. Senate (87th Cong., 2nd Sess.), 1962, pp. 268 et seq. Governor Tommy G. Thompson and Secretary of State Douglas La Follet, Proclamation of Christian Heritage Week October 3 - October 9, 1993, in the Capitol City of Madison. A similar Proclamation was also signed November 1, 1994. Courtesy of Bruce Barilla, Christian Heritage Week Ministry (P.O. Box 58, Athens, W.V. 24712; 304-384-7707, 304-384-9044 fax).

[119] Wyoming, State of. 1890, Constitution, Preamble. Charles E. Rice, The Supreme Court and Public Prayer (New York: Fordham University Press, 1964), p. 176; "Hearings, Prayers in Public Schools and Other Matters," Committee on the Judiciary, U.S. Senate (87th Cong., 2nd Sess.), 1962, pp. 268 et seq.

[120] Washington, John. An inscription on a tablet with the Ten Commandments that John Washington, the great-grandfather of George Washington, left, in his Last Will and Testament, as a gift to the church of the parish of Washington. William J. Johnson, George Washington - The Christian (St. Paul, MN: William J. Johnson, Merriam Park, February 23, 1919; Nashville, TN: Abingdon Press, 1919; reprinted Milford, MI: Mott Media, 1976; reprinted Arlington Heights, IL: Christian Liberty Press, 502 West Euclid Avenue, Arlington Heights, Illinois, 60004, 1992), p. 16.

[121] Washington, George. October 25, 1762, in an entry in the vestry book of the Pohick Church in Truro Parish, Virginia. W.M. Clark, Colonial Churches (1907), p. 126. William J. Johnson, George Washington - The Christian (St. Paul, MN: William J. Johnson, Merriam Park, February 23, 1919; Nashville, TN: Abingdon Press, 1919; reprinted Milford, MI: Mott Media, 1976; reprinted Arlington Heights, IL: Christian Liberty Press, 502 West Euclid Avenue, Arlington Heights, Illinois, 60004, 1992), p. 49.

Endnotes

[122] Washington, George. February 15, 1763, in the records of the Fairfax County Court. W.M. Clark, Colonial Churches (1907), p. 126. (Washington's position as a vestryman was again recorded on a leaf from the Pohick Church record, August 19, 1765; manuscripts in the library of the New York Historical Society. Benson J. Lossing, The Pictorial Field-Book of the Revolution, 2 vols. (1860), Vol. II, p. 215). William J. Johnson, George Washington - The Christian (St. Paul, MN: William J. Johnson, Merriam Park, February 23, 1919; Nashville, TN: Abingdon Press, 1919; reprinted Milford, MI: Mott Media, 1976; reprinted Arlington Heights, IL: Christian Liberty Press, 502 West Euclid Avenue, Arlington Heights, Illinois, 60004, 1992), pp. 49-50.

[123] Washington, George. 1768-1774, attendance at various Church and Vestry meetings recorded in his diary. W.M. Clark, Colonial Churches (1907), pp. 121-126. Rev. Randolph H. McKim, D.D., Rector of the Church of the Epiphany, Washington, D.C., New York Tribune (May 26, 1902), p. 7. E.C. M'guire, The Religious Opinions and Character of Washington (1836), p. 143. (E.C. M'Guire was the son-in-law of Mr. Robert Lewis, Washington's nephew and private secretary.) William J. Johnson, George Washington - The Christian (St. Paul, MN: William J. Johnson, Merriam Park, February 23, 1919; Nashville, TN: Abingdon Press, 1919; reprinted Milford, MI: Mott Media, 1976; reprinted Arlington Heights, IL: Christian Liberty Press, 502 West Euclid Avenue, Arlington Heights, Illinois, 60004, 1992), pp. 51-57, 66-67.

[124] Washington, George. James Madison's comments regarding Washington. Doctor Randolph H. McKim, New York Tribune (May 26, 1902), p. 7. William J. Johnson, George Washington - The Christian (St. Paul, MN: William J. Johnson, Merriam Park, February 23, 1919; Nashville, TN: Abingdon Press, 1919; reprinted Milford, MI: Mott Media, 1976; reprinted Arlington Heights, IL: Christian Liberty Press, 502 West Euclid Avenue, Arlington Heights, Illinois, 60004, 1992), p. 257.

[125] Washington, George. Paul F. Boller, Jr., George Washington & Religion (Dallas: Southern Methodist University, 1963), p. 27. A. James Reichley, Religion in American Public Life (Washington, D.C.: The Brookings Institution, 1985), p. 94. Pat Robertson, America's Dates With Destiny (Nashville, TN: Thomas Nelson Publishers, 1986), p. 108.

[126] Washington, George. January of 1790, in a letter to the Hebrew Congregations of Philadelphia, Newport, Charlestown and Richmond. William Barclay Allen, ed., George Washington - A Collection (Indianapolis: Liberty Classics, Liberty Fund, Inc., 7440 N. Shadeland, Indianapolis, Indiana 46250, 1988; based almost entirely on materials reproduced from The Writings of George Washington from the original manuscript sources, 1745-1799/ John Clement Fitzpatrick, editor), pp. 545-546. John Clement Fitzpatrick, ed., The Writings of George Washington, from the Original Manuscript Sources 1749-1799, 39 vols. (Washington, D.C.: United States Government Printing Office, 1931-1944). Norman Cousins, In God We Trust - The Religious Beliefs and Ideas of the Founding Fathers (NY: Harper & Brothers, 1958), p. 62.

[127] Washington, George. April 30, 1789, in his Inaugural Address. Charles W. Eliot, LL.D., ed., American Historical Documents 1000-1904 (New York: P.F. Collier & Son Company, The Harvard Classics, 1910), Vol. 43, pp. 241-245.

[128] Washington, George. June 1779, near his headquarters on the Hudson River, in a private prayer. E.C. M'guire, The Religious Opinions and Character of Washington (1836), pp. 162-167. (E.C. M'Guire was the son-in-law of Mr. Robert Lewis, Washington's nephew and private secretary.) William J. Johnson, George Washington - The Christian (St. Paul, MN: William J. Johnson, Merriam Park, February 23, 1919; Nashville, TN: Abingdon Press, 1919; reprinted Milford, MI: Mott Media, 1976; reprinted Arlington Heights, IL: Christian Liberty Press, 502 West Euclid Avenue, Arlington Heights, Illinois, 60004, 1992), pp. 126-127. Stephen Abbott Northrop, D.D., A Cloud of Witnesses (Portland, OR: American Heritage Ministries, 1987; Mantle Ministries, 228 Still Ridge, Bulverde, Texas), p. 484.

[129] Washington, George. May 15, 1776, in his issued orders. Jared Sparks, ed., The Writings of George Washington 12 vols. (Boston: American Stationer's Company, 1837; NY: F.

Andrew's, 1834-1847), Vol. III, p. 392. William J. Johnson, George Washington - The Christian (St. Paul, MN: William J. Johnson, Merriam Park, February 23, 1919; Nashville, TN: Abingdon Press, 1919; reprinted Milford, MI: Mott Media, 1976; reprinted Arlington Heights, IL: Christian Liberty Press, 502 West Euclid Avenue, Arlington Heights, Illinois, 60004, 1992), p. 81.

[130] Washington, George. May 15, 1796, in a letter written from Philadelphia to the Emperor of Germany. William Barclay Allen, ed., George Washington - A Collection (Indianapolis: Liberty Classics, Liberty Fund, Inc., 7440 N. Shadeland, Indianapolis, Indiana 46250, 1988; based almost entirely on materials reproduced from The Writings of George Washington from the original manuscript sources, 1745-1799/John Clement Fitzpatrick, editor), p. 633. John Clement Fitzpatrick, ed., The Writings of George Washington, from the Original Manuscript Sources 1749-1799, 39 vols. (Washington, D.C.: United States Government Printing Office, 1931-1944).

[131] Washington, George. May 5, 1778, orders issued from the headquarters at Valley Forge upon receiving intelligence that France had joined the War on the side of the Colonies. Henry Whiting, Revolutionary Orders of General Washington, selected from MSS. of John Whiting (1844), p. 77. William J. Johnson, George Washington - The Christian (St. Paul, MN: William J. Johnson, Merriam Park, February 23, 1919; Nashville, TN: Abingdon Press, 1919; reprinted Milford, MI: Mott Media, 1976; reprinted Arlington Heights, IL: Christian Liberty Press, 502 West Euclid Avenue, Arlington Heights, Illinois, 60004, 1992), pp. 112-113. Charles E. Kistler, This Nation Under God (Boston: Richard G. Badger, The Gorham Press, 1924), pp. 74-75. Peter Marshall and David Manuel, The Light and the Glory (Old Tappan, NJ: Fleming H. Revell Company, 1977), p. 326.

[132] Washington, George. December 8, 1795, Tuesday, in his Seventh Annual Message to Congress. Jared Sparks, ed., The Writings of George Washington 12 vols. (Boston: American Stationer's Company, 1837; NY: F. Andrew's, 1834-1847), Vol. XII, pp. 56-64. James D. Richardson (U.S. Representative from Tennessee), ed., A Compilation of the Messages and Papers of the Presidents 1789-1897, 10 vols. (Washington, D.C.: U.S. Government Printing Office, published by Authority of Congress, 1897, 1899; Washington, D.C.: Bureau of National Literature and Art, 1789-1902, 11 vols., 1907, 1910), Vol. I, pp. 182-184. William J. Johnson, George Washington - The Christian (St. Paul, MN: William J. Johnson, Merriam Park, February 23, 1919; Nashville, TN: Abingdon Press, 1919; reprinted Milford, MI: Mott Media, 1976; reprinted Arlington Heights, IL: Christian Liberty Press, 502 West Euclid Avenue, Arlington Heights, Illinois, 60004, 1992), p. 217. William Barclay Allen, ed., George Washington - A Collection (Indianapolis: Liberty Classics, Liberty Fund, Inc., 7440 N. Shadeland, Indianapolis, Indiana 46250, 1988; based almost entirely on materials reproduced from The Writings of George Washington from the original manuscript sources, 1745-1799/John Clement Fitzpatrick, editor), pp. 499-502. John Clement Fitzpatrick, ed., The Writings of George Washington, from the Original Manuscript Sources 1749-1799, 39 vols. (Washington, D.C.: United States Government Printing Office, 1931-1944).

[133] Washington, George. March 3, 1797, in a "Letter to the Clergy of Different Denominations Residing in and near the City of Philadelphia. Ashabel Green, The Life of Ashabel Green, by Himself (1849), p. 615. Paul F. Boller, Jr., George Washington and Religion (Dallas: Southern Methodist University Press, 1963), p. 82. John Eidsmoe, Christianity and the Constitution - The Faith of Our Founding Fathers (Grand Rapids, MI: Baker Book House, A Mott Media Book, 1987, 6th printing 1993), p. 120. Stephen McDowell and Mark Beliles, "The Providential Perspective" (Charlottesville, VA: The Providence Foundation, P.O. Box 6759, Charlottesville, Va. 22906, January 1994), Vol. 9, No. 1, p. 8. Norman Cousins, In God We Trust - The Religious Beliefs and Ideas of the Founding Fathers (NY: Harper & Brothers, 1958), p. 63. Ashabel Green, The Life of Ashabel Green (1849). p. 615. William J. Johnson, George Washington - The Christian (St. Paul, MN: William J. Johnson, Merriam Park, February 23, 1919; Nashville, TN: Abingdon Press, 1919; reprinted Milford, MI: Mott Media, 1976; reprinted Arlington Heights, IL: Christian Liberty

Endnotes

Press, 502 West Euclid Avenue, Arlington Heights, Illinois, 60004, 1992), pp. 224-225.
[134] Washington, George. June 14, 1783, in a "Circular Letter Addressed to the Governors of all the States on Disbanding the Army." Old South Leaflets, No. 51. Jared Sparks, ed., The Writings of George Washington 12 vols. (Boston: American Stationer's Company, 1837, NY: F. Andrew's, 1834-1847), Vol. VIII, pp. 440, 444, 452. Selim Peabody, ed., American Patriotism: Speeches, Letters, and Other Papers Which Illustrate the Foundation, the Development, the Preservation of the United States of America (NY: American Book Exchange, 1880), p. 142. William J. Johnson, George Washington - The Christian (St. Paul, MN: William J. Johnson, Merriam Park, February 23, 1919; Nashville, TN: Abingdon Press, 1919; reprinted Milford, MI: Mott Media, 1976; reprinted Arlington Heights, IL: Christian Liberty Press, 502 West Euclid Avenue, Arlington Heights, Illinois, 60004, 1992), pp. 139-141.John Clement Fitzpatrick, ed., The Writings of George Washington, from the Original Manuscript Sources 1749-1799, 39 vols. (Washington, D.C.: United States Government Printing Office, 1931-1944), Vol. 26, p. 483-496. William Barclay Allen, ed., George Washington - A Collection (Indianapolis: Liberty Classics, Liberty Fund, Inc., 7440 N. Shadeland, Indianapolis, Indiana 46250, 1988; based almost entirely on materials reproduced from The Writings of George Washington from the original manuscript sources, 1745-1799/ John Clement Fitzpatrick, editor), pp. 240, 241, 249. Saxe Commins, ed., The Basic Writings of George Washington (NY: Random House, 1948), p. 493. Norman Cousins, In God We Trust - The Religious Beliefs and Ideas of the American Founding Fathers (NY: Harper & Brothers, 1958), p. 55. The Annals of America, 20 vols. (Chicago, IL: Encyclopedia Britannica, 1968), Vol. 2, p. 60. D.P. Diffine, Ph.D., One Nation Under God - How Close a Separation? (Searcy, Arkansas: Harding University, Belden Center for Private Enterprise Education, 6th edition, 1992), p. 8. Stephen McDowell and Mark Beliles, "The Providential Perspective" (Charlottesville, VA: The Providence Foundation, P.O. Box 6759, Charlottesville, Va. 22906, January 1994), Vol. 9, No. 1, p. 4.
[135] Washington, George. May 30, 1778, from his headquarters at Valley Forge, to Landon Carter. Jared Sparks, ed., The Writings of George Washington 12 vols. (Boston: American Stationer's Company, 1837; NY: F. Andrew's, 1834-1847), Vol. V, p. 388. William J. Johnson, George Washington - The Christian (St. Paul, MN: William J. Johnson, Merriam Park, February 23, 1919; Nashville, TN: Abingdon Press, 1919; reprinted Milford, MI: Mott Media, 1976; reprinted Arlington Heights, IL: Christian Liberty Press, 502 West Euclid Avenue, Arlington Heights, Illinois, 60004, 1992), pp. 113-114.
[136] Washington, George. April 30, 1789, in his Inaugural Address. Charles W. Eliot, LL.D., ed., American Historical Documents 1000-1904 (New York: P.F. Collier & Son Company, The Harvard Classics, 1910), Vol. 43, pp. 241-245.
[137] Washington, George. January 1, 1795, from Philadelphia, in a Proclamation of a National Day of Public Thanksgiving and Prayer. Jared Sparks, ed., The Writings of George Washington 12 vols. (Boston: American Stationer's Company, 1837; NY: F. Andrew's, 1834-1847), Vol. XII, pp. 132-134. James D. Richardson (U.S. Representative from Tennessee), ed., A Compilation of the Messages and Papers of the Presidents 1789-1897, 10 vols. (Washington, D.C.: U.S. Government Printing Office, published by Authority of Congress, 1897, 1899; Washington, D.C.: Bureau of National Literature and Art, 1789-1902, 11 vols., 1907, 1910), Vol. I, pp. 179-180. William J. Johnson, George Washington - The Christian (St. Paul, MN: William J. Johnson, Merriam Park, February 23, 1919; Nashville, TN: Abingdon Press, 1919; reprinted Milford, MI: Mott Media, 1976; reprinted Arlington Heights, IL: Christian Liberty Press, 502 West Euclid Avenue, Arlington Heights, Illinois, 60004, 1992), pp. 215-217.
[138] Washington, George. May 2, 1778, orders issued to his troops at Valley Forge. George Washington, General Orders (Mount Vernon, VA: Archives of Mount Vernon). Henry Whiting, Revolutionary Orders of General Washington, selected from MSS. of John Whiting (1844), p. 74. Benson J. Lossing, The Pictorial Field-Book of the Revolution (1886), Vol. II, p. 140. John Clement Fitzpatrick, ed., The Writings of George Washington, from the Original

Manuscript Sources 1749-1799, 39 vols. (Washington, D.C.: United States Government Printing Office, 1931-1944), Vol. XI, p. 343. William J. Johnson, George Washington - The Christian (St. Paul, MN: William J. Johnson, Merriam Park, February 23, 1919; Nashville, TN: Abingdon Press, 1919; reprinted Milford, MI: Mott Media, 1976; reprinted Arlington Heights, IL: Christian Liberty Press, 502 West Euclid Avenue, Arlington Heights, Illinois, 60004, 1992), p. 112. Norman Cousins, In God We Trust - The Religious Beliefs and Ideas of the Founding Fathers (NY: Harper & Brothers, 1958), p. 51. Peter Marshall & David Manuel, The Glory of America (Bloomington, MN: Garborg's Heart 'N Home, 1991), 9.5. D.P. Diffine, Ph.D., One Nation Under God - How Close a Separation? (Searcy, Arkansas: Harding University, Belden Center for Private Enterprise Education, 6th edition, 1992), p. 8.

[139] Washington, George. May 18, 1789, Monday, in his Presidential reply to the United States Senate. James D. Richardson (U.S. Representative from Tennessee), ed., A Compilation of the Messages and Papers of the Presidents 1789-1897, 10 vols. (Washington, D.C.: U.S. Government Printing Office, published by Authority of Congress, 1897, 1899; Washington, D.C.: Bureau of National Literature and Art, 1789-1902, 11 vols., 1907, 1910), Vol. I, p. 55. William Barclay Allen, ed., George Washington - A Collection (Indianapolis: Liberty Classics, Liberty Fund, Inc., 7440 N. Shadeland, Indianapolis, Indiana 46250, 1988; based almost entirely on materials reproduced from The Writings of George Washington from the original manuscript sources, 1745-1799/John Clement Fitzpatrick, editor), p. 465. John Clement Fitzpatrick, ed., The Writings of George Washington, from the Original Manuscript Sources 1749-1799, 39 vols. (Washington, D.C.: United States Government Printing Office, 1931-1944).

[140] Washington, George. June 29, 1788, in a letter written from Mount Vernon to Benjamin Lincoln. John Clement Fitzpatrick, ed., The Writings of George Washington, from the Original Manuscript Sources 1749-1799, 39 vols. (Washington, D.C.: United States Government Printing Office, 1931-1944), Vol. XXX, p. 11. William Barclay Allen, ed., George Washington - A Collection (Indianapolis: Liberty Classics, Liberty Fund, Inc., 7440 N. Shadeland, Indianapolis, Indiana 46250, 1988; based almost entirely on materials reproduced from The Writings of George Washington from the original manuscript sources, 1745-1799/John Clement Fitzpatrick, editor), pp. 403-404. Peter Marshall and David Manuel, The Glory of America (Bloomington, MN: Garborg's Heart'N Home, Inc., 1991), 6.30.

[141] Washington, George. May 15, 1776, in his issued orders. Jared Sparks, ed., The Writings of George Washington 12 vols. (Boston: American Stationer's Company, 1837; NY: F. Andrew's, 1834-1847), Vol. III, p. 392. William J. Johnson, George Washington - The Christian (St. Paul, MN: William J. Johnson, Merriam Park, February 23, 1919; Nashville, TN: Abingdon Press, 1919; reprinted Milford, MI: Mott Media, 1976; reprinted Arlington Heights, IL: Christian Liberty Press, 502 West Euclid Avenue, Arlington Heights, Illinois, 60004, 1992), p. 81.

[142] Washington, George. March 6, 1776, from the headquarters at Cambridge, in his command for a Day of Prayer, Fasting, and Humiliation. Dorothy Dudley, The Cambridge of 1776, with the diary of Dorothy Dudley, (1876), p. 59. William J. Johnson, George Washington - The Christian (St. Paul, MN: William J. Johnson, Merriam Park, February 23, 1919; Nashville, TN: Abingdon Press, 1919; reprinted Milford, MI: Mott Media, 1976; reprinted Arlington Heights, IL: Christian Liberty Press, 502 West Euclid Avenue, Arlington Heights, Illinois, 60004, 1992), p. 77. John Eidsmoe, Christianity and The Constitution - The Faith of Our Founding Fathers (Baker Book House, 1987), p. 139.

[143] Washington, George. March 6, 1776, from the headquarters at Cambridge, in his command for a Day of Prayer, Fasting, and Humiliation. Dorothy Dudley, The Cambridge of 1776, with the diary of Dorothy Dudley, (1876), p. 59. William J. Johnson, George Washington - The Christian (St. Paul, MN: William J. Johnson, Merriam Park, February 23, 1919; Nashville, TN: Abingdon Press, 1919; reprinted Milford, MI: Mott Media, 1976; reprinted Arlington Heights, IL: Christian Liberty Press, 502 West Euclid Avenue, Arlington Heights, Illinois, 60004, 1992), p. 77. John Eidsmoe, Christianity and The Constitution - The Faith of Our

Endnotes

Founding Fathers (Baker Book House, 1987), p. 139.
[144] Washington, George. October 3, 1789, from the city of New York, President issued a Proclamation of a National Day of Thanksgiving. Jared Sparks, ed., The Writings of George Washington 12 vols. (Boston: American Stationer's Company, 1837, NY: F. Andrew's, 1834-1847), Vol. XII, p. 119. James D. Richardson (U.S. Representative from Tennessee), ed., A Compilation of the Messages and Papers of the Presidents 1789-1897, 10 vols. (Washington, D.C.: U.S. Government Printing Office, published by Authority of Congress, 1897, 1899; Washington, D.C.: Bureau of National Literature and Art, 1789-1902, 11 vols., 1907, 1910), Vol. 1, p. 64. William J. Johnson, George Washington - The Christian (St. Paul, MN: William J. Johnson, Merriam Park, February 23, 1919; Nashville, TN: Abingdon Press, 1919; reprinted Milford, MI: Mott Media, 1976; reprinted Arlington Heights, IL: Christian Liberty Press, 502 West Euclid Avenue, Arlington Heights, Illinois, 60004, 1992), pp. 172-174. William Barclay Allen, ed., George Washington - A Collection (Indianapolis: Liberty Classics, Liberty Fund, Inc., 7440 N. Shadeland, Indianapolis, Indiana 46250, 1988; based almost entirely on materials reproduced from The Writings of George Washington from the original manuscript sources, 1745-1799/John Clement Fitzpatrick, editor), pp. 534-353. John Clement Fitzpatrick, ed., The Writings of George Washington, from the Original Manuscript Sources 1749-1799, 39 vols. (Washington, D.C.: United States Government Printing Office, 1931-1944). John F. Schroeder, ed., Maxims of Washington (Mt. Vernon: Mt. Vernon Ladies' Association, 1942), pp. 275, 287. Anson Phelps Stokes and Leo Pfeffer, Church and State in the United States, 3 vols. (NY: Harper & Brothers, 1950), p. 87. Pat Robertson, America's Dates with Destiny (Nashville: Thomas Nelson Publishers, 1986), p. 112. Tim LaHaye, Faith of Our Founding Fathers (Brentwood, TN: Wolgemuth & Hyatt, Publishers, Inc., 1987), pp. 104-106. John Eidsmoe, Christianity and the Constitution - The Faith of Our Founding Fathers (Grand Rapids, MI: Baker Book House, A Mott Media Book, 1987, 6th printing 1993), p. 118. Gary DeMar, The Biblical Worldview (Atlanta, GA: An American Vision Publication - American Vision, Inc., 1992), Vol. 8, No. 12, p. 8. D.P. Diffine, Ph.D., One Nation Under God - How Close a Separation? (Searcy, Arkansas: Harding University, Belden Center for Private Enterprise Education, 6th edition, 1992), p. 9. Gary DeMar, America's Christian History: The Untold Story (Atlanta, GA: American Vision Publishers, Inc., 1993), pp. 76-77.
[145] Washington, George. April 30, 1789, Thursday, in his First Inaugural Address. National Archives, Original work and facsimile, (complete text), No. 22 (Washington: 1952). Jared Sparks, ed., The Writings of George Washington 12 vols. (Boston: American Stationer's Company, 1837, NY: F. Andrew's, 1834-1847), Vol. XII, pp. 2-5. James D. Richardson (U.S. Representative from Tennessee), ed., A Compilation of the Messages and Papers of the Presidents 1789-1897, 10 vols. (Washington, D.C.: U.S. Government Printing Office, published by Authority of Congress, 1897, 1899; Washington, D.C.: Bureau of National Literature and Art, 1789-1902, 11 vols., 1907, 1910), Vol. 1, pp. 52-53. Inaugural Addresses of the Presidents of the United States - From George Washington 1789 to Richard Milhous Nixon 1969 (Washington, D.C.: United States Government Printing Office; 91st Congress, 1st Session, House Document 91-142, 1969), pp. 1-4. Charles W. Eliot, LL.D., ed., American Historical Documents 1000-1904 (New York: P.F. Collier & Son Company, The Harvard Classics, 1910), Vol. 43, pp. 241-245. William J. Johnson, George Washington - The Christian (St. Paul, MN: William J. Johnson, Merriam Park, February 23, 1919; Nashville, TN: Abingdon Press, 1919; reprinted Milford, MI: Mott Media, 1976; reprinted Arlington Heights, IL: Christian Liberty Press, 502 West Euclid Avenue, Arlington Heights, Illinois, 60004, 1992), pp. 161-162. John Clement Fitzpatrick, ed., The Writings of George Washington, from the Original Manuscript Sources 1749-1799, 39 vols. (Washington, D.C.: United States Government Printing Office, 1931-1944), Vol. XXX, pp. 291-296. William Barclay Allen, ed., George Washington - A Collection (Indianapolis: Liberty Classics, Liberty Fund, Inc., 7440 N. Shadeland, Indianapolis, Indiana 46250, 1988; based almost entirely on materials reproduced from The Writings of George Washington from the original

manuscript sources, 1745-1799/John Clement Fitzpatrick, editor), pp. 460-463. John F. Schroeder, ed., Maxims of Washington (Mt. Vernon: Mt. Vernon Ladies' Association, 1942), pp. 287-288. Saxe Commins, ed., The Basic Writings of George Washington (NY: Random House, 1948), complete work, pp. 599-602. Frederick C. Packard, Jr., ed., Are You an American? - Great Americans Speak (NY: Charles Scribner's Sons, 1951), pp. 14-18. Paul M. Angle, ed., By These Words (NY: Rand McNally & Company, 1954), pp. 128-131. Davis Newton Lott, The Inaugural Addresses of the American Presidents (NY: Holt, Rinehart and Winston, 1961), p. 3-5. Charles E. Rice, The Supreme Court and Public Prayer (New York: Fordham University Press, 1964), p. 177-178. Daniel Boorstin, Jr., ed., An American Primer (Chicago: The University of Chicago Press, 1966), complete work, pp. 172-174. Henry Steele Commager, ed., Documents of American History, 2 vols. (NY: F.S. Crofts and Company, 1934; Appleton-Century-Crofts, Inc., 1948, 6th edition, 1958; Englewood Cliffs, NJ: Prentice Hall, Inc., 9th edition, 1973), Vol. I, pp. 152-154. Gary DeMar, God and Government, A Biblical and Historical Study (Atlanta, GA: American Vision Press, 1984), p. 127-28. Pat Robertson, America's Dates With Destiny (Nashville, TN: Thomas Nelson Publishers, 1986), p. 104. Tim LaHaye, Faith of Our Founding Fathers (Brentwood, TN: Wolgemuth & Hyatt, Publishers, Inc., 1987), pp. 63-64, 107. John Eidsmoe, Christianity and the Constitution - The Faith of Our Founding Fathers (Grand Rapids, MI: Baker Book House, A Mott Media Book, 1987, 6th printing 1993), pp. 117, 123. "Our Christian Heritage," Letter from Plymouth Rock (Marlborough, NH: The Plymouth Rock Foundation), p. 4. D.P. Diffine, Ph.D., One Nation Under God - How Close a Separation? (Searcy, Arkansas: Harding University, Belden Center for Private Enterprise Education, 6th edition, 1992), p. 2. J. Michael Sharman, J.D., Faith of the Fathers (Culpepper, Virginia: Victory Publishing, 1995), pp. 18-19.
[116] Washington, George. October 3, 1789, from the city of New York, President issued a Proclamation of a National Day of Thanksgiving. Jared Sparks, ed., The Writings of George Washington 12 vols. (Boston: American Stationer's Company, 1837, NY: F. Andrew's, 1834-1847), Vol. XII, p. 119. James D. Richardson (U.S. Representative from Tennessee), ed., A Compilation of the Messages and Papers of the Presidents 1789-1897, 10 vols. (Washington, D.C.: U.S. Government Printing Office, published by Authority of Congress, 1897, 1899; Washington, D.C.: Bureau of National Literature and Art, 1789-1902, 11 vols., 1907, 1910), Vol. 1, p. 64. William J. Johnson, George Washington - The Christian (St. Paul, MN: William J. Johnson, Merriam Park, February 23, 1919; Nashville, TN: Abingdon Press, 1919; reprinted Milford, MI: Mott Media, 1976; reprinted Arlington Heights, IL: Christian Liberty Press, 502 West Euclid Avenue, Arlington Heights, Illinois, 60004, 1992), pp. 172-174. William Barclay Allen, ed., George Washington - A Collection (Indianapolis: Liberty Classics, Liberty Fund, Inc., 7440 N. Shadeland, Indianapolis, Indiana 46250, 1988; based almost entirely on materials reproduced from The Writings of George Washington from the original manuscript sources, 1745-1799/John Clement Fitzpatrick, editor), pp. 534-353. John Clement Fitzpatrick, ed., The Writings of George Washington, from the Original Manuscript Sources 1749-1799, 39 vols. (Washington, D.C.: United States Government Printing Office, 1931-1944). John F. Schroeder, ed., Maxims of Washington (Mt. Vernon: Mt. Vernon Ladies' Association, 1942), pp. 275, 287. Anson Phelps Stokes and Leo Pfeffer, Church and State in the United States, 3 vols. (NY: Harper & Brothers, 1950), p. 87. Pat Robertson, America's Dates with Destiny (Nashville: Thomas Nelson Publishers, 1986), p. 112. Tim LaHaye, Faith of Our Founding Fathers (Brentwood, TN: Wolgemuth & Hyatt, Publishers, Inc., 1987), pp. 104-106. John Eidsmoe, Christianity and the Constitution - The Faith of Our Founding Fathers (Grand Rapids, MI: Baker Book House, A Mott Media Book, 1987, 6th printing 1993), p. 118. Gary DeMar, The Biblical Worldview (Atlanta, GA: An American Vision Publication - American Vision, Inc., 1992), Vol. 8, No. 12, p. 8. D.P. Diffine, Ph.D., One Nation Under God - How Close a Separation? (Searcy, Arkansas: Harding University, Belden Center for Private Enterprise Education, 6th edition, 1992), p. 9. Gary DeMar, America's Christian History: The Untold Story (Atlanta, GA: American Vision Publishers, Inc., 1993), pp. 76-77.

Endnotes

[147] Washington, George. September 1775, in a handbill written from the headquarters at Cambridge to be distributed in Canada prior to the arrival of Colonel Benedict Arnold. Jared Sparks, ed., The Writings of George Washington 12 vols. (Boston: American Stationer's Company, 1837; NY: F. Andrew's, 1834-1847), Vol. III, p. 92. William J. Johnson, George Washington - The Christian (St. Paul, MN: William J. Johnson, Merriam Park, February 23, 1919; Nashville, TN: Abingdon Press, 1919; reprinted Milford, MI: Mott Media, 1976; reprinted Arlington Heights, IL: Christian Liberty Press, 502 West Euclid Avenue, Arlington Heights, Illinois, 60004, 1992), p. 72. William Barclay Allen, ed., George Washington - A Collection (Indianapolis: Liberty Classics, Liberty Fund, Inc., 7440 N. Shadeland, Indianapolis, Indiana 46250, 1988; based almost entirely on materials reproduced from The Writings of George Washington from the original manuscript sources, 1745-1799/John Clement Fitzpatrick, editor), pp. 46-48. John Clement Fitzpatrick, ed., The Writings of George Washington, from the Original Manuscript Sources 1749-1799, 39 vols. (Washington, D.C.: United States Government Printing Office, 1931-1944).

[148] Washington, George. March 17, 1776, in reply to an address from the General Assembly of Massachusetts regarding the recent evacuation of Boston. Jared Sparks, ed., The Writings of George Washington 12 vols. (Boston: American Stationer's Company, 1837, NY: F. Andrew's, 1834-1847), Vol. IX, p. 337. William J. Johnson, George Washington - The Christian (St. Paul, MN: William J. Johnson, Merriam Park, February 23, 1919; Nashville, TN: Abingdon Press, 1919; reprinted Milford, MI: Mott Media, 1976; reprinted Arlington Heights, IL: Christian Liberty Press, 502 West Euclid Avenue, Arlington Heights, Illinois, 60004, 1992), pp. 77-78.

[149] Washington, George. November 27, 1783, in a letter to the ministers, elders, deacons, and members of the Reformed German Congregation of New York. William Barclay Allen, ed., George Washington - A Collection (Indianapolis: Liberty Classics, Liberty Fund, Inc., 7440 N. Shadeland, Indianapolis, Indiana 46250, 1988; based almost entirely on materials reproduced from The Writings of George Washington from the original manuscript sources, 1745-1799/John Clement Fitzpatrick, editor), pp. 270-271. John Clement Fitzpatrick, ed., The Writings of George Washington, from the Original Manuscript Sources 1749-1799, 39 vols. (Washington, D.C.: United States Government Printing Office, 1931-1944). Norman Cousins, In God We Trust - The Religious Beliefs and Ideas of the Founding Fathers (NY: Harper & Brothers, 1958), p. p. 58.

[150] Washington, George. July 31, 1788, from Mount Vernon, in a letter to James McHenry. Jared Sparks, ed., The Writings of George Washington 12 vols. (Boston: American Stationer's Company, 1837; NY: F. Andrew's, 1834-1847), Vol. IX, p. 406. William J. Johnson, George Washington - The Christian (St. Paul, MN: William J. Johnson, Merriam Park, February 23, 1919; Nashville, TN: Abingdon Press, 1919; reprinted Milford, MI: Mott Media, 1976; reprinted Arlington Heights, IL: Christian Liberty Press, 502 West Euclid Avenue, Arlington Heights, Illinois, 60004, 1992), p. 155.

[151] Washington, George. January 1, 1796, in answering a letter from P.A. Adet, the minister plenipotentiary of the French Republic. James D. Richardson (U.S. Representative from Tennessee), ed., A Compilation of the Messages and Papers of the Presidents 1789-1897, 10 vols. (Washington, D.C.: U.S. Government Printing Office, published by Authority of Congress, 1897, 1899; Washington, D.C.: Bureau of National Literature and Art, 1789-1902, 11 vols., 1907, 1910), Vol. X, p. 19.

[152] Washington, George. July 2, 1776, from his Head Quarters in New York the General Orders were issued to his troops. Jared Sparks, ed., The Writings of George Washington 12 vols. (Boston: American Stationer's Company, 1837, NY: F. Andrew's, 1834-1847), Vol. III, p. 449. John Bartlett, Bartlett's Familiar Quotations (Boston: Little, Brown and Company, 1863, 1980), p. 379. William J. Johnson, George Washington - The Christian (St. Paul, MN: William J. Johnson, Merriam Park, February 23, 1919; Nashville, TN: Abingdon Press, 1919; reprinted Arlington Heights, IL: Christian Liberty Press, 502 West Euclid Avenue, Arlington Heights, Illinois, 60004, 1992), p. 82. William

Barclay Allen, ed., George Washington - A Collection (Indianapolis: Liberty Classics, Liberty Fund, Inc., 7440 N. Shadeland, Indianapolis, Indiana 46250, 1988; based almost entirely on materials reproduced from The Writings of George Washington from the original manuscript sources, 1745-1799/John Clement Fitzpatrick, editor), p. 71. John Clement Fitzpatrick, ed., The Writings of George Washington, from the Original Manuscript Sources 1749-1799, 39 vols. (Washington, D.C.: United States Government Printing Office, 1931-1944). Henry Steele Commager and Richard B. Morris, ed., Spirit of '76 (New York: The Bobbs - Merrill Co., Inc., 1958), p. 32. Peter Marshall and David Manuel, The Glory of America (Bloomington, MN: Garborg's Heart'N Home, Inc., 1991), 11.18.

[153] Washington, George. April 20, 1789, in addressing the mayor, recorder, aldermen and Common Council of the City of Philadelphia. Jared Sparks, ed., The Writings of George Washington 12 vols. (Boston: American Stationer's Company, 1837; NY: F. Andrew's, 1834-1847), Vol. XII, p. 145. William J. Johnson, George Washington - The Christian (St. Paul, MN: William J. Johnson, Merriam Park, February 23, 1919; Nashville, TN: Abingdon Press, 1919; reprinted Milford, MI: Mott Media, 1976; reprinted Arlington Heights, IL: Christian Liberty Press, 502 West Euclid Avenue, Arlington Heights, Illinois, 60004, 1992), p. 158.

[154] Washington, George. April 16, 1789, in an address to the mayor, corporation and citizens of Alexandria. Lodge, George Washington, pp. 43-44. William Barclay Allen, ed., George Washington - A Collection (Indianapolis: Liberty Classics, Liberty Fund, Inc., 7440 N. Shadeland, Indianapolis, Indiana 46250, 1988; based almost entirely on materials reproduced from The Writings of George Washington from the original manuscript sources, 1745-1799/ John Clement Fitzpatrick, editor), pp. 436-437. John Clement Fitzpatrick, ed., The Writings of George Washington, from the Original Manuscript Sources 1749-1799, 39 vols. (Washington, D.C.: United States Government Printing Office, 1931-1944).

[155] Washington, George. December 3, 1793, in his Fifth Annual Address to Congress. James D. Richardson (U.S. Representative from Tennessee), ed., A Compilation of the Messages and Papers of the Presidents 1789-1897, 10 vols. (Washington, D.C.: U.S. Government Printing Office, published by Authority of Congress, 1897, 1899; Washington, D.C.: Bureau of National Literature and Art, 1789-1902, 11 vols., 1907, 1910), Vol. I, p. 139. William Barclay Allen, ed., George Washington - A Collection (Indianapolis: Liberty Classics, Liberty Fund, Inc., 7440 N. Shadeland, Indianapolis, Indiana 46250, 1988; based almost entirely on materials reproduced from The writings of George Washington from the original manuscript sources, 1745-1799/John Clement Fitzpatrick, editor), p. 487.

[156] Washington, George. In a letter to his mother during the French and Indian War. Marion Harland, The Story of Mary Washington (1892), p. 91. William J. Johnson, George Washington - The Christian (St. Paul, MN: William J. Johnson, Merriam Park, February 23, 1919; Nashville, TN: Abingdon Press, 1919; reprinted Milford, MI: Mott Media, 1976; reprinted Arlington Heights, IL: Christian Liberty Press, 502 West Euclid Avenue, Arlington Heights, Illinois, 60004, 1992), p. 39.

[157] Washington, George. September 14, 1775, in a personal letter to Colonel Benedict Arnold. Jared Sparks, ed., The Writings of George Washington 12 vols. (Boston: American Stationer's Company, 1837; NY: F. Andrew's, 1834-1847), Vol. III, p. 91. William J. Johnson, George Washington - The Christian (St. Paul, MN: William J. Johnson, Merriam Park, February 23, 1919; Nashville, TN: Abingdon Press, 1919; reprinted Milford, MI: Mott Media, 1976; reprinted Arlington Heights, IL: Christian Liberty Press, 502 West Euclid Avenue, Arlington Heights, Illinois, 60004, 1992), p. 71. John Eidsmoe, Christianity and the Constitution - The Faith of Our Founding Fathers (Grand Rapids, MI: Baker Book House, A Mott Media Book, 1987, 6th printing 1993), p. 122-123.

[158] Washington, George. November 2, 1783, in his Farewell Orders to the Armies of the United States issued from Rock Hill, near Princeton. Jared Sparks, ed., The Writings of George Washington 12 vols. (Boston: American Stationer's Company, 1837; NY: F. Andrew's, 1834-1847), Vol. VIII, pp. 492-496. William J. Johnson, George Washington -

Endnotes

The Christian (St. Paul, MN: William J. Johnson, Merriam Park, February 23, 1919; Nashville, TN: Abingdon Press, 1919; reprinted Milford, MI: Mott Media, 1976; reprinted Arlington Heights, IL: Christian Liberty Press, 502 West Euclid Avenue, Arlington Heights, Illinois, 60004, 1992), pp. 143-144. William Barclay Allen, ed., George Washington - A Collection (Indianapolis: Liberty Classics, Liberty Fund, Inc., 7440 N. Shadeland, Indianapolis, Indiana 46250, 1988; based almost entirely on materials reproduced from The Writings of George Washington from the original manuscript sources, 1745-1799/John Clement Fitzpatrick, editor), pp. 266-271. John Clement Fitzpatrick, ed., The Writings of George Washington, from the Original Manuscript Sources 1749-1799, 39 vols. (Washington, D.C.: United States Government Printing Office, 1931-1944). Saxe Commins, ed., The Basic Writings of George Washington (NY: Random House, 1948), complete work, pp. 499-502. Charles Wallis, ed., Our American Heritage (NY: Harper & Row, Publishers, Inc., 1970), p. 130.

[159] Washington, George. September 22, 1788, from Mount Vernon, in reply to Henry Lee in Congress, who had sent a letter urging him to accept the presidency. Jared Sparks, ed., The Writings of George Washington 12 vols. (Boston: American Stationer's Company, 1837; NY: F. Andrew's, 1834-1847), Vol. IX, p. 431. William J. Johnson, George Washington - The Christian (St. Paul, MN: William J. Johnson, Merriam Park, February 23, 1919; Nashville, TN: Abingdon Press, 1919; reprinted Milford, MI: Mott Media, 1976; reprinted Arlington Heights, IL: Christian Liberty Press, 502 West Euclid Avenue, Arlington Heights, Illinois, 60004, 1992), p. 155-156.

[160] Washington, George. April 30, 1789. In the President's Oath of Office given at his inauguration. John Eidsmoe, Christianity and The Constitution - The Faith of Our Founding Fathers (Baker Book House, 1987), p. 117. The World Book Encyclopedia 22 vols. (Chicago, IL: Field Enterprises Educational Corporation, 1976; Field Enterprises, Inc., 1957; W.F. Quarrie and Company, 8 vols., 1917), Vol. 21, p. 79. Edmund Fuller and David E. Green, God in the White House - The Faiths of American Presidents (NY: Crown Publishers, Inc., 1968), p. 15. Lucille Johnston, Celebrations of a Nation (Arlington, VA: The Year of Thanksgiving Foundation, 1987), p. 142. Pat Robertson, America's Dates with Destiny (Nashville: Thomas Nelson Publishers, 1986), p. 102.

[161] Washington, George. In writing to the Hebrew Congregations of the city of Savannah, Georgia. William Barclay Allen, ed., George Washington - A Collection (Indianapolis: Liberty Classics, Liberty Fund, Inc., 7440 N. Shadeland, Indianapolis, Indiana 46250, 1988; based almost entirely on materials reproduced from The Writings of George Washington from the original manuscript sources, 1745-1799/John Clement Fitzpatrick, editor), p. 549. John Clement Fitzpatrick, ed., The Writings of George Washington, from the Original Manuscript Sources 1749-1799, 39 vols. (Washington, D.C.: United States Government Printing Office, 1931-1944). John F. Schroeder, ed., Maxims of Washington (Mt. Vernon: Mt. Vernon Ladies' Association, 1942), p. 303. Tim LaHaye, Faith of Our Founding Fathers (Brentwood, TN: Wolgemuth & Hyatt, Publishers, Inc., 1987), p. 109.

[162] Washington, George. March 11, 1792, in a letter from Philadelphia to John Armstrong. Jared Sparks, ed., The Writings of George Washington 12 vols. (Boston: American Stationer's Company, 1837; NY: F. Andrew's, 1834-1847), Vol. X, p. 222. William J. Johnson, George Washington - The Christian (St. Paul, MN: William J. Johnson, Merriam Park, February 23, 1919; Nashville, TN: Abingdon Press, 1919; reprinted Milford, MI: Mott Media, 1976; reprinted Arlington Heights, IL: Christian Liberty Press, 502 West Euclid Avenue, Arlington Heights, Illinois, 60004, 1992), p. 210. John Clement Fitzpatrick, ed., The Writings of George Washington, from the Original Manuscript Sources 1749-1799, 39 vols. (Washington, D.C.: United States Government Printing Office, 1931-1944), Vol. XXXII, p. 2. "Our Christian Heritage," Letter from Plymouth Rock (Marlborough, NH: The Plymouth Rock Foundation), p. 4.

[163] Washington, George. Saturday, December 14, 1799, at about eleven o'clock in the evening, in speaking his final words to his secretary, Tobias Lear. Mason L. Weems, The Life

of General Washington (1808), p. 170. William J. Johnson, George Washington - The Christian (St. Paul, MN: William J. Johnson, Merriam Park, February 23, 1919; Nashville, TN: Abingdon Press, 1919; reprinted Milford, MI: Mott Media, 1976; reprinted Arlington Heights, IL: Christian Liberty Press, 502 West Euclid Avenue, Arlington Heights, Illinois, 60004, 1992), p. 234. D. James Kennedy, "The Faith of George Washington" (Fort Lauderdale, Florida: Coral Ridge Ministries), p. 10.

[164] Washington, George. Last Will and Testament. Original in Fairfax County Courthouse, Fairfax, Virginia. William Barclay Allen, ed., George Washington - A Collection (Indianapolis: Liberty Classics, Liberty Fund, Inc., 7440 N. Shadeland, Indianapolis, Indiana 46250, 1988; based almost entirely on materials reproduced from The Writings of George Washington from the original manuscript sources, 1745-1799/John Clement Fitzpatrick, editor), pp. 667-679. John Clement Fitzpatrick, ed., The Writings of George Washington, from the Original Manuscript Sources 1749-1799, 39 vols. (Washington, D.C.: United States Government Printing Office, 1931-1944).

[165] Washington, George. In writing to the Hebrew Congregations of the city of Savannah, Georgia. William Barclay Allen, ed., George Washington - A Collection (Indianapolis: Liberty Classics, Liberty Fund, Inc., 7440 N. Shadeland, Indianapolis, Indiana 46250, 1988; based almost entirely on materials reproduced from The Writings of George Washington from the original manuscript sources, 1745-1799/John Clement Fitzpatrick, editor), p. 549. John Clement Fitzpatrick, ed., The Writings of George Washington, from the Original Manuscript Sources 1749-1799, 39 vols. (Washington, D.C.: United States Government Printing Office, 1931-1944). John F. Schroeder, ed., Maxims of Washington (Mt. Vernon: Mt. Vernon Ladies' Association, 1942), p. 303. Tim LaHaye, Faith of Our Founding Fathers (Brentwood, TN: Wolgemuth & Hyatt, Publishers, Inc., 1987), p. 109.

[166] Washington, George. August 17, 1790, in an address to the Hebrew Congregation in Newport, Rhode Island. William Barclay Allen, ed., George Washington - A Collection (Indianapolis: Liberty Classics, Liberty Fund, Inc., 7440 N. Shadeland, Indianapolis, Indiana 46250, 1988; based almost entirely on materials reproduced from The Writings of George Washington from the original manuscript sources, 1745-1799/John Clement Fitzpatrick, editor), pp. 547-548. John Clement Fitzpatrick, ed., The Writings of George Washington, from the Original Manuscript Sources 1749-1799, 39 vols. (Washington, D.C.: United States Government Printing Office, 1931-1944). Paul F. Boller, Jr., George Washington and Religion (Dallas: Southern Methodist University Press, 1963), pp. 185-186. John Eidsmoe, Christianity and the Constitution - The Faith of Our Founding Fathers (Grand Rapids, MI: Baker Book House, A Mott Media Book, 1987, 6th printing 1993), p. 123.

[167] Penn, William. August 18, 1681, in his letter to the Indians before his arrival. Pennsylvania Historical Society Collection, Philadelphia.

[168] Franklin, Benjamin. Leonard Labaree, ed., The Papers of Benjamin Franklin (New Haven: Yale University Press, 1959), Vol. I, p. 213. Tim LaHaye, Faith of Our Founding Fathers (Brentwood, TN: Wolgemuth & Hyatt, Publishers, Inc., 1987), p. 120.

[169] Franklin, Benjamin. March 9, 1790, in a letter to Ezra Stiles, President of Yale University. Jared Sparks, editor, The Works of Benjamin Franklin (Boston: Tappan, Whittmore and Mason, 1838), Vol. X, p. 424. Tryon Edwards, D.D., The New Dictionary of Thoughts - A Cyclopedia of Quotations (Garden City, NY: Hanover House, 1852; revised and enlarged by C.H. Catrevas, Ralph Emerson Browns and Jonathan Edwards [descendent, along with Tryon, of Jonathan Edwards (1703-1758), president of Princeton], 1891; The Standard Book Company, 1955, 1963), p. 91. Albert Henry Smyth, ed., The Writings of Benjamin Franklin (New York: MacMillan, 1905-7), Vol. 10, p. 84. John Bigelow, Complete Words of Benjamin Franklin. Stephen Abbott Northrop, D.D., A Cloud of Witnesses (Portland, OR: American Heritage Ministries, 1987; Mantle Ministries, 228 Still Ridge, Bulverde, Texas), p. 159. Carl Van Dorn, ed., The Autobiography of Benjamin Franklin (NY: Viking Press, 1945), p. 783. Norman Cousins, In God We Trust - The Religious Beliefs and Ideas of the American Founding Fathers (NY: Harper & Brothers, Publishers, 1955), p. 42. Frank B. Carlson, Our

Endnotes

Presbyterian Heritage, (1973), p. 25. Raymond A. St. John, American Literature for Christian Schools (Greenville, SC: Bob Jones University Press, Inc., 1979), p. 131. Tim LaHaye, Faith of Our Founding Fathers (Brentwood, TN: Wolgemuth & Hyatt, Publishers, Inc., 1987), p. 116. John Eidsmoe, Christianity and The Constitution - The Faith of Our Founding Fathers (Grand Rapids, MI: Baker Book House, 1987), p. 210. D.P. Diffine, Ph.D., One Nation Under God - How Close a Separation? (Searcy, Arkansas: Harding University, Belden Center for Private Enterprise Education, 6th edition, 1992), p. 8. Henry M. Morris, "Sweet Land of Liberty" (El Cajon, CA: Institute for Creation Research, Back to Genesis, No. 91, July 1996), p. a.

[170] Franklin, Benjamin. 1754. Benjamin Franklin, Information on Those Who Would Remove to America (London: M. Gurney, 1754), pp. 22, 23. "Advice on Coming to America," George D. Youstra, ed., America in Person (Greenville, SC: Bob Jones University Press, 1975), p. 109. Tim LaHaye, Faith of Our Founding Fathers (Brentwood, TN: Wolgemuth & Hyatt, Publishers, Inc. 1987), p. 31. Benjamin Franklin, Works of the Late Doctor Benjamin Franklin Consisting of His Life, Written by Himself, Together with Essays, Humorous, Moral & Literary, Chiefly in the Manner of the Spectator, Richard Price, ed., (Dublin: P. Wogan, P. Byrne, J. Moore, and W. Jones, 1793), p. 289.

[171] Sherman, Roger. Lewis Henry Boutell, The Life of Roger Sherman (Chicago: A.C. McClure & Co., 1896), pp. 272-273. Tim LaHaye, Faith of Our Founding Fathers (Brentwood, TN: Wolgemuth & Hyatt, Publishers, Inc., 1987), pp. 136-137.

[172] Jefferson, Thomas. March 4, 1805, Monday, in his Second Inaugural Address. James D. Richardson (U.S. Representative from Tennessee), ed., A Compilation of the Messages and Papers of the Presidents 1789-1897, 10 vols. (Washington, D.C.: U.S. Government Printing Office, published by Authority of Congress, 1897, 1899; Washington, D.C.: Bureau of National Literature and Art, 1789-1902, 11 vols., 1907, 1910), Vol. I, p. 378-382. Inaugural Addresses of the Presidents of the United States - From George Washington 1789 to Richard Milhous Nixon 1969 (Washington, D.C.: United States Government Printing Office; 91st Congress, 1st Session, House Document 91-142, 1969), pp. 17-21. Saul K. Padover, ed., The Complete Jefferson, Containing His Major Writings, Published and Unpublished, Except His Letters (NY: Duell, Sloan & Pearce, 1943), p. 412. Adrienne Koch and William Paden, eds., The Life and Selected Writings of Thomas Jefferson (NY: Random House, 1944), p. 341. Davis Newton Lott, The Inaugural Addresses of the American Presidents (NY: Holt, Rinehart and Winston, 1961), p. 22. Charles E. Rice, The Supreme Court and Public Prayer (New York: Fordham University Press, 1964), p. 179. Arthur Schlesinger Jr., ed., The Chief Executive (NY: Chelsea House Publishers, 1965), p. 20. Richard Maxfield, K. De Lynn Cook, and W. Cleon Skousen, The Real Thomas Jefferson (Washington, D.C.: National Center for Constitutional Studies, 2nd edition, 1981, 1983), pp. 403-440. Gary DeMar, God and Government - A Biblical and Historical Study (Atlanta, GA: American Vision Press, 1982), p. 166. John Eidsmoe, Christianity and The Constitution - The Faith of Our Founding Fathers (Grand Rapids, MI: Baker Book House, 1987), pp. 227-228, 243. John Whitehead, The Rights of Religious Persons in Public Education (Wheaton, IL: Crossway Books, Good News Publishers, 1991), p. 45. Gary DeMar, America's Christian History: The Untold Story (Atlanta, GA: American Vision Publishers, Inc., 1993), p. 116. J. Michael Sharman, J.D., Faith of the Fathers (Culpepper, Virginia: Victory Publishing, 1995), pp. 25-26.

[173] Jefferson, Thomas. April 21, 1803, in a letter to Benjamin Rush. William Linn, The Life of Thomas Jefferson (Ithaca, NY: Mack & Andrus, 1834), p. 265. Norman Cousins, In God We Trust - The Religious Beliefs and Ideas of the American Founding Fathers (NY: Harper & Brothers, 1958), p. 170-171. Richard Maxfield, K. De Lynn Cook, and W. Cleon Skousen, The Real Thomas Jefferson (Washington, D.C.: National Center for Constitutional Studies, 2nd edition, 1981, 1983), pp. 495-496. John Eidsmoe, Christianity and The Constitution - The Faith of Our Founding Fathers (Grand Rapids, MI: Baker Book House, 1987), p. 230. Albert Ellery Bergh, editor, The Writings of Thomas Jefferson (Washington, D.C.: The Thomas Jefferson Memorial Association, 1904), Vol. X, pp. 380. Compiled for Senator A.

Willis Robertson, Letters of Thomas Jefferson on Religion (Williamsburg, VA: The Williamsburg Foundation, April 27, 1960). Burton Stevenson, The Home Book of Quotations-Classical & Modern (New York: Dodd, Mead and Company, 1967), p. 266.
[174] Pinckney, Charles Cotesworth. Article XXXVIII of the Constitution of South Carolina 1778. John J. McGrath, ed., Church and State in American Law: Cases and Materials (Milwaukee: The Bruce Publishing Co., 1962), p. 375.
[175] Pennsylvania, State of. 1776, Constitution, Frame of Government, Chapter 2, Section 10. The Constitutions of the Several Independent States of America (Boston: Norman and Bowen, 1785), p. 81. S.E. Morison, ed., Sources and Documents Illustrating the American Revolution 1764-1788 and the Formation of the Federal Constitution (NY: Oxford University Press, 1923), p. 166. Benjamin Franklin Morris, The Christian Life and Character of the Civil Institutions of the United States (Philadelphia, PA: L. Johnson & Co., 1863; George W. Childs, 1864), p. 233
[176] Vermont, State of. 1792, Constitution, Frame of Government, Chapter II, Section XII. The Constitutions of the Sixteen States (Boston: Manning and Loring, 1797), p. 257.
[177] Tocqueville, Alexis de. August 1831. Alexis de Tocqueville, The Republic of the United States of America and Its Political Institutions - Reviewed and Examined, Henry Reeves, trans., (Garden City, NY: A.S. Barnes & Co., 1851), Vol. I, p. 334. Alexis de Tocqueville, Democracy in America, 2 vols. (NY: Alfred A. Knopf, 1945), Vol. I, pp. 311, 319-320. Alexis de Tocqueville, Democracy in America, George Lawrence, translator, (NY: Harper & Row, 1988) p. 47. Tryon Edwards, D.D., The New Dictionary of Thoughts - A Cyclopedia of Quotations (Garden City, NY: Hanover House, 1852; revised and enlarged by C.H. Catrevas, Ralph Emerson Browns and Jonathan Edwards [descendent, along with Tryon, of Jonathan Edwards (1703-1758), president of Princeton], 1891; The Standard Book Company, 1955, 1963), p. 337. The Annals of America, 20 vols. (Chicago, IL: Encyclopedia Britannica, 1968, 1977), Vol. 5, pp. 486-487, 497. Sidney E. Ahlstrom, A Religious History of the American People (New Haven, CT: Yale University Press, 1972), p. 386. Frederick Kershner, Jr., ed., Tocqueville's America - The Great Quotations (Athens, Ohio: Ohio University Press, Cooper Industries, 1983), p. 62. Charles Colson, Kingdoms in Conflict (Grand Rapids, MI: Zondervan Publishing House, 1987), pp. 228-229, 273. John Eidsmoe, Christianity and the Constitution - The Faith of Our Founding Fathers (Grand Rapids, MI: Baker Book House, A Mott Media Book, 1987; 6th printing, 1993), p. 408. Pat Robertson, The Turning Tide (Dallas: Word Publishing, 1993), p. 270.
[178] Beaumont, Gustave de. 1835, in his work entitled, Marie ou l'Esclavage aux E'tas-Unis (Paris: 1835), Vol. II, p. 183ff. The Annals of America, 20 vols. (Chicago, IL: Encyclopedia Britannica, 1968), Vol. 6, p. 156.
[179] Grund, Francis J. 1837. Francis J. Grund, The Americans in Their Moral, Social and Political Relations, (1837), Vol. I, pp. 281, 292, 294. Anson Phelps Stokes and Leo Pfeffer, Church and State in the United States (NY: Harper and Row, Publishers, 1950, revised one-volume edition, 1964), p. 210.
[180] Matthew D. Staver, "The Ten Commandments in American Law and Government" (Orlando, FL: The Liberty Counsel, P.O. Box 540774, Orlando, FL 32854, 407-875-2100, 407-875-0770 Fax, http://www.lc.org, liberty@lc.org, 2002), pp. 3-4.
[181] Virginia, Second Charter of. May 23, 1609, granted by King James I. Ebenezer Hazard, Historical Collection: Consisting of State Papers and other Authentic Documents: Intended as Materials for an History of the United States of America (Philadelphia: T. Dobson, 1792), Vol. I, p. 72. Perley Poore, ed., The Federal and State Constitutions, Colonial Charters, and Other Organic Laws of the United States (Washington, 1877), Vol. II, p. 1893 ff. Henry Steele Commager, ed., Documents of American History, 2 vols. (NY: F.S. Crofts and Company, 1934; Appleton-Century-Crofts, Inc., 1948, 6th edition, 1958; Englewood Cliffs, NJ: Prentice Hall, Inc., 9th edition, 1973), Vol. I, pp. 10-11.
[182] Massachusetts, Body of Liberties of. 1641. Massachusetts Colonial Records, 1:174. Benjamin Fletcher Wright, Jr., American Interpretations of Natural Law (New York: Russell

Endnotes

& Russell, 1962), p. 33. John Eidsmoe, Christianity and the Constitution - The Faith of Our Founding Fathers (Grand Rapids, MI: Baker Book House, A Mott Media Book, 1987, 6th printing 1993), p. 33. "Our Christian Heritage," Letter from Plymouth Rock (Marlborough, NH: The Plymouth Rock Foundation), p. 2.

[183] Massachusetts Bay Colony, Cambridge Platform of. 1648, included the proposal of William Vassall and others, as recorded in the Plymouth Colony Records IX, 1663. Henry Steele Commager, ed., Documents of American History, 2 vols. (NY: F.S. Crofts and Company, 1934; Appleton-Century-Crofts, Inc., 1948, 6th edition, 1958; Englewood Cliffs, NJ: Prentice Hall, Inc., 9th edition, 1973), Vol. I, pp. 29-31. The Annals of America, 20 vols. (Chicago, IL: Encyclopedia Britannica, 1968), Vol. 1, pp. 90-94.

[184] Connecticut, Code of the General Court of. 1650, in the Capital Laws Section of the Code, which stated offenses and their punishments. The Code of 1650 - Being a Compilation of the Earliest Laws and Orders of the General Court of Connecticut, etc., etc., (Hartford: Silus Andrus, 1822), complete work pages, pp. 20-94. The Annals of America, 20 vols. (Chicago, IL: Encyclopedia Britannica, 1968, 1977), Vol. I, p. 200.

[185] Franklin, Benjamin. June 6, 1753, in a letter from Philadelphia to Joseph Huey. Jared Sparks, Works of Benjamin Franklin (Boston: 1840), Vol. VII. Albert Henry Smyth, ed., The Writings of Benjamin Franklin, 10 vols. (NY: The Macmillan Co., 1905-07), Vol. II, p. 144. Verna M. Hall, The Christian History of the American Revolution (San Francisco: Foundation for Christian Education, 1976), pp. 189-190. Perry Tanksley, To Love is to Give (Jackson, Mississippi: Allgood Books, Box 1329; Parthenon Press, 201 8th Ave., South, Nashville, Tennessee, 1972), p. 27. John Eidsmoe, Christianity and the Constitution - The Faith of Our Founding Fathers (Grand Rapids, MI: Baker Book House, A Mott Media Book, 1987; 6th printing, 1993), p. 200.

[186] Adams, Samuel. November 20, 1772, in a report for the Committees of Correspondence, entitled, The Rights of the Colonists; in the section: "The Rights of the Colonist as Men." Old South Leaflets. David C. Whitney, Signers of the Declaration of Independence - Founders of Freedom (1964), p. 49. The Annals of America, 20 vols. (Chicago, IL: Encyclopedia Britannica, 1968), Vol. 2, p. 217. Lucille Johnston, Celebrations of a Nation (Arlington, VA: The Year of Thanksgiving Foundation, 1987), p. 79.

[187] Jefferson, Thomas. 1786, Notes on the State of Virginia entitled "Republican Notes on Religion and an Act Establishing Religious Freedom, Passed in the Assembly of Virginia, in the Year 1786." H.A. Washington, ed., The Writings of Thomas Jefferson - Being His Autobiography, Correspondence, Reports, Messages, Addresses, and Other Writings, Official and Private, 9 vols. (NY: Derby & Jackson, 1859, Washington, 1853-54. Vol. 8, Philadelphia, 1871), Vol. III, p. 358-406. The Annals of America, 20 vols. (Chicago, IL: Encyclopedia Britannica, 1968), Vol. 2, p. 571. Norman Cousins, In God We Trust - The Religious Beliefs and Ideas of the American Founding Fathers (NY: Harper & Brothers, 1958), p. 123. Thomas Jefferson, Notes on the State of Virginia, Peden, ed., pp. 158-59.

[188] Washington, George. January 27, 1793, in a letter to the congregation of the New Church in Baltimore, Washington. Norman Cousins, In God We Trust - The Religious Beliefs and Ideas of the Founding Fathers (NY: Harper & Brothers, 1958), pp. 48, 62. John F. Schroeder, ed., Maxims of Washington (Mt. Vernon: Mt. Vernon Ladies' Association, 1942), pp. 301-302. Tim LaHaye, Faith of Our Founding Fathers (Brentwood, TN: Wolgemuth & Hyatt, Publishers, Inc., 1987), p. 110. Gary DeMar, America's Christian History: The Untold Story (Atlanta, GA: American Vision Publishers, Inc., 1993), p. 92.

[189] New Jersey, State of. 1776, Constitution, Article XVIII. The Constitutions of the Several Independent States of America (Boston: Norman and Bowen, 1785), p. 73, Section 19. Benjamin Franklin Morris, The Christian Life and Character of the Civil Institutions of the United States (Philadelphia, PA: L. Johnson & Co., 1863; George W. Childs, 1864), p. 234. Frances Newton Thorpe, ed., Federal and State Constitutions, Colonial Charters, and Other Organic Laws of the States, Territories, and Colonies now or heretofore forming the United States, 7 vols. (Washington: Government Printing Office, 1905; 1909; St. Clair Shores, MI:

Scholarly Press, 1968). Edwin S. Gaustad, Neither King nor Prelate - Religion and the New Nation, 1776-1826 (Grand Rapids, MI: William B. Eerdmans Publishing Company, 1993), p. 167-168.

[190] Maryland, State of. 1776, Constitution, Article XIX, XXXIII. Benjamin Franklin Morris, The Christian Life and Character of the Civil Institutions of the United States (Philadelphia, PA: L. Johnson & Co., 1863; George W. Childs, 1864), p. 234. Frances Newton Thorpe, ed., Federal and State Constitutions, Colonial Charters, and Other Organic Laws of the States, Territories, and Colonies now or heretofore forming the United States, 7 vols. (Washington: Government Printing Office, 1905; 1909; St. Clair Shores, MI: Scholarly Press, 1968). Gary DeMar, God And Government, A Biblical and Historical Study (Atlanta, GA: American Vision Press, 1982), p. 164. Edwin S. Gaustad, Neither King nor Prelate - Religion and the New Nation, 1776-1826 (Grand Rapids, MI: William B. Eerdmans Publishing Company, 1993), p. 164.

[191] North Carolina, State of. 1776, Constitution, Article XIX. Frances Newton Thorpe, ed., Federal and State Constitutions, Colonial Charters, and Other Organic Laws of the States, Territories, and Colonies now or heretofore forming the United States, 7 vols. (Washington: Government Printing Office, 1905; 1909; St. Clair Shores, MI: Scholarly Press, 1968), Vol. V, p. 2788. Edwin S. Gaustad, Neither King nor Prelate - Religion and the New Nation, 1776-1826 (Grand Rapids, MI: William B. Eerdmans Publishing Company, 1993), p. 168. Anson Phelps Stokes and Leo Pfeffer, Church and State in the United States (NY: Harper and Row, Publishers, 1950, revised one-volume edition, 1964), p. 54.

[192] North Carolina, State of. 1776, Constitution, Article XXXII. The Constitutions of the Several Independent States of America, Published by Order of Congress (Boston: Norman & Bowen, 1785) p. 138. The Constitutions of All the United States According to the Latest Amendments (Lexington, KY: Thomas T. Skillman, 1817), p. 224. Benjamin Franklin Morris, The Christian Life and Character of the Civil Institutions of the United States (Philadelphia, PA: L. Johnson & Co., 1863; George W. Childs, 1864), p. 233. Supreme Court Justice David Josiah Brewer, who served 1890-1910, in his work, The United States - Christian Nation (Philadelphia: The John C. Winston Company, 1905, Supreme Court Collection). Frances Newton Thorpe, ed., Federal and State Constitutions, Colonial Charters, and Other Organic Laws of the States, Territories, and Colonies now or heretofore forming the United States, 7 vols. (Washington: Government Printing Office, 1905; 1909; St. Clair Shores, MI: Scholarly Press, 1968). Gary DeMar, "Censoring America's Christian History" (Atlanta, GA: The Biblical Worldview, An American Vision Publication - American Vision, Inc., July 1990), p. 7. Gary DeMar, America's Christian History: The Untold Story (Atlanta, GA: American Vision Publishers, Inc., 1993), p. 68.

[193] Vermont, State of. 1777, Constitution, Declaration of Rights, III. Perley Poore, ed., The Federal and State Constitutions, Colonial Charters, and Other Organic Laws of the United States (Washington, 1877). Frances Newton Thorpe, ed., Federal and State Constitutions, Colonial Charters, and Other Organic Laws of the States, Territories, and Colonies now or heretofore forming the United States, 7 vols. (Washington: Government Printing Office, 1905; 1909; St. Clair Shores, MI: Scholarly Press, 1968). The Annals of America, 20 vols. (Chicago, IL: Encyclopedia Britannica, 1968), Vol. 2, p. 485. Edwin S.Gaustad, Neither King nor Prelate - Religion and the New Nation, 1776-1826 (Grand Rapids, MI: William B. Eerdmans Publishing Company, 1993), p. 173.

[194] South Carolina, State of. 1778, Constitution, Article XXXVIII. Benjamin Franklin Morris, The Christian Life and Character of the Civil Institutions of the United States (Philadelphia, PA: L. Johnson & Co., 1863; George W. Childs, 1864), pp. 230-231. Frances Newton Thorpe, ed., Federal and State Constitutions, Colonial Charters, and Other Organic Laws of the States, Territories, and Colonies now or heretofore forming the United States, 7 vols. (Washington: Government Printing Office, 1905; 1909; St. Clair Shores, MI: Scholarly Press, 1968), Vol. V, p. 3264. Edwin S. Gaustad, Neither King nor Prelate - Religion and the New Nation 1776-1826 (Grand Rapids, MI: William B. Eerdmans Publishing Company, 1993),

Endnotes

pp. 171-172. John J. McGrath, ed., Church and State in American Law: Cases and Materials (Milwaukee: The Bruce Publishing Co., 1962), p. 375. Anson Phelps Stokes and Leo Pfeffer, Church and State in the United States (NY: Harper and Row, Publishers, 1950, revised one-volume edition, 1964), p. 79.
[195] Massachusetts, State of. 1780, Constitution, Part I, Article II. The Constitutions of All the United States According to the Latest Amendments (Lexington, KY: Thomas T. Skillman, 1817), pp. 60, 62. Frances Newton Thorpe, ed., Federal and State Constitutions, Colonial Charters, and Other Organic Laws of the States, Territories, and Colonies now or heretofore forming the United States, 7 vols. (Washington: Government Printing Office, 1905; 1909; St. Clair Shores, MI: Scholarly Press, 1968), Vol. V, p. 38. Henry Steele Commager, ed., Documents of American History, 2 vols. (NY: F.S. Crofts and Company, 1934; Appleton-Century-Crofts, Inc., 1948, 6th edition, 1958; Englewood Cliffs, NJ: Prentice Hall, Inc., 9th edition, 1973), Vol. I, pp. 107-108. The Annals of America, 20 vols. (Chicago, IL: Encyclopedia Britannica, 1968), Vol. I, pp. 322-333. Jacob C. Meyer, Church and State in Massachusetts from 1740-1833 (Cleveland: Western Reserve Press, 1930) pp. 234-235. Anson Phelps Stokes and Leo Pfeffer, Church and State in the United States (NY: Harper and Row, Publishers, 1950, revised one-volume edition, 1964), p. 77. The Constitutions of the Several Independent States of America (Philadelphia: Bailey, published by order of the U.S. Continental Congress, 1781, in the Evans Collection, #17390), p. 138. Gary DeMar, "Censoring America's Christian History" (Atlanta, GA: The Biblical Worldview, An American Vision Publication - American Vision, Inc., July 1990), p. 7.
[196] New Hampshire, State of. 1838, cited in the Massachusetts Supreme Court case of Commonwealth v. Abner Kneeland, 37 Mass. (20 Pick) 206, 207, 216-218 (Sup. Ct. Mass. 1838).
[197] New Hampshire, State of. 1784, 1792, Part One, Article I, Section V. The Constitutions of All the United States According to the Latest Amendments (Lexington, KY: Thomas T. Skillman, 1817), pp. 27, 29. The Constitutions of the Several Independent States of America, Published by Order of Congress (Boston: Norman & Bowen, 1785) p. 3-4. Frances Newton Thorpe, ed., Federal and State Constitutions, Colonial Charters, and Other Organic Laws of the States, Territories, and Colonies now or heretofore forming the United States, 7 vols. (Washington: Government Printing Office, 1905; 1909; St. Clair Shores, MI: Scholarly Press, 1968). Charles E. Rice, The Supreme Court and Public Prayer (New York: Fordham University Press, 1964), p. 172; "Hearings, Prayers in Public Schools and Other Matters," Committee on the Judiciary, U.S. Senate (87th Cong., 2nd Sess.), 1962, pp. 268 et seq. New Hampshire Manuel (1937), pp. 9-10.5. Edwin S. Gaustad, Neither King nor Prelate - Religion and the New Nation, 1776-1826 (Grand Rapids, MI: William B. Eerdmans Publishing Company, 1993), p. 166.
[198] Tennessee, State of. 1796, Constitution, Article XI, Section 3. Frances Newton Thorpe, ed., Federal and State Constitutions, Colonial Charters, and Other Organic Laws of the States, Territories, and Colonies now or heretofore forming the United States, 7 vols. (Washington: Government Printing Office, 1905; 1909; St. Clair Shores, MI: Scholarly Press, 1968). Edwin S. Gaustad, Neither King nor Prelate - Religion and the New Nation, 1776-1826 (Grand Rapids, MI: William B. Eerdmans Publishing Company, 1993), pp. 172-73. Governor Ned McWherter and Secretary of State Riley C. Darnell, Proclamation declaring Christian Heritage Week, August 29 - September 4, 1993, signed June 21, 1993, in the Capitol City of Nashville. Courtesy of Bruce Barilla, Christian Heritage Week Ministry (P.O. Box 58, Athens, W.V. 24712; 304-384-7707, 304-384-9044 fax).
[199] Tennessee, State of. 1796, Constitution, Article VIII, Section II; Article XI, Section IV. The Constitutions of the Sixteen States (Boston: Manning and Loring, 1797), pp. 274, 277. The Constitutions of All the United States According to the Latest Amendments (Lexington, KY: Thomas T. Skillman, 1817), p. 287. The Constitutions of the United States of America, pp. 342, 344. Frances Newton Thorpe, ed., Federal and State Constitutions, Colonial Charters, and Other Organic Laws of the States, Territories, and Colonies now or heretofore

forming the United States, 7 vols. (Washington: Government Printing Office, 1905; 1909; St. Clair Shores, MI: Scholarly Press, 1968). Edwin S. Gaustad, Neither King nor Prelate - Religion and the New Nation, 1776-1826 (Grand Rapids, MI: William B. Eerdmans Publishing Company, 1993), p. 172.

[200] Georgia, State of. 1798, Constitution, Article IV, Section 10. Frances Newton Thorpe, ed., Federal and State Constitutions, Colonial Charters, and Other Organic Laws of the States, Territories, and Colonies now or heretofore forming the United States, 7 vols. (Washington: Government Printing Office, 1905; 1909; St. Clair Shores, MI: Scholarly Press, 1968). Edwin S. Gaustad, Neither King nor Prelate - Religion and the New Nation, 1776-1826 (Grand Rapids, MI: William B. Eerdmans Publishing Company, 1993), pp. 162-163.

[201] Connecticut, State of. 1818, Constitution, Article VII, Section 1. The Constitutions of the Several States Composing the Union (Philadelphia: Hogan and Thompson, 1838), p. 110. Benjamin Franklin Morris, The Christian Life and Character of the Civil Institutions of the United States (Philadelphia, PA: L. Johnson & Co., 1863; George W. Childs, 1864), p. 236. Charles E. Rice, The Supreme Court and Public Prayer (New York: Fordham University Press, 1964), p. 168; "Hearings, Prayers in Public Schools and Other Matters," Committee on the Judiciary, U.S. Senate (87th Cong., 2nd Sess.), 1962, pp. 268 et seq.

[202] Maine, State of. 1819, Constitution, Article I, Section 3. Charles E. Rice, The Supreme Court and Public Prayer (New York: Fordham University Press, 1964), p. 170; "Hearings, Prayers in Public Schools and Other Matters," Committee on the Judiciary, U.S. Senate (87th Cong., 2nd Sess.), 1962, pp. 268 et seq.

[203] Delaware, State of. 1831, Constitution, Article I. Frances Newton Thorpe, ed., Federal and State Constitutions, Colonial Charters, and Other Organic Laws of the States, Territories, and Colonies now or heretofore forming the United States, 7 vols. (Washington: Government Printing Office, 1905; 1909; St. Clair Shores, MI: Scholarly Press, 1968). Edwin S. Gaustad, Neither King nor Prelate - Religion and the New Nation, 1776-1826 (Grand Rapids, MI: William B. Eerdmans Publishing Company, 1993), pp. 161-162. Charles E. Rice, The Supreme Court and Public Prayer (New York: Fordham University Press, 1964), p. 168; "Hearings, Prayers in Public Schools and Other Matters," Committee on the Judiciary, U.S. Senate (87th Cong., 2nd Sess.), 1962, pp. 268 et seq. Gary DeMar, God and Government, A Biblical and Historical Study (Atlanta, Georgia: American Vision Press), Vol. 1, pp. 164-165. Church of the Holy Trinity v. U.S., 143 U.S. 457, 469-470. Recorded in The State of Delaware Executive Proclamation of November 14 - 20, 1993, as "Christian Heritage Week," signed by Governor Thomas R. Caper, and Lieutenant Governor Ruth Ann Minner. Courtesy of Bruce Barilla, Christian Heritage Week Ministry (P.O. Box 58, Athens, W.V. 24712; 304-384-7707, 304-384-9044 fax).

[204] Florida, State of. 1838. Constitution, Bill of Rights. Frances Newton Thorpe, ed., Federal and State Constitutions, Colonial Charters, and Other Organic Laws of the States, Territories, and Colonies now or heretofore forming the United States, 7 vols. (Washington: Government Printing Office, 1905; 1909; St. Clair Shores, MI: Scholarly Press, 1968), Vol. II, p. 664. Anson Phelps Stokes and Leo Pfeffer, Church and State in the United States (NY: Harper and Row, Publishers, 1950, revised one-volume edition, 1964), p. 156.

[205] Texas, State of. August 27, 1845, Constitution, Article I, Section 4. Journals of the Convention, Assembled at the City of Austin on the Fourth of July, 1845, for the purpose of framing a Constitution for the State of Texas (Austin, TX: Miner & Cruger, Printers to the Convention, 1845; A Facsimile Reproduction of the 1845 Edition with a Preface by Mary Bell Hart, Shoal Creek Publishers, 1974), p. 339.

[206] Wisconsin, State of. 1848, Constitution, Article I, Section 18. Charles E. Rice, The Supreme Court and Public Prayer (New York: Fordham University Press, 1964), p. 176; "Hearings, Prayers in Public Schools and Other Matters," Committee on the Judiciary, U.S. Senate (87th Cong., 2nd Sess.), 1962, pp. 268 et seq.

[207] Indiana, State of. 1851, Constitution, Article I, Section 2. Charles E. Rice, The Supreme Court and Public Prayer (New York: Fordham University Press, 1964), p. 169; "Hearings,

Endnotes

Prayers in Public Schools and Other Matters," Committee on the Judiciary, U.S. Senate (87th Cong., 2nd Sess.), 1962, pp. 268 et seq.

[208] Ohio, State of. 1852, Constitution, Bill of Rights, Article I, Section 7. The Constitutions of the United States of America with the Latest Amendments (Trenton: Moore & Lake, 1813), p. 334. Frances Newton Thorpe, ed., Federal and State Constitutions, Colonial Charters, and Other Organic Laws of the States, Territories, and Colonies now or heretofore forming the United States, 7 vols. (Washington: Government Printing Office, 1905; 1909; St. Clair Shores, MI: Scholarly Press, 1968). Charles E. Rice, The Supreme Court and Public Prayer (New York: Fordham University Press, 1964), pp. 173-174; "Hearings, Prayers in Public Schools and Other Matters," Committee on the Judiciary, U.S. Senate (87th Cong., 2nd Sess.), 1962, pp. 268 et seq.

[209] Minnesota, State of. 1857, Constitution, Bill of Rights, Article I, Section 16. Charles E. Rice, The Supreme Court and Public Prayer (New York: Fordham University Press, 1964), p. 171; "Hearings, Prayers in Public Schools and Other Matters," Committee on the Judiciary, U.S. Senate (87th Cong., 2nd Sess.), 1962, pp. 268 et seq.

[210] Oregon, State of. 1857, Constitution, Bill of Rights, Article I, Section 2. Charles E. Rice, The Supreme Court and Public Prayer (New York: Fordham University Press, 1964), p. 174; "Hearings, Prayers in Public Schools and Other Matters," Committee on the Judiciary, U.S. Senate (87th Cong., 2nd Sess.), 1962, pp. 268 et seq.

[211] Kansas, State of. 1859, Constitution, Bill of Rights, Section 7. Charles E. Rice, The Supreme Court and Public Prayer (New York: Fordham University Press, 1964), pp. 169-170; "Hearings, Prayers in Public Schools and Other Matters," Committee on the Judiciary, U.S. Senate (87th Cong., 2nd Sess.), 1962, pp. 268 et seq.

[212] Pennsylvania, State of. 1874, Constitution, Article I, Section 3. Charles E. Rice, The Supreme Court and Public Prayer (New York: Fordham University Press, 1964), p. 174; "Hearings, Prayers in Public Schools and Other Matters," Committee on the Judiciary, U.S. Senate (87th Cong., 2nd Sess.), 1962, pp. 268 et seq.

[213] Arkansas, State of. 1874, Constitution, Article II, Section 24. Constitutions of the United States - National and State (Dobbs Ferry, New York: Oceana Publications, Inc., published for Legislative Drafting Research Fund of Columbia University, Release 94-4, Issued October 1994), Vol. 1, Arkansas(October 1994), p. 4. Charles E. Rice, The Supreme Court and Public Prayer (New York: Fordham University Press, 1964), p. 167; "Hearings, Prayers in Public Schools and Other Matters," Committee on the Judiciary, U.S. Senate (87th Cong., 2nd Sess.), 1962, pp. 268 et seq.

[214] Arkansas, State of. 1874, Constitution, Article XIX, Section 1. Constitutions of the United States - National and State (Dobbs Ferry, New York: Oceana Publications, Inc., published for Legislative Drafting Research Fund of Columbia University, Release 94-4, Issued October 1994), Vol. 1, Arkansas(October 1994), p. 32. Charles E. Rice, The Supreme Court and Public Prayer (New York: Fordham University Press, 1964), p. 168; "Hearings, Prayers in Public Schools and Other Matters," Committee on the Judiciary, U.S. Senate (87th Cong., 2nd Sess.), 1962, pp. 268 et seq.

[215] Nebraska, State of. June 12, 1875, Constitution, Bill of Rights, Article I, Section 4. Charles E. Rice, The Supreme Court and Public Prayer (New York: Fordham University Press, 1964), p. 172; "Hearings, Prayers in Public Schools and Other Matters," Committee on the Judiciary, U.S. Senate (87th Cong., 2nd Sess.), 1962, pp. 268 et seq.

[216] South Dakota, State of. 1889, Constitution, Article VI, Section 3. Charles E. Rice, The Supreme Court and Public Prayer (New York: Fordham University Press, 1964), p. 175; "Hearings, Prayers in Public Schools and Other Matters," Committee on the Judiciary, U.S. Senate (87th Cong., 2nd Sess.), 1962, pp. 268 et seq.

[217] Michigan, State of. 1908, Constitution, Article II, Section 3. Charles E. Rice, The Supreme Court and Public Prayer (New York: Fordham University Press, 1964), p. 171; "Hearings, Prayers in Public Schools and Other Matters," Committee on the Judiciary, U.S. Senate (87th Cong., 2nd Sess.), 1962, pp. 268 et seq.

[218] New Mexico, State of. 1911, Constitution, Article II, Section 2. Charles E. Rice, The Supreme Court and Public Prayer (New York: Fordham University Press, 1964), p. 173; "Hearings, Prayers in Public Schools and Other Matters," Committee on the Judiciary, U.S. Senate (87th Cong., 2nd Sess.), 1962, pp. 268 et seq.

[219] Louisiana, State of. 1921, Constitution, Article I, Section 4. Charles E. Rice, The Supreme Court and Public Prayer (New York: Fordham University Press, 1964), p. 170; "Hearings, Prayers in Public Schools and Other Matters," Committee on the Judiciary, U.S. Senate (87th Cong., 2nd Sess.), 1962, pp. 268 et seq.

[220] Missouri, Constitution of the State of. 1945, Bill of Rights, Article I, Section 5. Charles E. Rice, The Supreme Court and Public Prayer (New York: Fordham University Press, 1964), p. 172; "Hearings, Prayers in Public Schools and Other Matters," Committee on the Judiciary, U.S. Senate (87th Cong., 2nd Sess.), 1962, pp. 268 et seq.

[221] Polk, James Knox. March 4, 1845, Tuesday, in his Inaugural Address. James D. Richardson (U.S. Representative from Tennessee), ed., A Compilation of the Messages and Papers of the Presidents 1789-1897, 10 vols. (Washington, D.C.: U.S. Government Printing Office, published by Authority of Congress, 1897, 1899; Washington, D.C.: Bureau of National Literature and Art, 1789-1902, 11 vols., 1907, 1910), Vol. 4, pp. 373-382. Benjamin Franklin Morris, The Christian Life and Character of the Civil Institutions of the United States (Philadelphia: George W. Childs, 1864), p. 607. Inaugural Addresses of the Presidents, House Document #540, 1952, p. 90. Inaugural Addresses of the Presidents of the United States - From George Washington 1789 to Richard Milhous Nixon 1969 (Washington, D.C.: United States Government Printing Office; 91st Congress, 1st Session, House Document 91-142, 1969), pp. 89-98. Arthur Schlesinger Jr., ed., The Chief Executive (NY: Chelsea House Publishers, 1965), p. 106. Charles E. Rice, The Supreme Court and Public Prayer (New York: Fordham University Press, 1964), pp. 182-183. Benjamin Weiss, God in American History: A Documentation of America's Religious Heritage (Grand Rapids, MI: Zondervan, 1966), p. 80. Willard Cantelon, Money Master of the World (Plainfield, NJ: Logos International, 1976), p. 120. Peter Marshall and David Manuel, The Glory of America (Bloomington, MN: Garborg's Heart 'N Home, Inc., 1991), 4.6. J. Michael Sharman, J.D., Faith of the Fathers (Culpepper, Virginia: Victory Publishing, 1995), pp. 47-48.

[222] Wilson, (Thomas) Woodrow. November 5, 1915, in an address celebrating the fiftieth Anniversary of the Manhattan Club, at the Biltmore Hotel, New York. A Compilation of the Messages and Papers of the Presidents 20 vols. (New York: Bureau of National Literature, Inc., prepared under the direction of the Joint Committee on Printing, of the House and Senate, pursuant to an Act of the Fifty-Second Congress of the United States, 1893, 1923), Vol. XVI, pp. 8083-8087. [see also: President Woodrow Wilson, July 4, 1913, in a message delivered at Gettysburg, Pennsylvania. A Compilation of the Messages and Papers of the Presidents 20 vols. (New York: Bureau of National Literature, Inc., prepared under the direction of the Joint Committee on Printing, of the House and Senate, pursuant to an Act of the Fifty-Second Congress of the United States, 1893, 1923), Vol. XVI, pp. 7883-7884.]

[223] Roosevelt, Franklin Delano. January 6, 1941, in his Four Freedoms Speech to Congress. Samuel I. Rosenman, ed., The Public Papers of Franklin D. Roosevelt (NY:1941) Vol. VI, p. 411. Paul M. Angle, ed., By These Words (NY: Rand McNally & Company, 1954), pp. 381-382. Richard D. Heffner, A Documentary History of the United States (New York: The New American Library of World Literature, Inc., 1961), pp. 282-289. The Annals of America, 20 vols. (Chicago, IL: Encyclopedia Britannica, 1968), Vol. 16, p. 456. Peter Marshall & David Manuel, The Glory of America (Bloomington, MN: Garborg's Heart 'N Home, 1991), 1.6.

[224] Truman, Harry S. March 6, 1946, at noon, in an addressed, nationally broadcast via radio, given to a Conference of the Federal Council of Churches in Deshler-Wallick Hotel, Columbus, Ohio. Public Papers of the Presidents: Harry S. Truman, 1946 - Containing Public Messages, Speeches, and Statements of the President, January 1 to December 31, 1946 (Washington, DC: United States Government Printing Office, 1962), Item 52, p. 141.

[225] Truman, Harry S. January 20, 1949, in his Inaugural Address. Harry S. Truman, Memoirs

Endnotes

by Harry S. Truman - Volume Two: Years of Trial and Hope (Garden City, NY: Doubleday & Company, Inc., 1956), pp. 226-227. Inaugural Addresses of the Presidents of the United States - From George Washington 1789 to Richard Milhous Nixon 1969 (Washington, D.C.: United States Government Printing Office; 91st Congress, 1st Session, House Document 91-142, 1969), pp. 251-256. Davis Newton Lott, The Inaugural Addresses of the American Presidents (NY: Holt, Rinehart and Winston, 1961), pp. 251-255. Charles E. Rice, The Supreme Court and Public Prayer (New York: Fordham University Press, 1964), pp. 191-192. Lillian W. Kay, ed., The Ground on Which We Stand - Basic Documents of American History (NY: Franklin Watts., Inc, 1969), p. 275. Benjamin Weiss, God in American History: A Documentation of America's Religious Heritage (Grand Rapids, MI: Zondervan, 1966), p. 141. Willard Cantelon, Money Master of the World (Plainfield, NJ: Logos International, 1976), p. 121. Proclaim Liberty (Dallas, TX: Word of Faith), p. 2. J. Michael Sharman, J.D., Faith of the Fathers (Culpepper, Virginia: Victory Publishing, 1995), pp. 102-104. T.S. Settel, and the staff of Quote, editors, The Quotable Harry Truman introduction by Merle Miller (NY: Droke House Publishers, Inc., Berkley Publishing Corporation, 1967), p. 76.
[226] Matthew D. Staver, "The Ten Commandments in American Law and Government" (Orlando, FL: The Liberty Counsel, P.O. Box 540774, Orlando, FL 32854, 407-875-2100, 407-875-0770 Fax, http://www.lc.org, liberty@lc.org, 2002), pp. 4-9.
[227] Massachusetts, Body of Liberties of. 1641. Massachusetts Colonial Records, 1:174. Benjamin Fletcher Wright, Jr., American Interpretations of Natural Law (New York: Russell & Russell, 1962), p. 33. John Eidsmoe, Christianity and the Constitution - The Faith of Our Founding Fathers (Grand Rapids, MI: Baker Book House, A Mott Media Book, 1987, 6th printing 1993), p. 33. "Our Christian Heritage," Letter from Plymouth Rock (Marlborough, NH: The Plymouth Rock Foundation), p. 2.
[228] Massachusetts Bay Colony, Cambridge Platform of. 1648, included the proposal of William Vassall and others, as recorded in the Plymouth Colony Records IX, 1663. Henry Steele Commager, ed., Documents of American History, 2 vols. (NY: F.S. Crofts and Company, 1934; Appleton-Century-Crofts, Inc., 1948, 6th edition, 1958; Englewood Cliffs, NJ: Prentice Hall, Inc., 9th edition, 1973), Vol. I, pp. 29-31. The Annals of America, 20 vols. (Chicago, IL: Encyclopedia Britannica, 1968), Vol. 1, pp. 90-94.
[229] Connecticut, Code of the General Court of. 1650, in the Capital Laws Section of the Code, which stated offenses and their punishments. The Code of 1650 - Being a Compilation of the Earliest Laws and Orders of the General Court of Connecticut, etc., etc., (Hartford: Silus Andrus, 1822), complete work pages, pp. 20-94. The Annals of America, 20 vols. (Chicago, IL: Encyclopedia Britannica, 1968, 1977), Vol. I, p. 200
[230] New York Colony, Colonial Legislature of the. 1665, in an act passed by the Legislature. Benjamin Franklin Morris, The Christian Life and Character of the Civil Institutions of the United States (Philadelphia: George W. Childs, 1864), p. 88. Peter G. Mode, Sourcebook and Bibliographical Guide for American Church History (Menasha, WI: George Banta Publishing Co., 1921), p. 133. Gary DeMar, God and Government-A Biblical and Historical Study (Atlanta, GA: American Vision Press, 1982), p. 116.
[231] New York, State of. 1777, 1821, Constitution, cited by the Massachusetts Supreme Court in the case of Commonwealth v. Abner Kneeland; 37 Mass. (20 Pick) 206, 207, 218. (Sup. Ct. Mass. 1838).
[232] Washington, George. August 3, 1776, in orders issued to the Continental Army. Jared Sparks, ed., The Writings of George Washington 12 vols. (Boston: American Stationer's Company, 1837; NY: F. Andrew's, 1834-1847), Vol. IV, p. 26. William J. Johnson, George Washington - The Christian (St. Paul, MN: William J. Johnson, Merriam Park, February 23, 1919; Nashville, TN: Abingdon Press, 1919; reprinted Milford, MI: Mott Media, 1976; reprinted Arlington Heights, IL: Christian Liberty Press, 502 West Euclid Avenue, Arlington Heights, Illinois, 60004, 1992), pp. 83-84. Norman Cousins, In God We Trust - The Religious Beliefs and Ideas of the American Founding Fathers (NY: Harper & Brothers, 1958), p. 51.

[233] Blackstone, Sir William. 1765-1770, in his work entitled, Commentaries on the Laws of England (Philadelphia: J.B. Lippincott and Co., 1879), Vol. II, p. 59; as cited in the case Updegraph v. The Commonwealth, 11 Ser. & R. 396 (1824).

[234] Massachusetts Supreme Court. 1838. Commonwealth v. Abner Kneeland, 37 Mass. (20 Pick) 206, 216-217 (1838).

[235] Massachusetts Supreme Court. 1838. Commonwealth v. Abner Kneeland, 37 Mass. (20 Pick) 206, 216-217 (1838).

[236] Story, Joseph. 1844. Vidal v. Girard's Executors, 43 U.S. 126, 132 (1844), pp. 198, 205-206. William W. Story, Life and Letters of Judge Story, Vol. II, Chap. XII. Stephen Abbott Northrop, D.D., A Cloud of Witnesses (Portland, OR: American Heritage Ministries, 1987; Mantle Ministries, 228 Still Ridge, Bulverde, Texas), p. 434.

[237] New York Supreme Court. 1811, The People v. Ruggles, 8 Johns 545 (1811).

[238] New York Supreme Court. 1811, The People v. Ruggles, 8 Johns 545 (1811).

[239] New York Supreme Court. 1811, The People v. Ruggles, 8 Johns 545-547 (1811). Church of the Holy Trinity v. United States, 143 US 457, 458, 465-471, 36 L ed 226, Justice David Josiah Brewer. "Our Christian Heritage," Letter from Plymouth Rock (Marlborough, NH: The Plymouth Rock Foundation), p. 6. Gary DeMar, America's Christian History: The Untold Story (Atlanta, GA: American Vision Publishers, Inc., 1993), p. 63.

[240] Matthew D. Staver, "The Ten Commandments in American Law and Government" (Orlando, FL: The Liberty Counsel, P.O. Box 540774, Orlando, FL 32854, 407-875-2100, 407-875-0770 Fax, http://www.lc.org, liberty@lc.org, 2002), pp. 9-13.

[241] Virginia, Colony of. "Our Christian Heritage," Letter from Plymouth Rock (Marlborough, NH: The Plymouth Rock Foundation), p. 2.

[242] Virginia, Commonwealth of. 1662. Benjamin Franklin Morris The Christian Life and Character of the Civil Institutions of the United States (Philadelphia, PA: L. Johnson & Co., 1863; George W. Childs, 1864), pp. 232-233

[243] New York Colony, Colonial Legislature of the. 1665, in an act passed by the Legislature. Benjamin Franklin Morris, The Christian Life and Character of the Civil Institutions of the United States (Philadelphia: George W. Childs, 1864), p. 88. Peter G. Mode, Sourcebook and Bibliographical Guide for American Church History (Menasha, WI: George Banta Publishing Co., 1921), p. 133. Gary DeMar, God and Government-A Biblical and Historical Study (Atlanta, GA: American Vision Press, 1982), p. 116.

[244] New Jersey, Colony of. 1697. Benjamin Franklin Morris, The Christian Life and Character of the Civil Institutions of the United States (Philadelphia: George W. Childs, 1864), p. 91. Gary DeMar, God and Government-A Biblical and Historical Study (Atlanta, GA: American Vision Press, 1982), p. 116. Stephen K. McDowell and Mark A. Beliles, America's Providential History (Charlottesville, VA: Providence Press, 1988), p. 61.

[245] Pennsylvania, Frame of Government of. April 25, 1682, Fundamental Constitutions written by William Penn, Article XXII. A Collection of Charters and Other Public Acts Relating to the Province of Pennsylvania (Philadelphia: B. Franklin, 1740), pp. 10-12. Frances Newton Thorpe, ed., Federal and State Constitutions, Colonial Charters, and Other Organic Laws of the States, Territories, and Colonies now or heretofore forming the United States, 7 vols. (Washington: Government Printing Office, 1905; 1909; St. Clair Shores, MI: Scholarly Press, 1968), Vol. V, p. 3059. The Annals of America, 20 vols. (Chicago, IL: Encyclopedia Britannica, 1968), Vol. 1, p. 2271.

[246] Warren, James. June 16, 1775, in a Resolution of the Provincial Congress of Massachusetts, James Warren, president. Copied from original, printed courtesy Essex Institute, Salem, Massachusetts. Verna M. Hall, The Christian History of the American Revolution (San Francisco, CA: Foundation For American Christian Education, 1976), p. 410.

[247] Adams, Abigail. June 25, 1775, in a letter to her husband, John Adams from their estate at Braintree, reporting the details of the battle at Charlestown, Massachusetts. L.H. Butterfield, Marc Frielander, and Mary-Jo King, eds., The Book of Abigail and John - Selected Letters of

Endnotes

The Adams Family 1762-1784 (Cambridge, Massachusetts and London, England: Harvard University Press, 1975), pp. 90, 93.
[248] Washington, George. November 11, 1751, in a journal kept of his trip accompanying his brother Lawrence Washington to the West Indies. J.M. Toner, M.D., Washington's Barbadoes Journal (1823), p. 49. William J. Johnson, George Washington - The Christian (St. Paul, MN: William J. Johnson, Merriam Park, February 23, 1919; Nashville, TN: Abingdon Press, 1919; reprinted Milford, MI: Mott Media, 1976; reprinted Arlington Heights, IL: Christian Liberty Press, 502 West Euclid Avenue, Arlington Heights, Illinois, 60004, 1992), p. 22.
[249] Washington, George. Sunday, November 8, 1789, in a diary entry while in Connecticut. Benson J. Lossing, The Diary of George Washington, from 1789 to 1791 (1860), p. 50. E.C. M'guire, The Religious Opinions and Character of Washington (1836), p. 175. (E.C. M'Guire was the son-in-law of Mr. Robert Lewis, Washington's nephew and private secretary.) William J. Johnson, George Washington - The Christian (St. Paul, MN: William J. Johnson, Merriam Park, February 23, 1919; Nashville, TN: Abingdon Press, 1919; reprinted Milford, MI: Mott Media, 1976; reprinted Arlington Heights, IL: Christian Liberty Press, 502 West Euclid Avenue, Arlington Heights, Illinois, 60004, 1992), p. 176.
[250] Franklin, Benjamin. 1781, in his second Autobiography. Benjamin Franklin, Autobiography, II (1784). Carl Van Dorn, ed.,Franklin's Autobiographical Writings, Carl Van Dorn, ed., (NY: Viking Press, 1945), p. 624. Norman Cousins, In God We Trust - The Religious Beliefs and Ideas of the American Founding Fathers (NY: Harper & Brothers, Publishers, 1955), pp. 25-26. Raymond A. St. John, American Literature for Christian Schools (Greenville, SC: Bob Jones University Press, Inc., 1979), pp. 121-122. John Eidsmoe, Christianity and the Constitution - The Faith of Our Founding Fathers (Grand Rapids, MI: Baker Book House, A Mott Media Book, 1987; 6th printing, 1993), pp. 195-195.
[251] Sherman, Roger. 1777, comments about Sherman by Benjamin Rush. George W. Corner, ed., Autobiography of Benjamin Rush - His "Travels Through Life" together with His Commonplace Book for 1789-1813 (Princeton, N.J.: Published for The American Philosophical Society by Princeton University Press, 1948), pp. 139-156. Henry Steele Commager, ed., The Great Declaration - A Book for Young Americans (Indianapolis: The Bobbs-Merrill Co., Inc., 1958), p. 26. Henry Steele Commager and Richard B. Morris, eds., The Spirit of 'Seventy-Six (NY: Bobbs-Merrill Co., Inc., 1958, reprinted, NY: Harper & Row, Publishers, 1967), p. 275.
[252] Columbia University. 1754. Columbia Rules (New York: Samuel Loudon, 1785), pp. 5-8. Frank Monaghan, John Jay: Defender of Liberty (Indianapolis: Bobbs-Merrill, 1935, 1972), p. 26. John Eidsmoe, Christianity and the Constitution - The Faith of Our Founding Fathers (Grand Rapids, MI: Baker Book House, A Mott Media Book, 1987; 6th printing, 1993), p. 22.
[253] Dwight, Timothy. July 4, 1798, as president of Yale College, in an address delivered at New Haven, entitled, "The Duty of Americans, at the Present Crisis, Illustrated in a Discourse, Preached on the Fourth of July, 1798. (#Ital original). The Annals of America, 20 vols. (Chicago, IL: Encyclopedia Britannica, 1968, 1977), Vol. 4, pp. 33-39. Peter Marshall and David Manuel, The Glory of America (Bloomington, MN: Garborg's Heart 'N Home, Inc., 1991), 1.11. Peter Marshall and David Manuel, From Sea to Shining Sea (Old Tappan, NJ: Fleming H. Revell Company, 1986).
[254] McGuffey, William Holmes. Mason L. Weems, "King Charles II and William Penn," William Holmes McGuffey, McGuffey's Fifth Eclectic Reader (Cincinnati and New York: Van Antwerp, Bragg & Co., revised edition, 1879), lesson XXIII, pp. 89-91
[255] Opukahai'a, Henry. In his memoirs. "Hawaii's Heroes of Faith" University of the Nations (Hawaii: Youth With a Mission Newsletter).
[256] Wanamaker, John. Gordon MacClennon - Pastor of Bethany Presbyterian Church in Philadelphia, Prayers of John Wanamaker.
[257] Dallas High Schools. September 1946, E.B. Comstock, Assistant Superintendent in Charge

of High Schools, "Foreword," Bible Study Course - New Testament Bulletin No.170 (Dallas, TX: Dallas Public Schools Printshop, Authorized by Board of Education, April 23, 1946; reprinted Aledo, TX: WallBuilder Press, 1993), p. iii.
[258] Vermont, State of. 1777, Constitution, Declaration of Rights, III. Perley Poore, ed., The Federal and State Constitutions, Colonial Charters, and Other Organic Laws of the United States (Washington, 1877). Frances Newton Thorpe, ed., Federal and State Constitutions, Colonial Charters, and Other Organic Laws of the States, Territories, and Colonies now or heretofore forming the United States, 7 vols. (Washington: Government Printing Office, 1905; 1909; St. Clair Shores, MI: Scholarly Press, 1968). The Annals of America, 20 vols. (Chicago, IL: Encyclopedia Britannica, 1968), Vol. 2, p. 485. Edwin S.Gaustad, Neither King nor Prelate - Religion and the New Nation, 1776-1826 (Grand Rapids, MI: William B. Eerdmans Publishing Company, 1993), p. 173.
[259] Madison, James. October 31, 1785, "Bill for Punishing Disturbers of Religious Worship and Sabbath Breakers." Edmund Fuller and David E. Green, God in the White House - The Faiths of American Presidents (NY: Crown Publishers, Inc., 1968), p. 41. Daniel L. Driesbach, Real Threat and Mere Shadow: Religious Liberty and the First Amendment (Westchester, IL: Crossway Books, 1987), pp. 120-122. Benjamin Hart, Faith & Freedom - The Christian Roots of American Liberty (Dallas, TX: Lewis and Stanley, 1988), p. 352. John Whitehead, The Rights of Religious Persons in Public Schools (Wheaton, IL: Crossway Books, Good News Publishers, 1991), pp. 41, 235.
[260] United States Congress. May 1, 1789, in the United States House of Representatives. "Our Christian Heritage," Letter from Plymouth Rock (Marlborough, NH: The Plymouth Rock Foundation), p. 4. Gary DeMar, America's Christian History: The Untold Story (Atlanta, GA: American Vision Publishers, Inc., 1993), p. 51.
[261] Alabama, State of. 1901, Constitution, Article V, Section 125. Approval, Veto of Bills. Constitutions of the United States - National and States (Dobbs Ferry, New York: Oceana Publications, Inc., published for Legislative Drafting Research Fund of Columbia University, Release 96-4, Issued November 1996), Vol. 1, Alabama, Booklet 1(March 1996), p. 19.
[262] Adams, John Quincy. In a diary entry. Charles Francis Adams (son of John Quincy Adams and grandson of John Adams), ed., Memoirs of John Quincy Adams, 2 vols. (Philadelphia: J.B. Lippincott & Co., 1874-77), IX:289. Peter Marshall and David Manuel, The Glory of America (Bloomington, MN: Garborg's Heart 'N Home, 1991), 11.7.
[263] Adams, John Quincy. July 11, 1841, in a diary entry on the occasion of his seventy-fourth birthday. Edmund Fuller and David E. Green, God in the White House - The Faiths of American Presidents (NY: Crown Publishers, Inc., 1968), p. 53.
[264] Harrison, William Henry. In commenting to visitors during his brief term in Washington, D.C. Benjamin Franklin Morris, The Christian Life and Character of the Civil Institutions of the United States (Philadelphia: George W. Childs, 1864), p. 605.
[265] Taylor, Zachary. March 5, 1849, Monday, in his Inaugural Address, which he moved from March 4, Sunday, as he refused to be sworn in on the Sabbath. James D. Richardson (U.S. Representative from Tennessee), ed., A Compilation of the Messages and Papers of the Presidents 1789-1897, 10 vols. (Washington, D.C.: U.S. Government Printing Office, published by Authority of Congress, 1897, 1899; Washington, D.C.: Bureau of National Literature and Art, 1789-1902, 11 vols., 1907, 1910), Vol. 5, pp. 5-6. Benjamin Franklin Morris, The Christian Life and Character of the Civil Institutions of the United States (Philadelphia: George W. Childs, 1864), p. 607. Inaugural Addresses of the Presidents of the United States - From George Washington 1789 to Richard Milhous Nixon 1969 (Washington, D.C.: United States Government Printing Office; 91st Congress, 1st Session, House Document 91-142, 1969), pp. 99-101. Davis Newton Lott, The Inaugural Addresses of the American Presidents (NY: Holt, Rinehart and Winston, 1961), p. 100. Charles E. Rice, The Supreme Court and Public Prayer (New York: Fordham University Press, 1964), p. 183. J. Michael Sharman, J.D., Faith of the Fathers (Culpepper, Virginia: Victory Publishing, 1995), p. 50.

Endnotes

[266] Fillmore, Millard. Member of the Episcopalian Church. John Wilson Taylor, M.A., Ph.D., et al., The Lincoln Library of Essential Information (Buffalo, New York: The Frontier Press Company, 1935), p. 391.

[267] Fillmore, Millard. Benjamin Franklin Morris, The Christian Life and Character of the Civil Institutions of the United States (Philadelphia: George W. Childs, 1864), p. 609.

[268] Lincoln, Abraham. September 3, 1864, from his Executive Mansion in Washington, D.C. James D. Richardson (U.S. Representative from Tennessee), ed., A Compilation of the Messages and Papers of the Presidents 1789-1897, 10 vols. (Washington, D.C.: U.S. Government Printing Office, published by Authority of Congress, 1897, 1899; Washington, D.C.: Bureau of National Literature and Art, 1789-1902, 11 vols., 1907, 1910), Vol. VI, pp. 238-239.

[269] Grant, Ulysses Simpson. June 6, 1876, in a letter from Washington during his term as President, to the Editor of the Sunday School Times in Philadelphia. Stephen Abbott Northrop, D.D., A Cloud of Witnesses (Portland, OR: American Heritage Ministries, 1987; Mantle Ministries, 228 Still Ridge, Bulverde, Texas), p. 195. Peter Marshall and David Manuel, The Glory of America (Bloomington, MN: Garborg's Heart 'N Home, Inc., 1991), 4.27. Tryon Edwards, D.D., The New Dictionary of Thoughts - A Cyclopedia of Quotations (Garden City, NY: Hanover House, 1852; revised and enlarged by C.H. Catrevas, Ralph Emerson Browns and Jonathan Edwards [descendent, along with Tryon, of Jonathan Edwards (1703-1758), president of Princeton], 1891; The Standard Book Company, 1955, 1963), p. 48. Henry Halley, Halley's Bible Handbook (Grand Rapids, MI: Zondervan, 1927, 1965), p. 18. W. David Stedman and LaVaughn G. Lewis, Our Ageless Constitution (Asheboro, NC: W. Stedman Associates, 1987), p. 162. Gary DeMar, America's Christian History: The Untold Story (Atlanta, GA: American Vision Publishers, Inc., 1993), pp. 59-60. Edmund Fuller and David E. Green, God in the White House - The Faiths of American Presidents (NY: Crown Publishers, Inc., 1968), p. 130. D.P. Diffine, Ph.D., One Nation Under God - How Close a Separation? (Searcy, Arkansas: Harding University, Belden Center for Private Enterprise Education, 6th edition, 1992), p. 16.

[270] Grant, Ulysses Simpson. 1884, during his final illness. James P. Boyd, Military and Civil Life of General Ulysses S. Grant, pp. 709-710. Stephen Abbott Northrop, D.D., A Cloud of Witnesses (Portland, OR: American Heritage Ministries, 1987; Mantle Ministries, 228 Still Ridge, Bulverde, Texas), p. 195.

[271] Johnson, Lyndon Baines. Sunday, November 2, 1966, after touring many Asian and Pacific nations, President Lyndon B. Johnson spoke to those waiting for him in Dulles Airport, recalling a prayer offered ten days earlier on October 23, 1966, while they attended service at the Cathedral Church of St. James, Townsville, northern Australia. Lyndon Baines Johnson, The Vantage Point - Perspectives of the Presidency 1963-1969 (New York: Holt, Rinehart and Winston, 1971), pp. 361-364.

[272] Johnson, Lyndon Baines. Sunday, March 31, 1968, after attending church at St. Dominic's in Washington D.C., President Lyndon B. Johnson noted his feeling concerning his daughter Lynda's husband, Chuck Robb, and his daughter Luci's husband, Pat Nugent. Lyndon Baines Johnson, The Vantage Point - Perspectives of the Presidency 1963-1969 (New York: Holt, Rinehart and Winston, 1971), p. 432.

[273] Reagan, Ronald Wilson. March 6, 1984, at the annual convention of the National Association of Evangelicals. David R. Shepherd, ed., Ronald Reagan: In God I Trust (Wheaton, Illinois: Tyndale House Publishers, Inc., 1984), pp. 47-54. Frederick J. Ryan, Jr., ed., Ronald Reagan - The Wisdom and Humor of the Great Communicator (San Francisco: Collins Publishers, A Division of Harper Collins Publishers, 1995), p. 112.

[274] Washington, George. August 3, 1776, in orders issued to the Continental Army. Jared Sparks, ed., The Writings of George Washington 12 vols. (Boston: American Stationer's Company, 1837; NY: F. Andrew's, 1834-1847), Vol. IV, p. 26. William J. Johnson, George Washington - The Christian (St. Paul, MN: William J. Johnson, Merriam Park, February 23, 1919; Nashville, TN: Abingdon Press, 1919; reprinted Milford, MI: Mott Media, 1976;

reprinted Arlington Heights, IL: Christian Liberty Press, 502 West Euclid Avenue, Arlington Heights, Illinois, 60004, 1992), pp. 83-84. Norman Cousins, In God We Trust - The Religious Beliefs and Ideas of the American Founding Fathers (NY: Harper & Brothers, 1958), p. 51.

[275] Washington, George. May 2, 1778, orders issued to his troops at Valley Forge. George Washington, General Orders (Mount Vernon, VA: Archives of Mount Vernon). Henry Whiting, Revolutionary Orders of General Washington, selected from MSS. of John Whiting (1844), p. 74. Benson J. Lossing, The Pictorial Field-Book of the Revolution (1886), Vol. II, p. 140. John Clement Fitzpatrick, ed., The Writings of George Washington, from the Original Manuscript Sources 1749-1799, 39 vols. (Washington, D.C.: United States Government Printing Office, 1931-1944), Vol. XI, p. 343. William J. Johnson, George Washington - The Christian (St. Paul, MN: William J. Johnson, Merriam Park, February 23, 1919; Nashville, TN: Abingdon Press, 1919; reprinted Milford, MI: Mott Media, 1976; reprinted Arlington Heights, IL: Christian Liberty Press, 502 West Euclid Avenue, Arlington Heights, Illinois, 60004, 1992), p. 112. Norman Cousins, In God We Trust - The Religious Beliefs and Ideas of the Founding Fathers (NY: Harper & Brothers, 1958), p. 51. Peter Marshall & David Manuel, The Glory of America (Bloomington, MN: Garborg's Heart 'N Home, 1991), 9.5. D.P. Diffine, Ph.D., One Nation Under God - How Close a Separation? (Searcy, Arkansas: Harding University, Belden Center for Private Enterprise Education, 6th edition, 1992), p. 8.

[276] Washington, George. March 22, 1783, from Newburg, New York, as recorded in the Orderly Book. Elizabeth Bryant Johnston, George Washington - Day by Day (1894), p. 44. William J. Johnson, George Washington - The Christian (St. Paul, MN: William J. Johnson, Merriam Park, February 23, 1919; Nashville, TN: Abingdon Press, 1919; reprinted Milford, MI: Mott Media, 1976; reprinted Arlington Heights, IL: Christian Liberty Press, 502 West Euclid Avenue, Arlington Heights, Illinois, 60004, 1992), pp. 138-139.

[277] United States Congress. Act passed in Congress. Benjamin Franklin Morris, The Christian Life and Character of the Civil Institutions of the United States (Philadelphia, PA: L. Johnson & Co., entered, according to Act of Congress, in the Clerk's Office of the District Court of the United States for the Eastern District of Pennsylvania, 1863; George W. Childs, 1864), pp. 315-316.

[278] Perry, Matthew Calbraith. 1853. Stephen Abbott Northrop, D.D., A Cloud of Witnesses (Portland, OR: American Heritage Ministries, 1987; Mantle Ministries, 228 Still Ridge, Bulverde, Texas), p. 350.

[279] Lincoln, Abraham. November 15, 1862, from his Executive Mansion in Washington, D.C., issued a General Order Respecting the Observance of the Sabbath Day in the Army and Navy. James D. Richardson (U.S. Representative from Tennessee), ed., A Compilation of the Messages and Papers of the Presidents 1789-1897, 10 vols. (Washington, D.C.: U.S. Government Printing Office, published by Authority of Congress, 1897, 1899; Washington, D.C.: Bureau of National Literature and Art, 1789-1902, 11 vols., 1907, 1910), Vol. VI, p. 125. [see General George Washington's July 9, 1776, order issued to the army in response to the reading of the Declaration of Independence by the Continental Congress. Jared Sparks, ed., The Writings of George Washington 12 vols. (Boston: American Stationer's Company, 1837; NY: F. Andrew's, 1834-1847), Vol. III, p. 456. Writings of George Washington, (Sparks ed.), Vol. XII, p. 401, citing Orderly Book; also orders of August 3, 1776, in ibid., IV, 28 n. William J. Johnson, George Washington - The Christian (St. Paul, MN: William J. Johnson, Merriam Park, February 23, 1919; Nashville, TN: Abingdon Press, 1919; reprinted Milford, MI: Mott Media, 1976; reprinted Arlington Heights, IL: Christian Liberty Press, 502 West Euclid Avenue, Arlington Heights, Illinois, 60004, 1992), p. 83. John Clement Fitzpatrick, ed., The Writings of George Washington, from the Original Manuscript Sources 1749-1799, 39 vols. (Washington, D.C.: United States Government Printing Office, 1931-1944), Vol. V, p. 245. William Barclay Allen, ed., George Washington - A Collection (Indianapolis: Liberty Classics, Liberty Fund, Inc., 7440 N. Shadeland, Indianapolis, Indiana 46250, 1988; based almost entirely on materials reproduced from The Writings of George

Endnotes

Washington from the original manuscript sources, 1745-1799/John Clement Fitzpatrick, editor), p. 73. John F. Schroeder, ed., Maxims of Washington (Mt. Vernon: Mt. Vernon Ladies' Association, 1942), p. 299. Saxe Commins, ed., The Basic Writings of George Washington (NY: Random House, 1948), p. 236. Anson Phelps Stokes and Leo Pfeffer, Church and State in the United States (NY: Harper and Row, Publishers, 1950, revised one-volume edition, 1964), p. 35. Norman Cousins, In God We Trust - The Religious Beliefs and Ideas of the Founding Fathers (NY: Harper & Brothers, 1958), p. 50. Paul F. Boller, Jr., George Washington and Religion (Dallas: Southern Methodist University Press, 1963), p. 69. Frank Donovan, Mr. Jefferson's Declaration (New York: Dodd Mead & Co., 1968), p. 192. A. James Reichley, Religion in American Public Life (Washington, D.C.: The Brookings Institute, 1985), p. 99. John Eidsmoe, Christianity and The Constitution - The Faith of Our Founding Fathers (Grand Rapids, MI: Baker Book House, A Mott Media Book, 1987, 6th printing 1993), pp. 120-121. Tim LaHaye, Faith of Our Founding Fathers (Brentwood, TN: Wolgemuth & Hyatt, Publishers, Inc., 1987), p. 108.

[280] Rosecrans, William Starke. His motto as a Union general in the Civil War. Jeffery Warren Scott, "Fighters of Faith" (Carol Stream, IL: Christian History, Issue 33-1992), Vol. XI, No. 1, p. 37.

[281] Howard, Oliver Otis. 1863, in an address to the 127th Pennsylvania Volunteers. Greg, Life, p. 87. Peter Marshall and David Manuel, The Glory of America (Bloomington, MN: Garborg's Heart'N Home, Inc., 1991), 2.19. D.P. Diffine, Ph.D., One Nation Under God - How Close a Separation? (Searcy, Arkansas: Harding University, Belden Center for Private Enterprise Education, 6th edition, 1992), p. 14.

[282] Jackson, Thomas Jonathan "Stonewall". In a letter to his pastor, Reverend Dr. White, concerning the Sunday School class General Jackson taught in Lexington. John G. Gittings, Personal Recollections of Stonewall Jackson (Cincinnati: The Editor Publishing Company, 1899), p. 65.

[283] Harrison, Benjamin. June 7, 1889, from his Executive Mansion. James D. Richardson (U.S. Representative from Tennessee), ed., A Compilation of the Messages and Papers of the Presidents 1789-1897, 10 vols. (Washington, D.C.: U.S. Government Printing Office, published by Authority of Congress, 1897, 1899; Washington, D.C.: Bureau of National Literature and Art, 1789-1902, 11 vols., 1907, 1910), Vol. IX, p. 29.

[284] Wilson, (Thomas) Woodrow. January 20, 1918, in an Executive Order to the Army and Navy enjoining Sabbath observance. A Compilation of the Messages and Papers of the Presidents 20 vols. (New York: Bureau of National Literature, Inc., prepared under the direction of the Joint Committee on Printing, of the House and Senate, pursuant to an Act of the Fifty-Second Congress of the United States, 1893, 1923), Vol. XVII, p. 8433.

[285] Churchill, Winston Leonard Spencer. August 10, 1941, in his records of the Mid-Atlantic Conference. Edmund Fuller and David E. Green, God in the White House - The Faiths of American Presidents (NY: Crown Publishers, Inc., 1968), p. 205.

[286] MacArthur, Douglas. September 2, 1945, in a prayer given aboard the battleship USS Missouri in Tokyo Bay, at a meeting with leaders of Allied forces to sign the treaty of surrender of Japan. Charles Colson, Kingdoms in Conflict (Grand Rapids, MI: Zondervan Publishing House, 1987), p. 178.

[287] United States Corp of Cadets. July 24, 1949, New York Times. Anson Phelps Stokes and Leo Pfeffer, Church and State in the United States (NY: Harper and Row, Publishers, 1950, revised one-volume edition, 1964), p. 473-474.

[288] United States Naval Academy. July 28, 1949, New York Times. Anson Phelps Stokes and Leo Pfeffer, Church and State in the United States (NY: Harper and Row, Publishers, 1950, revised one-volume edition, 1964), p. 473-474.

[289] Brewer, David Josiah. February 29, 1892, delivering the court's opinion in the case Church of the Holy Trinity v. United States, 143 US 457-458, 465-471, 36 L ed 226, (submitted and argued January 7, 1892). "Our Christian Heritage," Letter from Plymouth Rock (Marlborough, NH: The Plymouth Rock Foundation), p. 6. D.P. Diffine, Ph.D., One

Nation Under God - How Close a Separation? (Searcy, Arkansas: Harding University, Belden Center for Private Enterprise Education, 6th edition, 1992), p. 3. Gary DeMar, America's Christian History: The Untold Story (Atlanta, GA: American Vision Publishers, Inc., 1993), p. 21.

[290] South Carolina Supreme Court. 1846, City of Charleston v. S.A. Benjamin, 2 Strob. 508 (1846).

[291] South Carolina Supreme Court. 1846, City of Charleston v. S.A. Benjamin, 2 Strob. 518-520 (1846).

[292] South Carolina Supreme Court. 1846, City of Charleston v. S.A. Benjamin, 2 Strob. 521-524 (1846).

[293] United States Congress. January 19, 1853, Mr. Badger giving report of Congressional investigations in the Senate of the United States. The Reports of Committees of the Senate of the United States for the Second Session of the Thirty-Second Congress, 1852-53 (Washington: Robert Armstrong, 1853), pp. 1, 6, 8-9. Benjamin Franklin Morris, The Christian Life and Character of the Civil Institutions of the United States (Philadelphia: George W. Childs, 1864), pp. 324-327.

[294] Matthew D. Staver, "The Ten Commandments in American Law and Government" (Orlando, FL: The Liberty Counsel, P.O. Box 540774, Orlando, FL 32854, 407-875-2100, 407-875-0770 Fax, http://www.lc.org, liberty@lc.org, 2002), p. 13.

[295] Washington, George. 1745. 110 Rules of Civility and Decent Behavior in Company and Conversation - copied in his own handwriting. Moncure D. Conway, George Washington's Rules of Civility (1890), pp. 178, 180. William J. Johnson, George Washington - The Christian (St. Paul, MN: William J. Johnson, Merriam Park, February 23, 1919; Nashville, TN: Abingdon Press, 1919; reprinted Milford, MI: Mott Media, 1976; reprinted Arlington Heights, IL: Christian Liberty Press, 502 West Euclid Avenue, Arlington Heights, Illinois, 60004, 1992), p. 20. 110 Rules of Civility and Decent Behavior in Company and Conversation (Bedford, MA: Apple Books, 1988, distributed by The Globe Pequot Press, Chester, CT.), p. 30.

[296] Jefferson, Thomas. February 21, 1825, in a letter to Thomas Jefferson Smith. Dickenson Adams, ed., Jefferson's Extracts from the Gospels (Princeton: Princeton University Press, 1983), pp. 40-41. John Eidsmoe, Christianity and The Constitution - The Faith of Our Founding Fathers (Grand Rapids, MI: Baker Book House, 1987), p. 236. Robert Flood, The Rebirth of America (The Arthur S. DeMoss Foundation, 1986), p. 181.

[297] Franklin, Benjamin. 1754. Benjamin Franklin, Information on Those Who Would Remove to America (London: M. Gurney, 1754), pp. 22, 23. "Advice on Coming to America," George D. Youstra, ed., America in Person (Greenville, SC: Bob Jones University Press, 1975), p. 109. Tim LaHaye, Faith of Our Founding Fathers (Brentwood, TN: Wolgemuth & Hyatt, Publishers, Inc. 1987), p. 31. Benjamin Franklin, Works of the Late Doctor Benjamin Franklin Consisting of His Life, Written by Himself, Together with Essays, Humorous, Moral & Literary, Chiefly in the Manner of the Spectator, Richard Price, ed., (Dublin: P. Wogan, P. Byrne, J. Moore, and W. Jones, 1793), p. 289.

[298] Harvard University. 1636. Old South Leaflets. Benjamin Pierce, A History of Harvard University (Cambridge, MA: Brown, Shattuck, and Company, 1833), Appendix, p. 5. Peter G. Mode, ed., Sourcebook and Biographical Guide for American Church History (Menasha, WI: George Banta Publishing Co., 1921), pp. 74-75. Robert Flood, The Rebirth of America (Philadelphia: Arthur S. DeMoss Foundation, 1986), p. 41. "Our Christian Heritage," Letter from Plymouth Rock (Marlborough, NH: The Plymouth Rock Foundation), p. 2. Pat Robertson, America's Dates With Destiny (Nashville, TN: Thomas Nelson Publishers, 1986), pp. 44-45. Gary DeMar, America's Christian History: The Untold Story (Atlanta, GA: American Vision Publishers, Inc., 1993), p. 40. Rosalie J. Slater, "New England's First Fruits, 1643," Teaching and Learning America's Christian History (San Francisco: Foundation for Christian Education, 1980), p. vii. Stephen McDowell and Mark Beliles, "The Providential Perspective" (Charlottesville, VA: The Providence Foundation, P.O. Box 6759,

Endnotes

Charlottesville, Va. 22906, January 1994), Vol. 9, No. 1, p. 3. D.P. Diffine, Ph.D., One Nation Under God - How Close a Separation? (Searcy, Arkansas: Harding University, Belden Center for Private Enterprise Education, 6th edition, 1992), p. 4.

[299] Connecticut, Colony of. 1690, law passed in the legislature. Edward Kendall, Kendall's Travels (New York: I. Riley, 1809), Vol. I, pp. 270-271.

[300] Webster, Noah. 1839, in A Manual of Useful Studies (New Haven: S. Babcock, 1839), pp. 77-78. Stephen McDowell and Mark Beliles, "The Providential Perspective" (Charlottesville, VA: The Providence Foundation, P.O. Box 6759, Charlottesville, Va. 22906, January 1994), Vol. 9, No. 1, p. 1.

[301] Webster, Noah. Pat Robertson, America's Dates with Destiny (Nashville: Thomas Nelson Publishers, 1986), p. 48. Webster, An American Dictionary of the English Language, 1828, s.v.

[302] Adams, John Quincy. September 1811, in a letter to his son written while serving as U.S. Minister in St. Petersburg, Russia. James L. Alden, Letters of John Quincy Adams to His Son on the Bible and Its Teachings (1850), pp. 6-21. Henry H. Halley, Halley's Bible Handbook (Grand Rapids, MI: Zondervan Publishing House, 1927, 1965), p. 19. Verna M. Hall, The Christian History of the American Revolution - Consider and Ponder (San Francisco: Foundation for American Christian Education, 1976), pp. 615-616. Verna M. Hall and Rosalie J. Slater, The Bible and the Constitution of the United States of America (San Francisco: Foundation for American Christian Education, 1983), p. 17. Tim LaHaye, Faith of Our Founding Fathers (Brentwood, TN: Wolgemuth & Hyatt, Publishers, Inc., 1987), pp. 90-91. D.P. Diffine, Ph.D., One Nation Under God - How Close a Separation? (Searcy, Arkansas: Harding University, Belden Center for Private Enterprise Education, 6th edition, 1992), p. 6.

[303] Coolidge, (John) Calvin. May 1, 1926, before the National Council of the Boy Scouts of America, Washington, D.C. Calvin Coolidge, Foundations of the Republic - Speeches and Addresses (New York: Charles Scribner's Sons, 1926), pp. 389-398.

[304] Reagan, Ronald Wilson. May 20, 1981, in a Proclamation of Father's Day. David R. Shepherd, ed., Ronald Reagan: In God I Trust (Wheaton, Illinois: Tyndale House Publishers, Inc., 1984), p. 94.

[305] Reagan, Ronald Wilson. March 8, 1983, in a speech to the National Association of Evangelicals. William Safire, ed., Lend Me Your Ears - Great Speeches in History (NY: W.W. Norton & Company 1992), p. 464. David R. Shepherd, ed., Ronald Reagan: In God I Trust (Wheaton, Illinois: Tyndale House Publishers, Inc., 1984), pp. 35-38, 133-134. Frederick J. Ryan, Jr., ed., Ronald Reagan - The Wisdom and Humor of The Great Communicator (San Francisco: Collins Publishers, A Division of Harper Collins Publishers, 1995), p. 42.

[306] Smith, Jedediah Strong. December 24, 1829, from Wind River on the east side of the Rocky Mountains, his parents in Ashtabula County, Ohio. Dale L. Morgan, Jedediah Smith - and the Opening of the West (Lincoln, Nebraska: University of Nebraska Press, Bobbs - Merrill Company, 1953; Bison Books, 1964), pp. 350-351.

[307] Watts, J.C. February 4, 1997, Tuesday, Library of Congress, Washington, D.C., in the televised Republican response to President Clinton's State of the Union Address.

[308] Thatcher, Margaret Hilda. February 5, 1996, in New York City, prior to her trip to Utah where she addressed the U.K. - Utah Festival, in an interview with Joseph A. Cannon, entitled "The Conservative Vision of Margaret Thatcher," published in Human Events - The National Conservative Weekly, (Potomac, Maryland: Human Events Publishing, Inc., 7811 Montrose Road, Potomac, MD, 20854, 1-800-787-7557; Eagle Publishing, Inc.), March 29, 1996, Vol. 52, No. 12, pp. 12-14.

[309] New York Supreme Court. December 30, 1993, in the Appellate Division case of Alfonso v. Fernandez. "What Are They Teaching in the Public Schools?" The Phyllis Schlafly Report (Alton, IL: Eagle Trust Fund, January 1994), Vol. 27, No. 6, pp. 3-4.

[310] Matthew D. Staver, "The Ten Commandments in American Law and Government"

(Orlando, FL: The Liberty Counsel, P.O. Box 540774, Orlando, FL 32854, 407-875-2100, 407-875-0770 Fax, http://www.lc.org, liberty@lc.org, 2002), pp. 13-14.

[311] Washington, George. April of 1732, the baptism of George Washington, as recorded by his father, Augustine Washington, in the family Bible. James Walter, Memorials of Washington and Mary, His Mother, and Martha, His Wife (1887), p. 123. William J. Johnson, George Washington - The Christian (St. Paul, MN: William J. Johnson, Merriam Park, February 23, 1919; Nashville, TN: Abingdon Press, 1919; reprinted Milford, MI: Mott Media, 1976; reprinted Arlington Heights, IL: Christian Liberty Press, 502 West Euclid Avenue, Arlington Heights, Illinois, 60004, 1992), p. 18.

[312] Washington, George. April 12, 1743, the last words of his father, Augustine Washington. William H. Wilbur, The Making of George Washington (Caldwell, ID.: 1970, 1973), p. 92. Benjamin Hart, Faith & Freedom - The Christian Roots of American Liberty (Dallas, TX: Lewis and Stanley, 1988), p. 127.

[313] Webster, Noah. Noah Webster, The American Dictionary of the English Language (George and Charles Merrian, 1854). Russ Walton, One Nation Under God (NH: Plymouth Rock Foundation, 1993) p. 56.

[314] Dwight, Timothy. July 4, 1798, as president of Yale College, in an address delivered at New Haven, entitled, "The Duty of Americans, at the Present Crisis, Illustrated in a Discourse, Preached on the Fourth of July, 1798. (#Ital original). The Annals of America, 20 vols. (Chicago, IL: Encyclopedia Britannica, 1968, 1977), Vol. 4, pp. 33-39. Peter Marshall and David Manuel, The Glory of America (Bloomington, MN: Garborg's Heart 'N Home, Inc., 1991), 1.11. Peter Marshall and David Manuel, From Sea to Shining Sea (Old Tappan, NJ: Fleming H. Revell Company, 1986).

[315] Linn, William. May 1, 1789, as U.S. House Chaplain. Dickinson W. Adams, ed., Jefferson's Extracts from the Gospels (Princeton: Princeton University Press, 1983), p. 11. Quoting from William Linn, Serious Considerations on the Election of a President: Addressed to the Citizens of the United States (NY: 1800), p. 19. "Our Christian Heritage," Letter from Plymouth Rock (Marlborough, NH: The Plymouth Rock Foundation), p. 4.

[316] Alabama, State of. 1901, Constitution, Article VIII, Section 182. Disqualification of voters. Constitutions of the United States - National and States (Dobbs Ferry, New York: Oceana Publications, Inc., published for Legislative Drafting Research Fund of Columbia University, Release 96-4, Issued November 1996), Vol. 1, Alabama, Booklet 1(March 1996), p. 31.

[317] Alabama, State of. 1901, Constitution, Article IV, Section 86. Dueling. Constitutions of the United States - National and States (Dobbs Ferry, New York: Oceana Publications, Inc., published for Legislative Drafting Research Fund of Columbia University, Release 96-4, Issued November 1996), Vol. 1, Alabama, Booklet 1(March 1996), p. 12.

[318] Texas, State of. August 27, 1845, Constitution, Article VII, Section 1. Journals of the Convention, Assembled at the City of Austin on the Fourth of July, 1845, for the purpose of framing a Constitution for the State of Texas (Austin, TX: Miner & Cruger, Printers to the Convention, 1845; A Facsimile Reproduction of the 1845 Edition with a Preface by Mary Bell Hart, Shoal Creek Publishers, 1974), pp. 354-355.

[319] Hamilton, Alexander. M.E. Bradford, A Worthy Company (Marlborough, NH: Plymouth Rock Foundation, 1982), p. 49. Tim LaHaye, Faith of Our Founding Fathers (Brentwood, TN: Wolgemuth & Hyatt, Publishers, Inc., 1987), p. 141.

[320] California Supreme Court. May 16, 1994, San Francisco, California, in the majority opinion delivered by Chief Justice Malcolm Lucas. Los Angeles Times. "Court rules that killing fetus during crime can be murder," The Dallas Morning News, (Dallas, TX: Tuesday, May 17, 1994, p. 3A.

[321] Roosevelt, Theodore. December 3, 1906, in his Sixth Annual Message to Congress. A Compilation of the Messages and Papers of the Presidents 20 vols. (New York: Bureau of National Literature, Inc., prepared under the direction of the Joint Committee on Printing, of

the House and Senate, pursuant to an Act of the Fifty-Second Congress of the United States, 1893, 1923), Vol. XIV, pp. 7030-7032, 7046, 7048,

[322] Reagan, Ronald Wilson. February 2, 1984, a National Prayer Breakfast. David R. Shepherd, ed., Ronald Reagan: In God I Trust (Wheaton, Illinois: Tyndale House Publishers, Inc., 1984), pp. 73-75.

[323] Matthew D. Staver, "The Ten Commandments in American Law and Government" (Orlando, FL: The Liberty Counsel, P.O. Box 540774, Orlando, FL 32854, 407-875-2100, 407-875-0770 Fax, http://www.lc.org, liberty@lc.org, 2002), p. 14.

[324] Connecticut, Code of the General Court of. 1650, in the Capital Laws Section of the Code, which stated offenses and their punishments. The Code of 1650 - Being a Compilation of the Earliest Laws and Orders of the General Court of Connecticut, etc., etc., (Hartford: Silus Andrus, 1822), complete work pages, pp. 20-94. The Annals of America, 20 vols. (Chicago, IL: Encyclopedia Britannica, 1968, 1977), Vol. I, p. 200.

[325] New York Colony, Colonial Legislature of the. 1665, in an act passed by the Legislature. Benjamin Franklin Morris, The Christian Life and Character of the Civil Institutions of the United States (Philadelphia: George W. Childs, 1864), p. 88. Peter G. Mode, Sourcebook and Bibliographical Guide for American Church History (Menasha, WI: George Banta Publishing Co., 1921), p. 133. Gary DeMar, God and Government-A Biblical and Historical Study (Atlanta, GA: American Vision Press, 1982), p. 116.

[326] New York, State of. 1777, Constitution, Article XXXVIII. Davis v. Beason, 133 U.S. 333, 341-343, 348 n. (1890). Frances Newton Thorpe, ed., Federal and State Constitutions, Colonial Charters, and Other Organic Laws of the States, Territories, and Colonies now or heretofore forming the United States, 7 vols. (Washington: Government Printing Office, 1905; 1909; St. Clair Shores, MI: Scholarly Press, 1968). Edwin S. Gaustad, Neither King nor Prelate - Religion and the New Nation, 1776-1826 (Grand Rapids, MI: William B. Eerdmans Publishing Company, 1993), p. 168.

[327] Arizona, State of. 1912, Constitution, Article XX. Ordinance. First. Toleration of Religious Sentiment, Second. Polygamy. Constitutions of the United States - National and State (Dobbs Ferry, New York: Oceana Publications, Inc., published for Legislative Drafting Research Fund of Columbia University, Issued September 1993), Vol. 1, Arizona(September 1993), pp. 74-75.

[328] Texas, State of. August 27, 1845, Constitution, Article VII, Section 18. Journals of the Convention, Assembled at the City of Austin on the Fourth of July, 1845, for the purpose of framing a Constitution for the State of Texas (Austin, TX: Miner & Cruger, Printers to the Convention, 1845; A Facsimile Reproduction of the 1845 Edition with a Preface by Mary Bell Hart, Shoal Creek Publishers, 1974), p. 357.

[329] Alabama, State of. 1901, Constitution, Article VIII, Section 182. Disqualification of voters. Constitutions of the United States - National and States (Dobbs Ferry, New York: Oceana Publications, Inc., published for Legislative Drafting Research Fund of Columbia University, Release 96-4, Issued November 1996), Vol. 1, Alabama, Booklet 1(March 1996), p. 31.

[330] Pennsylvania Supreme Court. 1824. Updegraph v. The Commonwealth, 11 Serg. & Rawle, 393-394, 398-399, 400-401, 402-407 (1824); 5 Binn. R. 555; of New York, 8 Johns. R. 291; of Connecticut, 2 Swift's System. 321; of Massachusetts, Dane's Ab. vol. 7, c. 219, a. 2, 19. Church of the Holy Trinity v. United States, 143 US 457, 458, 465-471, 36 L ed 226, Justice David Josiah Brewer. Vide Cooper on the Law of Libel, 59 and 114, et seq.; and generally, 1 Russ. on Cr. 217; 1 Hawk, c. 5; 1 Vent. 293; 3 Keb. 607; 1 Barn. & Cress. 26. S. C. 8 Eng. Com. Law R. 14; Barnard. 162; Fitsgib. 66; Roscoe, Cr. Ev. 524; 2 Str. 834; 3 Barn. & Ald. 161; S. C. 5 Eng Com. Law R. 249 Jeff. Rep. Appx. See 1 Cro. Jac. 421 Vent. 293; 3 Keb. 607; Cooke on Def. 74; 2 How. S. C. 11-ep. 127, 197 to 201. "Our Christian Heritage," Letter from Plymouth Rock (Marlborough, NH: The Plymouth Rock Foundation), p. 6.

[331] United States Supreme Court. 1885, Murphy v. Ramsey & Others, 144 U.S. 15, 45 (1885).

[332] United States Supreme Court. 1889, Davis v. Beason, 133 U.S. 333, 341-343, 348 (1890).

John Eidsmoe, The Christian Legal Advisor (Milford, MI: Mott Media, 1984), p. 150. Gary DeMar, America's Christian History: The Untold Story (Atlanta, GA: American Vision Publishers, Inc., 1993), pp. 68, 106.
[333] United States Supreme Court. 1878, Reynolds v. United States, 98 U.S. 145, 165 (1878).
[334] United States Supreme Court. 1890, The Church of Jesus Christ of Latter Day Saints v. United States, 136 U.S. 1 (1890). Gary DeMar, America's Christian History: The Untold Story (Atlanta, GA: American Vision Publishers, Inc., 1993), p. 68. [The following related quotations are taken from James D. Richardson (U.S. Representative from Tennessee), ed., A Compilation of the Messages and Papers of the Presidents 1789-1897, 10 vols. (Washington, D.C.: U.S. Government Printing Office, published by Authority of Congress, 1897, 1899; Washington, D.C.: Bureau of National Literature and Art, 1789-1902, 11 vols., 1907, 1910).
On January 4, 1896, President Grover Cleveland issued the Proclamation: "Whereas said convention, so organized, did, by ordinance irrevocable without the consent of the United States and the people of said State, as required by said act, provide that perfect toleration of religious sentiment shall be secured and that no inhabitant of said State shall ever be molested in person or property on account of his or her mode of religious worship, but that polygamous or plural marriages are forever prohibited, and did also by said ordinance make the other various stipulations recited in section 3 of said act." (Vol. IX, p. 689).
On September 25, 1894, President Grover Cleveland issued the Proclamation: "Whereas Congress by a statute approved March 22, 1882, and by statutes in furtherance and amendment thereof defined the crimes of bigamy, polygamy, and unlawful cohabitation in the Territories and other places within the exclusive jurisdiction of the United States and prescribed a penalty for such crimes; and Whereas on or about the 6th day of October, 1890, the Church of the Latter-day Saints, commonly known as the Mormon Church, through its president issued a manifesto proclaiming the purpose of said church no longer to sanction the practice of polygamous marriages and calling upon all members and adherents of said church to obey the laws of the United States in reference to said subject-matter; and Whereas on the 4th day of January, A.D. 1893, Benjamin Harrison, then President of the United States, did declare and grant a full pardon and amnesty to certain offenders under said acts upon condition of future obedience to their requirements, as is fully set forth in said proclamation of amnesty and pardon; and Whereas upon the evidence now furnished me I am satisfied that the member and adherents of said church generally abstain from plural marriages and polygamous cohabitation and are now living in obedience to the laws, and that time has now arrived when the interests of public justice and morality will be promoted by granting of amnesty and pardon to all such offenders as have complied with the conditions of said proclamation, including such of said offenders as have been convicted under the provisions of said act: Now, therefore, I, Grover Cleveland, President of the United States, by virtue of the powers in me vested, do hereby declare and grant a full amnesty and pardon to all persons who have in violation of said acts committed either of the offenses of polygamy, bigamy, adultery, or unlawful cohabitation under the color of polygamous or plural marriage, or who, having been convicted of violations of said acts, are now suffering deprivation of civil rights in consequence of the same, excepting all persons who have not complied with the conditions contained in said executive proclamation of January 4, 1893. In witness whereof I have hereunto set my hand and caused the seal of the United States to be affixed. Done at the city of Washington, this 25th day of September, A.D. 1894, and of the Independence of the United States the one hundred and nineteenth. Grover Cleveland. By the President: W.Q. Gresham, Secretary of State." (Vol. IX, pp. 510-511).
On January 4, 1893, President Benjamin Harrison issued the Proclamation: "Whereas Congress by statute approved March 22, 1882, and by statutes in furtherance and amendment thereof defined the crimes of bigamy, polygamy, and unlawful cohabitation in the Territories and other places within the exclusive jurisdiction of the United States and prescribed a penalty for such crimes; and Whereas on or about the 6th day of October, 1890,

Endnotes

the Church of the Latter-day Saints, commonly known as the Mormon Church, through its president issued a manifesto proclaiming the purpose of said church no longer to sanction the practice of polygamous marriages and calling upon all members and adherents of said church to obey the laws of the United States in reference to said subject-matter; and Whereas it is represented that since the date of said declaration the members and adherents of said church have generally obeyed said laws and have abstained from plural marriages and polygamous cohabitation; and Whereas by a petition dated December 19, 1891, the officials of said church, pledging the membership thereof to a faithful obedience to the laws against plural marriage and unlawful cohabitation, have applied to me to grant amnesty for past offenses against said laws, which request a very large number of influential non-Mormons residing in the Territories have also strongly urged; and Whereas the Utah Commission in their report bearing date September 15, 1892, recommend that said petition be granted and said amnesty proclaimed, under proper conditions as to the future observance of the law, with a view to the encouragement of those now disposed to become law-abiding citizens; and Whereas during the past two years such amnesty has been granted to individual applicants in a very large number of cases, conditioned upon the faithful observance of the laws of the United States against unlawful cohabitation, and there are now pending many more such applications: Now, therefore, I, Benjamin Harrison, President of the United States, by virtue of the powers in me vested, do hereby declare and grant a full amnesty and pardon to all persons liable to the penalties of said act by reason of unlawful cohabitation under the color of polygamous or plural marriage who have since November 1, 1890, abstained from such unlawful cohabitation, but upon the express condition that they shall in the future faithfully obey the laws of the United States hereinbefore named and not otherwise. Those who shall fail to avail themselves of the clemency hereby offered will be vigorously prosecuted. In witness whereof I have hereunto set my hand and caused the seal of the United States to be affixed. Done at the city of Washington, this 4th day of January, A.D. 1893, and of the Independence of the United States the one hundred and seventeenth. Benj. Harrison. By the President: John W. Foster, Secretary of State." (Vol. IX, pp. 368-369).

On December 9, 1891, President Benjamin Harrison stated in his Third Annual Message: "The legislation of Congress for the repression of polygamy has, after years of resistance on the part of the Mormons, at last brought them to the conclusion that resistance is unprofitable and unavailing. The power of Congress over this subject should not be surrendered until we have satisfactory evidence that the people of the State to be created would exercise the exclusive power of the State over this subject in the same way. The question is not whether these people now obey the laws of Congress against polygamy, but rather would they make, enforce, and maintain such laws themselves if absolutely free to regulate the subject? We can not afford to experiment with this subject, for when a State in once constituted the act is final and any mistake irretrievable." (Vol. IX, p. 206).

On December 1, 1890, President Benjamin Harrison stated in his Second Annual Message: "The increasing numbers and influence of the non-Mormon population of Utah are observed with satisfaction. The recent letter of Wilford Woodruff, president of the Mormon Church, in which he advised his people to 'refrain from contracting any marriage forbidden by the laws of the land,' has attracted wide attention, and it is hoped that its influence will be highly beneficial in restraining infractions of the laws of the United States. But the fact should not be overlooked that the doctrine or belief of the church that polygamous marriages are rightful and supported by divine revelation remains unchanged. President Woodruff does not renounce the doctrine, but refrains from teaching it, and advises against the practice of it because the law is against it. Now, it is quite true that the law should not attempt to deal with faith or belief of anyone; but it is quite another thing, and the only safe thing, so to deal with the Territory of Utah as that those who believe polygamy to be rightful shall not have the power to make it lawful." (Vol. IX, p. 118).

On December 3, 1888, President Grover Cleveland stated in his Fourth Annual Message: "It also appears from this report that though prior to March, 1885, there had been but 6 convictions in the Territories of Utah and Idaho under the laws of 1862 and 1882, punishing polygamy and unlawful cohabitation as crimes, there have been since that date nearly 600 convictions under these laws and the statutes of 1887; and the opinion is expressed that under such a firm and vigilant execution of these laws and the advance of ideas opposed to the forbidden practices, polygamy within the United States is virtually at an end." (Vol. 8, p. 794).

On December 8, 1885, President Grover Cleveland stated in his First Annual Message to Congress: "In the Territory of Utah the law of the United States passed for suppression of polygamy has been energetically and faithfully executed during the past year, with measurably good results. A number of convictions have been secured for unlawful cohabitation, and in some cases pleas of guilty have been entered and a slight punishment imposed, upon a promise by the accused that they would not again offend against the law, nor advise, counsel, aid, or abet in any way its violation by others. The Utah commissioners express the opinion, based upon such information as they are able to obtain, that but few polygamous marriages have taken place in the Territory during the last year. They further report that while there can not be found upon the registration lists of voters the name of a man actually guilty of polygamy, and while none of that class are holding office, yet at the last election in the Territory all the officers elected, except in one county, were men who, though not actually living in the practice of polygamy, subscribe to the doctrine of polygamous marriages as a divine revelation and a law unto all higher and more binding upon the conscience than any human law, local or national. Thus is the strange spectacle presented of a community protected by a republican form of government, to which they owe allegiance, sustaining by their suffrages a principle and a belief which set at naught that obligation of absolute obedience to the law of the land which lies at the foundation of republican institutions. The strength, the perpetuity, and the destiny of the nation rest upon our homes, established by the law of God, guarded by parental care, regulated by parental authority, and sanctified by parental love. These are not the homes of polygamy. The mothers of our land, who rule the nation as they mold the characters and guide the actions of their sons, live according to God's holy ordinances, and each, secure and happy in the exclusive love of the father of her children, sheds the warm light of true womanhood, unperverted and unpolluted, upon all within her pure and wholesome family circle. These are not the cheerless, crushed, and unwomanly mothers of polygamy. The fathers of our families are the best citizens of the Republic. Wife and children are the sources of patriotism, and conjugal and parental affection beget devotion to the country. The man who, undefiled with plural marriage, is surrounded in his single home with his wife and children has a stake in the country which inspires him with respect for its laws and courage for its defense. These are not the fathers of polygamous families. There is no feature of this practice or system which sanctions it which is not opposed to all that is of value in our institutions. There should be no relaxation in the firm but just execution of the law now in operation, and I should be glad to approve such further discreet legislation as will rid the country of this blot upon its fair fame. Since the people upholding polygamy in our Territories are reenforced by immigration from other lands, I recommend that a law be passed to prevent the importation of Mormons into the country." (Vol. 8, pp. 361-362).

On March 4, 1885, President Grover Cleveland stated in his First Inaugural Address: "The conscience of the people demands that the Indians within our boundaries shall be fairly and honestly treated as wards of the Government and their education and civilization promoted with a view to their ultimate citizenship, and that polygamy in the Territories, destructive of the family relation and offensive to the moral sense of the civilized world, shall be repressed." (Vol. 8, p. 302).

On December 1, 1884, President Chester A. Arthur stated in his Fourth Annual Message: "The report of the Utah Commission will be read with interest. It discloses the results of recent legislation looking to the prevention and punishment of polygamy in that Territory. I still believe that if that abominable practice can be suppressed by law it can only be by the most radical legislation consistent with the restraints of the Constitution. I again recommend, therefore, that Congress assume absolute political control of the Territory of Utah and provide for the appointment of commissioners with such governmental powers as in its judgement may justly and wisely be put into their hands." (Vol. 8, p. 250).

On December 4, 1883, President Chester A. Arthur stated in his Third Annual Message: "The Utah Commission has submitted to the Secretary of the Interior its second annual report. As a result of its labors in supervising the recent election in that Territory, pursuant to the act of March 22, 1882, it appears that persons by that act disqualified to the number of about 12,000, were excluded from the polls. This fact, however, affords little cause for congratulation, and I fear that it is far from indicating any real and substantial progress toward the extirpation of polygamy. All the members elect of the legislature are Mormons. There is grave reason to believe that they are in sympathy with the practices that this Government is seeking to suppress, and that its efforts in that regard will be more likely to encounter their opposition than to receive their encouragement and support. Even if this view should happily be erroneous, the law under which the commissioners have been acting should be made more effective by the incorporation of some such stringent amendments as they recommend, and as were included in bill No. 2238 on the Calendar of the Senate at its last session. I am convinced, however, that polygamy has become so strongly intrenched in the Territory of Utah that it is profitless to attack it with any but the stoutest weapons which constitutional legislation can fashion. I favor, therefore, the repeal of the act upon which the existing government depends, the assumption by the National Legislature of the entire political control of the Territory, and the establishment of a commission with such powers and duties as shall be delegated to it by law." (Vol. 8, p. 184).

On December 6, 1881, President Chester A. Arthur stated in his First Annual Message to Congress: "For many years the Executive, in his annual message to Congress, has urged the necessity of stringent legislation for the suppression of polygamy in the Territories, and especially in the Territory of Utah. The existing statute for the punishment of this odious crime, so revolting to the moral and religious sense of Christendom, has been persistently and contemptuously violated ever since its enactment. Indeed, in spite of commendable efforts on the part of the authorities who represent the United States in that Territory, the law has in very rare instances been enforced, and, for a cause to which reference will presently be made, is practically a dead letter. The fact that adherents of the Mormon Church, which rests upon polygamy as its corner stone, have recently been peopling in large numbers Idaho, Arizona, and other of our Western Territories is well calculated to excite the liveliest interest and apprehension. It imposes upon Congress and the Executive the duty of arraying against this barbarous system all the power which under the Constitution and the law they can wield for its destruction. Reference has been already made to the obstacles which the United States officers have encountered in their efforts to punish violations of law. Prominent among these obstacles is the difficulty of procuring legal evidence sufficient to warrant a conviction even in the case of the most notorious offenders. Your attention is called to a recent opinion of the Supreme Court of the United States, explaining its judgement of reversal in the case of Miles, who had been convicted of bigamy in Utah. The court refers to the fact that the secrecy attending the celebration of marriages in that Territory makes the proof of polygamy very difficult, and the propriety is suggested of modifying the law of evidence which now makes a wife incompetent to testify against her husband. This suggestion is approved. I recommend also the passage of an act providing that in the Territories of the United States the fact that a woman has been married to a person charged with bigamy shall not disqualify her as a witness upon his trial for that offense. I further recommend legislation by which any person solemnizing a marriage in any of the Territories shall be required, under stringent penalties for neglect or refusal, to file a certificate of such marriage in the supreme court of the Territory. Doubtless Congress may devise other practicable measures for obviating the difficulties which have hitherto attended the efforts to suppress this iniquity. I assure you of my determined purpose to cooperate with you in any lawful and discreet measures which may be proposed to that end." (Vol. VIII, pp. 57-58).

On March 4, 1881, President James A. Garfield stated in his Inaugural Address: "The Constitution guarantees absolute religious freedom. Congress is prohibited from making any law respecting an establishment of religion or prohibiting the free exercise thereof. The Territories of the United States are subject to the direct legislative authority of Congress, and hence the General Government is responsible for any violation of the Constitution in any of them. It is therefore a reproach to the Government that in the most populous of the Territories the constitutional guaranty is not enjoyed by the people and the authority of Congress is set at naught. The Mormon Church not only offends the moral sense of manhood by sanctioning polygamy, but prevents the administration of justice through ordinary instrumentalities of law. In my judgement it is the duty of Congress, while respecting to the uttermost the conscientious convictions and religious scruples of every citizen, to prohibit within its jurisdiction all criminal practices, especially of that class which destroys the family relations and endanger social order." (Vol. 8, p. 11).

On December 6, 1880, President Rutherford B. Hayes stated in his Fourth Annual Message to Congress: "It is the recognized duty and purpose of the people of the United States to suppress polygamy where it now exists in our Territories and to prevent its extension. Faithful and zealous efforts have been made by the United States authorities in Utah to enforce the laws against it. Experience has shown that the legislation upon this subject, to be effective, requires extensive modification and amendment. The longer action is delayed the more difficult it will be to accomplish what is desired. Prompt and decided measures are necessary. The Mormon sectarian organization which upholds polygamy has the whole power of making and executing the local legislation of the Territory. By its control of the grand and petit juries it possesses large influence over the administration of justice. Exercising, as the heads of this sect do, the local power of the Territory, they are able to make effective their hostility to the law of Congress on the subject of polygamy, and, in fact, do prevent its enforcement. Polygamy will not be abolished if the enforcement of the law depends on those who practice and uphold the crime. It can only be suppressed by taking away the political power of the sect which encourages and sustains it. The power of Congress to enact suitable laws to protect the Territories is ample. It is not a case for halfway measures. The political power of the Mormon sect is increasing. It controls now one of our wealthiest and most populous Territories. It is extending steadily into other Territories. Wherever it goes it establishes polygamy and sectarian political power. The sanctity of marriage and the family relation are the corner stone of our American society and civilization. Religious liberty and the separation of church and state are among the elementary ideas of free institutions. To reestablish the interests and principles which polygamy and Mormonism have imperiled, and to fully reopen to intelligent and virtuous immigrants of all creeds that part of our domain which has been in a great degree closed to general immigration by intolerant and immoral institutions, it is recommended that the government of the Territory of Utah be reorganized. I recommend that Congress provide for the government of Utah by a governor and judges, or commissioners, appointed by the President and confirmed by the Senate - a government analogous to the provisional government established for the territory northwest of the Ohio by the ordinance of 1787. If, however, it is deemed best to continue the existing form of local government, I recommend that the right to vote, hold office, and sit on juries in the Territory of Utah be confined to those who neither practice nor uphold polygamy. If thorough measures are adopted, it is believed that within a few years the evils which now afflict Utah will be eradicated, and that this Territory will in good time become one of the most prosperous and attractive of the new States of the Union." (Vol. 7, pp. 605-606).

On December 1, 1879, President Rutherford B. Hayes stated in his Third Annual Message to Congress: "The continued deliberate violation by a large number of prominent and influential citizens of the Territory of Utah of the laws of the United States for the prosecution and punishment of polygamy demands the attention of every department of the Government. This Territory has a population sufficient to entitle it to admission as a State, and the general interests of the nation, as well as the welfare of the citizens of the Territory, require its advance from the Territorial form of government to the responsibilities and privileges of a State. This important change will not, however, be approved by the country while the citizens of Utah in very considerable number uphold a practice which is condemned as a crime by the laws of all civilized communities throughout the world. The law for the suppression of this offense was enacted with great unanimity by Congress more than seventeen years ago, but has remained until recently a dead letter in the Territory of Utah, because of the peculiar difficulties attending its enforcement. The opinion widely prevailed among the citizens of Utah that the law was in contravention of the constitutional guaranty of religious freedom. This objection is now removed. The Supreme Court of the United States has decided the law to be within the legislative power of Congress and binding as a rule of action for all who reside within the Territories. There is no longer any reason for delay or hesitation in its enforcement. It should be firmly and effectively executed. If not sufficiently stringent in its provisions, it should be amended; and in aid of the purpose in view I recommend that more comprehensive and more searching methods for preventing as well as punishing this crime be provided. If necessary to secure obedience to the law, the enjoyment and exercise of the rights and priviledges of citizenship in the Territories of the United States may be withheld or withdrawn from those who violate or oppose the enforcement of the law on this subject." (Vol. 7, pp. 559-569).

On December 7, 1875, President Ulysses S. Grant stated in his Seventh Annual Message to Congress: "In nearly every annual message that I have had the honor of transmitting to Congress I have called attention to the anomalous, not to say scandalous, condition of affairs existing in the Territory of Utah, and have asked for definite legislation to correct it. That polygamy should exist in a free, enlightened, and Christian country, without the power to punish so flagrant a crime against decency and morality, seems preposterous. True, there is no law to sustain this unnatural vice; but what is needed is a law to punish it as a crime, and at the same time to fix that status of the innocent children, the offspring of this system, and of the possibility innocent plural wives. But as an institution polygamy should be banished from the land....I deem of vital importance [to]....drive out licensed immorality, such as polygamy and the importation of women for illegitimate purposes." (Vol. 7, pp. 355-356).

On December 4, 1871, President Ulysses S. Grant stated in his Third Annual Message to Congress: "In Utah there still remains a remnant of barbarism, repugnant to civilization, to decency, and to the laws of the United States. Territorial officers, however, have been found who are willing to perform their duty in a spirit of equity and with a due sense of the necessity of sustaining the majesty of the law. Neither polygamy nor any other violation of existing statutes will be permitted within the territory of the United States. It is not with the religion of the self-styled Saints that we are now dealing, but with their practices. They will be protected in the worship of God according to the dictates of their consciences, but they will not be permitted to violate the laws under the cloak of religion. It may be advisable for Congress to consider what, in the execution of the laws against polygamy, is to be the status of plural wives and their offspring. The propriety of Congress passing an enabling act authorizing the Territorial legislature of Utah to legitimize all children born prior to a time fixed in the act might be justified by its humanity to these innocent children." (Vol. 7, p. 151).

On December 6, 1858, President James Buchanan stated in his Second Annual Message to Congress: "The present condition of the Territory of Utah, when contrasted with what it was one year ago, is a subject for congratulation. It was then in a state of open rebellion, and, cost what it might, the character of the Government required that this rebellion should be suppressed and the Mormons compelled to yield obedience to the Constitution and the laws. In order to accomplish this object, as I informed you in my last annual message, I appointed a new governor instead of Brigham Young, and other Federal officers to take the place of those who, consulting their personal safety, had found it necessary to withdraw from the Territory.

To protect these civil officers, and to aid them, as a posse comitatus, in the execution of the laws in case of need, I ordered a detachment of the Army to accompany them to Utah. The necessity for adopting these measures in now demonstrated. On the 15th of September, 1857, Governor Young issued his proclamation, in the style of an independent sovereign, announcing his purpose to resist by force of arms the entry of the United States troops into our own Territory of Utah. By this he required all the forces in the Territory to 'hold themselves in readiness to march at a moment's notice to repel any and all such invasion,' and established martial law from its date throughout the Territory. These proved to be no idle threats. Forts Bridger and Supply were vacated and burnt down by the Mormons to deprive our troops of a shelter after their long and fatiguing march. Orders were issued by Daniel H. Wells, styling himself 'Lieutenant-General, Nauvoo Legion,' to stampede the animals of the United States troops on their march, to set fire to their trains, to burn the grass and the whole country before them and on their flanks, to keep them from sleeping by night surprises, and to blockade the road by felling trees and destroying the fords of rivers, etc. These orders were promptly and effectually obeyed. On the 4th of October, 1857, the Mormons captured and burned, on Green River, three of our supply trains, consisting of seventy-five wagons loaded with provisions and tents for the army, and carried away several hundred animals. This diminished the supply of provisions so materially that General Johnston was obliged to reduce the ration, and even with this precaution there was only sufficient left to subsist the troops until the 1st of June. Our little army behaved admirably in their encampment at Fort Bridger under these trying privations. In the midst of the mountains, in a dreary, unsettled, and inhospitable region, more than a thousand miles from home, they passed the severe and inclement winter without a murmur. They looked forward with confidence for relief from their country in due season, and in this they were not disappointed. The Secretary of War employed all his energies to forward them the necessary supplies and to muster and send such a military force to Utah as would render resistance on the part of the Mormons hopeless, and thus terminate the war without the effusion of blood. In his efforts he war efficiently sustained by Congress. They granted appropriations sufficient to cover the deficiency thus necessarily created, and also provided for raising two regiments of volunteers 'for the purpose of quelling disturbances in the Territory of Utah, for the protection of supply and emigrant trains, and the suppression of Indian hostilities on the frontiers.' Happily, there was no occasion to call these regiments into service. If there had been, I should have felt serious embarrassment in selecting them, so great war the number of our brave and patriotic citizens anxious to serve their country in this distant and apparently dangerous expedition. Thus it has ever been, and thus may it ever be. The wisdom and economy of sending sufficient reinforcements to Utah are established, not only by the event, but in the opinion of those who from their position and opportunities are the most capable of forming a correct judgement. General Johnston, the commander of the forces, in addressing the Secretary of War from Fort Bridger under date of October 18, 1857, expresses the opinion that 'unless a large force is sent here, from the nature of the country a protracted war on their [the Mormon's] part is inevitable.' This he considered necessary to terminate the war 'speedily and more economically than if attempted by insufficient means.' In the meantime it was my anxious desire that the Mormons should yield obedience to the Constitution and the laws without rendering it necessary to resort to military force. To aid in accomplishing this object, I deemed it advisable in April last to dispatch two distinguished citizens of the United States, Messrs. Powell and McCulloch, to Utah. They bore with them a proclamation addressed by myself to the inhabitants of Utah, dated on the 6th day of that month, warning them of their true condition and how hopeless it was on their part to persist in rebellion against the United States, and offering all those who should submit to the laws a full pardon for their past seditions and treasons. At the same time I assured those who should persist in rebellion against the United States that they must expect no further lenity, but look to be rigorously dealt with according to their deserts. The instructions to these agents, as well as a copy of the proclamation and their reports, are herewith submitted. It will be seen by their report of the

3d of July last that they have fully confirmed the opinion expressed by General Johnston in the previous October as to the necessity of sending reinforcements to Utah. In this they state that they 'are firmly impressed with the belief that the presence of the Army here and the large additional force that had been ordered to this Territory were the chief inducements that caused the Mormons to abandon the idea of resisting the authority of the United States. A less decisive policy would probably have resulted in a long, bloody, and expensive war.' These gentlemen conducted themselves to my entire satisfaction and rendered useful services in executing the humane intentions of the Government. It also affords me great satisfaction to state that Governor Cumming has performed his duty in an able and conciliatory manner and with the happiest effect. I can not in this connection refrain from mentioning the valuable services of Colonel Thomas L. Kane, who, from motives of pure benevolence and without any official character or pecuniary compensation, visited Utah during the last inclement winter for the purpose of contributing to the pacification of the Territory. I am happy to inform you that the governor and other civil officers of Utah are now performing their appropriate functions without resistance. The authority of the Constitution and the laws has been fully restored and peace prevails throughout the Territory." (Vol. 5, pp. 503-506).

On April 6, 1858, President James Buchanan issued the Proclamation: "Whereas the Territory of Utah was settled by certain emigrants from the States and from foreign countries who have for several years past manifested a spirit of insubordination to the Constitution and laws of the United States. The great mass of those settlers, acting under the influence of leaders to whom they seem to have surrendered their judgement, refuse to be controlled by any other authority. They have been often advised to obedience, and these friendly counsels have been answered with defiance. The officers of the Federal Government have been driven from the Territory for no offense but an effort to do their sworn duty; others have been prevented from going there by threats of assassination; judges have been violently interrupted in the performance of their functions, and the records of the courts have been seized and destroyed or concealed. Many other acts of unlawful violence have been perpetrated, and the right to repeat them has been openly claimed by the leading inhabitants, with at least the silent acquiescence of nearly all the others. Their hostility to the lawful government of the country has at length become so violent that no officer bearing a commission from the Chief Magistrate of the Union can enter the Territory or remain there with safety, and all those officers recently appointed have been unable to go to Salt Lake or anywhere else in Utah beyond the immediate power of the Army. Indeed, such is believed to be the condition to which a strange system of terrorism has brought the inhabitants of that region that no one among them could express an opinion favorable to this Government, or even propose to obey its laws, without exposing his life and property to peril. After carefully considering this state of affairs and maturely weighing the obligation I was under to see the laws faithfully executed, it seemed to me right and proper that I should make such use of the military force at my disposal as might be necessary to protect the Federal officers in going into the Territory of Utah and in performing their duties after arriving there. I accordingly ordered a detachment of the Army to march for the city of Salt Lake, or within reach of that place, and to act in case of need as a posse for the enforcement of the laws. But in the meantime the hatred of that misguided people for the just and legal authority of the Government had become so intense that they resolved to measure their military strength with that of the Union. They have organized an armed force far from contemptible in point of numbers and trained it, if not with skill, at least with great assiduity and perseverance. While the troops of the United States were on their march a train of baggage wagons, which happened to be unprotected, was attacked and destroyed by a portion of the Mormon forces and the provisions and stores with which the train was laden were wantonly burnt. In short, their present attitude is one of decided and unreserved enmity to the United States and to all their loyal citizens. Their determination to oppose the authority of the Government by military force has not only been expressed in words, but manifested in overt acts of the most unequivocal character. Fellow-citizens of Utah, this is rebellion against the Government to which you owe allegiance; it is levying war against the United States, and involves you in the guilt of treason. Persistence in it will bring you to condign punishment, to ruin, and to shame; for it is mere madness to suppose that with your limited resources you can successfully resist the force of this great and powerful nation. If you have calculated upon the forbearance of the United States, if you have permitted yourselves to suppose that this Government will fail to put forth its strength and bring you to submission, you have fallen into a grave mistake. You have settled upon territory which lies, geographically, in the heart of the Union. The land you live upon was purchased by the United States and paid for our of their Treasury; the proprietary right and title to it is in them, and not in you. Utah is bounded on every side by States and Territories whose people are true to the Union. It is absurd to believe that they will or can permit you to erect in their very midst a government of your own, not only independent of the authority which they all acknowledge, but hostile to them and their interests. Do not deceive yourselves nor try to mislead others by propagating the idea that this is a crusade against your religion. The Constitution and laws of this country can take no notice of your creed, whether it be true or false. That is a question between your god and yourselves, in which I disclaim all right to interfere. If you obey the laws, keep the peace, and respect the just rights of others, you will be perfectly secure, and may live one in your present faith or change it for another at your pleasure. Every intelligent man among you knows very well that this Government has never, directly or indirectly, sought to molest you in your worship, to control you in your ecclesiastical affairs, or even to influence you in your religious opinions. This rebellion is not merely a violation of your legal duty; it is without just cause, without reason, without excuse. You never made a complaint that was not listened to with patience; you never exhibited a real grievance that was not redressed as promptly as it could be. The laws and regulations enacted for your government by Congress have been equal and just, and their enforcement was manifestly necessary for your own welfare and happiness. You have never asked their repeal. They are similar in every material respect to the laws which have been passed for the other Territories of the Union, and which everywhere else (with one partial exception) have been cheerfully obeyed. No people ever lived who were freer from unnecessary legal restraints than you. Human wisdom never devised a political system which bestowed more blessings or imposed lighter burdens than the Government of the United States in its operation upon the Territories. But being anxious to save the effusion of blood and to avoid the indiscriminate punishment of a whole people for crimes of which it is not probable that all are equally guilty, I offer now a free and full pardon to all who will submit themselves to the just authority of the Federal Government. If you refuse to accept it, let the consequences fall upon your own heads. But I conjure you to pause deliberately and reflect well before you reject this tender of peace and good will. Now, therefore, I, James Buchanan, President of the United States, have thought proper to issue this my proclamation, enjoining upon all public officers in the Territory of Utah to be diligent and faithful, to the full extent of their power, in the execution of the laws; commanding all citizens of the United States in said Territory to aid and assist the officers in the performance of their duties; offering to the inhabitants of Utah who shall submit to the laws a free pardon for the seditions and treasons heretofore by them committed; warning those who shall persist, after notice of this proclamation, in the present rebellion against the United States that they must expect no further lenity, but look to be rigorously dealt with according to their deserts; and declaring that the military forces now in Utah and hereafter to be sent there will not be withdrawn until the inhabitants of that Territory shall manifest a proper sense of the duty which they owe to this Government. In testimony whereof I have hereunto set my hand and caused the seal of the United States to be affixed to these presents. Done at the city of Washington the 6th day of April, 1858, and of the Independence of the United States the eighty-second. James Buchanan, By the President: Lewis Cass, Secretary of State." (Vol. 5, pp. 493-495).

On December 8, 1857, President James Buchanan stated in his First Annual Message to Congress: "A Territorial government was established for Utah by act of Congress approved the 9th September, 1850, and the Constitution and laws of the United States were thereby extended over it 'so far as the same of any provisions thereof may be applicable.' This act provided for the appointment by the President, by and with the advice and consent of the Senate, of a governor (who was to be ex officio superintendent of Indian affairs), a secretary, three judges of the supreme court, a marshal, and a district attorney. Subsequent acts provided for the appointment of the officers necessary to extend our land and our Indian system over the Territory. Brigham Young was appointed the first governor on the 20th September, 1850, and has held the office ever since. Whilst Governor Young has been both governor and superintendent of Indian affairs throughout this period, he has been at the same time the head of the church called the Latter-day Saints, and professes to govern its members and dispose of their property by direct inspiration and authority from the Almighty. His power has been, therefore, absolute over both church and state. The people of Utah almost exclusively belong to this church, and believing with a fanatical spirit that he is governor of the Territory by divine appointment, they obey his commands as if these were direct revelations from Heaven. If, therefore, he chooses that his government shall come into collision with the Government of the United States, the members of the Mormon Church will yield implicit obedience to his will. Unfortunately, existing facts leave but little doubt that such is his determination. Without entering upon a minute history of occurrences, it is sufficient to say that all the officers of the United States, judicial and executive, with the single exception of two Indian agents, have found it necessary for their own personal safety to withdraw from the Territory, and there no longer remains any government in Utah but the despotism of Brigham Young. This being the condition of affairs in the Territory, I could not mistake the path of duty. As Chief Executive Magistrate I was bound to restore the supremacy of the Constitution and laws within its limits. In order to effect this purpose, I appointed a new governor and other Federal officers for Utah and sent with them a military force for their protection and to aid as a posse comitatus in case of need in the execution of laws. With the religious opinions of the Mormons, as long as they remained mere opinions, however deplorable in themselves and revolting to the moral and religious sentiments of all Christendom, I had no right to interfere. Actions alone, when in violation of the Constitution and laws of the United States, become the legitimate subjects for the jurisdiction of the civil magistrate. My instructions to Governor Cummings have therefore been framed in strict accordance with these principles. At their date a hope was indulged that no necessity might exist for employing the military in restoring and maintaining the authority of the law, but this hope has now vanished. Governor Young has by proclamation declared his determination to maintain his power by force, and has already committed acts of hostility against the United States. Unless he should retrace his steps the Territory of Utah will be in a state of open rebellion. He has committed these acts of hostility notwithstanding Major Van Vliet, an officer of the Army, sent to Utah by the Commanding General to purchase provisions for the troops, had given him the strongest assurances of the peaceful intentions of the Government, and that the troops would only be employed as a posse comititus when called on by the civil authority to aid in the execution of the laws. There is reason to believe that Governor Young has long contemplated this result. He knows that the continuance of his despotic power depends upon the exclusion of all settlers from the Territory except those who will acknowledge his divine mission and implicitly obey his will, and that an enlightened public opinion there would soon prostrate institutions at war with the laws both of God and man. He has therefore for several years, in order to maintain his independence, been industriously employed in collecting and fabricating arms and munitions of war and in disciplining the Mormons for military service. As superintendent of Indian affairs he has had an opportunity of tampering with the Indian tribes and exciting their hostile feelings against the United States. This, according to our information, he has accomplished in regard to some of these tribes, while others have remained true to their allegiance and have communicated his intrigues to our Indian agents. He has laid in a store of provisions for three years, which in case of necessity, as he informed Major Van Vliet, he will conceal, 'and then take to the mountains and bid defiance to all powers of the Government.' A great part of all this may be idle boasting, but yet no wise government will lightly estimate the efforts which may be inspired by such frenzied fanaticism as exists among the Mormon in Utah. This is the first rebellion which has existed in our Territories, and humanity itself requires that we should put it down in such a manner that it shall be the last. To trifle with it would be to encourage it and to render it formidable. We ought to go there with such an imposing force as to convince these deluded people that resistance would be vain, and thus spare the effusion of blood. We can in this manner best convince them that we are their friends, not their enemies. In order to accomplish this object it will be necessary, according to the estimated of the War Department, to raise four additional regiments; and this I earnestly recommend to Congress. At the present moment of depression in the revenues of the country I am sorry to be obliged to recommend such a measure; but I feel confident of the support of Congress, cost what it may, in suppressing the insurrection and in restoring and maintaining the sovereignty of the Constitution and laws over the Territory of Utah." (Vol. 5, pp. 454-456).]

[335] United States Supreme Court. 1986, in the case of Bowers v. Hardwick, 478 U.S. 186, 92 L Ed 2d 140, 106 S. Ct. 2841, p. 149, (Chief Justice Warren E. Burger). Gary DeMar, America's Christian History: The Untold Story (Atlanta, GA: American Vision Publishers, Inc., 1993), p. 68.

[336] United States Supreme Court. 1986, in the case of Bowers v. Hardwick, 478 U.S. 186, 92 L Ed 2d 140, 106 S. Ct. 2841, reh den (US) 92 L Ed 2d 779, 107 S. Ct. 29. pp. 147-148 (Chief Justice Warren E. Burger). Gary DeMar, America's Christian History: The Untold Story (Atlanta, GA: American Vision Publishers, Inc., 1993), pp. 102-103.

[337] Tocqueville, Alexis de. Alexis De Tocqueville, Democracy in America (New York: Vintage Books, 1945), Vol. I, p. 314-315. Tim LaHaye, Faith of Our Founding Fathers (Brentwood, TN: Wolgemuth & Hyatt, Publishers, Inc., 1987), p. 98.

[338] Greeley, Horace. Autobiography of Horace Greeley, p. 71. Stephen Abbott Northrop, D.D., A Cloud of Witnesses (Portland, OR: American Heritage Ministries, 1987; Mantle Ministries, 228 Still Ridge, Bulverde, Texas), p. 197.

[339] Washington, George. May 26, 1777, in a circular to the brigadier-generals Jared Sparks, ed., The Writings of George Washington 12 vols. (Boston: American Stationer's Company, 1837; NY: F. Andrew's, 1834-1847), Vol. IV, p. 436. William J. Johnson, George Washington - The Christian (St. Paul, MN: William J. Johnson, Merriam Park, February 23, 1919; Nashville, TN: Abingdon Press, 1919; reprinted Milford, MI: Mott Media, 1976; reprinted Arlington Heights, IL: Christian Liberty Press, 502 West Euclid Avenue, Arlington Heights, Illinois, 60004, 1992), p. 98.

[340] Washington, George. March 10, 1778. The Writings of George Washington - Bicentennial Edition (March 1 through May 31, 1778, 11:83-84, published by the U.S. Government Printing Office, 1934. Howard Phillips, The Howard Phillips Issues and Strategy Bulletin (March 31, 1993, Vienna, Virginia 22182). Gary DeMar, The Biblical Worldview (Atlanta, GA: An American Vision Publication - American Vision, Inc., May 1993), Vol. 9, No. 5, p. 8. John Clement Fitzpatrick, ed., The Writings of George Washington, from the Original Manuscript Sources 1749-1799, 39 vols. (Washington, D.C.: United States Government Printing Office, 1931-1944), Vol. XI, p. 83-84.

[341] Ulysses S. Grant, December 4, 1871, in his Third Annual Message to Congress.

[342] Grant, Ulysses Simpson. December 7, 1875, in his Seventh Annual Message to Congress. James D. Richardson (U.S. Representative from Tennessee), ed., A Compilation of the Messages and Papers of the Presidents 1789-1897, 10 vols. (Washington, D.C.: U.S. Government Printing Office, published by Authority of Congress, 1897, 1899; Washington, D.C.: Bureau of National Literature and Art, 1789-1902, 11 vols., 1907, 1910), Vol. 7, pp. 336, 355-356.

[343] Arthur, Chester Alan. December 6, 1881, in his First Annual Message to Congress. James D. Richardson (U.S. Representative from Tennessee), ed., A Compilation of the Messages and Papers of the Presidents 1789-1897, 10 vols. (Washington, D.C.: U.S. Government

Endnotes

Printing Office, published by Authority of Congress, 1897, 1899; Washington, D.C.: Bureau of National Literature and Art, 1789-1902, 11 vols., 1907, 1910), Vol. 8, pp. 25-26, 37, 39, 40, 42, 57.

[344] Cleveland, (Stephen) Grover. December 8, 1885, in his First Annual Message to Congress. James D. Richardson (U.S. Representative from Tennessee), ed., A Compilation of the Messages and Papers of the Presidents 1789-1897, 10 vols. (Washington, D.C.: U.S. Government Printing Office, published by Authority of Congress, 1897, 1899; Washington, D.C.: Bureau of National Literature and Art, 1789-1902, 11 vols., 1907, 1910), Vol. 8, pp. 361-362.

[345] Roosevelt, Theodore. January 30, 1905, in a message to Congress. A Compilation of the Messages and Papers of the Presidents 20 vols. (New York: Bureau of National Literature, Inc., prepared under the direction of the Joint Committee on Printing, of the House and Senate, pursuant to an Act of the Fifty-Second Congress of the United States, 1893, 1923), Vol. XIV, pp. 6942-6943.

[346] Roosevelt, Theodore. December 3, 1906, in his Sixth Annual Message to Congress. A Compilation of the Messages and Papers of the Presidents 20 vols. (New York: Bureau of National Literature, Inc., prepared under the direction of the Joint Committee on Printing, of the House and Senate, pursuant to an Act of the Fifty-Second Congress of the United States, 1893, 1923), Vol. XIV, pp. 7030-7032, 7046, 7048,

[347] Eisenhower, Dwight David. In the magazine, Episcopal Churchnews. Edmund Fuller and David E. Green, God in the White House - The Faiths of American Presidents (NY: Crown Publishers, Inc., 1968), pp. 215-216.

[348] Truman, Harry S. December 5, 1950, in an address at the Mid-Century White House Conference on Children and Youth. T.S. Settel, and the staff of Quote, editors, The Quotable Harry Truman introduction by Merle Miller (NY: Droke House Publishers, Inc., Berkley Publishing Corporation, 1967), pp. 43-44.

[349] Reagan, Ronald Wilson. March 8, 1983, in a speech to the National Association of Evangelicals. William Safire, ed., Lend Me Your Ears - Great Speeches in History (NY: W.W. Norton & Company 1992), p. 464. David R. Shepherd, ed., Ronald Reagan: In God I Trust (Wheaton, Illinois: Tyndale House Publishers, Inc., 1984), pp. 35-38, 133-134. Frederick J. Ryan, Jr., ed., Ronald Reagan - The Wisdom and Humor of The Great Communicator (San Francisco: Collins Publishers, A Division of Harper Collins Publishers, 1995), p. 42.

[350] Reagan, Ronald Wilson. March 6, 1980, Los Angeles Times.

[351] Reagan, Ronald Wilson. July 12, 1984, in answer to a questionnaire from The Scoreboard.

[352] Reagan, Ronald Wilson. May 7, 1983, in a Radio address to the Nation. David R. Shepherd, ed., Ronald Reagan: In God I Trust (Wheaton, Illinois: Tyndale House Publishers, Inc., 1984), pp. 108-111.

[353] Matthew D. Staver, "The Ten Commandments in American Law and Government" (Orlando, FL: The Liberty Counsel, P.O. Box 540774, Orlando, FL 32854, 407-875-2100, 407-875-0770 Fax, http://www.lc.org, liberty@lc.org, 2002), pp. 14-15.

[354] Lowell, James Russell. November 20, 1885, in his International Copyright. John Bartlett, Bartlett's Familiar Quotations (Boston: Little, Brown and Company, 1855, 1980), p. 569.

[355] Twain, Mark. 1876, in The Adventures of Tom Sawyer, chapter 13. John Bartlett, Bartlett's Familiar Quotations (Boston: Little, Brown and Company, 1855, 1980), p. 622.

[356] Matthew D. Staver, "The Ten Commandments in American Law and Government" (Orlando, FL: The Liberty Counsel, P.O. Box 540774, Orlando, FL 32854, 407-875-2100, 407-875-0770 Fax, http://www.lc.org, liberty@lc.org, 2002), p. 15.

[357] Franklin, Benjamin. Leonard Labaree, ed., The Papers of Benjamin Franklin (New Haven: Yale University Press, 1959), Vol. I, pp. 104-105. Carl Becker, Benjamin Franklin (New York: Cornell University, 1946), p. 81. Tim LaHaye, Faith of Our Founding Fathers (Brentwood, TN: Wolgemuth & Hyatt, Publishers, Inc., 1987), pp. 119, 122.

[358] Franklin, Benjamin. List of Virtues. The Autobiography of Benjamin Franklin.

[359] Jefferson, Thomas. August 19, 1785, in a letter to Peter Carr. John Bartlett, Bartlett's Familiar Quotations (Boston: Little, Brown and Company, 1855, 1980), p. 388.
[360] Morris, Gouverneur. 1785, in An Address on the Bank of North America given in the Pennsylvania State Assembly. Jared Sparks, ed., The Life of Gouverneur Morris, with Selections from His Correspondence and Miscellaneous Papers, 3 vols. (Boston: Gray and Bowen, 1832), Vol. III, p. 465. Stephen McDowell and Mark Beliles, "The Providential Perspective" (Charlottesville, VA: The Providence Foundation, P.O. Box 6759, Charlottesville, Va. 22906, January 1994), Vol. 9, No. 1, p. 5. John Eidsmoe, Christianity and The Constitution - The Faith of Our Founding Fathers (Baker Book House, 1987), pp. 183-84.
[361] Hill, Benjamin Harvey. In a Tribute to Robert E. Lee. Thomas Nelson Page, Robert E. Lee, (1911). John Bartlett, Bartlett's Familiar Quotations (Boston: Little, Brown and Company, 1855, 1980), p. 592.
[362] Wilson, (Thomas) Woodrow. 1911, statement. George Otis, The Solution to the Crisis in America, Revised and Enlarged Edition (Van Nuys, CA.: Fleming H. Revell Company; Bible Voice, Inc., 1970, 1972, foreword by Pat Boone), p. 28.
[363] Blackstone, Sir William. 1765-1770, in his work entitled, Commentaries on the Laws of England. Wendell's Blackstone's Commentaries, Vol. IV, p. 43. Stephen Abbott Northrop, D.D., A Cloud of Witnesses (Portland, Oregon: American Heritage Ministries, 1987; Mantle Ministries, 228 Still Ridge, Bulverde, Texas), p. 33.
[364] Massachusetts Supreme Court. 1838. Commonwealth v. Abner Kneeland, 37 Mass. (20 Pick) 206, 216-217 (1838).
[365] South Carolina, State of. 1778, Constitution, Article XXXVIII. Benjamin Franklin Morris, The Christian Life and Character of the Civil Institutions of the United States (Philadelphia, PA: L. Johnson & Co., 1863; George W. Childs, 1864), pp. 230-231. Frances Newton Thorpe, ed., Federal and State Constitutions, Colonial Charters, and Other Organic Laws of the States, Territories, and Colonies now or heretofore forming the United States, 7 vols. (Washington: Government Printing Office, 1905; 1909; St. Clair Shores, MI: Scholarly Press, 1968), Vol. V, p. 3264. Edwin S. Gaustad, Neither King nor Prelate - Religion and the New Nation 1776-1826 (Grand Rapids, MI: William B. Eerdmans Publishing Company, 1993), pp. 171-172. John J. McGrath, ed., Church and State in American Law: Cases and Materials (Milwaukee: The Bruce Publishing Co., 1962), p. 375. Anson Phelps Stokes and Leo Pfeffer, Church and State in the United States (NY: Harper and Row, Publishers, 1950, revised one-volume edition, 1964), p. 79.
[366] Tocqueville, Alexis de. August 1831. Alexis de Tocqueville, The Republic of the United States of America and Its Political Institutions - Reviewed and Examined, Henry Reeves, trans., (Garden City, NY: A.S. Barnes & Co., 1851), Vol. I, p. 334. Alexis de Tocqueville, Democracy in America, 2 vols. (NY: Alfred A. Knopf, 1945), Vol. I, pp. 311, 319-320. Alexis de Tocqueville, Democracy in America, George Lawrence, translator, (NY: Harper & Row, 1988) p. 47. Tryon Edwards, D.D., The New Dictionary of Thoughts - A Cyclopedia of Quotations (Garden City, NY: Hanover House, 1852; revised and enlarged by C.H. Catrevas, Ralph Emerson Browns and Jonathan Edwards [descendent, along with Tryon, of Jonathan Edwards (1703-1758), president of Princeton], 1891; The Standard Book Company, 1955, 1963), p. 337. The Annals of America, 20 vols. (Chicago, IL: Encyclopedia Britannica, 1968, 1977), Vol. 5, pp. 486-487, 497. Sidney E. Ahlstrom, A Religious History of the American People (New Haven, CT: Yale University Press, 1972), p. 386. Frederick Kershner, Jr., ed., Tocqueville's America - The Great Quotations (Athens, Ohio: Ohio University Press, Cooper Industries, 1983), p. 62. Charles Colson, Kingdoms in Conflict (Grand Rapids, MI: Zondervan Publishing House, 1987), pp. 228-229, 273. John Eidsmoe, Christianity and the Constitution - The Faith of Our Founding Fathers (Grand Rapids, MI: Baker Book House, A Mott Media Book, 1987; 6th printing, 1993), p. 408. Pat Robertson, The Turning Tide (Dallas: Word Publishing, 1993), p. 270.
[367] Arkansas, State of. 1874, Constitution, Article XIX, Section 1. Constitutions of the United

Endnotes

States - National and State (Dobbs Ferry, New York: Oceana Publications, Inc., published for Legislative Drafting Research Fund of Columbia University, Release 94-4, Issued October 1994), Vol. 1, Arkansas(October 1994), p. 32. Charles E. Rice, The Supreme Court and Public Prayer (New York: Fordham University Press, 1964), p. 168; "Hearings, Prayers in Public Schools and Other Matters," Committee on the Judiciary, U.S. Senate (87th Cong., 2nd Sess.), 1962, pp. 268 et seq.

[368] South Carolina Supreme Court. 1846, City of Charleston v. S.A. Benjamin, 2 Strob. 521-524 (1846).

[369] Washington, George. September 19, 1796, in his Farewell Address. Address of George Washington, President of the United States, and Late Commander in Chief of the American Army. To the People of the United States, Preparatory to His Declination. Published in the American Daily Advertiser, Philadelphia, September, 1796. Jared Sparks, ed., The Writings of George Washington 12 vols. (Boston: American Stationer's Company, 1837; NY: F. Andrew's, 1834-1847), Vol. XII, pp. 227-228. James D. Richardson (U.S. Representative from Tennessee), ed., A Compilation of the Messages and Papers of the Presidents 1789-1897, 10 vols. (Washington, D.C.: U.S. Government Printing Office, published by Authority of Congress, 1897, 1899; Washington, D.C.: Bureau of National Literature and Art, 1789-1902, 11 vols., 1907, 1910), Vol. 1, pp. 205-216, 220

[370] Madison, James. July 23, 1813, in a Proclamation of a National Day of Public Humiliation and Prayer. James D. Richardson (U.S. Representative from Tennessee), ed., A Compilation of the Messages and Papers of the Presidents 1789-1897, 10 vols. (Washington, D.C.: U.S. Government Printing Office, published by Authority of Congress, 1897, 1899; Washington, D.C.: Bureau of National Literature and Art, 1789-1902, 11 vols., 1907, 1910), Vol. I, pp. 532-533. Irving Brant, James Madison (Indianapolis: Bobbs-Merrill, 1941), V:19, VI:198. John Eidsmoe, Christianity and the Constitution - The Faith of Our Founding Fathers (Grand Rapids, MI: Baker Book House, A Mott Media Book, 1987, 6th printing 1993), p. 111.

[371] Jackson, Andrew. March 4, 1837, in his Farewell Address. James D. Richardson (U.S. Representative from Tennessee), ed., A Compilation of the Messages and Papers of the Presidents 1789-1897, 10 vols. (Washington, D.C.: U.S. Government Printing Office, published by Authority of Congress, 1897, 1899; Washington, D.C.: Bureau of National Literature and Art, 1789-1902, 11 vols., 1907, 1910), Vol. II, pp. 292-308. The Annals of America, 20 vols. (Chicago, IL: Encyclopedia Britannica, 1968), Vol. VI, p. 310. Peter Marshall and David Manuel, The Glory of America (Bloomington, MN: Garborg's Heart 'N Home, Inc., 1991), 3.3. D.P. Diffine, Ph.D., One Nation Under God - How Close a Separation? (Searcy, Arkansas: Harding University, Belden Center for Private Enterprise Education, 6th edition, 1992), p. 11.

[372] Buchanan, James. March 28, 1860, in a formal Protest to the House of Representatives. James D. Richardson (U.S. Representative from Tennessee), ed., A Compilation of the Messages and Papers of the Presidents 1789-1897, 10 vols. (Washington, D.C.: U.S. Government Printing Office, published by Authority of Congress, 1897, 1899; Washington, D.C.: Bureau of National Literature and Art, 1789-1902, 11 vols., 1907, 1910), Vol. 5, p. 618.

[373] Lincoln, Abraham. March 30, 1863, in a Proclamation of a National Day of Humiliation, Fasting and Prayer. James D. Richardson (U.S. Representative from Tennessee), ed., A Compilation of the Messages and Papers of the Presidents 1789-1897, 10 vols. (Washington, D.C.: U.S. Government Printing Office, published by Authority of Congress, 1897, 1899; Washington, D.C.: Bureau of National Literature and Art, 1789-1902, 11 vols., 1907, 1910), Vol. VI, pp. 164-165. Benjamin Franklin Morris, The Christian Life and Character of the Civil Institutions of the United States (Philadelphia: George W. Childs, 1864), pp. 558-559. Anson Phelps Stokes, Church and State in the United States (New York: Harper and Brothers, 1950), Vol. III, p. 186. Roy P. Basler, ed., The Collected Works of Abraham Lincoln, 9 vols. (New Brunswick, NJ: Rutgers University Press, 1953), Vol. 6, p. 179. Benjamin Weiss, God in American History: A Documentation of America's Religious Heritage (Grand Rapids, MI:

Zondervan, 1966), p. 92. Willard Cantelon, Money Master of the World (Plainfield, NJ: Logos International, 1976), p. 120. Gary DeMar, God and Government, A Biblical and Historical Study (Atlanta, GA: American Vision Press, 1984), p. 128-29. "Our Christian Heritage," Letter from Plymouth Rock (Marlborough, NH: The Plymouth Rock Foundation), p. 6. D.P. Diffine, Ph.D., One Nation Under God - How Close a Separation? (Searcy, Arkansas: Harding University, Belden Center for Private Enterprise Education, 6th edition, 1992), pp. 14-15. Gary DeMar, America's Christian History: The Untold Story (Atlanta, GA: American Vision Publishers, Inc., 1993), pp. 53, 99. George Otis, The Solution to the Crisis in America, Revised and Enlarged Edition (Van Nuys, CA.: Fleming H. Revell Company; Bible Voice, Inc., 1970, 1972, foreword by Pat Boone), pp. 47-48.

[374] Colfax, Schuyler. O.J. Hollister, Life of Schuyler Colfax, p. 453. Stephen Abbott Northrop, D.D., A Cloud of Witnesses (Portland, OR: American Heritage Ministries, 1987; Mantle Ministries, 228 Still Ridge, Bulverde, Texas), p. 93.

[375] Eisenhower, Dwight David. January 20, 1953, in his Inaugural Address. New York Times, January 21, 1953. Inaugural Addresses of the Presidents of the United States - From George Washington 1789 to Richard Milhous Nixon 1969 (Washington, D.C.: United States Government Printing Office; 91st Congress, 1st Session, House Document 91-142, 1969), pp. 257-262. Paul M. Angle, ed., By These Words (NY: Rand McNally & Company, 1954), pp. 400-408. Davis Newton Lott, The Inaugural Addresses of the American Presidents (NY: Holt, Rinehart and Winston, 1961), pp. 257-261. Charles Hurd, ed., A Treasury of Great American Speeches (NY: Hawthorne Books, 1959), (paragraphs 2-4), pp. 305-306. D.D. Eisenhower, The Inaugural Prayer (Denison, TX: on display at the Eisenhower Birthplace Memorial, 208 E. Day, Denison, Texas, 75020). Charles E. Rice, The Supreme Court and Public Prayer (New York: Fordham University Press, 1964), pp. 192-193. Edmund Fuller and David E. Green, God in the White House - The Faiths of American Presidents (NY: Crown Publishers, Inc., 1968), p. 217. Edward L.R. Elson, D.D., Lit.D., LL.D., America's Spiritual Recovery (Westwood, N.J.: Fleming H. Revell Company, 1954), p. 56. January 20, 1953, Scripture choice at his Inauguration, January 20, 1953: "If my people, who are called by my name, will humble themselves and pray and seek my face, and turn from their wicked ways, then I will hear from heaven, will forgive their sin, and heal their land."(II Chronicles 7:14). J. Michael Sharman, J.D., Faith of the Fathers (Culpepper, Virginia: Victory Publishing, 1995), pp. 106-108.

[376] Bush, George Herbert Walker. February 22, 1990, in a Presidential Proclamation declaring 1990 the International Year of Bible Reading, concurring with the request of Congress, Senate Joint Resolution 164. Courtesy of Bruce Barilla, Christian Heritage Week Ministry (P.O. Box 58, Athens, W.V. 24712; 304-384-7707, 304-384-9044 fax).

[377] Holland, Josiah Gilbert. 1872, in his work, Wanted, l. I. John Bartlett, Bartlett's Familiar Quotations (Boston: Little, Brown and Company, 1855, 1980), p. 566. Carl Van Dorn, ed., Patriotic Anthology (NY: Literary Guild of America, Inc, 1941), p. 390. Charles Wallis, ed., Our American Heritage (NY: Harper & Row, Publishers, Inc., 1970), p. 163. Peter Marshall & David Manuel, The Glory of America (Bloomington, MN: Garborg's Heart 'N Home, 1991), 7.24.

[378] William McGuffey's Third Eclectic Reader contains Lesson 31, entitled "On Speaking Truth"

[379] Dwight, Timothy. July 4, 1798, as president of Yale College, in an address delivered at New Haven, entitled, "The Duty of Americans, at the Present Crisis, Illustrated in a Discourse, Preached on the Fourth of July, 1798. (#Ital original). The Annals of America, 20 vols. (Chicago, IL: Encyclopedia Britannica, 1968, 1977), Vol. 4, pp. 33-39. Peter Marshall and David Manuel, The Glory of America (Bloomington, MN: Garborg's Heart 'N Home, Inc., 1991), 1.11. Peter Marshall and David Manuel, From Sea to Shining Sea (Old Tappan, NJ: Fleming H. Revell Company, 1986).

[380] Matthew D. Staver, "The Ten Commandments in American Law and Government" (Orlando, FL: The Liberty Counsel, P.O. Box 540774, Orlando, FL 32854, 407-875-2100,

Endnotes

407-875-0770 Fax, http://www.lc.org, liberty@lc.org, 2002), pp. 15-16.
[381] Adams, John. October 11, 1798, in a letter to the officers of the First Brigade of the Third Division of the Militia of Massachusetts. Charles Francis Adams (son of John Quincy Adams and grandson of John Adams), ed., The Works of John Adams - Second President of the United States: with a Life of the Author, Notes, and Illustration (Boston: Little, Brown, & Co., 1854), Vol. IX, pp. 228-229. Charles E. Rice, The Supreme Court and Public Prayer (New York: Fordham University Press, 1964), p. 47. Senator A. Willis Robertson, "Report on Prayers in Public Schools and Other Matters, Senate Committee on the Judiciary (87th Congress, 2nd Session), 1962, 32. Richard John Neuhaus, The Naked Public Square (Grand Rapids, MI: William B. Eerdman Publishing Company, 1984), p. 95. War on Religious Freedom (Virginia Beach, Virginia: Freedom Council, 1984), p. 1. A. James Reichley, Religion in American Public Life (Washington, D.C.: The Brookings Institute, 1985), p. 105. Pat Robertson, America's Dates With Destiny (Nashville, TN: 1986), pp. 93-95. Charles Colson, Kingdoms in Conflict (Grand Rapids, MI: Zondervan Publishing House, 1987), pp. 47, 120. Tim LaHaye, Faith of Our Founding Fathers (Brentwood, TN: Wolgemuth & Hyatt, Publishers, Inc., 1987), p. 194. John Eidsmoe, Christianity and the Constitution - The Faith of Our Founding Fathers (Grand Rapids, MI: Baker Book House, A Mott Media Book, 1987; 6th printing, 1993), pp. 273, 292, 381. Gary DeMar, "Is the Constitution Christian?" (Atlanta, GA: The Biblical Worldview, An American Vision Publication - American Vision, Inc., December 1989), p. 2. Peter Marshall and David Manuel, The Glory of America (Bloomington, MN: Garborg's Heart 'N Home, 1991), 8.11. Kerby Anderson, "Christian Roots of the Declaration" (Dallas, TX: Freedom Club Report, July 1993), p. 6. Rush H. Limbaugh III, See, I Told You So (New York, NY: reprinted by permission of Pocket Books, a division of Simon & Schuster Inc., 1993), pp. 73-76. Stephen McDowell and Mark Beliles, "The Providential Perspective" (Charlottesville, VA: The Providence Foundation, P.O. Box 6759, Charlottesville, Va. 22906, January 1994), Vol. 9, No. 1, p. 4.
[382] Webster, Noah. 1823, in his Letters to a Young Gentleman Commencing His Education (New Haven: Howe & Spalding, 1823), pp. 18-19. Stephen McDowell and Mark Beliles, "The Providential Perspective" (Charlottesville, VA: The Providence Foundation, P.O. Box 6759, Charlottesville, Va. 22906, January 1994), Vol. 9, No. 1, p. 6.
[383] Cleveland, (Stephen) Grover. 1903. Edmund Fuller and David E. Green, God in the White House - The Faiths of American Presidents (NY: Crown Publishers, Inc., 1968), p. 149.
[384] Bacon, Sir Francis. In his work entitled, Essays: Of Goodness. Tryon Edwards, D.D., The New Dictionary of Thoughts - A Cyclopedia of Quotations (Garden City, NY: Hanover House, 1852; revised and enlarged by C.H. Catrevas, Ralph Emerson Browns and Jonathan Edwards [descendent, along with Tryon, of Jonathan Edwards (1703-1758), president of Princeton], 1891; The Standard Book Company, 1955, 1963), p. 91. Burton Stevenson, The Home Book of Quotations - Classical & Modern (New York: Dodd, Mead and Company, 1967), p. 265
[385] Grotius, Hugo. James Madison, Examination of the British Doctrine, 1806. Verna M. Hall, Christian History of the Constitution of the United States of America: Christian Self-Government (San Francisco: Foundation for American Christian Education, 1966, 1980), p. 250. John Eidsmoe, Christianity and the Constitution - The Faith of Our Founding Fathers (Grand Rapids, MI: Baker Book House, A Mott Media Book, 1987; 6th printing, 1993), p. 62.
[386] Grotius, Hugo. 1625. Hugo Grotius, The Rights of War and Peace, (Amsterdam, 1933), 1:4.1.3. William Vasilio Sotirovich, Grotius' Universe: Divine Law and a Quest for Harmony (New York: Vantage Press, 1978), p. 51. John Eidsmoe, Christianity and the Constitution - The Faith of Our Founding Fathers (Grand Rapids, MI: Baker Book House, A Mott Media Book, 1987; 6th printing, 1993), p. 63.
[387] Cotton, John. 1636. Benjamin Fletcher Wright, Jr., American Interpretations of Natural Law (New York: Russell & Russell, 1962), pp. 17-18. John Eidsmoe, Christianity and the Constitution - The Faith of Our Founding Fathers (Grand Rapids, MI: Baker Book House, A

Mott Media Book, 1987; 6th printing, 1993), p. 32.

[388] Locke, John. Donald S. Lutz and Charles S. Hyneman, "The Relative Influence of European Writers on Late Eighteenth-Century American Political Thought," American Political Review 189 (1984): 189-197. (Courtesy of Dr. Wayne House of Dallas Theological Seminary.) John Eidsmoe, Christianity and the Constitution - The Faith of Our Founding Fathers (Grand Rapids, MI: Baker Book House, A Mott Media Book, 1987, 6th printing 1993), pp. 51-53. Stephen K. McDowell and Mark A. Beliles, America's Providential History (Charlottesville, VA: Providence Press, 1988), p. 156. [1760-1805], Origins of American Constitutionalism, (1987).

[389] Locke, John. John Locke, Of Civil Government, Book Two, II:11, III:56; V:25, 55; XVIII:200. John Eidsmoe, Christianity and the Constitution - The Faith of Our Founding Fathers (Grand Rapids, MI: Baker Book House, A Mott Media Book, 1987, 6th printing 1993), p. 61.

[390] Locke, John. 1690, John Locke, Of Civil Government, Book Two, XI:136n. John Locke, The Second Treatise on Civil Government, 1690 (reprinted Buffalo, NY: Prometheus Books, 1986), p. 76, n. 1. Richard Hooker, Of the Laws of Ecclesiastical Polity, Book 1, section 10. John Eidsmoe, Christianity and the Constitution - The Faith of Our Founding Fathers (Grand Rapids, MI: Baker Book House, A Mott Media Book, 1987, 6th printing 1993), p. 62.

[391] Blackstone, Sir William. 1826-1830, as cited in a work written by Chancellor James Kent of New York entitled, Commentaries on American Law, (1826-1830). Hon. Robert K. Dornan and Csaba Vedlik, Jr., Judicial Supremacy: The Supreme Court on Trial (Massachusetts: Plymouth Rock Foundation, 1986), p. 10.

[392] Blackstone, Sir William. 1765-1770, in his work entitled, Commentaries on the Law of England (Oxford: Clarendon Press, 1769). Sir William Blackstone, Commentaries on the Laws of England (Philadelphia: J.B. Lippincott and Co., 1879), Vol. I, pp. 39, 41, 42. Verna M. Hall, The Christian History of the Constitution of the United States of America - Christian Self-Government with Union (San Francisco: Foundation for American Christian Education, 1962, 1976, 1979), pp. 140-146. John Eidsmoe, Christianity and the Constitution - The Faith of Our Founding Fathers (Grand Rapids, MI: Baker Book House, A Mott Media Book, 1987; 6th printing, 1993), pp. 57-58.

[393] Blackstone, Sir William. 1765-1770, in his work entitled, Commentaries on the Laws of England (Oxford: Clarendon Press, 1769). Sir William Blackstone, Commentaries on the Laws of England (Philadelphia: J.B. Lippincott and Co., 1879), Vol. I, pp. 39, 41, 42. Verna M. Hall, The Christian History of the Constitution of the United States of America - Christian Self-Government with Union (San Francisco: Foundation for American Christian Education, 1962, 1976, 1979), pp. 140-146. John Whitehead, The Second American Revolution (Elgin, IL: David C. Cook, 1982), pp. 30-32. Tim LaHaye, Faith of Our Founding Fathers (Brentwood, TN: Wolgemuth & Hyatt, Publishers, Inc., 1987) pp. 86-87. John Eidsmoe, Christianity and the Constitution - The Faith of Our Founding Fathers (Grand Rapids, MI: Baker Book House, A Mott Media Book, 1987; 6th printing, 1993), pp. 57-58.

[394] Connecticut, Fundamental Orders (Constitution) of. January 14, 1639. Old South Leaflets, No. 8. John Fiske, The Beginning of New England (Boston: Houghton, Mifflin & Co., 1889, 1898), p. 127-128.

[395] Connecticut, Fundamentals Orders (Constitution) of. January 14, 1639. Old South Leaflets, No. 8.The World Book Encyclopedia, 18 vols. (Chicago, IL: Field Enterprises, Inc., 1957; W.F. Quarrie and Company, 8 vols., 1917; World Book, Inc., 22 vols., 1989), Vol. 3, p. 1675.

[396] Connecticut, Fundamental Orders (Constitution) of. January 14, 1639. John Wingate Thornton, The Pulpit of the American Revolution, 1860 (reprinted NY: Burt Franklin, 1970), p. XIX.

[397] Montesquieu, Baron Charles Louis Joseph de Secondat. 1748. The Spirit of the Laws (New York: Hafner, 1949, 1962), 1:1-3. John Eidsmoe, Christianity and the Constitution - The Faith of Our Founding Fathers (Grand Rapids, MI: Baker Book House, A Mott Media

Endnotes

Book, 1987, 6th printing 1993), pp. 54-55.

[398] Franklin, Benjamin. 1790, in a letter to Thomas Paine. Jared Sparks, editor, The Works of Benjamin Franklin (Boston: Tappan, Whittemore, and Mason, 1840), Vol. X, pp. 281-282.

[399] Burke, Edmund. 1791, in "A Letter to a Member of the National Assembly." Theodore Roosevelt, "Fifth Annual Message to Congress," December 5, 1905. A Compilation of the Messages and Papers of the Presidents 20 vols. (New York: Bureau of National Literature, Inc., prepared under the direction of the Joint Committee on Printing, of the House and Senate, pursuant to an Act of the Fifty-Second Congress of the United States, 1893, 1923), Vol. XIV, p. 6986. Keith Fournier, In Defense of Liberty (Virginia Beach, VA: Law & Justice, 1993), Vol. 2, No. 2, p. 5. Rush H. Limbaugh III, See, I Told You So (New York, NY: reprinted by permission of Pocket Books, a division of Simon & Schuster Inc., 1993), pp. 73-76.

[400] Washington, George. September 19, 1796, in his Farewell Address. Address of George Washington, President of the United States, and Late Commander in Chief of the American Army. To the People of the United States, Preparatory to His Declination. Published in the American Daily Advertiser, Philadelphia, September, 1796. Jared Sparks, ed., The Writings of George Washington 12 vols. (Boston: American Stationer's Company, 1837; NY: F. Andrew's, 1834-1847), Vol. XII, pp. 227-228. James D. Richardson (U.S. Representative from Tennessee), ed., A Compilation of the Messages and Papers of the Presidents 1789-1897, 10 vols. (Washington, D.C.: U.S. Government Printing Office, published by Authority of Congress, 1897, 1899; Washington, D.C.: Bureau of National Literature and Art, 1789-1902, 11 vols., 1907, 1910), Vol. 1, pp. 205-216, 220.

[401] Adams, Abigail. November 5, 1775(circa), in a letter to her friend, Mercy Warren). Warren-Adams Letters, 1743-1777 (Massachusetts Historical Society Collections), Vol. I, p. 72. L.H. Butterfield, ed., Adams Family Correspondence (Cambridge, MA: The Belknap Press of Harvard University Press, 1963), Vol. I, p. 323. Edmund Fuller and David E. Green, God in the White House - The Faiths of American Presidents (NY: Crown Publishers, Inc., 1968), p. 22. Jan Payne Pierce, The Patriot Primer III (Fletcher, NC: New Puritan Library, Inc., 1987), p. 44. Peter Marshall and David Manuel, The Glory of America (Bloomington, MN: Garborg's Heart'N Home, Inc., 1991), 3.11. D.P. Diffine, Ph.D., One Nation Under God - How Close a Separation? (Searcy, Arkansas: Harding University, Belden Center for Private Enterprise Education, 6th edition, 1992), p. 7. Stephen McDowell and Mark Beliles, "The Providential Perspective" (Charlottesville, VA: The Providence Foundation, P.O. Box 6759, Charlottesville, Va. 22906, January 1994), Vol. 9, No. 1, p. 7.

[402] Baldwin, Abraham. 1785, Charter of the College of Georgia. Charles C. Jones, Biographical Sketches of the Delegates from Georgia (Tustin, CA: American Biography Service), pp. 6-7. Tim LaHaye, Faith of Our Founding Fathers (Brentwood, TN: Wolgemuth & Hyatt, Publishers, Inc., 1987), pp. 146-147.

[403] Morse, Jedediah. April 25, 1799, in Jedediah Morse's Election Sermon given at Charleston, Mass., taken from an original in the Evans collection compiled by the American Antiquarian Society. Verna M. Hall, Christian History of the Constitution of the United States of America (San Francisco: Foundation for America Christian Education, 1975), pp. v, 145. Peter Marshall and David Manuel, The Glory of America (Bloomington, MN: Garborg's Heart'N Home, Inc., 1991), 4.25, 8.5. Stephen McDowell and Mark Beliles, "The Providential Perspective" (Charlottesville, VA: The Providence Foundation, P.O. Box 6759, Charlottesville, Va. 22906, January 1994), Vol. 9, No. 1, p. 7.

[404] Madison, James. Federalist Paper #39. Alexander Hamilton, John Jay and James Madison, The Federalist, on the New Constitution Written in 1788 (Philadelphia: Benjamin Warner, 1818), pp. 203-204, James Madison, Number 39.

[405] Madison, James. 1778, attributed. Harold K. Lane, Liberty! Cry Liberty (Boston: Lamb and Lamb Tractarian Society, 1939), pp. 32-33. Frederick Nymeyer, First Principles in Morality and Economics: Neighborly Love and Ricardo's Law of Association (South Holland: Libertarian Press, 1958), p. 31. Frederick Nymeyer, Progressive Calvinism,

(January, 1958), Vol. 4, p. 31. Spiritual Mobilization Calendar (Los Angeles, CA: Spiritual Mobilization, First Congregational Church, 1958), inscription. Rousas J. Rushdoony Institutes of Biblical Law (1973). Gary DeMar, God and Government-A Biblical and Historical Study (Atlanta, GA: American Vision Press, 1982), pp. 137-138. Russ Walton, Biblical Principles of Importance to Godly Christians (Marlborough, New Hampshire: Plymouth Rock Foundation, 1984), 361. Stephen K. McDowell and Mark A. Beliles, America's Providential History (Charlottesville, VA: Providence Press, 1988), p. 221. Benjamin Hart, Faith & Freedom - The Christian Roots of American Liberty (Dallas, TX: Lewis and Stanley, 1988), p. 18. D.P. Diffine, Ph.D., One Nation Under God - How Close a Separation? (Searcy, Arkansas: Harding University, Belden Center for Private Enterprise Education, 6th edition, 1992), p. 7. Rush H. Limbaugh III, See, I Told You So (New York, NY: reprinted by permission of Pocket Books, a division of Simon & Schuster Inc., 1993), pp. 73-76. Liberty and Justice for All (Virginia Beach, VA: Regent University, 1993), p. 6. D. James Kennedy, What if Jesus had never been born? (Nashville, TN: Thomas Nelson Inc., 1994), p. 71. Kirk Fordice, Governor of the State of Mississippi, along with the Secretary of State, D.M., in an Executive Proclamation By The Governor of the State of Mississippi, declaring November 20 - November 26, 1994, as "Christian Heritage Week," signed in the Capitol City of Jackson, August 24, 1994; August 23, 1993. Christine Tod Whitman, Governor of the State of New Jersey, along with Secretary of State Lonna R. Hooks, in an Executive Proclamation by the Governor of the State of New Jersey, declaring November 19 - November 25, 1995, as "Christian Heritage Week," signed October 31, 1995. Courtesy of Bruce Barilla, Christian Heritage Week Ministry (P.O. Box 58, Athens, W.V. 24712; 304-384-7707, 304-384-9044 fax). Adrian Rogers, Ten Secrets for a successful family (Wheaton, IL: Crossway, 1996), p. 30.

[406] Webster, Noah. 1832. The History of the United States (New Haven: Durrie & Peck, 1832), p. 309, paragraph 53. Gary DeMar, God and Government, A Biblical and Historical Study (Atlanta, GA: American Vision Press, 1984), p. 4. "Our Christian Heritage," Letter from Plymouth Rock (Marlborough, NH: The Plymouth Rock Foundation), p. 5. Noah Webster, The American Dictionary of the English Language (NY: S. Converse, 1828; reprinted, San Francisco: Foundation for American Christian Education, facsimile edition, 1967), preface, p. 22. Gary DeMar, God and Government - A Biblical and Historical Study (Atlanta: American Vision Press, 1982), p. 4. Robert Flood, The Rebirth of America (The Arthur S. DeMoss Foundation, 1986), p. 33.

[407] Webster., Noah 1834, in his work Value of the Bible and Excellence of the Christian Religion. (1834, reprinted; San Francisco: Foundation for Christian Education, republished 1988), p. 78. Stephen McDowell and Mark Beliles, "The Providential Perspective" (Charlottesville, VA: The Providence Foundation, P.O. Box 6759, Charlottesville, Va. 22906, January 1994), Vol. 9, No. 1, p. 6.

[408] Webster, Noah. 1834, in his work Value of the Bible and Excellence of the Christian Religion. (San Francisco: Foundation for Christian Education, republished 1988), p. 78. Stephen McDowell and Mark Beliles, "The Providential Perspective" (Charlottesville, VA: The Providence Foundation, P.O. Box 6759, Charlottesville, Va. 22906, January 1994), Vol. 9, No. 1, pp. 6-7.

[409] Webster, Noah. 1839, in A Manual of Useful Studies (New Haven: S. Babcock, 1839), p. vi. Stephen McDowell and Mark Beliles, "The Providential Perspective" (Charlottesville, VA: The Providence Foundation, P.O. Box 6759, Charlottesville, Va. 22906, January 1994), Vol. 9, No. 1, p. 3.

[410] Webster, Noah. Verna M. Hall and Rosalie J. Slater, The Bible and the Constitution of the United States (San Francisco: Foundation for American Christian Education, 1983), p. 27. Tim LaHaye, Faith of Our Founding Fathers (Brentwood, TN: Wolgemuth & Hyatt, Publishers, Inc., 1987), pp. 76-78.

[411] Adams, Samuel. November 20, 1772, in a report for the Committees of Correspondence, entitled, The Rights of the Colonists; in the section: "The Rights of the Colonist as Men."

Endnotes

Old South Leaflets. David C. Whitney, Signers of the Declaration of Independence - Founders of Freedom (1964), p. 49. The Annals of America, 20 vols. (Chicago, IL: Encyclopedia Britannica, 1968), Vol. 2, p. 217. Lucille Johnston, Celebrations of a Nation (Arlington, VA: The Year of Thanksgiving Foundation, 1987), p. 79.

[412] Adams, John Quincy. September 1811, in a letter to his son written while serving as U.S. Minister in St. Petersburg, Russia. James L. Alden, Letters of John Quincy Adams to His Son on the Bible and Its Teachings (1850), pp. 6-21. Henry H. Halley, Halley's Bible Handbook (Grand Rapids, MI: Zondervan Publishing House, 1927, 1965), p. 19. Verna M. Hall, The Christian History of the American Revolution - Consider and Ponder (San Francisco: Foundation for American Christian Education, 1976), pp. 615-616. Verna M. Hall and Rosalie J. Slater, The Bible and the Constitution of the United States of America (San Francisco: Foundation for American Christian Education, 1983), p. 17. Tim LaHaye, Faith of Our Founding Fathers (Brentwood, TN: Wolgemuth & Hyatt, Publishers, Inc., 1987), pp. 90-91. D.P. Diffine, Ph.D., One Nation Under God - How Close a Separation? (Searcy, Arkansas: Harding University, Belden Center for Private Enterprise Education, 6th edition, 1992), p. 6.

[413] Adams, John Quincy. Statement. John Wingate Thornton, The Pulpit of the American Revolution 1860 (NY: Burt Franklin, 1860; 1970), p. XXIX. D.P. Diffine, Ph.D., One Nation Under God - How Close a Separation? (Searcy, Arkansas: Harding University, Belden Center for Private Enterprise Education, 6th edition, 1992), p. 11.

[414] McHenry, James. Bernard Steiner, One Hundred and Ten Years of Bible Society in Maryland (Maryland: Maryland Bible Society, 1921), p. 14. Tim LaHaye, Faith of Our Founding Fathers (Brentwood, TN: Wolgemuth & Hyatt, Publishers, Inc., 1987), pp. 171-172. Peter Marshall & David Manuel, The Glory of America (Bloomington, MN: Garborg's Heart 'N Home, 1991), 8.17.

[415] Tocqueville, Alexis de. Robert N. Bellah, et. al., Habits of the Heart, p. viii. Gary DeMar, The Biblical Worldview (Atlanta, GA: An American Vision Publication - American Vision Inc., 1993), Vol. 9, No. 2, p. 14.

[416] Tocqueville, Alexis de. Statement. Alexis de Tocqueville, The Republic of the United States of America and Its Political Institutions, Reviewed and Examined, Henry Reeves, trans., (Garden City, NY: A.S. Barnes & Co., 1851), Vol. I, p. 337. Alexis de Tocqueville, Democracy in America (New York: Vintage Books, 1945), Vol. I, p. 319. Tim LaHaye, Faith of Our Founding Fathers (Brentwood, TN: Wolgemuth & Hyatt, Publishers, Inc., 1987), p. 97. Francis J. Grund, a publicist, wrote his work The Americans in Their Moral, Social and Political Relations in 1837, in which he observed the trends of religious influence in America: "The religious habits of the Americans form not only the basis of their private and public morals, but have become so thoroughly interwoven with their whole course of legislation, that it would be impossible to change them, without affecting the very essence of their government." Francis J. Grund, The Americans in Their Moral, Social and Political Relations, (1837), Vol. I, pp. 281, 292, 294. Anson Phelps Stokes and Leo Pfeffer, Church and State in the United States (NY: Harper and Row, Publishers, 1950, revised one-volume edition, 1964), p. 210.

[417] Tocqueville, Alexis de. Alexis de Tocqueville, The Republic of the United States of America and Its Political Institutions, Reviewed and Examined, Henry Reeves, trans., (Garden City, NY: A.S. Barnes & Co., 1851), Vol. I, p. 334. Alexis de Tocqueville, Democracy in America (New York: Vintage Books, 1945), Vol. I, p. 316. Francis J. Grund, a publicist, wrote his work The Americans in Their Moral, Social and Political Relations in 1837, in which he observed the trends of religious influence in America: "The Americans look upon religion as a promoter of civil and political liberty; and have, therefore, transferred to it a large portion of the affection which they cherish for the institutions of their country." Francis J. Grund, The Americans in Their Moral, Social and Political Relations, (1837), Vol. I, pp. 281, 292, 294. Anson Phelps Stokes and Leo Pfeffer, Church and State in the United States (NY: Harper and Row, Publishers, 1950, revised one-volume edition, 1964), p. 210.

Tim LaHaye, Faith of Our Founding Fathers (Brentwood, TN: Wolgemuth & Hyatt, Publishers, Inc., 1987), p. 97. Verna M. Hall, Christian History (San Francisco: Foundation for Christian Education), Vol. I, p. 372.

[418] Tocqueville, Alexis de. Alexis de Tocqueville, The Republic of the United States of America and Its Political Institutions, Reviewed and Examined, 2 vols. (New York: Alfred A. Knopf, 1945), Vol. I, p. 303. Alexis de Tocqueville, Democracy in America (New York: Vintage Books, 1945), Vol. I, pp. 314-315. Gary DeMar, The Biblical Worldview (Atlanta, GA: An American Vision Publication - American Vision, Inc., 1993), Vol. 9, No. 2, p. 14. "Our Christian Heritage," Letter from Plymouth Rock (Marlborough, NH: The Plymouth Rock Foundation), p. 5. Tim LaHaye, Faith of Our Founding Fathers (Brentwood, TN: Wolgemuth & Hyatt, Publishers, Inc., 1987), p. 97.

[419] Tocqueville, Alexis de. 1835, 1840. Alexis de Tocqueville, The Republic of the United States and Its Political Institutions, Reviewed and Examined, Henry Reeves, translator (Garden City, NY: A.S. Barnes & Co., 1851), Vol. I, p. 331-332. Alexis de Tocqueville, Democracy in America, 2 vols. (NY: Alfred A. Knopf, 1945), Vol. I, p. 303. Alexis de Tocqueville, Democracy in America (New York: Vintage Books, 1945), Vol. I, pp. 314-315. Gary DeMar, "The Christian America Debate" (Atlanta, GA: The Biblical Worldview, An American Vision Publication - American Vision, Inc., February 1993), Vol. 9, No. 2, p. 14. Tim LaHaye, Faith of Our Founding Fathers (Brentwood, TN: Wolgemuth & Hyatt, Publishers, Inc., 1987), p. 97. "Our Christian Heritage," Letter from Plymouth Rock (Marlborough, NH: The Plymouth Rock Foundation), p. 5.

[420] Tocqueville, Alexis de. Statement. Alexis de Tocqueville, Democracy in America, Henry Reeve, translator, Francis Bowen ed., (Cambridge: 2nd edition, 1876). Alexis de Tocqueville, Democracy in America, George Lawrence, translator, (NY: Harper & Row, 1988) p. 291. John Whitehead, The Second American Revolution (Wheaton, Illinois: Crossway Books, 1982), p. 34.

[421] Tocqueville, Alexis de. 1830, Alexis de Tocqueville, Democracy in America, 2 vols. (NY: Alfred A. Knopf, 1945), Vol. 2, pp. 152-153. Frederick Kershner, Jr., ed., Tocqueville's America - The Great Quotations (Athens, Ohio: Ohio University Press, Cooper Industries, 1983), p. 64.

[422] Tocqueville, Alexis de. Alexis De Tocqueville, Democracy in America (New York: Vintage Books, 1945), Vol. I, p. 314-315. Tim LaHaye, Faith of Our Founding Fathers (Brentwood, TN: Wolgemuth & Hyatt, Publishers, Inc., 1987), p. 98. Alexis de Tocqueville, The Republic of the United States of America and Its Political Institutions, Reviewed and Examined, Henry Reeves, trans., (Garden City, NY: A.S. Barnes & Co., 1851), Vol. I, p. 333.

[423] Tocqueville, Alexis de. The Republic of the United States of America and Its Political Institutions, Reviewed and Examined, Henry Reeves, trans., (Garden City, NY: A.S. Barnes & Co., 1851), Vol. I, p. 335.

[424] Tocqueville, Alexis de. 1831. Alexis de Tocqueville, Journey to America, George Lawrence, translator, J.P. Mayer, ed., (New Haven, CT: Yale University Press, 1959), p. 114. Frederick Kershner, Jr., ed., Tocqueville's America - The Great Quotations (Athens, Ohio: Ohio University Press, Cooper Industries, 1983), p. 64.

[425] Beecher, Lyman. 1831, in a newspaper article he wrote entitled, "The Spirit of the Pilgrims." Perry Miller, The Life of the Mind in America from the Revolution to the Civil War-Books 1-3 (New York: Harcourt, Brace & World, 1966), p. 36. Peter Marshall and David Manuel, The Glory of America (Bloomington, MN: Garborg's Heart'N Home, Inc., 1991), 12.5.

[426] Webster, Daniel. 1851. Robert Flood, The Rebirth of America (Philadelphia: Arthur S. DeMoss Foundation, 1986), p. 21. The Works of Daniel Webster (Boston: Little, Brown and Company, 1853), Vol. II, p. 615, July 4, 1851.

[427] Webster, Daniel. Tryon Edwards, D.D., The New Dictionary of Thoughts - A Cyclopedia of Quotations (Garden City, NY: Hanover House, 1852; revised and enlarged by C.H. Catrevas, Ralph Emerson Browns and Jonathan Edwards [descendent, along with Tryon, of

Endnotes

Jonathan Edwards (1703-1758), president of Princeton], 1891; The Standard Book Company, 1955, 1963), p. 49. Charles Lanman, Private Life of Daniel Webster, p. 104. Stephen Abbott Northrop, D.D., A Cloud of Witnesses (Portland, OR: American Heritage Ministries, 1987; Mantle Ministries, 228 Still Ridge, Bulverde, Texas), p. 491.

[428] Webster, Daniel. Statement. George Otis, The Solution to the Crisis in America, Revised and Enlarged Edition (Van Nuys, CA.: Fleming H. Revell Company; Bible Voice, Inc., 1970, 1972, foreword by Pat Boone), p. 51.

[429] Wayland, Francis. Tryon Edwards, D.D., The New Dictionary of Thoughts - A Cyclopedia of Quotations (Garden City, NY: Hanover House, 1852; revised and enlarged by C.H. Catrevas, Ralph Emerson Browns and Jonathan Edwards [descendent, along with Tryon, of Jonathan Edwards (1703-1758), president of Princeton], 1891; The Standard Book Company, 1955, 1963), p. 47.

[430] Bryant, William Cullen. John Bigelow, Life of William Cullen Bryant, p. 275. Stephen Abbott Northrop, D.D., A Cloud of Witnesses (Portland, OR: American Heritage Ministries, 1987; Mantle Ministries, 228 Still Ridge, Bulverde, Texas), pp. 57-58.

[431] Parker, Theodore. Tryon Edwards, D.D., The New Dictionary of Thoughts - A Cyclopedia of Quotations (Garden City, NY: Hanover House, 1852; revised and enlarged by C.H. Catrevas, Ralph Emerson Browns and Jonathan Edwards [descendent, along with Tryon, of Jonathan Edwards (1703-1758), president of Princeton], 1891; The Standard Book Company, 1955, 1963), p. 46.

[432] Winthrop, Robert Charles. May 28, 1849, in an address, entitled "Either by the Bible or the Bayonet," at the Annual Meeting of the Massachusetts Bible Society in Boston. Addresses and Speeches on Various Occasions (Boston: Little, Brown & Company, 1852), p. 172. Benjamin Franklin Morris, The Christian Life and Character of the Civil Institutions of the United States (Philadelphia, PA: L. Johnson & Co., 1863; George W. Childs, 1864), pp. 227-228. Stephen McDowell and Mark Beliles, "The Providential Perspective" (Charlottesville, VA: The Providence Foundation, P.O. Box 6759, Charlottesville, Va. 22906, January 1994), Vol. 9, No. 1, p. 1. Verna M. Hall, The Christian History of the American Revolution (San Francisco: Foundation for American Christian Education, 1976), p. 20. Marshall Foster and Mary-Elaine Swanson, The American Covenant - The Untold Story (Roseburg, OR: Foundation for American Christian Self-Government, 1981; Thousand Oaks, CA: The Mayflower Institute, 1983, 1992), p. 7. Gary DeMar, America's Christian History: The Untold Story (Atlanta, GA: American Vision Publishers, Inc., 1993), p. 58. John Whitehead, The Separation Illusion (Milford, Michigan: Mott Media, 1977), p. 90.

[433] Merritt, Wesley. Stephen Abbott Northrop, D.D., A Cloud of Witnesses (Portland, OR: American Heritage Ministries, 1987; Mantle Ministries, 228 Still Ridge, Bulverde, Texas), p. 316.

[434] Roosevelt, Theodore. December 5, 1905, in his Fifth Annual Message to Congress. A Compilation of the Messages and Papers of the Presidents 20 vols. (New York: Bureau of National Literature, Inc., prepared under the direction of the Joint Committee on Printing, of the House and Senate, pursuant to an Act of the Fifty-Second Congress of the United States, 1893, 1923), Vol. XIV, pp. 6973, 6975-6976, 6980, 6984-6986, 6992-6994, 7003, 7008, 7015-7016.

[435] Wilson, (Thomas) Woodrow. October 24, 1914, in an address entitled "The Power of Christian Young Men," delivered at the Anniversary Celebration of the Young Men's Christian Association in Pittsburgh, Pennsylvania. A Compilation of the Messages and Papers of the Presidents 20 vols. (New York: Bureau of National Literature, Inc., prepared under the direction of the Joint Committee on Printing, of the House and Senate, pursuant to an Act of the Fifty-Second Congress of the United States, 1893, 1923), Vol. XVI, pp. 7993-8000. Charles J. Herold, The Wisdom of Woodrow Wilson: Being Selections from his Thoughts and Comments on Political, Social and Moral Questions (NY: Brentano's, 1919), p. 122.

[436] Dulles, John Foster. April 11, 1955, in a speech delivered to the Fifth Annual All-Jesuit

Alumni Dinner, during his tenure as Secretary of State. Charles Hurd, ed., A Treasury of Great American Speeches (NY: Hawthorne Books, 1959), pp. 325-330.
[437] Hoover, J. (John) Edgar. 1954, in the introduction of the book by Edward L.R. Elson, D.D., Lit.D., LL.D., America's Spiritual Recovery (Westwood, N.J.: Fleming H. Revell Company, 1954), pp. 9-11. (Biographical note: Edward L.R. Elson was the pastor of The National Presbyterian Church in Washington, D.C., after having been a Colonel in the military, serving as a Chaplain during World War II, 1941-1946.)
[438] United States Congress. March 27, 1854, Mr. Meacham giving report of the House Committee on the Judiciary. Reports of Committees of the House of Representatives Made During the First Session of the Thirty-Third Congress (Washington: A.O.P. Nicholson, 1854), pp. 1, 6, 8-9. Benjamin Franklin Morris, The Christian Life and Character of the Civil Institutions of the United States (Philadelphia, PA: L. Johnson & Co., entered, according to Act of Congress, in the Clerk's Office of the District Court of the United States for the Eastern District of Pennsylvania, 1863; George W. Childs, 1864), pp. 317-324. "Our Christian Heritage," Letter from Plymouth Rock (Marlborough, NH: The Plymouth Rock Foundation), pp. 5-6.
[439] Pennsylvania Supreme Court. 1817. The Commonwealth v. Wolf, 3 Serg.& R. 48, 50 (1817).
[440] Maryland, State of. 1851, Constitution. Supreme Court Justice David Josiah Brewer, who served 1890-1910, in his work, The United States - A Christian Nation (Philadelphia: The John C. Winston Company, 1905, Supreme Court Collection). "Our Christian Heritage," Letter from Plymouth Rock (Marlborough, NH: The Plymouth Rock Foundation), p. 6.
[441] Maryland, State of. 1864, Constitution. Benjamin Franklin Morris, The Christian Life and Character of the Civil Institutions of the United States (Philadelphia: George W. Childs, 1864). Supreme Court Justice David Josiah Brewer, who served 1890-1910, in his work, The United States - Christian Nation (Philadelphia: The John C. Winston Company, 1905, Supreme Court Collection). "Our Christian Heritage," Letter from Plymouth Rock (Marlborough, NH: The Plymouth Rock Foundation), p. 6.
[442] South Carolina, State of. 1778, Constitution, Article XII. The Constitutions of the Several Independent States of America (Boston: Norman and Bowen, 1785), South Carolina, 1776, Section 13, p. 146. Frances Newton Thorpe, ed., Federal and State Constitutions, Colonial Charters, and Other Organic Laws of the States, Territories, and Colonies now or heretofore forming the United States, 7 vols. (Washington: Government Printing Office, 1905; 1909; St. Clair Shores, MI: Scholarly Press, 1968). Edwin S. Gaustad, Neither King nor Prelate - Religion and the New Nation, 1776-1826 (Grand Rapids, MI: William B. Eerdmans Publishing Company, 1993), p. 171.
[443] South Carolina, State of. 1778, Constitution, Article XXXVIII. Benjamin Franklin Morris, The Christian Life and Character of the Civil Institutions of the United States (Philadelphia, PA: L. Johnson & Co., 1863; George W. Childs, 1864), pp. 230-231. Frances Newton Thorpe, ed., Federal and State Constitutions, Colonial Charters, and Other Organic Laws of the States, Territories, and Colonies now or heretofore forming the United States, 7 vols. (Washington: Government Printing Office, 1905; 1909; St. Clair Shores, MI: Scholarly Press, 1968), Vol. V, p. 3264. Edwin S. Gaustad, Neither King nor Prelate - Religion and the New Nation 1776-1826 (Grand Rapids, MI: William B. Eerdmans Publishing Company, 1993), pp. 171-172. John J. McGrath, ed., Church and State in American Law: Cases and Materials (Milwaukee: The Bruce Publishing Co., 1962), p. 375. Anson Phelps Stokes and Leo Pfeffer, Church and State in the United States (NY: Harper and Row, Publishers, 1950, revised one-volume edition, 1964), p. 79.
[444] South Carolina, State of. 1778, Constitution, Article XXXVIII. The Constitutions of the Several Independent States of America, Published by Order of Congress (Boston: Norman & Bowen, 1785) p. 152.
[445] Tennessee, State of. 1796, Constitution, Article VIII, Section II; Article XI, Section IV. The Constitutions of the Sixteen States (Boston: Manning and Loring, 1797), pp. 274, 277.

Endnotes

The Constitutions of All the United States According to the Latest Amendments (Lexington, KY: Thomas T. Skillman, 1817), p. 287. The Constitutions of the United States of America, pp. 342, 344. Frances Newton Thorpe, ed., Federal and State Constitutions, Colonial Charters, and Other Organic Laws of the States, Territories, and Colonies now or heretofore forming the United States, 7 vols. (Washington: Government Printing Office, 1905; 1909; St. Clair Shores, MI: Scholarly Press, 1968). Edwin S. Gaustad, Neither King nor Prelate - Religion and the New Nation, 1776-1826 (Grand Rapids, MI: William B. Eerdmans Publishing Company, 1993), p. 172.

[446] Tennessee, State of. 1870, Constitution, Article IX, Section 2. Charles E. Rice, The Supreme Court and Public Prayer (New York: Fordham University Press, 1964), p. 175; "Hearings, Prayers in Public Schools and Other Matters," Committee on the Judiciary, U.S. Senate (87th Cong., 2nd Sess.), 1962, pp. 268 et seq.

[447] Mississippi, State of. 1817. Constitution. Supreme Court Justice David Josiah Brewer, who served 1890-1910, in his work, The United States - Christian Nation (Philadelphia: The John C. Winston Company, 1905, Supreme Court Collection).

[448] Beaumont, Gustave de. 1835, in work entitled, Marie ou l'Esclavage aux E'tas-Unis (Paris, 1835), Vol. II, p. 183ff. The Annals of America, 20 vols. (Chicago, IL: Encyclopedia Britannica, 1968), Vol. 6, p. 156.

[449] Franklin, Benjamin. Leonard Labaree, ed., The Papers of Benjamin Franklin (New Haven: Yale University Press, 1959), Vol. I, p. 213. Tim LaHaye, Faith of Our Founding Fathers (Brentwood, TN: Wolgemuth & Hyatt, Publishers, Inc., 1987), p. 120.

[450] Blackstone, Sir William. 1765-1770, in his work entitled, Commentaries on the Laws of England. Wendell's Blackstone's Commentaries, Vol. IV, p. 43. Stephen Abbott Northrop, D.D., A Cloud of Witnesses (Portland, Oregon: American Heritage Ministries, 1987; Mantle Ministries, 228 Still Ridge, Bulverde, Texas), p. 33.

[451] McHenry, James. Bernard Steiner, One Hundred and Ten Years of Bible Society in Maryland (Maryland: Maryland Bible Society, 1921), p. 14. Tim LaHaye, Faith of Our Founding Fathers (Brentwood, TN: Wolgemuth & Hyatt, Publishers, Inc., 1987), pp. 171-172. Peter Marshall & David Manuel, The Glory of America (Bloomington, MN: Garborg's Heart 'N Home, 1991), 8.17.

[452] Adams, Samuel. April 30, 1776, in a letter to John Scollay of Boston. Norman Cousins, In God We Trust - The Religious Beliefs and Ideas of the American Founding Fathers (NY: Harper & Brothers, 1958), pp. 351-352. Stephen McDowell and Mark Beliles "Providential Perspective" (The Providence Foundation, P.O. Box 6759, Charlottesville, VA. 22906, January 1994), Vol. 9, No. 1, p. 2.

[453] Adams, John. March 6, 1799, in a Proclamation of a National Day of Humiliation, Fasting, and Prayer. James D. Richardson (U.S. Representative from Tennessee), ed., A Compilation of the Messages and Papers of the Presidents 1789-1897, 10 vols. (Washington, D.C.: U.S. Government Printing Office, published by Authority of Congress, 1897, 1899; Washington, D.C.: Bureau of National Literature and Art, 1789-1902, 11 vols., 1907, 1910), Vol. 1, pp. 284-286. Benjamin Franklin Morris, The Christian Life and Character of the Civil Institutions of the United States (Philadelphia: George W. Childs, 1864), pp. 547-548. Gary DeMar, The Biblical Worldview (Atlanta, GA: An American Vision Publication - American Vision, Inc., 1992), Vol. 8, No. 12, p. 9. Gary DeMar, America's Christian History: The Untold Story (Atlanta, GA: American Vision Publishers, Inc., 1993), p. 78. Stephen McDowell and Mark Beliles, "The Providential Perspective" (Charlottesville, VA: The Providence Foundation, P.O. Box 6759, Charlottesville, Va. 22906, January 1994), Vol. 9, No. 1, pp. 4, 6.

[454] Adams, John. January 13, 1815, in a letter to Judge F.A. Van der Kemp. Norman Cousins, In God We Trust - The Religious Beliefs and Ideas of the American Founding Fathers (NY: Harper & Brothers, 1958), p. 104.

[455] Adams, John. December 27, 1816, in a letter to Judge F.A. Van de Kemp. Norman Cousins, In God We Trust - The Religious Beliefs and Ideas of the American Founding

Fathers (NY: Harper & Brothers, 1958), pp. 104-105. John Eidsmoe, Christianity and the Constitution - The Faith of Our Founding Fathers (Grand Rapids, MI: Baker Book House, A Mott Media Book, 1987; 6th printing, 1993), p. 286. Gary DeMar, "Why the Religious Right is Always Right - Almost" (Atlanta, GA: The Biblical Worldview, An American Vision Publication - American Vision, Inc., November 1992), p. 6. Gary DeMar, America's Christian History: The Untold Story (Atlanta, GA: American Vision Publishers, Inc., 1993), p. 95.

[456] Adams, John. Life and Works of John Adams, Vol. X, p. 390. Stephen Abbott Northrop, D.D., A Cloud of Witnesses (Portland, Oregon: American Heritage Ministries, 1987; Mantle Ministries, 228 Still Ridge, Bulverde, Texas), pp. 2-3.

[457] Jefferson, Thomas. Shmucher, Life of Jefferson. Stephen Abbott Northrop, D.D., A Cloud of Witnesses (Portland, OR: American Heritage Ministries, 1987; Mantle Ministries, 228 Still Ridge, Bulverde, Texas), pp. 252-253.

[458] Rush, Benjamin. 1798. 1786, in "Thoughts upon the Mode of Education Proper in a Republic," published in Early American Imprints. Benjamin Rush, Essays, Literary, Moral and Philosophical (Philadelphia: Thomas and Samuel F. Bradford, 1798), p. 8, "Of the Mode of Education Proper in a Republic." The Annals of America, 20 vols. (Chicago, IL: Encyclopedia Britannica, 1968), Vol. 4, pp. 28-29. Stephen McDowell and Mark Beliles, "The Providential Perspective" (Charlottesville, VA: The Providence Foundation, P.O. Box 6759, Charlottesville, Va. 22906, January 1994), Vol. 9, No. 1, p. 3.

[459] Kent, James. Extracts from an Address before the American Bible Society. Stephen Abbott Northrop, D.D., A Cloud of Witnesses (Portland, Oregon: American Heritage Ministries, 1987; Mantle Ministries, 228 Still Ridge, Bulverde, Texas), pp. 265-266.

[460] Pinckney, Charles Cotesworth. Article XXXVIII of the Constitution of South Carolina 1778. John J. McGrath, ed., Church and State in American Law: Cases and Materials (Milwaukee: The Bruce Publishing Co., 1962), p. 375.

[461] Webster, Noah. Noah Webster, The American Dictionary of the English Language (George and Charles Merrian, 1854).

[462] Matthew D. Staver, "The Ten Commandments in American Law and Government" (Orlando, FL: The Liberty Counsel, P.O. Box 540774, Orlando, FL 32854, 407-875-2100, 407-875-0770 Fax, http://www.lc.org, liberty@lc.org, 2002), p. 16

AMERICA'S GOD AND COUNTRY ENCYCLOPEDIA OF QUOTATIONS
By William J. Federer
$29.99 Hardcover (ISBN 1-880563-09-6)
$19.99 Paperback (ISBN 1-880563-05-3)

Best-selling resource of profound quotes highlighting America's noble heritage. Over 200,000 in print! 845 pages of quotations from Presidents, Statesmen, Acts of Congress, Supreme Court Decisions, State Constitutions, Colonial Charters, Scientists, Explorers, Pioneers, Business Leaders, Military Leaders... on topics such as: God, religion, morality, Deity, virtue, character, providence, faith...

Easy to use, alphabetically arranged, fully footnoted, with subject and entry index. A favorite of national leaders, politicians, teachers, etc. No American library is complete without this classic!

CPSIA information can be obtained at www.ICGtesting.com
Printed in the USA
LVOW071426190911

246890LV00001B/12/A